D1442876

On Press

On Press

The Liberal Values That Shaped the News

MATTHEW PRESSMAN

Harvard University Press

Cambridge, Massachusetts
London, England
2018

Copyright © 2018 by the President and Fellows of Harvard College
All rights reserved
Printed in the United States of America

First Printing

Library of Congress Cataloging-in-Publication Data

Names: Pressman, Matthew, 1981– author.
Title: On press : the liberal values that shaped the news / Matthew Pressman.
Description: Cambridge, Massachusetts : Harvard University Press, 2018. |
Includes bibliographical references and index.
Identifiers: LCCN 2018002541 | ISBN 9780674976658 (hardcover : alk. paper)
Subjects: LCSH: New York Times Company. | Los Angeles Times (Firm) |
Journalistic ethics—United States—History—20th century. | Journalistic Ethics—
United States—History—21st century. | Liberalism—United States—History—20th century. |
Liberalism—United States—History—21st century. | American newspapers—Objectivity.
Classification: LCC PN4888.E8 P74 2018 | DDC 174/.907—dc23
LC record available at https://lccn.loc.gov/2018002541

For Lauren, with love and gratitude

Contents

On Press

Introduction

Liberal Values, Not Liberal Bias

COVERING THE NEWS involves countless decisions. Which stories matter most? Who should be interviewed? What questions should be asked? How should a situation be described? What should the headline say? Journalists make decisions like these based on their news judgments, and behind those news judgments lies a set of values. Those values usually remain constant over the years, but once in a while there is a period of revolutionary change. That is what happened between 1960 and 1980—during these two decades, American journalism adopted the characteristics that would guide it into the twentieth century. It is happening again today.

To some observers, the overriding characteristic of American journalism is liberal bias. But that is inaccurate, because it suggests either a deliberate effort to slant the news or a complete obliviousness to the political implications of news coverage. What truly defines contemporary American journalism is a set of values that determine news judgments. Some are political values: mistrust of the wealthy and powerful, sympathy for the dispossessed, belief in the government's responsibility to address social ills. Others are journalistic values: the beliefs that journalists must analyze the news, must serve their readers, must try to be evenhanded.

These values are not designed to serve any ideological agenda, but they help create a news product more satisfying to the center-left than to those who are right of center.

To examine the changing values behind the news, consider an edition of the country's leading newspaper, the *New York Times,* from a random day in 1960: Thursday, April 21. On the front page, all fourteen stories concerned the actions of governmental bodies or officials—indeed, all fourteen mentioned governmental bodies or officials in the very first sentence. Pages 2 and 4 featured transcripts of official statements and speeches. Nearly every article in the main news section began the same way: by recounting what a prominent person or group—usually affiliated with government—had said or done the day before. Although a few of the dispatches from abroad analyzed the meaning behind news events, most stories confined themselves to verifiable facts and a modicum of background information.

Any reader wishing to satisfy interests beyond politics and foreign affairs would find limited offerings. Like most newspapers, the *New York Times* had sections devoted to sports and business. The sports pages gave the previous day's results and reported on personnel changes at major professional teams. The business pages consisted mainly of articles summarizing companies' earnings reports or expansion plans (along with voluminous tables of market data). In business and sports alike, the news subjects received overwhelmingly favorable treatment; the sole exception was a business article about the annual meeting of an aircraft company, at which disgruntled shareholders complained to the chief executive about a cut in their dividend.[1] Three partial pages toward the back of the first section dealt with theater, dance, classical music, and books—interspersed with articles about politics that had not fit onto the pages closer to the front. A single page about television included program listings, a review, and a brief item about new shows in production. A two-page section targeting women readers, labeled "Food Fashions Family Furnishings," featured elaborate recipes (shad stuffed with sole mousse; roasted leg of lamb with fresh coconut pudding) and short articles about homemaking. The lead story in the "Four F's" section concerned an exhibition of British fashions that had originally been presented to the Queen Mother and Princess Margaret (heavy on ball gowns and tiaras).[2]

The values behind the news judgments in this 1960 edition of the *New York Times* are readily apparent. The editors' mission was to inform readers about what they considered the most consequential events in public life. That translated into a narrow definition of newsworthiness: foreign affairs, government and politics, business, and, to a lesser extent, science, religion, and education (a handful of articles on those topics were peppered throughout the first section, but none ran longer than a half-column of text). Reporters did not challenge the people they covered or judge their motivations, beliefs, and competence. The paper's secondary function—an afterthought, really—was to inform its readers about developments they might consider important in their personal lives: how their favorite sports team had fared, which Broadway show had people talking, what gourmet recipes they could try out.

Two decades later, the *New York Times* had changed dramatically, as the edition of Thursday, April 17, 1980, shows.[3] The front page had become more reader-friendly, with seven articles (down from fourteen), larger pictures, and fewer, wider columns of type. Most articles on the front page focused on governmental activities, but some did not—a dispatch from Moscow discussed how "ordinary Soviet citizens" felt about the likely U.S. boycott of the 1980 Olympics in Moscow.[4] Furthermore, the coverage of public officials scrutinized and challenged them. One front-page article, for instance, suggested that the head of New York City's mass-transit system had misrepresented the cost of a new union contract under consideration.[5] In 1960 the *New York Times* had reported allegations of wrongdoing against public officials only when they were formally charged; in 1980 the paper's own reporters were the ones asking the transit chief tough questions, pointing out inconsistencies in his answers, and levying informal charges.

Instead of simply recounting the previous day's developments, the reporters in 1980 tried to explain them. One front-page piece was labeled "news analysis," a format that the paper had inaugurated in the 1950s but used sparingly for years, and never on page one. Even the articles not labeled "news analysis" often took an analytical approach. The lead sentence of a front-page article about a Supreme Court ruling, rather than paraphrasing what the Justices said, explained what their decision meant: "The Supreme Court made private civil rights suits against local governments substantially easier to win today," reporter Linda Green-house began.[6] Flipping past the front page, a reader would find two more articles labeled "analysis" inside the paper, but zero transcripts of speeches or official statements.[7] Articles in which the lead sentence simply stated what an important person or group had done the day before were the exception, rather than the rule. A story on page 7 began, "The spring thaw that breaks the grip of the Russian winter renews the spirit, and into the exile of Andrei D. Sakharov, spring has brought a glimmer of hope."[8] In 1960 a lead like that might have appeared in a literary magazine, but not in the *New York Times*.

The adversarial approach apparent in the front-page article about New York's transit head was evident inside the paper as well—even in the sports and business sections, once unabashedly boosterish. That day's "Sports of the Times" column lambasted both of New York's Major League Baseball teams, the Yankees and the Mets, for extracting generous financial arrangements for their stadiums that "help keep the city poor."[9] The writer, Jim Naughton, had formerly been one of the paper's top political reporters, an indication of the hard-hitting sensibility the *Times* wished to bring to all areas of the paper. Likewise, the lead article in the business section was sure to rankle its subjects. It described how the billionaire Hunt brothers had lobbied (unsuccessfully) against changes in the government's regulation of futures trading. Although there was no suggestion that the Hunts had acted illegally, the article showed them attempting to manipulate the political system and, through their greed, recklessly endangering the stability of financial markets.[10]

What had been a peripheral function of the *New York Times* in 1960—catering to readers' personal interests—was central in 1980. The two pages on "Food Fashions Family Furnishings" had morphed into an eighteen-page stand-alone section called "Home," one of five rotating weekday sections about leisure interests (the others: entertainment, "living," sports, and science and technology). An additional ten pages at the back of the Home section covered the arts and entertainment. The *New York Times* as a whole had grown larger—112 pages, compared to 64 in 1960—but even so, the proportion of it devoted to "soft news" was far greater. And throughout the paper, the quality of writing had improved enormously since 1960—it had become livelier, more concise, more engaging.

Although the *New York Times,* as the country's most prestigious journalistic institution, was an atypical newspaper, others underwent a similar transformation between 1960 and 1980. The shift at the *Los Angeles Times* was equally profound. Most noticeably, the amount of space devoted to readers' personal lives increased enormously. On April 21, 1960, the *Los Angeles Times* had a section titled "Family," with roughly ten pages about food, weddings, and "society" news; four additional pages covering the arts and entertainment were split between the back of the Family section and the back of the metropolitan-news sections. That amounted to more soft-news coverage than in the 1960 *New York Times,* but it was nothing compared to the *Los Angeles Times* of April 17, 1980. In that issue, the daily View section—the descendent of the Family section—contained 32 pages. On top of that, the daily Calendar section (covering film, theater, and television) clocked in at 12 pages, followed by a two-part Food section (a regular Thursday feature) with 38 ad-filled pages. Whereas the entire 1960 edition contained 92 pages, the corresponding edition from 1980 contained 81 pages devoted to soft news alone.[11]

Moreover, the content of the 1980 View section would have scandalized a reader of its 1960 predecessor. The main articles in the Family section on April 21, 1960, concerned wedding etiquette, advice for high school students, Lebanese cuisine, and a UCLA psychologist who warned of the perils of too much leisure time. On April 17, 1980, the View section contained a report on the characteristics of women who have affairs with married men, a column about how middle-aged men wished to have more exciting sex lives, and a column about the impact of divorce on children. Such frank discussions of topics recently considered taboo appeared occasionally, but less frequently, in the more socially conservative *New York Times.* Most of the articles in the *New York Times* Home section of April 17, 1980, in fact, could have appeared in 1960. The stories on the section's front page extolled the joys of house tours, eulogized a recently deceased Park Avenue hostess, and explained the process of obtaining a green card for one's housekeeper.[12]

Like the *New York Times,* the *Los Angeles Times* in 1960 had relied heavily on articles that simply described what government officials had said and done the day before. That genre of story was increasingly hard to find in 1980. Yes, there was an article on the front page about California governor Jerry Brown, but it did not center on any official pronouncement he had made. Instead, it reported, to Brown's likely annoyance, that his car might be seized to pay off medical claims against the state.[13] Another front-page story reported on the shortage of safe-deposit boxes at U.S. banks, using that fact as an opening to explore Americans' anxieties about inflation and crime.[14] Not only did these two stories rely far more on the reporter's initiative and the reporter's voice than articles from 1960 had, but both of the bylines belonged to women—something that could not have occurred twenty years earlier, when no female reporters worked on the main news staff.

The political orientation of the *Los Angeles Times* also changed dramatically. In the edition of April 21, 1960, headlines in the first few pages played up the communist threat and hailed the efforts of Republican leaders and groups to combat it.[15] The lead editorial that day blasted the American Civil Liberties Union for proposing a police practices review board for Los Angeles—this represented a "usurpation of power" that could lead to "anarchy," the paper warned.[16] On April 17, 1980, by contrast, the headlines revealed no political favoritism, and the editorial page contained an appreciation of Jean-Paul Sartre, the French writer-philosopher—and radical leftist activist—who had died two days earlier. Drawings from each of the two *Los Angeles Times* editorial cartoonists appeared that day; one, by Paul Conrad, paid tribute to Sartre, while the other, by Frank Interlandi, implied that Ronald Reagan was telling lies on the campaign trail.

This comparison of two major newspapers on randomly selected dates in 1960 and 1980 shows how dramatically the American press changed during those two decades.[17] A different set of values reigned in 1980. Interpretation replaced transmission, and adversarialism replaced deference, as core values of reporting. Journalists also embraced a much broader definition of newsworthiness. The fundamental goal was no longer simply to inform readers as citizens, but also to cater to readers as consumers.

These changes did not all advance left-wing ideological goals. Adversarial reporting, as the examples above show, could rankle a Democratic politician like Jerry Brown or undermine a left-wing cause like increased funding for public transit. And the emphasis on soft news and consumerism, while not overtly political, runs counter to the anticorporate ethos that animates many people on the left. Nevertheless, it is fair to say that the press became "liberal" during these two decades. Journalism's revised values gave left-leaning reporters more license to analyze the news; they encouraged questioning the status quo and challenging those in power; they advocated an inclusive approach to coverage. People on the left generally approved of these changes—many on the right did not.

• • •

THE PRESS'S SHIFT toward a new set of values began, as Chapter 1 shows, a few years before 1960, with an increasing focus on interpretation and analysis in news coverage. Although journalists had been talking about the need for interpretive reporting since the 1930s, they only began to put it into practice, gradually, in the second half of the 1950s. Ever-increasing numbers of Americans were getting their news from television, radio, and weekly newsmagazines, so newspapers needed to provide more complete, meaningful coverage. They needed, as one industry analyst urged in 1961, "to put the facts in perspective, to provide interpretation in the news columns, not just on the editorial pages."[18] The newsmagazines, primarily *Time* and *Newsweek,* made interpretive reporting their trademark from their inception, and as TV news expanded in the 1960s, analysis and commentary constituted an increasing portion of the airtime. Throughout the 1960s, delivering more interpretive coverage remained a top priority of the *New York Times* and the *Los Angeles Times* as they attempted to stave off their competition.

The press's move toward interpretation contributed to deeper changes in American society and politics. For decades scholars have argued that the initial years of the Cold War—from the end of World War II until the early 1960s—were a time of widespread consensus in American public life.[19] Although subsequent historians have pointed out that the consensus was far from universal, it nevertheless pervaded the country's middle and upper classes. The press, by reporting in a straightforward manner on what the elites said and did, helped to create and sustain the Cold War consensus. The world as portrayed in the newspapers of the 1950s was certainly not untroubled, but it was relatively uncomplicated: statements were made, measures taken, reports issued. Interpretive reporting suggested that the superficial clarity of such news events masked ambiguities. It implied that the true meaning of the news was neither self-evident nor universally agreed upon.

The press did not foist this increasingly nuanced view of the world on readers who longed for simplicity. As *New York Times* executive editor Turner Catledge said in a 1965 speech, a "revolutionary change"—what he called "the knowledge explosion"—was reshaping newspaper audiences. The typical reader, according to Catledge, "is much better educated, his interests are more sophisticated, his tastes are more likely to be international, he has a grounding in culture which the older generation did not have."[20] To be sure, the buyers of elite newspapers had always been relatively well educated, but as of 1966, 48 percent of *New York Times* readers had never attended college.[21] That percentage was sure to decrease considerably as the nation moved toward what the sociologist Daniel Bell termed "post-industrial society"—meaning the decline of semiskilled occupations and "the pre-eminence of the technical and professional class," a group that was growing twice as fast as the overall labor force in 1970.[22] This burgeoning class of knowledge workers wished to understand the news in its full complexity. The newspaper publisher Charles Scripps, trying to explain in 1959 why magazine circulation was skyrocketing while newspaper circulation stagnated, said, "Our modern world is getting almost hopelessly complex and confusing." According to Scripps, magazines were "doing the job of helping people understand," but newspapers were not.[23]

Newspapers had resisted interpretive reporting because many journalists believed it ran counter to the profession's most cherished principle: objectivity. The press's efforts to reconcile interpretation and objectivity set off a pitched battle over what objectivity meant and whether or not it was a worthy ideal. Chapters 2 and 3 discuss this conflict, which had profound ramifications not only for the practice of journalism but also for American politics writ large.

Chapter 2 shows how the press responded to a right-wing critique that, while novel at the time, retains a prominent place in conservative ideology today. Before interpretation became a major element of news reports, conservatives' objections to the press centered on columnists and editorials expressing views they disliked. Reporters may have held liberal views, but the conventions of the trade prevented those views from influencing coverage, because most news articles were devoid of analysis. By the late 1960s, however, many conservatives had adopted a viewpoint that was most forcefully expressed by Vice President Spiro Agnew in a series of speeches in 1969 and 1970. They believed journalists had abandoned objectivity and were slanting the news to reflect their left-wing biases. The managers of the *New York Times* and the *Los Angeles Times* rejected this critique. While they acknowledged the left-wing leanings of their newsrooms, they maintained that reporters exercising professional judgment and editors guarding against bias usually kept the news coverage straight. Few conservatives were convinced, partly because the views expressed in editorials and by opinion columnists moved steadily leftward in the 1960s and 1970s (especially at the *Los Angeles Times*).

If the attacks from Agnew and his supporters had constituted the only major criticism leveled against the press, editors and publishers might have felt compelled to change their practices. However, as Chapter 3 explains, the unprecedentedly vehement right-wing critique coincided with an equally vehement critique from the left, often coming from within the news profession. Many journalists, especially younger ones, argued that trying to achieve objectivity led to reporting that favored the Establishment and stifled the truth. They preferred a more opinionated style of journalism that could sometimes veer into advocacy. The management of the *New York Times* and *Los Angeles Times* felt strongly that they should take a balanced approach to the news; if their coverage had to be placed on an ideological spectrum, it should be squarely in the center. Therefore, the fact that partisans on each side found fault with their approach to objectivity helped convince them that they were pursuing the proper course.

They accepted that some minor alterations might be required. At the *New York Times,* the definition of objectivity expanded to allow for a considerable degree of interpretation in news articles. At the *Los Angeles Times,* the term "objectivity" fell out of favor in the 1970s, as the publisher, editors, and many reporters thought its meaning had become too murky. They preferred to speak of "fairness." Their definition of fairness, however, was almost identical to the way other journalists defined objectivity: refraining from advocacy, correcting for one's personal prej-udices, being evenhanded. Objectivity itself, even for those who earnestly attempt to achieve it, may be considered a liberal value. It reflects an op-timistic belief in people's fundamental goodness, and faith in technocratic ideals like empiricism and detachment.

Although newspaper managers tried to strike a balance between two extremes—the conservatives claiming that liberal bias had displaced ob-jectivity and the New Leftists claiming that objectivity must be jettisoned—they paid more heed to critics on the left than to those on the right. They reasoned that readers who agreed with the right-wing critique were older and that their numbers were declining, particularly in the circulation areas of the *New York Times* and the *Los Angeles Times*. Conversely, the young, well-educated readers these papers needed to attract in order to grow were presumably sympathetic to the radical ideas flourishing on college cam-puses in the 1960s and 1970s. Executives laughed it off when angry conservatives wrote in to cancel their subscriptions, confident that the addition of new readers would more than offset the loss of some crotchety reactionaries.[24] These disgruntled ex-subscribers would not be content unless news coverage reverted to the days before interpretive reporting or provided a blatantly conservative slant—measures that no editor at a major metropolitan newspaper in America would even consider.

Partly because the press declined to make significant concessions to conservatives who believed it exhibited a liberal bias, conservative in-dignation continued to grow. Casting the "liberal media" as a foil was crucial to the self-perception of the New Right and to its rise. As many historians and other commentators have argued, the modern conserva-tive movement has long viewed itself as an insurgent group being victim-ized by the liberal establishment.[25] In this view, no institution is more emblematic of the liberal establishment and its power than the news media. By dismissing conservative complaints—although many journalists would concede that they had some validity—the press unwittingly fueled the modern conservative movement.

But even as the press helped inspire the right, it also helped bolster the shrinking center. In the late 1960s and throughout the 1970s, almost every major institution in American society experienced a crisis of authority. People lost faith in the effectiveness, trustworthiness, and essential value of not only government but also organized religion, education, corporations, even medical science.[26] The press was no exception to this trend, yet its leaders continued to behave as if they enjoyed the public's trust and spoke on behalf of all the people—news organizations that wished to retain a mass audience had little other choice. Whatever biases they perceived, most Americans recognized that the press intended to represent the vast middle of American politics. The press delineated the boundaries of respectable political discourse and helped to define the areas of broad consensus in American life; it had performed these functions to a far greater degree in the 1950s, but it continued to do so in the 1970s, 1980s, and 1990s. As the influence of "legacy media" (metropolitan newspapers, network news, national magazines) dwindled beginning in the 2000s, and the influence of more partisan and niche-oriented media grew, U.S. politics became more polarized and the center seemed to fade. Abandoning centrist news outlets in favor of ideological ones, Americans began enclosing themselves in "filter bubbles" or "information cocoons"; as a result, people with differing political views disagree not only about policy but also about basic, seemingly verifiable facts.[27]

Chapter 4 pivots away from questions of objectivity and politics to address the most readily apparent change in newspapers between 1960 and 1980: the increased prominence of "soft news," the unfairly dismissive label often applied to material meant to entertain readers or enrich their lives. This was the central element in the creation of a more reader-oriented newspaper (other elements included an increase in suburban coverage and in service material such as entertainment listings and practical advice). As with the growth of interpretive journalism, the growth of soft news represented an effort to stave off competition from other media and to halt the decline in newspaper readership, especially among the young. Additionally, and equally important to newspaper finances, expanded soft-news sections provided an attractive new option for advertisers.

The change in the newspaper's role, from informing readers to informing, entertaining, and serving them, corresponded to a shift in the American public's primary role: from citizens to consumers. With the decline of political-party organizations and civic groups in the late twentieth century, metropolitan newspapers—especially those with prestigious, national reputations, such as the *New York Times* and the *Los Angeles*

Times—became the primary link between voters and their community, state, and nation. The increasing amount of newspaper content about leisure activities and things to buy implied that the reader was being addressed primarily as a consumer, not as a citizen. For example, the *Los Angeles Times* in 1976 began including with every Tuesday's paper a magazine called *You*. It would be "an exciting new concept in consumer information," the promotional materials promised, with features devoted to hobbies, personal finance, personal health, romance, shopping, and do-it-yourself projects.[28] This and similar offerings sent readers a clear message: the press, a major institution in American public life, caters to *you*—especially if "you" are someone with disposable income.

As newspapers became increasingly reader-oriented, the scope of news broadened considerably. Important news, journalists began to realize, did not always revolve around government officials, business leaders, or prominent intellectuals. Social movements, changes in the culture, the condition of disadvantaged groups—these could be even more momentous. Articles on such topics began appearing with increasingly frequency in the 1960s and 1970s, and the trend continued into the 1980s and 1990s. The mainstream press had previously overlooked these stories in part because of the homogeneity of its newsrooms, which were composed of white men almost exclusively. Although white men would continue to predominate in positions of editorial responsibility throughout the 1970s and beyond, having to reckon with other perspectives helped them arrive at a different definition of what constituted important news. The process of making these institutions more inclusive did not always proceed smoothly, however, as Chapter 5 demonstrates.

Chapter 5 examines how the movements for equality by women and racial minorities changed newsrooms and news coverage. The *New York Times* and the *Los Angeles Times*, like most employers and institutions, practiced systemic discrimination in the early 1960s. Women who wished to be reporters were restricted to writing about fashion, society, and the family; if there were any black reporters (the *Los Angeles Times* had none, the *New York Times* had between one and three), they covered the black community almost exclusively. The content reflected the staffing: "women's news" meant stories related to homemaking, and the meager amount of news about minority communities focused mainly on issues that might concern whites. Starting from this low bar, the situation improved considerably by 1980, thanks to pressure from within the newsroom and without. Women and minorities at the *New York Times* filed two separate discrimination lawsuits against the paper; a women's caucus at the *Los Angeles Times* threatened to do the same. Gradually both papers increased the number of women and minorities on their reporting staffs, although nearly all high-ranking editors continued to be white men.

Newspapers' treatment of women and minorities, in the newsroom and in news coverage, shifted with the political climate. From the early 1960s until the early 1970s, the civil rights movement, urban unrest, and Black Power struck editors as major national stories of significant interest to all their readers (the vast majority of whom were white). They could not cover those stories effectively with an all-white staff, so hiring black reporters became a top priority, and the black reporters' stories often made the front page. By the late 1970s the situation had changed. Most major newspapers had a handful of minority reporters on staff—still far below the proportion of minorities in the general population, but not an indefensibly low number. The Black Power movement had waned, and suburbanites had become disengaged, mentally and geographically, from the problems of the inner city—a phenomenon historian Kevin Kruse has called "suburban secession."[29] Minorities and their grievances were perceived as a topic of special interest, not general interest. Editors wanted to have in-depth, quality stories on the topic occasionally, but it was no longer a priority. As C. Gerald Fraser, an African-American reporter at the *New York Times,* said in 1979, "No one can succeed here as a reporter of black affairs because there is no interest in that subject."[30]

By contrast, newspaper managers treated women and their concerns dismissively throughout the 1960s. Hiring more women was an afterthought tacked on to memos about hiring more blacks. Coverage of the feminist movement depicted it as an amusing curiosity. Sexism was so deeply ingrained that the *New York Times* publisher, in a 1967 Christmas message in the company newsletter, felt comfortable asking Santa for "shorter skirts on the young girls with the good legs and longer skirts on the ladies with the old legs."[31] But as feminism gained support and legal victories in the 1970s, editors began to reevaluate news stories that they formerly considered marginal. That included not only stories about women's political activism but also stories about women in the workplace, rape, abortion, parenting, and gender relations. Moreover, articles on such topics advanced the mission at many papers to broaden their reporting beyond the traditional arenas of government, politics, business, and sports with stories that would appeal to affluent suburbanites (especially women) and the younger generation. In an attempt to attract that audience and add some heft to their soft-news offering, editors often kept major stories having to do with women out of the main news section and published them instead on pages devoted mainly to entertainment, food, or life-style trends. To many, that amounted to a devaluation of such stories, and by 1980 this was the primary criticism that feminists raised about news coverage in the *New York Times* and the *Los Angeles Times*. Valid though that point is, a decade earlier it had been a secondary concern, given the many more flagrant examples of sexism that permeated most newspapers.

As Chapter 5 shows, the "rights revolutions" of the 1960s and 1970s resulted in significant, lasting changes in the press. Journalists and their employers generally came to accept the liberal viewpoints on race and gender, even if news organizations rarely managed to achieve their diversity goals. But another cultural change that emerged from the period between 1965 and 1975 had an even greater impact: the rise of a skeptical, antiestablishment ethos among journalists and the public at large. Chapter 6 describes and analyzes how the press's attitude toward powerful people and institutions shifted from deferential to adversarial. Although many people on the right would attribute this change to liberal bias, it had less to do with journalists' personal politics than with their professional practices. As far back as the muckraking era (approximately 1890–1914), reporters had prided themselves on challenging the powerful—the newspaper's role, according to a famous saying, was to "afflict the comfortable and comfort the afflicted."[32] The emphasis on this aspect of journalism faded during times of national crisis and consensus: World War I, the Great Depression, World War II, the early Cold War years. It came roaring back, however, in the late 1960s and early 1970s, thanks to an unpopular war about which the government routinely lied, a presidential administration that treated the press as a political enemy, and an urge to "question authority" (as a prominent slogan of the era said) then permeating American society.

This adversarial posture extended beyond coverage of Vietnam or the Nixon White House, however. Reporting on state and local government, law enforcement, business, and even sports became far tougher and more skeptical. By 1975 some editors and news executives believed the press had become *too* adversarial. As *Los Angeles Times* publisher Otis Chandler said that year, "the press . . . have gone bananas following Watergate. We seem to have lost our sense of balance, our sense of proportion." Journalists had become consumed, he continued, with "the drive for the jugular, the assumption that all politicians and all businessmen are crooks and thieves."[33] The pendulum swung back somewhat by 1980, but as evidenced by the sample issues of the *Los Angeles Times* and the *New York Times* discussed above, an adversarial edge remained.

Adversarial journalism helped reinforce a broader public cynicism about powerful institutions, especially government. This cynicism, in turn, bolstered the antigovernment philosophy of the right wing, which struck the conservative commentator Irving Kristol as highly ironic in 1975. He struggled to reconcile his belief that journalists had an ideological bias in favor of liberal big government with his observation that adversarial journalism undermined public support for liberal big government. "If government is unworthy of [the average citizen's] confidence, why should he want more powerful and more extensive government?" asked Kristol in an opinion column.[34] The answer to this apparent paradox is that professional norms, not ideological goals, dictated the tenor of news coverage.

Those professional norms were firmly entrenched by the end of the 1970s, thanks in part to the healthy profits they had helped to create at major news organizations. Chapter 7 brings the story of the media's values from 1980 to the present. The 1980s and 1990s were boom years for the media business, and as a result few news organizations felt inclined to fundamentally alter an approach that seemed to be working well. Even after the Internet upended the prevailing business model of journalism in the 2000s, most continued to cling to the values that they had established three or four decades earlier. Since about 2015, however, a subtle change seems to be occurring in "legacy" media. The growth of partisan news outlets and the ascent of Donald Trump have combined to cause many journalists and news executives to reassess their values and practices more deeply than at any time since the 1960s.

• • •

To EXPLORE HOW AMERICAN journalism changed between 1960 and 1980, it is instructive to look at the *New York Times* and the *Los Angeles Times.* Then, as now, the *New York Times* was almost universally regarded as the United States' leading journalistic institution. Other news organizations looked to it as a model of the profession's highest standards. The subtitle of Gay Talese's landmark 1969 history of the *New York Times* called it "the institution that influences the world," but it was also the institution that influences the press, as countless other newspapers strove to emulate it.[35]

In 1960 the *New York Times* was one of seven major dailies published in New York City, along with three other high-brow broadsheets and three tabloids. It had the highest circulation of the broadsheets—roughly 686,000 during the week and 1,372,000 on Sunday—and commanded the highest advertising rates of any paper, given the size and affluence of its readership.[36] The editors aimed to be scrupulously fair and incomparably complete in their news coverage, adhering to slogans that former publisher Adolph Ochs had adopted in the 1890s and 1900s: to "give the news impartially, without fear or favor," and to be a "paper of record" providing "all the news that's fit to print." Long transcripts of speeches and official statements constituted a significant portion of news material—"*The Times* likes texts. We print more than anybody," one editor proudly proclaimed in 1960.[37] Interpretations and explanations of the news appeared only in the Sunday edition and on the editorial page, which espoused moderate positions usually aligned with the Democratic Party (although the paper endorsed Dwight Eisenhower for president both times he ran). One newspaper editor, summarizing the way many readers likely felt about the *Times,* remarked, "Some days I pick it up and I say, 'I'm going to read you, you son of a bitch, if it kills me!'"[38]

The top editors at the *New York Times* in the early to mid-1960s—Turner Catledge and Clifton Daniel, two courtly Southerners—wished to make the paper more readable, perhaps even enjoyable. They took tentative steps toward doing so (more analytical reporting, better writing, broader coverage), but the process kicked into high gear when A. M. (Abe) Rosenthal began rising through the newsroom ranks. A distinguished foreign correspondent for the *Times*, he returned to New York to become the paper's metropolitan editor in 1963, earned a promotion to assistant managing editor in 1967, and became managing editor—in charge of the entire daily newspaper—in 1969. Seven years later, when the formerly separate Sunday edition merged with the daily, Rosenthal took the title of executive editor, overseeing all aspects of the news operation. A hard-driving, temperamental editor with a keen journalistic sense, Rosenthal bears more responsibility than any other individual for the transformation of the *New York Times* during the late 1960s and the 1970s.[39]

Rosenthal's boss, publisher Arthur Ochs "Punch" Sulzberger—a grandson of Adolph Ochs who took over the paper's business operations in 1963—rarely involved himself with news coverage. But on major issues Sulzberger usually backed Rosenthal. Two occasions stand out. In 1971 Sulzberger agreed to publish material from the Pentagon Papers, the military's secret history of U.S. involvement in Vietnam; in 1976, exasperated with an editorial page that he felt was too stridently liberal and antibusiness, Sulzberger forced the page's editor, his cousin John Oakes, into an early retirement and changed the composition of the editorial board—a move that met with the hearty approval of Rosenthal, who believed the editorials' hectoring, left-wing tone undermined the newspaper's reputation for objectivity.

As publisher, Sulzberger concerned himself mainly with the paper's financial health. Two newspaper strikes in New York—one in 1962–1963, the other in 1966—contributed to the demise of the *New York Times*'s main competitors in the local market, and by 1970 its daily circulation approached 1 million. The resolution of those strikes, however, left the *Times* with costly union contracts for production department staff whose jobs might otherwise have been phased out due to new technology. In the mid-1970s, with operating costs rising precipitously at the same time as the overall economy declined and affluent New Yorkers fled to the suburbs, the paper faced its gravest financial crisis since Adolph Ochs purchased it in 1896. It recovered quickly, however, thanks in large part to new special sections for each day of the week, devoted mainly to leisure interests such as food, entertainment, and the home. As the *New York Times* entered the 1980s, it was flourishing both financially and journalistically.[40]

The *Los Angeles Times* by 1980 had a reputation as one of the country's three leading general-interest newspapers, alongside the *New York Times* and the *Washington Post*. In 1960, however, most journalists considered it a provincial, reactionary rag. It employed few correspondents abroad, in Washington, or around the country; the typical headline, some journalists liked to joke, was "L.A. Dog Chases L.A. Cat over L.A. Fence."[41] And the paper had no qualms, prior to the 1960s, about slanting its news coverage to favor right-wing causes and politicians. For instance, *L.A. Times* editor-in-chief L. D. Hotchkiss, issuing his annual summary of the newspaper's performance in 1952, wrote, "In a news way the year 1952 was outstanding," primarily because "candidates endorsed by this newspaper won." He added, "Perhaps a small amount of credit at least should be given this newspaper for the overwhelming GOP vote in California."[42] The man who succeeded Hotchkiss as editor-in-chief, Nick Williams, admitted that the paper in this earlier era was "a propaganda organ . . . of the Republican Party."[43] Three generations of strong-willed publishers from the Chandler family had molded the *L.A. Times* into this shape, but fourth-generation publisher Otis Chandler, who took over in 1960, departed dramatically from the formula of his father, grandfather, and great-grandfather.

Thanks largely to the phenomenal growth that the Los Angeles area experienced in the twentieth century, the *L.A. Times* had always been highly profitable—in 1960 it led the country in advertising volume, as it had for many years running.[44] Nevertheless, Otis Chandler, thirty-two years old upon becoming publisher, determined to remake his family's paper. He may have feared that it could not maintain its success if it continued to put out a mediocre, highly partisan product. But concerned though he was with profits, he cared even more about prestige. He wanted the *Los Angeles Times* to become as good as or better than the *New York Times*.

To achieve that goal, Chandler needed to upgrade the staff and change the paper's political orientation, which he did with the help of editor-in-chief Nick Williams. Chandler made enormous investments in the *L.A.*

Times's news-gathering operation. He and Williams hired top journalists away from the country's leading newspapers and magazines, offering not only ample salaries but also assurances that the formerly hidebound paper had made a new commitment to openness and evenhandedness. The news staff doubled from 1961 to 1971, increasing even faster in high-visibility areas such as Washington reporters (three in 1962, eighteen in 1970) and foreign correspondents (one in 1962, twelve in 1965, more than twenty by the mid-1970s).[45] In addition to hiring more journalists to cover the city of Los Angeles, the *Times* greatly expanded its investment in "zoned" sections with news from each of L.A.'s sprawling suburban areas. Overall, the news budget increased from roughly $3 million to $12 million between 1960 and 1970.[46]

Moving the *Los Angeles Times* away from its traditional conservatism carried risks for Otis Chandler—he would alienate many longtime readers, certainly, but he would also incur the wrath of his extended family, who might oust him from the board of directors. Nevertheless, he decided that the potential rewards—in prestige and in new readers—outweighed the risks. In 1962 the paper published a five-part exposé on the ultra-right-wing John Birch Society, infuriating Chandler's relatives, some of whom were members. In 1964 the editorial page endorsed the moderate Nelson Rockefeller over the staunch conservative Barry Goldwater in the Republican presidential primary, then offered only a tepid endorsement of Goldwater in the general election. That same year the *Times* chose as its new editorial cartoonist the liberal Paul Conrad, whose scathing visual commentaries outraged Republican readers (and sometimes Democratic readers too). Chandler and Williams made their hires on the basis of talent, not politics—Conrad was, by consensus, the nation's best cartoonist apart from the *Washington Post*'s Herblock—and many talented journalists happened to be committed liberals. By the end of the 1960s, although the editor-in-chief (Nick Williams) and editorial page director (James Bassett) were both moderate Republicans, the paper's overall orientation was slightly left of center.

A year and a half after his retirement, Nick Williams wrote to Otis Chandler's mother, Dorothy "Buff" Chandler, an indomitable influence on the paper during her husband's tenure as publisher (and to a lesser extent during her son's). The overriding mission of his editorship, Williams said, was to gain "national prestige" for the *L.A. Times.* "The first essential of national prestige, and the fastest route to it, is a newspaper's prestige among other journalists," he explained. "So to gain the recognition of other journalists, two things had to be done. First, to begin recruiting—pirating—newspapermen with national reputations among their kind. . . . The second thing: newspaper prestige, not always but usually, is a function of liberal estimation. Most intellectuals are liberal, and editorial prestige depends on what intellectuals judge it to be."[47] Williams was oversimplifying somewhat, probably because he wished to justify the measures to which Buff Chandler objected most strongly: the paper's leftward shift and its hiring of several high-profile journalists whom she disliked (Williams also, with characteristic modesty, failed to mention the importance of a savvy, far-sighted editor). But on the whole, Williams summed up his tenure accurately. He hired top-notch journalists and did not impede their work. He eliminated the conservative bias from the news pages, encouraged his expensive new staff to cover the news aggressively, and condoned the inclusion of more left-wing views on the editorial pages—exemplified by Paul Conrad's cartoons.

The *Los Angeles Times* earned more than simply prestige during the years of Otis Chandler and Nick Williams's partnership, from 1960 to 1971. The daily paper's circulation increased from 537,000 to 981,000, and its revenues rose from $63 million to more than $160 million.[48] Management used those immense profits, in part, to generously reward the paper's staff. Unlike most newspapers, the *L.A. Times* had never been unionized, in large part because it paid higher salaries than its unionized competitors. By the 1970s the jobs had become so cushy, with lavish pay and benefits, that people referred to the paper as "the velvet coffin"—the staff stayed on until they retired or died.

Nick Williams's successor as editor-in-chief, Bill Thomas, continued to increase the *Los Angeles Times*'s prestige and profitability. Under Thomas, the paper placed a greater emphasis on investigative and "enterprise" journalism (ferreting out stories rather than simply responding to events) while also adding more of its soft-news coverage, including the same kinds of special sections that the *New York Times* launched. Thomas advocated the concept of the newspaper as a daily news magazine: it would provide interpretive coverage on nearly every topic of interest to a wide audience, it would contain elegant writing by strong authorial voices, and it would provide useful information to help readers in their everyday lives.

Comparing the *Los Angeles Times* and the *New York Times* during the 1960s and 1970s, some significant differences emerge. The *L.A. Times* was a "writer's paper." Journalists sometimes quipped that it was "edited with a shovel," meaning that material was simply dumped onto the page without being trimmed or refined—a luxury afforded by the vast amounts of advertising the paper brought in, which translated into vast amounts of editorial space to fill.[49] That was an exaggeration, to be sure, but many of the paper's most favored reporters had the freedom to write at great length, and editors were discouraged from cutting or changing their copy substantially.[50] The *New York Times,* by contrast, was an "editor's paper." Once again a newsroom quip may best illustrate what that meant: "They would scour the country for the most talented writers with the strongest voice, and then you would come in and they would beat it out of you."[51] A similarly harsh assessment, but it indicates the degree to which editors, mindful of the paper's reputation, tried to impose uniformity on editorial content and to excise any perceived biases. The similarities between the two papers' development during the 1960s and 1970s stand out far more than the differences, however. In their journalistic values, their changing approach to the news, and their response to business challenges, these two leading news organizations mirrored each other to a remarkable degree.

• • •

MOST AMERICANS have firm beliefs about the characteristics of the country's news media and the values that guide journalists' work. People who have been news consumers for all of their adult lives feel comfortable making judgments about what shapes news coverage. Similarly, most historians use newspapers and magazines from earlier eras as source material for their research, and their familiarity with this material can lead them to form assumptions about how journalism has (or has not) changed over the years. But to truly understand how the American press became what it is, one must consider the drama behind the headlines—the internal and external pressures that journalists contend with while making the thousands of decisions that will determine how they present the news.

The values that define contemporary American journalism are not timeless. Rather, this book will show, they took shape in the 1960s and 1970s—a period when technological change threatened the business model of traditional media and when the press found itself at the center of a vitriolic national political debate. A period, in other words, that was strikingly similar to our own. Examining this revolution in the newsroom yields valuable insights into history. And for those who believe that the past is prologue, it can help illuminate American journalism's current parlous state and its possible future.

❈ 1 ❈

Opening the Door to Interpretation

I N 1958 the Associated Press Managing Editors Association invited the esteemed journalist Louis M. Lyons to give a speech about how newspapers had changed in the previous quarter-century. His answer? They hadn't. "A candid look at the last 25 years would show them as . . . largely a holding operation," Lyons declared. However, Lyons noted one sign of innovation: the rise of "the interpretive story."[1]

Ever since major American newspapers began adopting the ideal of objectivity in the 1910s and 1920s, they had allowed only a select few journalists to interpret the news: editorial writers, opinion columnists, and those writing for special sections in the Sunday edition (such as the *New York Times* Week in Review). Foreign correspondents—at the few newspapers that employed any—also had the privilege of including some analysis in their stories. Workaday reporters, however, had to stick to the four W's and one H: who, what, when, where, and how. The "why" question was beyond their purview. With interpretive reporting, that began to change.

The move toward interpretation that began in the 1950s continues today, and it has had far-reaching implications. It caused journalists to redefine objectivity, contributed to the public's mistrust of the news

media, and shifted the balance of power in news organizations from editors to reporters. But at the outset, it was—like most profound changes
in big, established institutions—simply an attempt to keep pace with the
competition.

When newspapers had a monopoly on breaking news, there was little
reason for them to provide interpretation. A desire to know what had happened the day before provided reason enough for most Americans to buy
a daily paper. Radio news, however, broke that monopoly in the 1930s,
in spite of fierce resistance from newspaper publishers (they tried to pro-
hibit radio announcers from reading Associated Press dispatches on the
air, and to force stations to limit their newscasts to ten minutes per day).[2]
Partly as a result, the American Society of Newspaper Editors (ASNE)
in 1933 urged its members to "devote a larger amount of attention and
space to explanatory and interpretative news"; in 1938 journalism professor Curtis MacDougall published a textbook titled *Interpretative
Reporting*.[3]

In addition to the economic justification for interpretive reporting, it
made sense journalistically. Ever since the end of World War I, intellectuals had warned that facts without context could be deceptive or could
turn into propaganda.[4] As Walter Lippmann argued in *Public Opinion*
(1922), "News and truth are not the same thing, and must be clearly distinguished."[5] Although Lippmann did not explicitly propose interpretive
reporting as a solution, others did. During World War II, Time Inc. publisher Henry Luce assembled a commission of experts led by University
of Chicago chancellor Robert Hutchins to report on freedom of the press
in the United States. The Hutchins Commission Report, released in 1947,
concluded that press freedom was in danger, in large part because the
news media were not providing "a service adequate to the needs of the
society." The first requirement of the American press, the report stated,
was to provide "a truthful, comprehensive, and intelligent account of the
day's events in a context that gives them meaning." Without that context,
isolated "facts" could be misleading or untrue, the Hutchins Commission argued, and therefore the norms of news reporting must change. In
a line that subsequent advocates of interpretive reporting often quoted,
the commission declared, "It is no longer enough to report *the fact* truth-
fully. It is now necessary to report *the truth about the fact*."[6]

At the *New York Times*, the country's most prestigious newspaper, Washington correspondent James "Scotty" Reston (who would later become Washington bureau chief, executive editor, and a columnist) enthusiastically endorsed the Hutchins Commission's viewpoint on interpretation, and he urged other newspapers to do the same. Addressing the Associated Press Managing Editors in 1948, Reston said, "Explanatory writing is the field in which we can excel. You cannot merely report the literal truth. You have to explain it."[7] Reston himself had gained the unusual privilege of writing interpretive stories at the *New York Times*, which generally restricted such articles to certain parts of the Sunday edition. And even that allowance had not come easily. Sunday editor Lester Markel began advocating for interpretation in the 1920s, but publisher Adolph Ochs did not acquiesce until 1935, shortly before his death.[8]

Although Reston was writing for the daily paper and not the Sunday edition (two separate operations in those days), his articles did not merely report what officials said and did. They often included Reston's informed judgments about the motivations and strategies of world leaders, along with broad analyses of geopolitics. Foreign affairs were Reston's specialty; because editors and readers knew (and cared) more about what was happening in the United States, interpretive reporting about the international scene was relatively uncontroversial, and foreign correspondents had more freedom to interpret the news than did stateside reporters.[9] Casting judgments about American leaders was far more sensitive than playing Kremlinologist or analyzing the British prime minister's cabinet appointments.

However, as the 1950s progressed, Reston began writing interpretive stories about American politics, too. This sometimes made the paper's publisher, Arthur Hays Sulzberger, uneasy—for example, when Reston wrote an interpretive article prior to the 1952 presidential election that was critical of Dwight Eisenhower, Sulzberger's preferred candidate. Nevertheless, in a speech that same year, Sulzberger came out strongly in favor of interpretive reporting. Newspapers should provide "more interpretation, explanation, and presentation of background," he said. But Sulzberger stressed that interpretation "does not take the place of the factual news report. It is supplementary, and, essential as it is, it is dangerous if not watched and done correctly within rigid limits. The balance between interpretation and opinion is delicate and it must be preserved."[10]

With this proviso in mind, the *New York Times* proceeded cautiously on interpretive reporting. Only Reston and a few other trusted senior correspondents, such as military specialist Hanson Baldwin, were allowed to do it, and the editors felt compelled to clearly label interpretive articles as such.[11] In the mid-1950s they began inserting the words "an analysis" or "an appraisal" into the subheadlines of major interpretive stories, and setting the headlines in italics in order to distinguish them from the other articles on the page.[12] By 1958 the editors had decided to make the distinction even clearer. They indented a portion of the text at the beginning of the article and inserted a box that read, "News Analysis"—a usage that continues in the *New York Times* to this day.[13]

The trickle of interpretive stories in the 1950s eventually turned into a flood, at the *New York Times* and at many other American newspapers. Several studies have quantified the trend. Examining the front pages of the *New York Times,* the *Washington Post,* and the *Milwaukee Journal-Sentinel,* Katherine Fink and Michael Schudson found a marked increase in what they called "contextual stories" (those that are "explanatory in nature" and go "beyond the who-what-when-where of a recent event") and a concomitant decline in "conventional stories." Whereas conventional stories outnumbered contextual ones by more than 10 to 1 in 1955, by 2003 the ratio had become roughly 1-to-1. The shift "was most pronounced between 1955 and 1979."[14]

Kevin Barnhurst and Diana Mutz performed a similar analysis, looking at three newspapers at twenty-year intervals from 1894 to 1994. The categories of news they considered—crime, accidents, and employment—seem least ripe for interpretation, yet the results showed that the "emphasis on analysis and context" increased more during the years between 1954 and 1974 than in any other two-decade period.[15] Thomas Patterson took a narrower view, examining front-page stories about presidential elections in the *New York Times* between 1960 and 1992. He concluded that in 1960 more than 90 percent of stories relied on a descriptive rather than interpretive framework, but by 1976 interpretive stories accounted for more than half of the total.[16]

Prominent voices such as those of Walter Lippmann, Curtis MacDougall, the American Society of Newspaper Editors, and the Hutchins Commission had been pleading for interpretive reporting throughout the

1930s and 1940s, so why didn't it take off until the 1950s? The key obstacle was objectivity. Interpretive reporting, by definition, must include the reporter's judgments, and many journalists felt that would violate the profession's sacrosanct principle: that reporting should be objective. To take such a drastic step—to jettison or radically alter the objectivity ideal—would require a more compelling rationale than the middling threat posed by radio or philosophical musings about the nature of truth. That rationale came at last in the 1950s and 1960s, in the form of a television antenna and a blustering senator.

• • •

SENATOR JOSEPH MCCARTHY of Wisconsin rocketed from obscurity to national fame in the early 1950s thanks in large part to his astute exploitation of journalistic norms. When McCarthy made shocking accusations about communist agents inside the U.S. government, newspapers following the dictates of objectivity put his statements on the front page. Although many reporters doubted the truthfulness of McCarthy's claims (given the scant evidence he provided), they felt that expressing those doubts would be tantamount to editorializing. To be sure, the editorial pages and columnists of many leading newspapers denounced McCarthy, but their news pages dutifully amplified his charges.[17]

The spectacle of journalists abetting the rise of a man whom most of them considered a demagogue convinced many in the press that American reporting practices were badly broken. As early as 1950, prominent journalists were lamenting the press's adherence to "straight reporting" and limited use of "interpretive reporting," which made it easy for McCarthy to get the coverage he wanted.[18] The famous radio commentator Elmer Davis declared in 1953 that "the rise of McCarthy has compelled newspapers of integrity to develop a form of reporting which puts into context what men like McCarthy have to say."[19] This new form of reporting had to mix fact and interpretation. "Dead-pan objectivity" devoid of analysis, Davis said, "makes the news business merely a transmission belt for pretentious phonies."[20]

However, the press was far from unanimous in its support for interpretive reporting, especially if that would mean redefining objectivity. This was the topic of fierce debate at newspaper conventions in the early 1950s.

As Edwin Bayley found in his landmark study of McCarthy and the press, the debate broke down along partisan lines: "All of the 'fundamentalists' on objectivity were from newspapers that supported McCarthy editorially, and all of the editors who defended interpretive reporting were from newspapers that were critical of McCarthy."[21]

In short, the more liberal newspapers supported interpretive reporting and opposed McCarthy, while the more conservative newspapers opposed interpretive reporting and supported McCarthy. With McCarthy's fall from grace in 1954, the advocates of interpretation felt vindicated. By the mid-1950s the question at hand shifted from "Should newspapers do interpretive reporting?" to "How can newspapers do a good job of interpretive reporting?" Because the practice of interpretive reporting remained somewhat unfamiliar and controversial, journalists still had to justify it. They stressed the need to rethink the notion of objectivity while maintaining a distinction between interpretation and opinion.

"I recognize the danger of deviating from the straight and narrow road of objectivity," said Ernest Linford, the chief editorial writer of the *Salt Lake Tribune*, in a 1955 speech. When reporters with "strong prejudices" and "a cavalier attitude toward truth and responsibility" attempt interpretive reporting, Linford said, "they may do more damage than if they had not tried to explain the news." And yet, he argued, "one-dimensional news reporting is inadequate now. . . . Objectivity is still a good thing but it is not enough anymore."[22]

A year later, in 1956, the New York University journalism professor Hillier Krieghbaum echoed that viewpoint, declaring, "The old journalistic god of an impersonal, absolute objectivity for news reporting has largely failed its modern believers." However, he warned that it was "extremely difficult" to adapt "conventional objectivity" to allow for interpretation—it required reporters to describe "the nine-tenths of the iceberg of a news happening that is not easily visible above the surface."[23] Elmer Davis, a strong proponent of interpretive reporting, acknowledged that it "entails serious dangers." Journalists, he wrote, "must walk a tightrope between two great gulfs—on one side the false objectivity that takes everything at face value and lets the public be imposed on by the charlatan with the most brazen front; on the other, the 'interpretive' reporting which fails to draw the line between objective and subjective, between a well-established fact and what the reporter or editor wishes were the fact. To say that is easy; to do it is hard."[24]

· · ·

GIVEN THE DIFFICULTY of interpretive reporting, and the fact that it required a fundamental change in the principle of objectivity, few newspaper publishers and editors would have attempted it solely to prevent the rise of another Joe McCarthy. But when that public-spirited (or perhaps ideological) motivation was coupled with business considerations, the decision to embrace interpretation became much easier.

Television news grew slowly in the 1950s, but print journalists quickly recognized its potential to change their business. TV, even more than radio, threatened to make obsolete the newspaper's traditional role of simply describing what had happened the day before. "The press has lost to radio and television the first impact of a news event," wrote *Louisville Courier-Journal* publisher Barry Bingham in 1959. Therefore, he said, "newspapers must do what television cannot or does not do"—which meant "covering the news better, more fully, and in greater depth."[25] At the *New York Times*, Scotty Reston used the same argument several years earlier to reinforce his publisher's support for interpretive reporting. "A case can be made that there should be no critical analysis in the news columns," he allowed, "though I would consider that a great mistake, since this is about the only thing the television camera does not seem to be able to do as yet."[26]

As TV news expanded in the 1960s, newspaper editors continued to cite the competitive pressure as a reason to step up their efforts at interpreting the news. At the *Los Angeles Times* editor-in-chief Nick Williams felt interpretive reporting was the newspaper's only hope if it wished to remain relevant in the television age. In a 1966 memo he told publisher Otis Chandler, "Since we cannot match TV's capability for the live picture, we must then concentrate on a comparatively GREATER skill in the wordage, *and* in programming the substance of our interpretives, *and* in giving them comparatively greater insight than the TV boys give them."[27] A few months earlier, Chandler had expressed a similar sentiment in a memo to the heads of the *Los Angeles Times*'s parent company: "Let us face it, many people do not need The Times or any other newspaper.

They get their hard news from other media and many even wait for specialized magazines for recaps and interpretations of the news."[28] In 1968 a *Chicago Sun-Times* editor complimented a *New York Times* editor on what he considered an especially good interpretive article about the presidential campaign. "With that kind of campaign story, we'll all beat the electronic apes yet," the Chicago editor wrote.[29]

When an established business faces a new rival offering a similar product, it usually has two basic options: imitation or differentiation. The established business can offer the same thing that its new competitor provides, or it can provide something different that the competitor cannot match. For newspapers trying to adapt to the rise of TV news, imitation was not an option; they could never emulate the immersive audiovisual experience of watching television. In trying to differentiate themselves from TV, however, the daily newspaper imitated another rival that was nipping at its heels: magazines.

Weekly news magazines—primarily *Time, Newsweek,* and *U.S. News and World Report*—made tremendous circulation gains in the 1940s and 1950s, while nationwide newspaper circulation declined slightly. *Time* had essentially invented the concept of interpretive reporting in the 1920s, and its competitors successfully imitated that approach. (*Time* also showed that interpretive reporting has no inherent left-wing leaning, as its content generally reflected the internationalist, Republican views of publisher Henry Luce.) Charles Scripps, chairman of the newspaper chain that bore his name, warned in 1959 that newspapers needed to adopt a magazine-like approach to the news. "The people want someone to help them not only to know the events of the day—but to help them understand and relate them," Scripps said. The solution, he argued, was for newspapers to emulate magazines by doing "better, more interpretive and expository writing."[30]

As justifications for a journalistic revolution, however, the lessons of McCarthy and the competitive threat from rival news media left something to be desired. Citing the McCarthy saga made the press seem like patsies (for letting McCarthy manipulate them) or partisans (for disparaging a Republican senator whom many Americans admired). Citing the media competition made the press seem crass and self-interested. Fortunately for the proponents of interpretive reporting, there was a third rationale upon which they could rely: the world, they said, had become much more complicated, and to understand it, readers needed more explanation.

Every generation likely thinks that the world was simpler in the past, but Americans in the 1950s and 1960s had more grounds than most for believing that. The pace of discovery in science, technology, and medicine seemed to quicken each year—atomic bombs, vaccines, satellites. The United States became a global superpower, with strategic interests in nearly every corner of the world. In this new age, many journalists argued, the old methods of reporting would not keep the public adequately informed.

In 1961 *Arizona Republic* managing editor J. Edward Murray coined a term for the press's dilemma: he called it "the crisis of meaning." Murray explained, "The changes in the world are coming faster and faster, and newspapers are doing no better than anyone else in keeping up with them." This demanded reporting with "more depth, more perspective, more interpretation and explanation."[31] Nearly every plea for interpretive reporting included some version of this claim.[32]

This three-part justification for interpretive reporting—prevent unscrupulous politicians like McCarthy from exploiting the press, stave off the threat from TV news and magazines, and help readers understand their increasingly complex world—carried the day at most major news organizations by the early 1960s. At the *New York Times,* Turner Catledge, the top editor from 1951 to 1964, considered himself a "hard news man" and initially opposed interpretive reporting and "news analysis" stories. But as he recalled in his memoir, his views changed: "As political issues grew more complex and more personal to readers, and as politicians became more adept at distorting them, I increasingly saw the need for analysis of the news. Television was another important factor, for it increasingly gave people their hard news, while adding to their need for explanations."[33]

Even the Associated Press in the 1960s accepted the need for interpretive reporting. Since its creation in 1846, the wire service had been doggedly devoted to objective reporting that provided "just the facts"—a necessity, given that the AP wished to sell articles to newspapers with a wide range of political positions. But the AP general manager explained in 1962, "Spot news . . . is no longer enough. The worldwide public needs to know the 'why' of complex news situations; people need the background and appraisal which qualified specialists and experienced newsmen can provide." To that end, the wire service had recently introduced interpretive articles labeled "an AP news analysis."[34]

It is plausible that readers hungered for explanation, perspective, and analysis. In the mid-1960s a much greater proportion of Americans were college-educated than had been the case two decades earlier. Moreover, as Michael Schudson has noted, the nature of a college education had changed: it emphasized critical analysis and skepticism rather than reverence for the "accepted canons of high culture."[35] But those who made the case for interpretive reporting based on the public's supposed demand for it seem to have been operating on a hunch—they did not cite surveys or letters or any specific data. Rather, they may have been projecting their own desires and the desires of their colleagues. Reporters, like their audience, were increasingly well educated and schooled in the need to analyze the world critically—they wanted to read interpretive reporting, and they wanted to write interpretive stories. As *New York Times* executive editor Max Frankel recalled in his memoir, "Those of us knocking at newspaper doors in the 1950s aspired to be not just stenographic reporters but 'correspondents' like [Scotty] Reston."[36]

Although most decision makers in major news organizations got behind interpretive reporting in the 1960s, some holdouts remained. Richard Pourade, editor and publisher of the conservative *San Diego Union-Tribune,* opposed interpretive journalism on ideological grounds. He viewed it as a stalking horse for left-wing bias. During the 1960 presidential campaign, Pourade set up what he called "a special operation" to screen wire-service articles "for every sign of bias, slanting, and interpretative reporting"—three things that he apparently believed went hand in hand. He sent a batch of examples to *Los Angeles Times* editor-in-chief Nick Williams—all of them either favorable to John F. Kennedy or damaging to Richard Nixon—with a note that said, "This is the result of interpretive writing."[37]

By 1960, however, political ideology was no longer a reliable indicator of whether a journalist supported interpretive journalism. Some conservatives, like Pourade, insisted on the traditional definition of objectivity and rejected interpretation, but many did not. In a 1961 speech, *Los Angeles Times* editor-in-chief Nick Williams—a moderate Republican in charge of a conservative paper—argued that "reporting *has* to be interpreting" and that interpretive writing often "comes much nearer the truth than any so-called factual reporting could do." Editors who claimed to be opposed to interpretation, Williams suggested, actually just "do not like the way their reporters are writing. And my answer to that problem is as simple as a severance check."[38]

Irving Kristol, a founding father of neoconservatism, argued in a 1967 article that objective journalism without interpretation was "a rationalization for 'safe' and mindless reporting." He continued, "To keep a reporter's prejudices out of a story is commendable; to keep his judgment out of a story is to guarantee that truth will be emasculated."[39] This was a key distinction. Like most advocates of interpretive reporting, Kristol wished to redefine objectivity, not to dismiss it entirely. The traditionalists, on the other hand, would brook no changes to their most cherished ideal, and they based their opposition to interpretive reporting on the threat it posed to objectivity—and by extension, to press credibility.

At the *New York Times,* the leading opponent of interpretive reporting was also one of the paper's leading liberal thinkers: John Oakes, the editorial-page editor and cousin of publisher Arthur Ochs ("Punch") Sulzberger. As the man in charge of the lone section of the paper explicitly dispensing opinions, he regarded any feints toward interpretation as trespassing on his turf. Moreover, he felt that tampering with the line between news and opinion would undercut the paper's credibility and objectivity. Oakes's expansive definition of "opinion" included what most others considered interpretation. He regularly pleaded with his cousin the publisher to crack down on what he called "editorialization." In a 1963 letter Oakes wrote, "I suppose I am butting my head against a stone wall; but again I feel I must call your attention to the editorialization in the news columns, which in my view is steadily eroding the Times' reputation for objective news reporting." Punch Sulzberger forwarded the letter to the editor-in-chief, who disputed that there was any trend toward editorializing. Responding to Oakes, Sulzberger wrote, "I guess my philosophy lies somewhere between the two of you. I don't want to see editorializing in the news columns, but I would give a far wider latitude

John B. Oakes, editorial page
editor of the *New York Times*
from 1961 to 1976. A liberal in
his political beliefs but a
traditionalist in his journalistic beliefs, he opposed
interpretive reporting in
the 1960s and opposed the
expansion of soft news in the
1970s. Photo: © The New
York Times / Redux.

in this complex day and age to the reporter in permitting him to explain
complicated problems."[40]

Perhaps the fiercest opponent of interpretation in the news columns
was James S. Pope, executive editor of the *Louisville Courier-Journal*—
which Joe McCarthy had included on his list of "left-wing" newspapers.[41]
In 1961 Pope took to the pages of the *Columbia Journalism Review* to offer
an extended rebuttal of interpretive reporting. He acknowledged that it
arose from a "benevolent" intent: "Newspapers faced rough competition
from television and 'news' magazines; they should respond by giving
readers more, better information. Very admirable. A good, good invention. But then something Frankensteinish happened." When interpretive
reporting took root, he said, "the basic news-editorial duality sought by
good newspapers for decades began to fade" and editors began receiving
"copy in which news is intermingled with the writer's personal notions
about it." Pope scolded editors who believed the "fallacy" that "news-
column interpretation is proper if it is objective," reminding them that
"by definition interpretation is subjective." There was no room in his view

for a new category of reporting between straight news and editorial opinion, as the proponents of interpretation would have it: "A label like 'News Analysis' is cryptic, and seems to be inadequate to expose what is often outright editorial-page matter."[42]

Pope seems to have recognized, however, that his was a minority view and that interpretive reporting was already entrenched. He wrote in the present tense that "news now gets considerable interpretation before you know what it is" and admitted that views he abhorred "have gained credence among eminent editors."[43] He represented an ultratraditionalist perspective; when mentioning the competition from news magazines, he put the word "news" in quotation marks, indicating that he did not consider the likes of *Time* and *Newsweek* to be true purveyors of news (presumably because of their emphasis on analysis).

By the early 1960s the advocates for interpretive reporting had prevailed in their battle with the journalism profession's traditionalists. The rise of McCarthy was the sine qua non, the essential condition that made it possible for journalists to adjust the principle of objectivity to allow for interpretation. But it was the competitive threat from television that prompted newspapers to actively encourage interpretation and analysis instead of just paying it lip service. In 1963 an article in the *Bulletin of the American Society of Newspaper Editors* celebrated the ascendancy of interpretive reporting. A "quiet revolution" had occurred in American newspapers, wrote David Starr, a managing editor who had worked at several New York–area papers. The press, as he described it, had awakened from the Dark Ages:

> Once upon a time, news stories were like tape recorders. They echoed the words of the speaker and dittoed the words of the document. If the speaker lied, or the document distorted the truth, so be it—even if the reporter knew better. . . . That was Objectivity, and newsmen—especially editors—bowed low to it. No more. A whole generation of events has taught us better—Hitler and Goebbels, Stalin and McCarthy, automation and analog computers and missiles. The world is just too complicated for bare facts. . . . Objectivity, we realize now, includes calling a lie a lie. Objectivity includes putting facts in perspective.[44]

The fruit of this epiphany, this "search for truth," was "the interpretive story," Starr continued. "It put the news in its proper setting. It told what was being thought as well as what was being said."[45]

Starr's revised definition of objectivity, and his grandiose view of what interpretive stories could and should do, might well raise some objections. His casual conflation of McCarthy with Hitler, Goebbels, and Stalin could rankle conservatives, even as it showed the degree to which "McCarthy proved that objectivity was broken" had become journalistic dogma. Moreover, Starr presumed that reporters are in a position to know "what was being thought as well as what was being said." He implied that lies are easy to detect, and that everyone can agree on what is a lie and what is not. This might trouble not only conservatives but also nonideological journalists who simply worried about the press's credibility. It would give reporters a tremendous amount of discretion to judge the facts and frame the news. In short, interpretive reporting would place greater demands upon reporters, but it would also give them greater power.

• • •

SIMPLY ADDING MORE INTERPRETATION to news articles, however, would not be enough to help readers make sense of a complicated world and to stave off the competition from TV, magazines, and radio. In addition to changing *how* they reported the news, editors wanted to change *what* they reported as news. The front-page mainstays of politics, government, and war were not the only important stories. As for accidents, crime, and scandal, they came to be considered tabloid fodder at high-brow papers like the *New York Times* and the *Los Angeles Times*. The way forward, said Turner Catledge in a 1965 speech, was to adapt to "the knowledge explosion," by which he meant the increasing education level of readers and the increasing complexity of the information they had to digest. As a result, Catledge argued,

> Newspapers must throw away old definitions of what makes news—
> petty crime, local fires, the chitchat which provided so much of the
> stuff of our father's newspaper. Today the prime subjects of news are
> those which are on the frontiers of man's expanding knowledge: cy-
> bernetics, the new mathematics, the structure of the chromosome, the

deep philosophical and religious implications of man's expanded universe, the tidal movements in human relations, such as we have witnessed in the civil rights struggle in this country, [the] evolution [in] the Roman Catholic Church, . . . the complex splintering and elaboration of Marxism in many parts of the world.[46]

Other editors had been making similar arguments. To address the "crisis of meaning," said J. Edward Murray of the *Arizona Republic* in 1961, newspapers had to provide not only more interpretive reporting but also "better selection of stories." He elaborated: "First, more science, more education, more economics, more religion. More serious, useful news generally. Second, less perishable news that is only entertaining and time-consuming. Less spot news whose only virtue is its meaningless immediacy. Less crime and catastrophe that is like all the other crime and catastrophe."[47]

Los Angeles Times publisher Otis Chandler had a similar prescription in 1964 for newspapers that wished to thrive in the future. Addressing the American Society of Newspaper Editors, he recommended "*less* emphasis on cheap crime and sensational news. This type of news play does not hold readers." Instead, "a *greater news* package should be the basic core of your product, along with detailed reports on the meaning of the news." That package, he said, should include not only spot news but also "trends in government, water, air pollution, automation, civil rights, schools, freeways—special interest material having to do with people and how they live, think, react." As justification for these changes, he made the obligatory reference to pressure from other media: "The major challenge to metropolitan newspapers is that today television, radio, and magazines are providing stiff competition."[48]

The need for interpretive reporting and the need for a broader selection of stories reinforced each other. If an article about science, economics, or (in Catledge's words) "the deep philosophical and religious implications of man's expanded universe" were to be comprehensible and interesting, the reporter would have to provide plenty of explanation. At the same time, topics that had once been considered straightforward—like politics and foreign affairs—became subject to greater interpretation too. Rather than simply describing what was said or done the previous day in inverted-pyramid style (providing the most basic information at the top, then arranging the remaining details in order of their importance), news articles needed to provide insights that could not be gleaned from TV or radio reports. This also meant that news articles would need to become longer. Although editors stressed the need for concise writing, multiple studies have shown that the average length of news articles increased considerably in the 1960s and 1970s.[49]

So in addition to interpreting the familiar news topics and knowledgeably explaining the unfamiliar ones, reporters needed to write essay-length articles without leaving the reader bored or confused. That required tremendous skill. The archetypical reporter of the 1930s and 1940s was the sort depicted in the 1928 play *The Front Page* (and subsequent movie adaptations like *His Girl Friday*): hard-drinking, high-school-educated, and tasked mainly with getting a hot scoop and spelling names correctly. As more Americans began attending college in the 1940s and 1950s, however, the journalism business became more professionalized.[50] By the 1960s nearly all reporters on big-city newspapers had a college education, and at top-tier papers like the *New York Times* and the *Los Angeles Times,* they came increasingly from elite universities.[51] As *L.A. Times* editor-in-chief Nick Williams wrote to publisher Otis Chandler in 1962, "Newspapers are now attracting by far the best all-around talent they have ever attracted. This used to be a business for showoffs, crackpots, and drunks, with an occasional brilliant reporter. It isn't that way now."[52]

This deeper pool of talent enabled newspaper managers to ask more of their reporters. A 1961 article about the challenges of interpretive journalism observed, "It is one thing for a Scotty Reston . . . to offer some insight into the meaning of a Cabinet shift or a Congressional maneuver. It is an altogether different matter for every Tom, Dick and Harry in every newsroom from Olympia to Miami to try his unsure hand at explaining what the news means."[53] Similarly, covering specialized topics (science, law, education, religion) required specialized knowledge. Some intellectual observers in the 1960s argued that the main shortcoming of the American press—including the *New York Times*—was its reporters' lack of expertise in the topics they covered: business reporters had no training in economics, crime reporters had no knowledge of sociology, and foreign correspondents rarely spoke the language of the country about which they reported.[54]

Editors at the *New York Times* and the *Los Angeles Times* recognized the need to hire and promote the most knowledgeable reporters and the most skilled writers. At the *L.A. Times,* when Otis Chandler became publisher in 1960, he told Nick Williams that he wanted to create a world-class newspaper that would rival the *New York Times.* To achieve that goal, the paper went on a hiring spree, plucking gifted journalists— especially young ones—from leading newspapers and magazines, instead of hiring them away from smaller California papers as they had done in the past.[55] The need to compete with television, as always, helped spur this emphasis on employing top talent. As Nick Williams told a group of journalists in 1963, "Newspapers can no longer afford to say that they cannot buy the best in editorial work." Every newspaper, he said, must have "at least one man who is as fine a reporter-writer as any other medium can boast . . . whose work everyone in town must read."[56] Otis Chandler referred to the same challenge in a 1966 memo. "It is much easier to watch and listen to a Chet Huntley than it is to read a Bob Elegant [the leading *L.A. Times* foreign correspondent], and this is our problem," he wrote. "This means that we have to find better and better people to write for The Times. . . . Not only do we have to have brilliant people, but we have to make sure that they write the news and comment on the news in a way and style that will appeal to a large percentage of the [public]."[57]

The hiring spree at the *Los Angeles Times* had the desired effect. In 1969 Williams spoke frankly to a magazine reporter about how his newsroom had changed. "We didn't have the staff before to do the kind of reporting we do now," Williams said, referring specifically to interpretive reporting. He explained, "It usually takes new people to change a newspaper. We get very good ones now right out of college. Within a five-year period all our old editors and key reporters retired."[58] Washington bureau chief Bob Donovan agreed, telling author David Halberstam that in the 1960s the *L.A. Times* had "more good young newspapermen . . . more college graduates," which enabled them to do more analytical and investigative reporting. "If you tried to do this kind of paper 30 years ago, there might not have been the talent to do it with," Donovan said.[59]

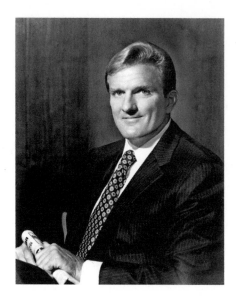

Otis Chandler, publisher of the
Los Angeles Times from 1960 to
1980. He was determined to
transform the newspaper, founded
by his great-grandfather in 1881,
into a world-class publication.
Photo: Copyright © Los Angeles
Times. Used with permission.

The *New York Times* also emphasized hiring reporters who could analyze the news and specialize in complex topics. A 1968 memo about
staffing from assistant managing editor Harrison Salisbury is suffused
with references to those kinds of journalists. He wanted people "who can
think and dig [into] . . . the *why* of the story," who can provide "analysis"
of "socio-politics," who can report on the "vast areas we do not cover,"
who would be "picked for special qualifications."[60] Newspaper managers
had been saying such things for at least a decade by 1968, but they were
dissatisfied with the results of their efforts. In September 1968 the
New York Times convened a group of senior editors called the News Committee to decide how to change the paper's coverage and presentation of
news. There was "a unanimous feeling" that they needed to drastically
reduce the amount of space allotted to "the formalistic or automatic
story—a piece of legislation is moved one step through Congress," for example. Instead, that space could be used give more prominent display to
subjects readers found more appealing—a step that "would make the
newspaper better able to compete with television, magazines, and so on."[61]
New areas of emphasis, the committee proposed at a subsequent meeting,
should include "business, finance, science and technology," along with
"thought, culture, ideas, creativity."[62]

In a 1970 announcement to readers, *New York Times* managing editor Abe Rosenthal took stock of the changes the paper had made in recent years. "Our definition of news, and our techniques of handling news, have been changing and broadening," he wrote. "We have learned that news is not simply what people say and do, but what they think, what motivates them, their styles of living, the movements, trends, and forces acting upon society and on a man's life."[63] This change in emphasis was evident to the reporters at the time. Joe Lelyveld, who joined the *New York Times* in the early 1960s (and later became its executive editor), recalled, "When I first became a reporter, most news was daily news. You went out and covered something in the morning and reported on it in the evening. Not too many people took more than a day to do a story." But in the mid-1960s, he said, that began to change, and "articles [became] much broader than that."[64]

As with the shift toward interpretation, the inclusion of unconventional topics among the day's top news disturbed some traditionalists. At the *New York Times,* John Oakes once again took the lead in cautioning the publisher against bending the paper's principles. For Oakes the last straw came in December 1967, when the paper published a front-page article headlined "More Coeds Find Less Guilt in Sex." This, he told Punch Sulzberger, represented "the nadir, the low point hit in long slide of the *Times'* standard of news presentation." He admitted, "Of course I read the story from first word to last, as I'm sure every single one of our readers with normal (or even abnormal) sexual instincts did. . . . [But] to treat this story as page one news, and handle it as we did, seems to me to be a deliberate effort to obliterate any distinction between the news philosophy of the Times and that of the Daily News, Journal American or Daily Mirror [all sensationalistic New York tabloids]."[65] Sulzberger, too, evinced some concern about moving too far in the direction of "soft news." In 1969 he asked Scotty Reston to assign someone to study the mix between "hard and soft" news stories in the *New York Times* versus the *Washington Post* (the results showed 94 percent hard news in the *Times* versus 79 percent in the *Post*).[66]

In spite of such reservations, by the end of the 1960s newspapers throughout the country had begun broadening their news coverage. In 1971 *Saturday Review* writer M. L. Stein talked to editors at twenty-eight major papers to determine how their newsrooms were changing, and he found that most were deemphasizing the traditional staple of big-city news: a one-day crime story written by a general-assignment reporter. Instead, they were assigning what some editors called "reporter-experts" or "subject specialists" to more specific news beats, producing in-depth articles about issues like hospitals, housing, and the court system. Many papers had also created beats devoted to topics such as "consumer affairs, natural resources, media, transportation, urban renewal, and space technology." Stein applauded these developments, partly because he sensed that they would help fulfill the "crying need for probing, interpretive journalism. It is not suggested here that newspapers drop straight news reporting, but analytical, explanatory, and background stories should get equal billing."[67] He viewed the shifts toward interpretive reporting and toward broader, more specialized coverage as the keys to the press's future success and observed approvingly that they were already well under way.

• • •

THE PRESS'S INCREASED focus on interpretation and its broadening of news coverage had several long-term effects. Above all, these changes made newspapers more interesting and useful, and contributed to their robust financial health in the late twentieth century. But interpretive reporting also shifted the balance of power within newsrooms from editors to writers. As one editor told the *Saturday Review* in 1971, "Fifteen years ago, the iron-handed city editor dealt out assignments like a stud poker player. . . . No longer must the reporter accept without question what he feels is a waste of time. . . . [He has] the option of tossing in his hand, dealing himself a new hand, or calling the game."[68] *L.A. Times* editor-in-chief Bill Thomas reflected on reporters' newfound importance in a 1973 memo to Otis Chandler:

> In little more than a decade, we've seen a transformation of the writer's role here at The Times which all the evidence shows has been duplicated across the country. Ten or 15 years ago a large city room . . . could count no more than a small percentage of literate writers. . . . It worked all right in those days, when newspapers consisted pri-

marily of "who, what, when, and where" stories. . . . Our reading
public [today] is better educated and better informed and thus
demands more sophisticated, more varied, and more meaningful
reporting. . . . To state the obvious, this evolution made the newspaper much more dependent on the writing skills of its reporters. No
longer could a bevy of editors pencil a reporter's story into an acceptable product, when such a product now requires interpretation,
background, and often a considerable literary skill. . . . All this is not
to say that the editors are not still indispensable to a quality newspaper, but it is at the same time true that the writer is *more important*
in producing it than he was just a short while ago.[69]

At the root of the change, as Thomas observed, lay the desire for "more
sophisticated, more varied, and more meaningful reporting." More meaningful reporting translated to reporting that included analysis and interpretation. More varied reporting meant reporting that covered a broader
range of topics. "More sophisticated reporting" is a more ambiguous
phrase—but it might mean detailed reporting, investigative reporting, or
reporting informed by specialized knowledge—it likely entailed the reporter providing interpretation.

The *Los Angeles Times* had a reputation for indulging its reporters, especially the stars among them, but reporters at the *New York Times* also
saw their power increase relative to editors. For many years the copy editors in what was known as the "bullpen" exercised great power to cut,
change, and determine the placement of articles. These editors had rarely
worked as reporters themselves, and many reporters raged at the way their
copy got "butchered" by the bullpen. Apart from the bullpen were the
desk editors—the individuals in charge of each department, and their
lieutenants—who handed out assignments, shaped stories, and awarded
promotions. Most of them were career editors who had worked only briefly
as reporters. In the 1950s, however, the bullpen's power started to wane,
and retiring desk editors were frequently replaced by people who had
worked primarily as reporters.[70] David R. Jones, who joined the *New York
Times* as a reporter in 1963 and later became a senior editor, noted that a
"basic change that started to take place in the Sixties was the transition
of control of the newsroom from career editors to career reporters." Men

who had had distinguished reporting careers, such as Harrison Salisbury and Abe Rosenthal, took on new roles overseeing major portions of the paper. Jones recalled, "It got to the point where almost all of the key positions were held by former reporters."[71] This sent a not-so-subtle message about which job the *Times* held in greater esteem.

By the mid- to late 1960s, a new set of consensus beliefs reigned among senior figures in the newsrooms of leading papers like the *New York Times* and the *Los Angeles Times*. They believed that news articles must include interpretation, and that good editors could prevent that interpretation from veering into opinion and thus damaging the paper's credibility. They believed broader categories of news—science, religion, urban affairs, education—must receive in-depth coverage from reporters with expertise in those topics.

However, journalists arrived warily at this new consensus. Some worried that allowing reporters to interpret the news would compromise the press's reputation for objectivity. Some worried that broadening news coverage would lead to a profusion of "soft news"—giving people what they wanted to know about instead of telling them what they needed to know about. Although the decision makers at news organizations shared these concerns, most felt they had no choice but to change—the marketplace and the audience demanded it. Those decision makers were right, but so were the naysayers. The press had started down a path—or a slippery slope, the traditionalists might have said—that would lead to the redefinition of its role.

❋ 2 ❋

Objectivity and the Right

A Worthy Ideal Abandoned

THE IDEA OF LIBERAL bias in the news media is relatively new. For most of the twentieth century, conservatives had few major complaints about the press. They griped occasionally about left-wing journalists, but in the days before interpretive reporting became commonplace, it would have been difficult for politically motivated reporters to put their own slant on the news even if they wanted to do so. Any slanting that occurred came from the decisions editors made regarding story selection, emphasis, and headlines; news-writing norms discouraged reporters from including any judgments that might be construed as bias. Most newspapers were essentially conservative institutions. They reported on the statements and actions of politicians, businessmen, clergy, academics, and prominent people in the local community. While news articles might provide some background or context, rarely did they challenge those statements and actions or attempt to analyze them in depth. Expressions of opinion were restricted to columnists and to the editorial page, which reflected the views of the publisher—a conservative, in most cases.

If conservative politicians or readers objected to something they saw in a newspaper, it was usually something a columnist had written rather than perceived bias in the news coverage. Such objections reached a new height in 1964, when the Republican nominee for president, Barry Goldwater, was criticized more harshly by columnists than any major-party candidate since the decline of the party press and the rise of objectivity in the early twentieth century. One of the most memorable moments of that year's GOP convention came when former president Dwight Eisenhower disparaged "sensation-seeking columnists and commentators"—to his apparent surprise, this elicited one of the longest and most enthusiastic ovations of the entire convention, a display of the party faithful's scorn for Goldwater critics in the press.[1]

Goldwater and his surrogates complained occasionally during the 1964 campaign about news reporting; they claimed that Goldwater was being misquoted or his views misrepresented (many journalists argued, and some Goldwater aides acknowledged, that Goldwater's tendency to mis-speak or speak very bluntly was to blame for this).[2] For the most part, however, the ire was directed at columnists, commentators, and editorial writers. In remarks after his concession speech, Goldwater said, "I've never seen or heard in my life such vitriolic unbased [*sic*] attacks one on man as has been directed to me"—but he made clear that those attacks came from columnists. Addressing news reporters, he said, "I think you've been fair."[3]

The *New York Times*, as the most prominent newspaper in the country, received its share of criticism in the early to mid-1960s, but few accused it of intentionally slanting its coverage to favor the left. When the right-wing magazine *National Review* wrote about the *Times* between 1962 and 1966, it registered only minor complaints—about its editorial stance on Communist China, its pessimistic analysis of the consequences of American bombing in Vietnam, or its tendency to reject advertisements from right-wing groups on questionable grounds.[4] In 1967 the conservative intellectual Irving Kristol wrote a long, detailed article about the short-comings of the *New York Times*.[5] He mentioned as an aside that the paper had biases—in favor of peace negotiations in Vietnam and against the Black Power movement—but regarded that as a normal, trivial issue (and the bias against Black Power was one that most white Americans shared). The real problem with the paper, Kristol argued, was that its reporters had no specialized knowledge about their news beats.[6]

The *Los Angeles Times,* conversely, did earn the enmity of many Republicans in the early to mid-1960s, but that resulted from publisher Otis Chandler's decision to make a swift break from the paper's past. For decades the *L.A. Times* had been unapologetically biased in its news reporting, favoring right-wing candidates and causes. Suddenly, under its new publisher, it moved to the center. In 1961 the *Times* published a major investigative series on the far-right-wing John Birch Society, accompanied by an editorial headlined "Peril to Conservatives," which slammed the group's leader, Robert Welch, as "radical and dictatorial."[7] The Birch Society represented the extremist fringe of right-wing opinion—its publications accused mainstream Republicans such as Dwight Eisenhower and California governor turned Supreme Court Justice Earl Warren of being communist agents. Nevertheless, it shocked many readers to see the *L.A. Times* report critically on this secretive organization. The most visible shift in the paper's political posture came in 1964, when Otis Chandler and editor-in-chief Nick Williams hired the Pulitzer Prize–winning editorial cartoonist Paul Conrad away from the *Denver Post.* Although Conrad skewered targets on all sides of the political spectrum occasionally, his overall outlook was that of a liberal, and he infuriated readers on the right. As *L.A. Times* Washington bureau chief Robert Donovan told David Halberstam, hiring Conrad "was almost like bringing in the arch enemy and putting him there to draw every day."[8]

The John Birch exposé and Paul Conrad's daily presence on the editorial page were the most visible signs of the *L.A. Times*'s new orientation, but day-to-day news coverage changed also. Most notably, Democratic politicians and ideas inimical to conservatism received respectful coverage in the news pages, instead of being ignored or treated dismissively. Loyal Republican readers took umbrage at this, as did Republican politicians who were accustomed to highly favorable treatment from the *L.A. Times*—in particular, Richard Nixon.

The *L.A. Times* and its longtime political editor, Kyle Palmer, had been instrumental in helping Nixon get elected as a congressman and senator, but by the time Nixon decided to run for governor of California in 1962, Palmer was gone and the *Times* was no longer a Republican organ. They assigned a tough, nonpartisan reporter named Richard Bergholz to cover his campaign. As David Halberstam wrote, Nixon "had never encountered equal treatment before in California and he found it devastating."[9] After losing the election, Nixon gave what he famously called his "last press conference," in which he complained about his press coverage during the campaign and told the assembled reporters they would not "have Nixon to kick around anymore." He had specific complaints about the *Los Angeles Times,* noting that while they had printed a misstatement on his part (Nixon said he was running for "governor of the United States"), they did not print a similar gaffe by his opponent, Pat Brown.[10] Referring to that discrepancy, Nixon said, "I think that it's time that our great newspapers have the same objectivity, the same fullness of coverage, that television has."[11] Nixon may have had a valid complaint about the gaffes, but more generally, objectivity to him meant, as he said repeatedly in that press conference, that reporters should simply "write what I say . . . every word"—without questioning or analyzing it too much, he implied.

But however much California Republicans felt betrayed by the *L.A. Times,* the paper did not immediately become a major target of conservatives elsewhere in the country. Barry Goldwater spoke highly of the *L.A. Times* in private and in public in 1964, despite the fact that the paper endorsed his opponent, Nelson Rockefeller, in the Republican primary.[12] However, the five years that elapsed between the Goldwater campaign and the Richard Nixon's inauguration in 1969 witnessed social change and upheaval the likes of which the United States has rarely experienced. Much of it—the antiwar movement, youth counterculture, Black Power—was deeply disturbing to conservative Americans. Indeed, concerns about this upheaval enabled Richard Nixon and his conservative third-party rival, George Wallace, to win 57 percent of the popular vote in the 1968 election, whereas four years earlier Goldwater had polled only 38.5 percent. Even though the Nixon administration would later launch a frontal assault against the press, during the campaign the "new Nixon," as his supporters styled him, refrained from inflammatory rhetoric. He portrayed himself and his running mate, Maryland governor Spiro Agnew, as moderate pragmatists who could unite the country.

In 1968 it was George Wallace, the segregationist Alabama governor, who stoked right-wing fury at the press. Many of the applause lines during his speeches foreshadowed what Vice President Agnew would say the following year—and what Donald Trump would say in 2016, appealing to a similar base of working-class whites. "The average American is sick and tired of all these over-educated, ivory-tower folks with pointed heads looking down their noses at the rest of us, and the left-wing liberal press writing editorials and guidelines," Wallace declared on the campaign trail.[13] The press dismissed Wallace as a fringe figure, a dangerous extremist—which fueled much of Wallace's anti-press sentiment in the first place—and therefore did not take his attacks too seriously. When similar comments were made by the vice president of the United States, however, they demanded far greater attention.

On November 13, 1969, speaking before a Republican audience in Des Moines, Agnew laid out a detailed critique of television news. He began by protesting the coverage of a major televised address on Vietnam that President Nixon had given on November 3. Normally the media-savvy Nixon designed his televised speeches to fit neatly into a block of airtime, but in this instance he spoke for thirty-two minutes. That left the networks with an additional twenty-eight minutes of airtime to fill before the next program, and they did so by presenting commentators who offered their take on Nixon's remarks—many of them critical. While acknowledging that "every American has a right to disagree with the President of the United States, and to express publicly that disagreement," Agnew asserted that "the people of this country have the right to make up their own minds and form their own opinions about a presidential address without having the president's words and thoughts characterized through the prejudices of hostile critics before they can even be digested." This was just one example, Agnew said, of the power and influence concentrated "in the hands of a tiny and closed fraternity of privileged men, elected by no one, and enjoying a monopoly sanctioned and licensed by government." He added, "The views of this fraternity do not represent the views of America."[14]

Agnew asked, "Do they allow their biases to influence the selection and presentation of the news?" He answered the question by citing statements from two network news anchors: "Objectivity is impossible to normal human behavior," he quoted NBC News's David Brinkley as saying; and he quoted a second, unnamed anchorman as admitting that his "private convictions" were reflected in his program. Such left-wing biases, Agnew claimed, were distorting the picture of America that the networks presented. "The American who relies upon television for his news," the vice president said, "might conclude that the majority of American students are embittered radicals, that the majority of black Americans feel no regard for their country, that violence and lawlessness are the rule, rather than the exception, on the American campus."[15] Agnew concluded his remarks—which were carried live by the three major TV networks—by reminding his audience, "The people can let the networks know that they want their news straight and objective. The people can register their complaints on bias through mail to the networks and phone calls to local stations."

Although the Nixon administration's communications team thought Agnew's speech was misguided, the president himself loved it—he had helped speechwriter Pat Buchanan draft it, along with a follow-up address that expanded the critique from TV news to print media.[16] Agnew delivered that salvo a week later, on November 20, in Montgomery, Alabama. He lamented the dwindling number of metropolitan newspapers, especially in New York and Washington, which had led to "the growing monopolization of the voices of public opinion on which we all depend." He singled out the *New York Times* and the *Washington Post* for criticism. The *Times,* he said, ignored news that was favorable to the Nixon administration, or buried it in the back pages. The *Post* he cited as an egregious example of monopolization, because its parent company also owned *Newsweek,* a news-radio station, and a local TV station—"all grinding out the same editorial line," Agnew claimed.[17]

These speeches catapulted Agnew to a level of prominence that few vice presidents have ever enjoyed. Agnew became "the High Priest of the Great Silent Majority," wrote the journalist Jules Witcover, and for a time was "bigger news than the president himself."[18] As the Nixon administration had hoped, TV networks, local stations, and major newspapers were inundated with letters and phone calls, most of them critical (although only 42 percent of the letters that the *New York Times* received were pro-Agnew, according to editorial page editor John Oakes).[19] Many commentators and Democratic politicians admonished Agnew for trying to intimidate or censor the media, but he brushed off their criticisms or accused them of trying to "silence" him. Never again after the fall of 1969 did Agnew make the news media the centerpiece of a speech; his mission had been accomplished, and the Nixon team felt it would be more advantageous to impose a "temporary armistice" in its anti-press war. A White House memo from November 27, 1969, reasoned, "We have discovered an issue on which we can rally a majority of the country and the South—why waste it now piling up our poll results."[20]

Although Agnew scaled back his offensive against the press, he lobbed grenades at them when he spoke about other topics, rarely missing an opportunity to remind the public that journalists were narrow-minded, liberal, elitist, and anti-Nixon. He often lumped them in with his other preferred targets: student protesters and the permissive parents and university administrators who enabled them.[21] In May 1970, two weeks after National Guardsmen killed four students during a protest at Kent State University, Agnew declared, "I have sworn I will uphold the Constitution against all enemies, foreign and domestic. Those who would tear our country apart or try to bring down its government are enemies."[22] It is not clear whether he was referring to violent demonstrators or to the press, but the implication was that those two groups were allied against the government. Such statements fit in perfectly with Nixon's message that he represented the Silent Majority against the elites, patriotism and law and order against radicals and dividers.

In his public remarks throughout 1970, Agnew called out individual journalists by name when he disagreed with them; he labeled *Washington Post* cartoonist Herblock "that master of sick invective" and took issue with the "irrational raving" of *New York Post* columnist Pete Hamill.[23] But unlike Barry Goldwater, he did not limit his criticism to cartoonists and columnists, whose role is to express personal opinions. Instead, Agnew argued that the press as a whole was biased and irresponsible. Agnew led the Nixon administration's public charge against the press, but he was not alone. In April 1971 Attorney General John Mitchell charged the press with "shocking contempt for the truth" in its reporting on new crime legislation and the Black Panther Party. Deploring a "sharp erosion of professionalism" in the news media, Mitchell said, "We find emotion and intuition in the saddle, while truth is trampled in the dust."[24] These attacks on the press all came prior to the two episodes the Nixon administration found most objectionable: reporting on Watergate and on the Pentagon Papers (the U.S. military's confidential history of the Vietnam War).

There are several possible explanations for the virulence of the Nixon administration's anti-press campaign. In part it was a genuine expression of outrage from men who believed the press had wronged them—most prominently Nixon, whom the *Los Angeles Times* had so abruptly jilted. Although the idea for Agnew to give a speech lambasting the news media had originated with Pat Buchanan, Nixon "couldn't contain his mirth" as he worked on the draft, according to the diary of his aide H. R. Haldeman. The president was "really pleased and highly amused."[25] Political calculations surely played a role too. Although attacking the press for liberal bias was not yet the time-honored technique of stirring up the conservative faithful that it would later become, Republican strategists had begun to realize its promise after Dwight Eisenhower's address at the 1964 GOP convention.[26] Nixon reportedly told his staff that it was "good politics for us to kick the press around."[27] The Agnew speeches were a test of just how good, and the results, for Republicans, were quite encouraging.

In addition, the Nixon administration likely hoped that the press would soften its coverage in response to the rebukes from Agnew and from the wider public. To some extent that is what happened—especially on television news, whose stations depended on government licenses for their continued existence. While Agnew stated that the administration had no intention of revoking or refusing to renew stations' broadcast licenses, many TV news executives feared that possibility—especially after Federal Communications Commission chairman Dean Burch called the network heads to request transcripts of the commentary they had aired following Nixon's Vietnam address on November 3, 1969.[28] When Nixon gave subsequent televised speeches, the networks offered only the mildest commentary afterward; sometimes they provided no commentary at all.[29] And part of the reason the unfolding Watergate scandal had so little impact on the 1972 election was that it received so little coverage from television news.[30] The difficulty of representing the Watergate story visually may have contributed to the scant TV coverage it received, but the chilling effect of Agnew's veiled threats was undoubtedly a major factor as well.

Regardless of the political motivations behind Agnew's remarks, many Americans shared his wish that the press would return to the kind of journalism that most newspapers had practiced in the 1940s and 1950s. Much of what he chalked up to liberal bias resulted from three of the major changes in journalistic practice that had recently occurred. First, inter-pretation had become a much bigger part of the news, in print and on television. Television networks, newspapers, and magazines would no longer simply air or print what the president said and then quote reac-tions from other politicians or public figures. They felt compelled to pro-vide analysis from their own staff and contributors. Second, journalists approached people in power in a far more skeptical, even adversarial, manner than they had done during World War II and the early years of the Cold War. As former *New York Times* executive editor Max Frankel put it, there was "a slow recognition that simply siding with our govern-ment against hostile forces, which was sort of the posture of the World War II generation, was no longer valid."[31] Therefore, journalists would question not only the wisdom of Nixon administration policies but also the motives behind them (as they had done with the Lyndon Johnson ad-ministration too).[32] Third, the scope of what was considered important news, and whose voices merited inclusion in the news, had broadened considerably. In particular, the grievances of protesters and dissidents received greater attention.

To Agnew, these changes were deeply regrettable. He alluded to all three in his initial critique of the news media, on November 13, 1969, in Des Moines. The first two changes, analysis and skepticism, went hand in hand. He deplored that the president's "words and policies were sub-jected to instant analysis and querulous criticism" by "self-appointed an-alysts, the majority of whom expressed, in one way or another, hostility to what he had to say." Agnew also made clear his view that the news media were inflating the importance of violence and dissent in the United States, and giving too great of a platform to people outside of the political main-stream. It was the networks, he noted, "that elevated Stokely Carmichael [the Black Power advocate] and George Lincoln Rockwell [founder of the American Nazi Party] from obscurity to national prominence." In another speech, Agnew mused, "If a theology student in Iowa should get up at a PTA luncheon in Sioux City and attack the president's Vietnam policy, you would probably find it reported somewhere in the next morning's issue of the *New York Times*."[33]

Such exaggerations aside, Agnew was correct that the press paid greater heed to dissenters than it had done in previous decades. In part this reflected the increasing size and frequency of protests, along with more effective tactics, but it also reflected a shift in journalistic values. To Agnew and many of his supporters, this shift was wholly unwarranted. The protesters were just a few misguided malcontents, they believed— "rotten apples" who should be discarded from the barrel of American society, as Agnew said in one speech.[34] In reality, according to this view, the United States was the same virtuous, harmonious nation it had been in the 1950s, the only difference being that in the 1960s and 1970s the rotten apples were receiving abundant, sympathetic coverage from the news media. *New York Times* columnist James Reston detected this sentiment in the letters his paper received in the wake of Agnew's attacks. Many letter writers, Reston noted, issued a "general indictment of reporters and commentators . . . for 'stirring up trouble' among the poor, the blacks, and the rebellious young on the university campuses."[35]

In addition to lamenting the press's newfound interest in America's internal strife, Agnew pined in another way for the journalistic climate of the 1940s and 1950s. Despite his public hostility toward the press, Agnew missed the days when politicians enjoyed chummy relationships with the reporters who covered them, and could expect to get the benefit of the doubt. Much of the press greeted his nomination for vice president with derision, referring to him as "Spiro who?" A *Washington Post* editorial said his nomination might become known as "perhaps the most eccentric political appointment since the Roman emperor Caligula named his horse a consul."[36]

Nevertheless, Agnew tried to ingratiate himself with the reporters covering him. As his campaign plane was about to depart from Las Vegas in September 1968, Agnew walked to the rear of the cabin for a chat with the traveling press. He noticed that one of them, a Japanese-American correspondent for the *Baltimore Sun* named Gene Oishi, had fallen asleep. "What's the matter with the fat Jap?" Agnew jokingly asked the other journalists, who, somewhat taken aback by his casual use of the racial slur, informed him that Oishi had been up late in the casino. Agnew was appalled when the remark was reported two days later in the *Washington Post*, in the last paragraph of a story about his positions on national issues. He had simply assumed that the reporters would consider the remark off the record. A few years earlier they almost certainly would have, but journalistic norms had changed. Additionally, at a press conference the previous week Agnew had referred to Polish-Americans as "Polacks," so some reporters thought the "fat Jap" remark showed a pattern of insensitivity on racial and ethnic matters. When forced to explain his use of the slur, Agnew said that he considered Oishi a friend and was simply kidding around with him.[37]

Even after launching his critique of the press, Agnew apparently believed he could rely on the good will of individual newspapermen. In January 1970, two months after condemning the *New York Times* in a major speech, Agnew invited the paper's publisher, Arthur Ochs Sulzberger, its top editor, A. M. (Abe) Rosenthal, and an executive vice president, Ivan Veit, to a dinner at the exclusive Manhattan restaurant "21." Agnew was concerned that he was getting a reputation for being anti-Semitic, so he hosted a dinner for about twenty-five prominent Jews and asked them to help him dispel the rumors. (Sulzberger was vacationing in the Caribbean and could not attend, but Rosenthal and Veit did.) In the course of the evening, Rosenthal wrote in a memo, Agnew told him "that he had met many Times reporters and never had had any complaints about any of them."[38]

Agnew had other private communications with the *New York Times* that belie the hostility he expressed in his public comments. In early December 1969, two weeks after the vice president lambasted the paper in his Montgomery, Alabama, remarks, his press secretary had lunch with an editor and reporter from the *Times* Washington bureau and informed them that Agnew "has long considered The Times the fairest paper around."[39] And on January 30, 1970, upon his return from a trip to visit U.S. allies in Asia, Agnew wrote Abe Rosenthal an almost fawning letter, saying:

> As a sometime critic of the press, I would be remiss if I did not express to you my deep appreciation of the news coverage given my recent Southeast Asia-Pacific trip by the New York Times. . . . I am very impressed with and appreciative of the fair, detailed, and objective coverage by Jim Naughton. In my opinion he is a credit to the Times editorial staff and compares favorably with some of the better reporters I have known. Jim also got along well with all of the other

members of our traveling party and it was a pleasure to have him with us. I enjoyed meeting you and talking with you at "21" last week.

In his response, Rosenthal picked up on Agnew's use of the terms "fair, detailed, and objective," telling Agnew, "In those three words I think you summed up the purpose of our professional existence."[40]

Agnew's conciliatory approach may have been part of a Nixon administration attempt to show that they bore no ill will toward the *New York Times,* despite having given the paper a public dressing-down. Also in January 1970, President Nixon wrote a personal letter to *Times* reporter Alden Whitman expressing his gratitude for a front-page article Whitman wrote about a group of New York-area businessmen who were close friends of Nixon. "I want you to know how much I enjoyed your article," Nixon began. "You were very kind and I thought objective in describing my friends in New York and their relationship with me, and I am most grateful."[41] Like Agnew, Nixon chose the word "objective" to describe an article he approved of, and that contained no criticism of him.[42]

Agnew had no complaints about the press coverage of his ten-country Asia trip. Did journalists intentionally go easy on him, knowing that he might publicly excoriate them for any perceived unfairness? Perhaps, but the more likely explanation for Agnew's satisfaction has to do with the nature of the trip itself. Visiting foreign dignitaries makes a politician look less like a political figure and more like a representative of the entire nation. Additionally, diplomatic coverage was one of the few areas in which the journalistic norms of the 1950s still held some sway. Official statements from political leaders were considered automatically newsworthy, and journalists generally assumed that U.S. officials were working on behalf of a national interest that most of the public was behind. The glaring exception, by the late 1960s, was the Vietnam War. Agnew mostly sidestepped that topic during his trip—he spent one day in Vietnam and said only that he felt the Nixon administration's policy was the right one.[43]

• • •

REGARDLESS OF AGNEW'S private assurances that he felt the *New York Times* was covering him fairly, his remarks raised alarms inside the paper. Publisher Arthur Ochs Sulzberger (known to his friends and colleagues

Arthur Ochs (Punch) Sulz-
berger, publisher of the *New
York Times* from 1963 to 1992.
Photo: Tim Kantor / The New
York Times / Redux. Reproduc-
tion from New York Times
Company Records, General
Files, MssCol 17802, Box 330,
Folder 3. Manuscripts and
Archives Division, The New
York Public Library, Astor,
Lenox and Tilden Foundations.

as "Punch") felt that his staff should not fan the flames by responding publicly to Agnew. The day after the vice president's speech in Alabama
criticizing the paper by name, Sulzberger issued a memo advising all
Times journalists to "stay off the air this week in order to avoid refuting
Vice President Agnew."[44] In late November, Punch Sulzberger tasked
Theodore Bernstein, the paper's assistant managing editor in charge of the
copy desk, with performing a comprehensive review of the *Times* for two
weeks to look for evidence of bias or unfairness. (Bernstein found fourteen potentially problematic examples but concluded that "virtually all"
were "trivial.")[45] Some *Times* editors also urged Sulzberger to appoint an
ombudsman to look for lapses in journalistic standards at the paper
and report back to readers.[46] (The *Washington Post* did this in the aftermath of Agnew's attacks, but the *New York Times* did not follow suit
until 2003.)

Agnew never singled out the *Los Angeles Times* for criticism, and his
focus on the media's East Coast bias may have provided the *L.A. Times*

some cover—indeed, Otis Chandler was asked in a TV interview whether he was "offended not to have been included when the vice president came out against the Washington and New York papers."[47] Still, Agnew's remarks caused a stir at the *L.A. Times* as well. In an editorial, the paper accused Agnew and the Nixon administration of trying to stifle criticism and of "assaulting the constitutionally-protected institution of free speech itself."[48] Rather than send a form-letter response to readers who wrote in to say they agreed with Agnew, editor-in-chief Nick Williams responded with detailed, personalized letters.[49]

In their public responses to Agnew's comments, journalists and news executives objected primarily to the vice president's apparent attempt to intimidate or censor the news media.[50] This was undoubtedly a serious concern—especially for the TV networks, which required government licenses in order to broadcast. However, many news organizations privately shared a separate concern: that Agnew's attacks could further damage their credibility. This derived in particular from Agnew's claim that news coverage was biased and inaccurate. More than anything else he said, this struck at the heart of the news media's mission, calling into question their most basic function of providing reliable information.

Public trust in the news media had been declining sharply throughout the 1960s. In a 1966 poll, only 29 percent of Americans said they had a "great deal of confidence" in the press, and by 1971 the number was down to 18 percent.[51] This trend worried many newspaper publishers and editors even before Nixon and Agnew were elected. In a 1966 memo to publisher Otis Chandler about the challenges facing journalism, *Los Angeles Times* editor-in-chief Nick Williams emphasized "the credibility factor," by which he meant "the feeling on the part of a large segment of the public that newspapers slant their news, or select their news, to accomplish a specific and not always honorable purpose." Williams noted, "We sell credibility . . . [it is] probably our most important asset."[52] The following year Chandler devoted an entire speech to the topic of the credibility gap between the public and the news media, in which he felt compelled to raise the question, "Are the media, in fact, deliberately distorting, deliberately poisoning, the flow of information to the public they serve?" His answer was "an emphatic no," and he labeled "the so-called credibility gap" a "molehill" and a "cliché."[53]

That was in 1967. A few years later—after the turbulent events of 1968, the Nixon administration's assault on the press, and increased social and political turmoil throughout the country—the *L.A. Times* leadership was much less cavalier about the credibility question. In 1971 Nick Williams reflected on the state of journalism in a letter to his Washington correspondent Stuart Loory, who was taking a leave from the paper. "I have a terribly uneasy feeling that journalism has reached both a pinnacle and a crossroads," Williams wrote. "I suspect it has gained enormously in power and has lost credibility, per se, with an alarming percentage of the people." If the loss of credibility were to continue, he mused, "we [will] have destroyed or weakened a keystone of our Constitution." But Williams rejected Agnew's suggestion that retreating from interpretive reporting would restore the press's credibility. On the contrary, he argued that the press needed to provide even *more* analysis—"to expound as thoroughly as we can . . . what we think has happened or will happen"—but in doing so, "beware of our own prejudices" and "reexamine them constantly."[54] Bill Thomas, who took over for Williams as editor-in-chief in 1971, told

Nick Williams, editor-in-chief of the *Los Angeles Times* from 1958 to 1971. Photo: Copyright © 1962 Los Angeles Times. Used with permission.

the *L.A. Times* business managers at a 1972 meeting, "We must above all else remain credible, or we are of no value to anyone."[55]

At the *New York Times,* the concern about credibility was even greater. It was the central preoccupation of the paper's top editor, Abe Rosenthal, who made it his mission to "keep the paper straight," as he liked to say, and to preserve the *Times*'s reputation for trustworthy, unbiased coverage. But Rosenthal was hardly alone in his concern. In 1973 the *New York Times* sales and marketing department took the problem seriously enough to prepare a detailed report for the publisher in which they took the unusual step of suggesting editorial changes. The report informed Punch Sulzberger that the paper's image had "suffered deterioration in the minds of a substantial portion of the public" since the 1950s and early 1960s. It advised considering changes "in news coverage and presentation that would add to The Times' credibility."[56]

The question of credibility, of course, cannot be separated from the question of objectivity. Most readers would trust a newspaper if they believed its coverage to be objective, and they would distrust it if they believed otherwise. And newspapers, by proclaiming their objectivity loudly and proudly for years, had created an expectation on the part of readers that they would rarely encounter anything biased or unfair in the paper. This expectation became much harder to meet in an age of interpretive reporting, riots, protests, and tumultuous social change. In early 1969, during his short stint as executive editor of the *New York Times,* James Reston was sufficiently worried about charges of bias to send a memo to the paper's twenty-two most senior editors telling them to be especially watchful: "For thirty years on The Times," Reston wrote, "I've been hearing complaints from inside and outside the paper of editorializing in the news columns, but lately the charges seem to have increased."[57] When several months later the vice president of the United States voiced such complaints—telling the public that the press was biased, unfair, and inaccurate—that compounded the challenges faced by organizations like the *New York Times* and the *Los Angeles Times* in trying to convince readers to trust them.

Despite their concerns about credibility, these newspapers did not change their practices in any fundamental ways because of Agnew's charges. They did, however, give careful consideration to each of his main complaints—after all, they had heard most of them before, and would hear them with increasing frequency from conservative critics in the ensuing decades.

In essence, Agnew had four main arguments:

1. The press focused too much on analysis and not enough on simply reporting the facts.
2. Stories about conflict, violence, and dissent—in short, "bad news"—featured much too prominently in domestic news coverage.
3. Too many commentators, columnists, and editorial pages were liberal or leftist, and they often made unfair or unfounded attacks on the Nixon administration.
4. News coverage (as opposed to editorials and opinion columns) was slanted to reflect journalists' liberal bias, whether consciously or unconsciously.

Very few print journalists took seriously Agnew's first complaint, about analysis and commentary. Interpretive and analytical reporting had become mainstays of newspaper coverage. Reporters wanted to do it, and the public wanted to read it—although some occasionally protested when they disagreed with the analysis. One of the few people in a prominent position at either *Times* who, like Agnew, wanted less of it, was editorial page editor John Oakes, a staunch liberal and the first cousin of publisher Arthur Ochs Sulzberger (John's father had anglicized the spelling of his family name amid the Germanophobia of World War I). Oakes was poles apart from Agnew politically. But as an old-fashioned newsman, he felt very strongly about the strict separation between the news pages and the editorial pages, coupled with a proprietary feeling that the editorial pages he controlled were the only place in the paper where anything resembling an opinion should appear. On many occasions throughout the 1960s he sent memos to Sulzberger and to fellow editors arguing that "news analysis" stories and interpretive articles in the Sunday Week in Review section were really just editorials in disguise, and that they should be published on the editorial pages or not at all. However, the publisher generally seems to have dismissed or ignored these suggestions.[58]

At the *Los Angeles Times,* some of the older reporters—holdovers from the pre–Otis Chandler days—likely felt the same way John Oakes did about interpretive reporting. But as the paper's former managing editor George Cotliar recalled, those were "9-to-5 kind of people" who were nearing retirement, and "none of them had the wherewithal to challenge anyone."[59] Besides, Nick Williams had been a staunch advocate of interpretive reporting at least as far back as 1961, so anyone opposed to it would have had trouble finding a sympathetic ear from the paper's editor.[60]

Agnew's criticism about a surfeit of "negative" news stories was similarly easy for most reporters to dismiss. In addition to the tendency among many to sympathize with protesters and dissenters, they understood that conflict and controversy made for good stories. But editors and publishers likely saw some validity to the complaint about negativity. One week *before* Agnew's opening salvo against the press in Des Moines, Abe Rosenthal sent a memo to his national editor and metropolitan editor foreshadowing the very point Agnew would make: "I think we continue to give an awry picture of America in our coverage," Rosenthal began, before pointing out how many stories in that day's paper were about protests, trials, poverty, or discrimination. He continued:

> I get the impression, reading The Times, that the image we give of America is largely of demonstrations, discrimination, antiwar movements, rallies, protests, etc. Obviously all these things are an important part of the American scene. But I think that because of our own liberal interest and because of our reporters' inclination, we overdo this. I am not suggesting eliminating any one of these stories. I am suggesting that reporters and editors look a bit more around them to see what is going on in other fields and to try to make an effort to represent other shades of opinion than those held by the new Left, the old Left, the middle-aged Left, and the antiwar people.[61]

It is unclear how much heed Rosenthal's staff paid to this suggestion, because it seems to have been a relatively low priority for the editor-in-chief. Combative though he was, he knew he had to pick his battles, so he devoted the most energy to "keeping the paper straight," as he often said, which meant preventing reporters from editorializing in news articles. Moreover, he could not count on the support of his boss, the publisher, for trying to rein in coverage of America's ills. In May 1970, for instance, when six black men were killed during a riot in Augusta, Georgia, one week after the deaths of four students at Kent State University, Punch Sulzberger sent the following brief but pointed memo to Rosenthal: "Abe, I am curious: why it is that when the National Guard kills four white students we put it on page 1, and when the National Guard kills six black people we put it on page 32?" Rosenthal responded that the Augusta story was mistakenly taken off the front page, and a follow-up article appeared on page one of the next day's paper.[62]

Even after Agnew had faded from the political scene, Rosenthal echoed another one of his complaints about the press's tendency to emphasize bad news. Just as Agnew in 1969 blasted the media for elevating the neo-Nazi George Lincoln Rockwell to national prominence, Rosenthal in 1974 took issue with a *Times* article about a twenty-year-old woman named Sandra Silva who had joined the American Nazi Party. In a memo to the editor responsible for the piece, he acknowledged that "we should report on the activities of political dissidents, left or right." But the paper must not, he said, "make celebrities out of them simply because of their political points of view. . . . There was nothing intrinsically interesting in Silva aside from the fact that she is a political kook. Does that entitle a person to command major attention—which we gave her—in the press? This kind of thing has always bothered me. Five hundred people hold a meeting and seven people picket them, and the seven get, often, as much attention as the five hundred."[63]

At the *Los Angeles Times,* Otis Chandler also anticipated Agnew's critique about bad news before Agnew delivered his remarks. The main reason for the press's unpopularity, Chandler argued in an April 1969 speech, was "the nature of the news we must report today." He mentioned Vietnam, student protests, and crime, noting that readers "do not want to think about" such problems and "do not want to believe [they] are happening." Nevertheless, Chandler said, "I do not believe we should stop reporting the news, negative and dreary and controversial as most of it is. Our mandate is to inform the public. If, in the process, we frustrate and anger them, this is a risk of our business."[64]

Other journalists shared Chandler's concern about negative news. In late November 1969, shortly after Agnew's first two speeches about the media, NBC-TV journalist Bob Abernethy raised the question in a lengthy interview with Chandler: "People say to us again and again, and I'm sure they say the same thing to you, 'Why can't you tell us some good news?' We go on covering riots and protests, because we consider that the news. What's your policy on this?" In his response, Chandler struck a different tone than he had in his speech earlier in 1969. He noted that the *Times* had been making "a conscious effort" to report "so-called good news stories— a black dress shop in Watts, or a foster mother in . . . East Los Angeles." However, Chandler continued, such articles typically generated little interest among readers: "They're like Bible stories: they're nice to have, but they're not very interesting. Because—say 1,000 children went to school yesterday, but there was one child that was hurt going to school. Why, that's the news, and that's what they want to hear about and read about, even though they say they don't and even though they say, 'All you're doing is tell[ing] us bad news.'"[65]

Chandler's statement in April 1969 that people do not want to read disturbing news is difficult to reconcile with his statement in November 1969 that people *do* want to read disturbing news and tend to skim over "good news stories." In both cases, he glossed over two key distinctions. First is the distinction between politically controversial news and relatively depoliticized news. People are unlikely to get angry at their local news outlet for reporting that a child from their area was hurt going to school, because that news carries few political implications. On the other hand, some people might get angry at their local news outlet for reporting on political protests in another city, because they view such reporting as amplifying the protesters' voices and giving them a platform they do not deserve (this was Agnew's view). The second distinction is between whether or not something is reported and *how* it is reported. For example, most *Los Angeles Times* readers surely considered the Black Power movement and the Berkeley Free Speech movement newsworthy. They wanted to read about such movements, but they wanted to read coverage that reflected their political opinions.

Whatever their reservations about focusing too relentlessly on negative news, no news organization that hoped to achieve or maintain a national reputation for excellence would demote disturbing stories from the front page or the top of the broadcast. Doing so would damage its reputation in the industry. As journalism became increasingly professionalized in the mid-twentieth century, its practitioners placed ever-greater importance on the respect of their peers. Perceptive observers in the early 1970s noted that journalists valued the esteem of their colleagues more than that of their readers—that they wrote primarily for other journalists.[66] Journalists at prestigious news organizations—and the people handing out Pulitzer Prizes and other industry awards—valued stories that tackled difficult problems. They disdained simple feel-good pieces, just as they belittled spot news about localized crime and fires (even though that qualifies as "bad news"). Along with professionalization came a consensus about what was newsworthy. Stories about political violence, protests, and threats to the prevailing social order—"social disorder stories" and "moral disorder stories," as sociologist Herbert Gans has called them—qualified as major news, and journalists felt a professional obligation to treat them as such.[67]

Editors would always discuss how to handle individual stories, and they might decide that some bad-news stories were less newsworthy than others. But throughout the 1970s, as the U.S. economy sputtered, cities decayed, and divisions over race, gender, and politics deepened, there was no effort at the *New York Times* or the *Los Angeles Times* to downplay or mitigate such news. Indeed, sometimes there was an effort to do the reverse. In the late 1970s some *Los Angeles Times* editors were concerned about criticism that they were not devoting enough coverage to the problem of poverty in Southern California. So they appointed a new City-County bureau chief, Bill Boyarsky, whom they knew to be sympathetic to the plight of the poor. He was allowed to recruit his own staff and was given a mandate to remedy this perceived deficit in the paper's local coverage.[68]

Agnew's point about columnists and editorials being overwhelmingly liberal and anti-Nixon merited serious consideration inside the two papers. It was an issue that the *New York Times* was already wrestling with, but it became a greater priority after Agnew's speeches. Deputy editorial page editor Abe Raskin felt they could address the issue without changing the political orientation of the editorials or columnists. "The most effective answer to criticism of the Agnew variety," Raskin wrote in a memo to Punch Sulzberger, would be to create an op-ed page, print more letters to the editor, and appoint an ombudsman—adding, "All these are things we should have done on our own initiative long ago."[69] Sulzberger acted upon only one of those three suggestions: in 1970 the *New York Times* launched an op-ed page. In addition to providing additional space for staff columnists, the page showcased think pieces from outside contributors of various political persuasions—mostly academics and intellectuals, who tended to occupy the center-left. Op-ed (short for "opposite the editorial page") quickly became one of the best-read parts of the paper, but it did little to change the overall ideological tilt of the opinion pages.[70]

In the wake of Agnew's complaint about left-wing commentators, Sulzberger made a change that went against the wishes of Abe Raskin and editorial-page editor John Oakes: he decided to hire a conservative columnist for the *Times* opinion pages. At the time, all of the opinion columns had a centrist or left-wing viewpoint (with the possible exception of C. L. "Cy" Sulzberger—the publisher's cousin—who wrote about foreign affairs). Although it took him three years to make the decision, Punch Sulzberger wound up selecting Agnew's speechwriter William Safire, who began writing for the *Times* in 1973.[71] But this bit of tokenism (Safire would be the lone conservative on the editorial page for many years) hardly changed the character of the *New York Times* opinion pages. The columnists remained overwhelming liberal in the years to come; as of 2018, ten of the paper's thirteen regular columnists were left-leaning, and the three conservatives (David Brooks, Ross Douthat, and Bret Stephens) were anti–Donald Trump—the type of conservative most palatable to liberals.

New York Times editors in the 1960s and 1970s recognized that their liberal opinion pages contributed to the impression that the entire paper was liberal. In December 1969, shortly after Agnew's public attack on the paper, his press secretary had lunch with two members of the *New York Times* Washington bureau Afterward, they reported to deputy managing editor Seymour Topping, "It is the 'goddam editorial page' that [Agnew] always complains about, and that colors his judgment of the whole corporation— as it the case also, of course, with [National Security Adviser Henry] Kissinger and most other people around the White House."[72]

Abe Rosenthal felt certain that the editorial page's left-wing stances were damaging the reputation of the paper as a whole. As he wrote in his personal journal in March 1971, he worried that readers perceived the *Times* as a "political journal" rather than "an information medium." He attributed this to the "strongly liberal point of view" of most *Times* columnists and to the stridency of the editorials—he claimed that most readers, including powerful figures in Washington, focused their attention on the paper's opinions and editorials and ignored the rest.[73] Rosenthal was not someone to keep such opinions to himself. He had written to Sulzberger on December 8, 1969, "I have strong reservations about the tone of our editorials and the antagonisms it has engendered toward the paper."[74] Despite such reservations, there would be no major shakeup in the opinion department until 1976, when Sulzberger pushed out John Oakes and much of his staff in favor of Max Frankel.[75] But this change mainly altered the tone and style of the editorials; the political positions that the paper espoused remained fairly consistent.[76]

The opinion pages at the *Los Angeles Times,* like most other parts of the paper, changed drastically between 1960 and 1970. They began featuring some liberal columnists and, most notably, when the paper's longtime editorial cartoonist died, his replacement, hired in 1964, was the acerbic liberal Paul Conrad.[77] The paper received so many complaints from aggravated conservative readers that Williams developed a form letter for his response. It began by stating, "The free press is like a free market. The press offers to its readers the work of reporters, editors, columnists, cartoonists, and photographers. And the reader accepts that which he believes is good and rejects that which he dislikes or doubts."[78]

When the powerful, conservative friends of the Chandler family complained about the new orientation of the *L.A. Times,* they sometimes received a more forthright explanation. As Otis Chandler wrote to one such individual in 1964, "The Times has changed its general news policies in recent years in that we do now cover both sides of most major issues of the day, political and non-political. . . . Our news coverage is not slanted or managed anymore in favor of the conservative viewpoint." But when it came to the "independent Republican philosophy" of the paper's editorials, Chandler added, "Let me say flatly that it hasn't changed! And it will not change!"[79] Despite Chandler's insistence in this letter, the editorial page *had* changed. That same month, editorial-page editor Jim Bassett wrote a memo acknowledging "our swing from conservative to moderate. Our turning from black-and-white editorializing to rather more reasoned writing."[80]

Chandler, Bassett, and editor-in-chief Nick Williams wanted to change the reputation of the *L.A. Times* from right-wing to centrist, not to liberal. They were fairly sensitive, therefore, to accusations that the paper had become rabidly leftist. In August 1969 an article in the trade journal *Editor & Publisher* printed the results of a survey indicating that 79 percent of *L.A. Times* columnists were "liberal," "radical liberal," or "extreme liberal." Nick Williams, a southerner who was normally unfailingly courteous in his correspondence, responded with an irate letter. He began, "How the hell did Editor & Publisher ever get suckered into printing, as it appeared, that article on Page 14 of your August 16 issue?" Williams pointed out problems with the survey's methodology and its purported facts, and expressed his fury that *Editor & Publisher* would "take such a handout which was deliberately planned to discredit The Times . . . and print it verbatim—never bothering to ask The Times itself if it had any comment on the poll's conclusions."[81] The article likely rankled Williams so much because he knew that, as with Agnew's critiques, it had some validity. While it was surely an exaggeration to say that 79 percent of *Los Angeles Times* columnists were on the left, more than half leaned in that direction—a fact that Williams may not have been entirely comfortable with.

The shift in the editorial page infuriated many conservative Californians who had subscribed to the *Los Angeles Times* since its days as a Republican organ. "I sometimes wonder if you really are Americans. If so, are you for this country or against it?" one reader wrote to the editorial page staff after an editorial he perceived as too sympathetic to the student protesters at Kent State. Assailing the paper's "left wing (liberal) coverage," he asked to know the background of the editorial writers, whom he urged to "cut your hair [and] take off your beads."[82] Jim Bassett evidently took some pleasure in referring this reader to his entry in *Who's Who in America:* "There you will find, among other things, that I am a retired Naval captain, served in the Pacific on Admiral Halsey's staff, and on four occasions worked with Nixon and the Republican

Party. If that makes me a left-wing liberal, I will eat the current volume of *Who's Who.*"[83]

The leaders of the *L.A. Times* were not particularly worried about losing conservative readers who preferred the pre-1960 version of the paper. Analyzing the results of a 1972 survey about canceled subscriptions, Bill Thomas acknowledged the "random comments from unhappy conservatives." However, he said, "the few quoted here could be balanced by what others like most about the paper. In other words, if we pleased these people, it's possible—even likely—that we would lose the others." Besides, Thomas noted, only 2 percent of those who canceled stated as their primary reason "too opinionated: inconsistent reporting."[84] In addition, the *L.A. Times* knew that readers who wanted a comprehensive, high-brow local newspaper had no other good options. The Hearst Corporation had shuttered its morning newspaper the *Los Angeles Examiner* in 1962, leaving only its declining afternoon paper, the renamed *Los Angeles Herald Examiner*, as a competing broadsheet. (In New York, similarly, the closing of the *New York Herald Tribune* in 1966 had removed the *New York Times*'s main competitor.) When trying to sway readers who canceled their subscriptions to protest the *Los Angeles Times* editorial cartoons, Nick Williams often reminded them of the paper's unmatched news coverage. He told one in 1970, "If at any time you feel that the overall coverage of The Times from its 18 foreign bureaus, its 7 national bureaus, and its staff in California reporting exclusively to Times readers, outweighs the work of two controversial cartoonists whose work occupies less than a column each day, the Editorial Department of The Times will be happy to welcome you back among our subscribers."[85]

The *L.A. Times* provoked a slew of outraged letters from longtime readers when it published an editorial in 1970 headlined "Get Out of Vietnam NOW." Overall, however, the paper received seven times as many letters supporting the editorial than opposing it.[86] And despite the accusations of some Republican readers, the editorials rarely took any radical leftist positions. Editorials about big business and organized labor generally expressed a conservative viewpoint.[87] And every year from 1964 to 1972, the *L.A. Times* endorsed the Republican candidate for president—the paper's decision to endorse Richard Nixon for reelection in 1972 so dismayed many staff members that they wrote a letter to the editor protesting it and expressing their support for the Democrat George McGovern.[88]

The 1972 Nixon endorsement, however, was the last presidential endorsement that the *Los Angeles Times* would make in the twentieth century; in 1973 the paper announced that it would no longer endorse candidates for president, governor, or senator.[89] An editorial explaining the decision said that even though the news and editorial departments were strictly separated, "some readers . . . find it hard to believe that this newspaper's editorial page endorsements really don't affect the news columns."[90] Editors at the *New York Times* were acutely aware of this problem too. As Seymour Topping wrote to Punch Sulzberger in 1971, "The average reader still does not understand that there is a separation of the Editorial and News departments."[91]

Given the concerns that both newspapers had about credibility, making endorsements in high-profile statewide or national elections (about which most readers had plenty of information) could be seen as unnecessarily fanning the flames of reader mistrust. Internal memos at the *L.A. Times* discussing the nonendorsement policy emphasized that the "credibility factor" would rise and that "our news product should also gain a great deal in credibility."[92] In a further attempt to dampen the perception that its editorial position was staunchly left-wing, the *L.A. Times* in 1973 moved Paul Conrad's daily editorial cartoon from the editorial page to the op-ed page. This put a little distance between Conrad's provocative work (which did not necessarily represent the views of the paper) and the more measured arguments of the editorial board (which did).[93]

Despite changes such as these, most people who looked at the opinion pages of the *New York Times* and the *Los Angeles Times* would characterize them as left-wing. This made practical sense, as it reflected the views of the audience both papers sought: educated coastal urbanites, especially younger ones. But it also gave ammunition to critics who wished to depict the press as monolithically liberal. That was not the case—nationwide, left-wing views were far from dominant on the opinion pages. Newspapers away from the coasts and in smaller cities usually had conservative editorial positions; and nationwide, conservative columnists were more widely syndicated than liberal ones. The headline of a 1984 article by *L.A. Times* media reporter David Shaw summed up the situation: "Political Columnists: What Became of the Liberals?" Columns by conservatives (led by James J. Kilpatrick and George F. Will) appeared in far more papers than columns by liberals.[94] Conservative dominance in syndicated columns continued into the twenty-first century.[95] Yet because the country's most prominent newspapers were based in major coastal cities and had liberal opinion pages—especially the *New York Times*, the *Washington Post*, and the *Los Angeles Times*—right-wing critics could successfully reinforce the perception that the press as a whole expressed overwhelmingly liberal views.

The most controversial charge that Agnew and other Republicans made, and the charge that vexed journalists the most, was that straight-news coverage, not just editorials and columns, exhibited a liberal slant. The Nixon White House and conservative activists devoted considerable energy to advancing this claim, in Agnew's speeches and by other means.[96] Agnew had a straightforward explanation for liberal bias: that journalists had become more left-wing, and that the press's increasing emphasis on interpretive reporting enabled them to inject more of their left-wing views into their articles, whether intentionally or unconsciously.[97] It was impossible to dispute the first part of that explanation (that journalists had become more left-wing). And while news organizations certainly tried to dispute the second part—insisting that journalists did not allow their personal views to influence news coverage—it is unlikely that they convinced many conservatives.

In California the name Chandler was synonymous with conservatism, and Otis Chandler, in his early years as publisher, was superficially devoted to upholding his family's traditional principles. But his personal politics ranged from moderate to liberal. He became a close friend of Robert F. Kennedy in the mid-1960s, so much so that in 1967 his assistant warned him that he might be perceived as a "Kennedy man."[98] In 1969, reflecting on RFK's assassination a year earlier, Chandler supposedly lamented to a friend, "I guess there's no one who represents us anymore." Asked whom he meant by "us," Chandler replied, "the black and the young and the poor."[99] In a 1969 speech Chandler described an encounter he had with a hippie on a plane ride as a collision of two entirely different perspectives. "I was flattered that even though I am over 30, he was willing to talk to me," Chandler said, and went on to explain the

young man's background and antiestablishment worldview the way a social scientist might.[100] But in 1978, after the ferment of the late 1960s and
early 1970s had died down, Chandler addressed an audience of graduate
students and presented a view of America's problems with which most left-
wingers would have agreed: sexism, racism, poverty, and spoliation of
the environment were the era's greatest ills, he said. He said the graduates should have "a commitment to change" the wrongs of society and applauded those law students who intended to become public defenders or
enter the fields of environmental and consumer law.[101]

During Chandler's tenure as publisher, several editors who moved
into top positions happened to be liberals in their personal politics:
Edwin Guthman, the former aide to Robert F. Kennedy who became
national editor in 1965; Jim Bellows, the former *New York Herald
Tribune* editor who became editor for soft news in 1966; Anthony Day,
who succeeded the former Nixon campaign manager Jim Bassett as
editorial page editor in 1971; and Bill Thomas, a moderate Democrat
who succeeded the moderate Republican Nick Williams as editor-in-
chief, also in 1971. Some conservatives remained—most notably managing
editor Frank Haven, who retired in 1978—but they were increasingly
outnumbered.

Some of the most prominent non-editor positions also came to be oc-
cupied by people whose backgrounds or beliefs would have disqualified
them from working at the *L.A. Times* under the previous, conservative
regime. Cartoonist Paul Conrad was the most visible example, but others
abounded. Phil Kerby, a longtime writer for the left-wing weekly *The
Nation,* became an editorial writer for the *Times* in 1971, despite having
been turned down for the job two years earlier. "In '69 I was too radical,
a few years later I was not," Kerby told David Halberstam.[102] Journalist
Robert Scheer certainly would have been too radical for the old *L.A.
Times,* having been editor of the revolutionary-leftist magazine *Ramparts.*
But in 1976 he became one of the paper's most high-profile additions, fresh
off the stir created by his *Playboy* interview with Jimmy Carter (in which
the presidential candidate admitted to having "committed adultery in my
heart").[103] Scheer received a higher salary than any of the paper's other
California-based reporters, along with assurances that the copy desk
would not tamper with his work.[104]

Scheer, Kerby, Conrad, and others were hired because of their journalistic abilities, not their political views. Bill Thomas and Otis Chandler both dismissed the idea that Scheer would bring a far-left sensibility to the *L.A. Times,* pointing out that his work since joining the paper had not exhibited any "radical" or "anti-establishment" bent.[105] It just so happened that, as Nick Williams observed in 1969, "the preponderance of people of ability who have any interest in the work of the media happen to be of a liberal persuasion."[106] It had been true for decades that most reporters held liberal political views, especially those at the top of their profession: Washington correspondents and reporters for prestigious big-city papers.[107] But in earlier years the relative conservatism of the senior editors and the copy desk (responsible for rewriting articles and creating headlines) offset the liberalism of the reporters. By the late 1960s the editors and the copy desk had become less conservative and less powerful, while many young reporters had become more radical, shifting the ideological balance and the balance of power leftward. In order to make the newsroom governable, *L.A. Times* management needed to allow some freedom to the talented, left-leaning journalists they had hired. After his retirement, Nick Williams explained to the Chandler family matriarch Dorothy "Buff" Chandler how he guided the newsroom. He acknowledged that, in her eyes, "sometimes I seemed—or the Times seemed—to be rocking the boat. Sometimes I had to choose between rocking the boat and rocking the staff's morale, and I thought (and still think, perhaps more than ever) that the boat could take it better."[108]

Summing up the power dynamic in the newsroom in 1973, Bill Thomas told Otis Chandler, "This is the writer's day."[109] The changing nature of newspaper content in the 1960s created a demand for a different kind of reporter than the city room denizens of an earlier era, who could perform the job adequately as long as they wrote quickly and kept their facts straight. By the 1970s, newspapers wanted outstanding writers who could interpret the news effectively and tell engaging stories; they also wanted specialists with deep knowledge of a particular beat, such as health, the law, or consumer affairs. For talented young reporters seeking newspaper jobs, it was a seller's market. As one twenty-five-year-old journalist wrote in 1971, "bright young journalism prospects do not want to start out writing obits, rewriting handouts, and covering an occasional fire or drowning." They wanted to skip these entry-level assignments and cover more exciting beats of their own choosing—a privilege some, like that young journalist, felt they were in a position to demand. He explained that he had turned down jobs at two top newspapers because it was so easy for him to earn a good living as a freelance writer. Many of his peers, he said, were being lured away from newspaper jobs by "alternative lifestyles and other communications media."[110]

At the *New York Times,* Abe Rosenthal lamented in 1971 that "we have pretty much dried up the pipeline on getting into the paper first-rate young or youngish reporters."[111] He recognized that, because of the climate on college campuses, more and more of them would "reflect the philosophy of their age group and times—personal engagement, militancy and radicalism."[112] But given the paper's need for young talent, that would not be a disqualifying factor. In early 1973, for instance, Rosenthal and his top lieutenants discussed hiring Mary Breasted, a young reporter working for the *Village Voice,* the alternative weekly that was the *Times*'s toughest left-wing critic. One editor wrote, "She will inevitably bring a left-of-center viewpoint to reporting, which I do not consider a pressing need at The Times now." Another said, "Her writing does have a bias, and it is simply impossible to tell how much of that bias will eventually show through."[113] She was hired in spite of these reservations.

Steve Roberts, a young reporter who had worked as Scotty Reston's assistant, twice infuriated the editors in New York by writing opinionated articles in left-wing publications, but he received only gentle reprimands. As the paper's Los Angeles bureau chief in 1970, he wrote a harshly critical article about California governor Ronald Reagan in *Change* magazine, prompting Reagan's press secretary to say, "You have made it impossible for me to cooperate in any way regarding news or stories concerning the governor."[114] Roberts's boss was asked to inform him, "If reporting for The Times loses you any source, including your prime source, we can certainly live with that. It is more difficult for us to accept that your reporting opportunities become prejudiced because of work for outside publications."[115] Asked about the incident many years later, Roberts had no recollection of it.[116] In 1973 investigative reporter Seymour Hersh—whom the *New York Times* had hired a year earlier—was quoted in a *Washington Star* article as saying, "Watergate has been freeing. I have a very strong bias against the Nixon administration and I don't worry about it anymore." When the conservative columnist John Lofton wrote to the paper suggesting that this statement made it impossible for Hersh to cover the White House objectively, Abe Rosenthal disagreed and refused to criticize Hersh, one of the paper's most high-profile reporters.[117]

In defending Hersh, Rosenthal relied on the same argument that Otis Chandler and Bill Thomas made about Robert Scheer: if the journalist's work is accurate and fair, his or her personal views are irrelevant. "The very basis of our existence is the belief that a reporter or an editor who works for this paper can and does submerge or put aside his own biases when he addresses the typewriter or makes an editorial decision," Rosenthal wrote. "Therefore, the test of the objectivity of our reporters and editors is not in their personal opinions, but in their work."[118] Even a relatively conservative journalist such as Rosenthal could look at the work of a Hersh or a Scheer and recognize it as good reporting. He believed that, like most journalists in the mainstream press, they were trying to report the truth, not to advance any political agenda.

But conservatives such as John Lofton, Spiro Agnew, and the millions of Americans who shared their views saw things differently. The press was becoming more adversarial, and its most frequent targets, it seemed, were institutions that people on the right revered: law enforcement, big business, the military, a Republican presidential administration. Add to this the fact that most journalists' personal politics were on the left, and conservatives considered the case for liberal bias open and shut.

Most conservatives fail to make a distinction, however, between a journalistic ethos influenced by left-wing ideas and a blatant advocacy of left-wing ideas. Several authors have tried to explain the ethos that emerged in the 1960s and 1970s. Political scientist Thomas Patterson argues, "Journalists had been silent skeptics. They became vocal cynics. This was particularly true among the 'elite' national journalists."[119] *Washington Post* reporter Paul Taylor noted of his fellow journalists, "We are progressive reformers, deeply skeptical of all the major institutions in society except our own."[120] Irving Kristol, in the midst of his transformation from liberal to neoconservative in 1972, offered a way to think about the recent changes in journalistic practice: "Journalism used to be primarily a craft"—like carpentry or picture framing—"but many journalists now see themselves as enlisted in a calling"—like preaching or politics.[121]

All of these explanations contain an element of truth. Journalists certainly became more vocal, as Patterson argues—the trend toward interpretation made the reporter's voice and judgments central to news coverage. In the 1960s, Patterson noted, quotes from news subjects usually set the tone for news articles, but by the 1970s the reporter's own words usually set the tone.[122] But the evidence for a shift from skepticism to cynicism is shakier, for, as Paul Taylor noted, there remained a reformist impulse, a hope among journalists that their work could help bring about positive change. In an essay about the press and politics in 1971, the *Wall Street Journal*'s Robert Bartley (then associate editor of the editorial page, later editorial-page editor and editor-in-chief) argued that the defining characteristic of most journalists was not liberalism or cynicism but idealism. Yes, Bartley said, journalists tend to be politically liberal, but more to the point, on a scale of practical to idealistic, they are generally "situated well toward the idealistic extreme."[123]

For many journalists, that idealism manifested itself in a commitment to the lofty goal of objectivity. For others, however—especially in the 1960s and 1970s—objectivity seemed like an obstacle to higher ideals, such as truth, justice, and social change. At same time that Agnew and his followers were telling the press, "Be more objective," other influential voices were telling them, "Stop trying to be objective."

❧ 3 ❧

Objectivity and the Left

An Ideal Worth Abandoning

O N MARCH 20, 1970, the *New York Times* published an unusual full-page ad. It was a message from A. M. Rosenthal, who had become managing editor (the top job in the news department at the time) the previous year. Rosenthal explained to readers that the *Times* was changing in significant ways—in particular, performing more investigative journalism and reporting "not simply what people say and do, but what they think, what motivates them, their styles of living, the movements, trends and forces acting upon society." That is to say, the paper's reporting was becoming more adversarial, more analytical, and broader in scope. But in spite of those changes, Rosenthal emphasized, the paper remained more devoted than ever to its "personality and purpose," which derived above all from its "most important" commitment:

> The Times is a newspaper of objectivity. Time was when objectivity was taken for granted as a newspaper's goal, if not always an attained goal. But we live in a time of commitment and advocacy, when "tell it like it is" really means "tell it like I say it is" or "tell it as I want it to be." For precisely that reason, it is more important than ever that The Times keeps objectivity in its news columns as its number one, bedrock

principle. We are all quite aware that since every story is written by a human being and that the decision on how to play it is made by other human beings, total pristine objectivity is impossible clinically. But we struggle to achieve the highest possible degree of objectivity.[1]

This message was obviously aimed at readers who might doubt the paper's fairness or credibility. But they were not the only constituency who needed to hear it, Rosenthal believed. He originally intended it for his colleagues and subordinates inside the *New York Times* newsroom; the text of the ad was adapted from an internal memo that Rosenthal had sent to the entire staff in October 1969, two months after becoming managing editor. In it he laid out a list of seven core beliefs on which "the character of the paper" rested. Five of those seven beliefs concerned objectivity:

> The belief that although total objectivity may be impossible because every story is written by a human being, the duty of every reporter and editor is to strive for as much objectivity as humanly possible.
> The belief that no matter how engaged the reporter is emotionally he tries as best he can to disengage himself when he sits down at the typewriter.
> The belief that expression of personal opinion should be excluded from the news columns.
> The belief that our own pejorative phrases should be excluded, and so should anonymous charges against people or institutions.
> The belief that presenting both sides of the issue is not hedging but the essence of responsible journalism.[2]

In his staff memo, Rosenthal did not accuse anyone of failing to honor those beliefs. "I am bringing all this up," he wrote, "not as a warning nor as a cry of alarm, because neither is needed, but simply as a reaffirmation of the determination to maintain the character of The Times as we grow and develop." That was disingenuous—privately, he felt there was indeed cause for alarm. He had adapted the memo from a letter he wrote the year before, when he was still metropolitan editor, to James Reston, then the paper's executive editor. In that letter, Rosenthal listed the same core beliefs and emphasized the need for the paper to maintain its character, but he also said that that character was under serious threat from inside the newsroom. "There are more reporters on the paper who seem to question or challenge the duty of the reporter, once taken for granted, to be above the battle," Rosenthal wrote to Reston. "Inevitably, more young reporters reflect the philosophy of their age group and times—personal engagement, militancy and radicalism. . . . It is also inevitable as time goes on that the radical or militant element in The Times staff will increase in size." A staunch anticommunist, Rosenthal even worried that some young subversives would secretly try to radicalize the paper from within—"radicalization of an establishment institution is an accepted and proper goal for militants, even an obligation," he noted.[3]

Rosenthal may have been lapsing into paranoia with that last concern, but he and other like-minded editors and publishers were facing a serious rebellion from within their ranks. Many young journalists (and some not-so-young ones) simply did not believe in the notion of objectivity. Far from considering it journalism's noblest principle, they believed it was foolish at best and deeply harmful at worst. This conflict existed at news organizations throughout the country. A June 1970 headline in the newspaper trade journal *Editor & Publisher* described the situation succinctly: "Attack on Objectivity Increases from Within."[4] After an article in the *Wall Street Journal* mentioned Rosenthal's staff memo and quoted excerpts from it, numerous requests came in to Rosenthal's office for a copy of the complete memo.[5] "We wrestle with the same problem here," wrote the Washington bureau chief of the *Minneapolis Tribune.* The general manager of the Associated Press told Rosenthal, "I have spoken to some young groups recently and expect some day to run into a militant with all the pat arguments for involvement [i.e., advocacy or activism]. I'd like to gather all the material I can on the reasons for objectivity." Many other editors and several journalism professors also wrote Rosenthal to thank him for sending them the memo and to say how heartily they agreed with his sentiments.[6]

During the period from the mid-1960s to the mid-1970s, activists were calling for systemic change in nearly every societal institution, and the press was no exception. A main obstacle to positive change, many felt, was journalists' unquestioning belief in objectivity. Writing in the fall of 1969, the longtime *Hartford Courant* editor-in-chief Herbert Brucker noted that, a decade earlier, "everyone agreed with what had been taught those of us who went into newspaper work in the first half of the century: that an accurate, unbiased account of the event reported was journalism's purest gem. . . . Today objective news has become anathema to young activists in journalism."[7] In a May 1970 speech the editor-in-chief of the *Wichita Eagle* observed that many journalism students "regard . . . objectivity as obscene."[8]

The reasons for these vociferous objections to objectivity varied. Some rejected the ideal because it was so plainly unachievable—although even its defenders, such as Rosenthal, acknowledged that "total pristine objectivity" was impossible. The "gonzo" journalist Hunter S. Thompson declared of objective journalism, "The phrase itself is a pompous contradiction in terms" and cracked, "The only thing I ever saw that came close to Objective Journalism was a closed-circuit TV setup that watched shoplifters at the General Store in Woody Creek, Colorado."[9]

Other skeptics noted that objectivity is in the eye of the beholder—a reader is more likely to perceive a news article as biased when its judgments run counter to the reader's personal views. For proof of this, *New York Times* journalists needed to look no further than Rosenthal, who held conservative beliefs on many topics. He issued dozens of memos flagging examples of bias that he found in the *New York Times,* and in nearly every instance it was left-wing bias that he detected. Because most *Times* reporters were left-leaning, one would expect liberal bias to be more common than conservative bias, and in many of the passages to which Rosenthal objected, the reporter's left-wing sympathies are quite evident. For instance, a 1973 article about the political mood on college campuses began: "Political activism is moribund at colleges and universities in New York, New Jersey, and Connecticut, and students have taken on the superficial appearance of their self-centered, socially indifferent, All-American campus counterparts of the 1950s." The following two paragraphs continued in a similar vein.[10] Rosenthal wrote to the two section editors responsible for it, saying, "I really couldn't believe my eyes when I read those first few paragraphs," calling them "editorialized in the extreme" for taking a negative view of students who did not engage in political activism. Reminding his colleagues that the credibility of the paper was under constant threat, he noted, "If we lose our reputation for non-editorialization, we are lost."[11]

In other instances, however, Rosenthal seized on seemingly inoffensive phrasing and insisted that it betrayed a liberal bias on the part of the reporter. In a 1972 article about the U.S. Senate, reporter John Finney wrote that the absenteeism of many liberal Democratic senators "is now threatening to shift the balance of power back to a conservative coalition."[12] This prompted a letter from Rosenthal to Finney and the two top editors in the Washington bureau: "It strikes me that the use of this word ['threatening'] was such an obvious indication of political bias that I am rather stunned that it was written, passed through the Washington desk and passed through at least two editors in New York. To whom is it threatening? Surely not the conservatives. . . . I cannot overemphasize the importance of guarding against this kind of thing. It not only damages a reporter's credibility but the paper's and confirms readers in their belief that news columns can be as biased as editorial columns."[13]

There were undoubtedly many *Times* articles that someone to the left of Rosenthal would have found to exhibit a conservative bias. But among his voluminous written complaints about editorializing, only once does he appear to have noticed editorializing from a right-wing perspective. It was in 1972, when the retired *Times* columnist and longtime Washington bureau chief Arthur Krock wrote a scathing article about the state of the Democratic Party.[14] It was essentially an opinion column, full of provocative arguments, but it ran on the news pages—this was about the most flagrant example of editorializing that one could imagine, and that is what it took to get Rosenthal to acknowledge that conservative bias might occasionally appear in his paper. "We don't print editorials in The New York Times news columns no matter who they come from," Rosenthal reminded the responsible editors.[15]

One prominent example of conservative bias escaped Rosenthal's notice because he authored it himself. As someone who grew up in poverty and cherished the free education he had received at City College of New York, Rosenthal deplored the wave of campus radicalism that he felt was overshadowing the universities' educational mission. Rosenthal was the *New York Times* metropolitan editor in April 1968, when student protesters at Columbia took over several university buildings, including the office of the president, Grayson Kirk. Although he was no longer a reporter and had not personally covered a news story in more than two years, Rosenthal took the unusual step of going to Columbia the night that police forcibly removed the students. His resulting front-page article sided openly with Kirk and the police, whom many accused of using excessive force; he depicted the student protesters, for the most part, as violent and hate-filled.[16]

Many *Times* journalists, especially younger ones, sympathized with the student movement and were appalled by Rosenthal's piece. Steve Roberts, at the time a twenty-five-year-old reporter who worked under Rosenthal on the metropolitan desk, remembered the situation vividly decades later. "The younger reporters were identifying very strongly with the protesters, [and Rosenthal] was identifying very strongly with the police and the authorities at Columbia," Roberts said. "We felt that the coverage of Columbia was heavily influenced and tilted toward the police version and the administration version, and that the Times would not allow us to give voice to the protesters' side of things."[17] So instead Roberts presented the protesters' side, and excoriated Grayson Kirk, in an article in the *Village Voice,* the alternative weekly that was sharply critical of the Establishment press and especially the *New York Times.*[18] This earned Roberts a rebuke from Rosenthal, who scolded the young reporter for using "extremely bad judgment in taking a sharp editorial position on a story which he was covering."[19]

But in spite of their opposing views on the situation at Columbia, Roberts and Rosenthal shared the same fundamental concern about the *New York Times*'s credibility and reputation for objectivity. Roberts and other reporters of his generation did not necessarily object to airing the viewpoint of the police and the Columbia administration, but Roberts "felt strongly—and I was not alone—that this coverage was not balanced." Rosenthal became managing editor a year later, and his article about Columbia, according to Roberts, contributed greatly to the *Times*'s lack of credibility among young people throughout Rosenthal's editorship. "I can't tell you how many dozens of times that piece was thrown up in my face," said Roberts, who spent many years covering students and youth movements for the paper. "Writing that story was an act of terrible misjudgment that harmed the paper for years afterward."[20]

Objective reporting, as Rosenthal and others defined it, should not favor one valid viewpoint over others. But which viewpoints get a hearing and which do not? On controversial issues, there are certain viewpoints that journalists feel merit inclusion in their coverage—these viewpoints fall into what the political scientist Daniel Hallin calls the "sphere of legitimate controversy." Other viewpoints journalists consider unfounded, or too extreme—these fall into the "sphere of deviance" and rarely get discussed. Noncontroversial views are contained in the "sphere of consensus."[21] In the case of Columbia, some *Times* journalists (most notably Rosenthal) felt the views of radical leftist students fell into the sphere of deviance, whereas others (such as Roberts) felt they belonged in the sphere of legitimate controversy.

Even if they did not think of it in these precise terms, working journalists understood that objectivity in practice entailed deciding which viewpoints deserved serious consideration and which did not. This recognition caused journalists who sympathized with the New Left or other political ideologies outside the mainstream to become disillusioned with and often to reject the doctrine of objectivity. Many African-American journalists were deeply skeptical about it for the same reason. C. Gerald Fraser, who was hired as a *New York Times* reporter in 1967, was disappointed when the paper declined to publish a story he had written in the late 1960s about black college students. "I just went out and asked the black students what they thought, and that's not what the *Times* wanted," Fraser recalled. "Had I interviewed the deans and college presidents and said, 'How are you dealing with the black students now?,' [my editor] would have liked that." But his mission at the *Times*, Fraser felt, was to convey perspectives that might not otherwise appear in the paper. "You can always get the white college president to talk," Fraser noted, "but what does the black student have to say?"[22]

Fraser and his fellow black reporters at the *Times* recognized "that our viewpoint was different than the general viewpoint on the news." Along with African-American journalists working for other publications in New York, they formed a group called Black Perspective, which met regularly in the offices of Kenneth Clark, the renowned African-American psychologist at City College.[23] In that forum as well as in others, they discussed objectivity frequently. Most agreed, as reporter Earl Caldwell recalled, that the press was hopelessly biased in its coverage of issues affecting people of color—that made it hard to take seriously the notion that black reporters should adhere to their white editors' standards. Said Caldwell, "The objectivity thing—I never got caught up on that. I always just said, 'I'm going to try to be honest, and I'm going to try to be fair.'"[24]

Many black journalists felt that objectivity was often synonymous with coverage that represented the mainstream white perspective. Gerald Fraser cited an example from his time at the New York *Daily News*, where he worked for four years as a copy editor before moving to the *New York Times*. The *Daily News* often referred to Adam Clayton Powell Jr., the U.S. representative from Harlem, as "the flamboyant Harlem congressman." One day, Fraser recalled, "I just drew a line through the word 'flamboyant.' I said to myself, I'm sick of this. Just say 'the Harlem congressman.'" Fraser's boss overruled him and insisted that the word "flamboyant" be restored. "That was the attitude of the news media," said Fraser. "They could call him 'the flamboyant congressman' and think they were being objective. Because after all, he was tall, good-looking, well-spoken, took no stuff from them, and so forth, so something had to be wrong with him!"[25] Rather than try to follow the vague dictates of objectivity, Fraser said, he simply tried to be "fair" and "honest"—the same terms used by Caldwell other journalists who had qualms about the concept.[26]

At the *New York Times*, too, black employees took exception to what they considered condescending coverage of Adam Clayton Powell Jr. When the paper published a negative editorial assessment of Powell after his death, the Afro-American Employees Association of the *Times* wrote to editorial page editor John Oakes to express their dissatisfaction—and to charge the *Times* with a lack of objectivity. "It seems that in the *Times*'s rush to criticize Powell, it failed to make an objective assessment of his influence and impact on Black America," the letter stated, adding that "the editorial establishes itself as another one of those pieces on Blacks that suffer from an egregious lack of perspective and scope."[27] This charge is similar to Fraser's, and to the complaint that Steve Roberts had about the *Times*'s coverage of the Columbia student revolt: that by giving some perspectives the greatest prominence and by ignoring or downplaying others, the paper was exhibiting a kind of bias, perhaps without realizing it.

This was the most frequent and most effective argument against objectivity: that it was, ironically, biased in its own way. In a 1970 column about the folly of objectivity, the iconoclastic *Washington Post* writer Nicholas von Hoffman skipped over the obvious point that it is not truly achievable. Instead he argued that because objectivity entailed taking at face value "the words and deeds of most of the men on our front pages," it was inherently biased. "This kind of objectivity rejects information that tends to throw doubt on ancient institutions and established practice," von Hoffman wrote.[28] In other words, it created a bias in favor of the Establishment. Many journalists felt this way, but most were young and did not hold high-level positions at major news organizations. The senior editors generally dismissed that criticism, as von Hoffman acknowledged. The *New York Times*, however, had on its masthead a vocal advocate for the anti-objectivity viewpoint: associate editor and columnist Tom Wicker.

A North Carolina native who joined the *Times* in 1960, Wicker became a favorite of Washington bureau chief James Reston and distinguished himself with his vivid writing and analytical verve. He succeeded Reston as bureau chief in 1964, but he turned out to be an ineffective manager, and he left Washington after four years in order to devote himself full-time to the opinion column he had begun writing in 1966 (his left-wing voice replaced that of the conservative Arthur Krock on the opinion page). As a consolation for losing the prestigious job of Washington bureau chief, Wicker received the title of associate editor. Although he had no editing or managerial responsibilities, his name appeared on the editorial-page masthead alongside the names of the paper's publisher and top editors.

Wicker had no use for the concept of objectivity, and he had no qualms about saying so publicly. Writing in the *Columbia Journalism Review* in 1971, he declared objectivity—by which he meant "reliance on and . . . acceptance of official sources"—to be the American press's "biggest weakness." Wicker explained, "The tradition of objectivity is bound to give a special kind of weight to the official source, the one who speaks from a powerful institutional position." That is, it privileged the perspective of the powerful, which gave the press an "orientation toward nationalism . . . and establishmentarianism." Wicker blamed this orientation for what he considered some of the press's greatest failings in recent years, such as

Tom Wicker, who derided
objectivity as a prominent
New York Times colum-
nist and associate editor
in the 1970s. Photo: April 14,
1976, File Photo. © The
New York Times / Redux.

raising few questions about American strategy in Vietnam and dismissing
as "a joke" the 1968 presidential campaign of the liberal Democratic senator Eugene McCarthy.[29]

Wicker acknowledged that he had no ready-made solution for the
problem of objectivity, no new model with which to replace it. But in his
CJR article and in a subsequent speech on the same themes, he suggested
that the press needed "an intellectual tradition"—meaning that journalists should have more freedom to include their judgments in articles and
to experiment with different literary forms.[30] That suggestion overlapped
with another frequent complaint about objectivity: that it placed
unnecessary constraints on journalists. It prevented them from reporting everything they knew, and it prevented them from following
their consciences.

Many young American journalists in the late 1960s and early 1970s, dissatisfied with the doctrine of objectivity, looked at the European press
and found what they considered a superior approach. In Europe, most
newspapers openly espoused a certain ideological viewpoint, and reporters were permitted to make far-reaching claims and judgments on

their own authority, without having to quote a specific source. Reporters remained on the same beat for many years and became experts, so they had the knowledge to make such judgments and claims. Rather than quoting several people with different views on a certain situation, European journalists could simply tell the reader, "This is the situation," and decide whether or not it was worth quoting the sources to whom they had spoken. Journalists who worked for major American news organizations such as the *Boston Globe*, the *Minneapolis Tribune*, the *Philadelphia Bulletin*, and the *New York Times* felt that the European model was in many ways superior, and they argued that point not only inside their newsrooms but also in journalism reviews and left-wing magazines.[31]

The debate over objectivity among newspaper staffs centered on politics and writerly freedom, but it was also about control. The editors, who were generally older and more conservative than the reporters, were the ones with the power to dole out assignments, change the text of articles, write headlines, and determine what would appear on the front page. As with most large organizations, newspapers were organized hierarchically. In this respect, too, many journalists found a more appealing model in European newspapers—in particular *Le Monde*, the respected Parisian daily that was run as a cooperative, with reporters sharing in decisions about editing and story placement, and with the journalists themselves each owning a share of the paper.[32] Sometime around 1970 a group of *New York Times* staffers who were dissatisfied with the paper's hierarchical decision-making process invited a representative from *Le Monde* to address the newsroom. Metropolitan editor Arthur Gelb, who was Abe Rosenthal's longtime right-hand man, found the presentation something of a joke, recalling that as the man from *Le Monde* spoke, it became obvious to the *Times* staffers in attendance that this model would never work for them.[33] It is unclear whether the people who initiated the meeting felt the same way, but in the end the decision on whether to try out any of *Le Monde*'s methods rested with people like Gelb and Rosenthal, and they never seriously considered it.

The avuncular Gelb was open to hearing challenges to the paper's traditional structure and ideals, even if he wound up dismissing them. Rosenthal, however, had no patience for challenges to his authority or for proposed experiments in participatory democracy. In 1972 an editor in his twenties, David Schneiderman, sent Rosenthal a letter arguing that the talents of young *Times* staffers were being wasted in menial jobs, and that young people in general did not find the *Times* worthwhile or trustworthy. It was a thoughtful, well-meaning letter, although it was blunt and somewhat presumptuous. It sent Rosenthal into a rage. He wrote Schneiderman a curt memorandum in reply: "Oh, no, Mr. Schneiderman, I will engage in no discussion, ever, with anybody who opens with hostility, insult, arrogance, and assault. I would demean myself by writing further." Rosenthal confided to a colleague the following day that before sending this memo to Schneiderman, he had dictated three much harsher ones that he discarded. He said there was "a warp in Mr. Schneiderman," and that Schneiderman's letter had made him physically ill, forcing him to skip the daily front-page meeting.[34]

Viewed in isolation, Rosenthal's response to Schneiderman's letter seems like a bizarre overreaction. But the letter came at a time when Rosenthal felt he and his values were under attack, including and perhaps especially from people within the *New York Times*. In 1970, *New York* magazine published an article titled "The Cabal at the New York Times: Which Way to the Revolution?" It reported on a group of prominent *Times* journalists—star reporters such as J. Anthony (Tony) Lukas and Joseph Lelyveld, cultural critics John Leonard and Clive Barnes, women's-news editor Charlotte Curtis—who wished to challenge "the current political and journalistic directions of the Times." They had been holding informal meetings during which they shared their grievances about heavyhanded editing and the paper's top-down decision-making process. Rosenthal got wind of it and invited the members of the "cabal" to a dinner at which he listened to their complaints and shot back with some criticisms of his own. The cabal petered out shortly thereafter.[35] According to Lelyveld, the cabal meetings were simply an opportunity for people to vent their frustrations, not a serious effort to change the character of the paper. But Rosenthal, he said, took it quite seriously. "It lingered for years in his mind as a great rebellion he put down," said Lelyveld.[36]

In 1971, one year after the cabal episode, Rosenthal began for the first time in his life to keep a journal. He mused about his motivations for doing

A. M. (Abe) Rosenthal, left, and Arthur Gelb, two years before Rosenthal became managing editor of the *New York Times*. Photo: October 27, 1967, File Photo. © The New York Times / Redux.

so in his first entry. The most likely reason, he wrote, was "the incessant attacks on The Times from the left and the liberal community. Somehow, the attacks from the right do not bother me—they never liked the paper or what it was trying to do. But the past few years the antagonism of the far left—which also never bothered me very much—has spread rightward into the center." Journalists from *New York* magazine, the *Village Voice,* and elsewhere who criticized the *Times* were "filled with hatred," he wrote, which he found greatly disturbing.[37] Rosenthal's displeasure must have deepened when, four months after that journal entry, reporter Tony Lukas left the *Times* to cofound the journalism review *[More]*. Like most other editors, Rosenthal was a great admirer of Lukas's vividly written investigative articles, one of which—about a young woman from a wealthy Connecticut family living a double life in Greenwich Village, where she was murdered—won the Pulitzer Prize in 1968. *[More]* would criticize the *Times* frequently and caustically; many prominent *Times* alumni (and some journalists who still worked at the paper) would write for *[More]* or participate in its annual conventions.

Rosenthal found the barbs from *[More]* and other left-wing publications so galling because they flippantly rejected the journalistic values he held dear. The mission statement in *[More]*'s first issue declared that it would cover the press "fairly but not 'objectively.'"[38] Putting the word in quotation marks conveyed the editors' belief that any sophisticated person would recognize journalistic objectivity as a ridiculous or phony concept; they dismissed it without bothering to explain why. For them, and for the many journalists who shared their views, the question of objectivity had been settled. The real question when it came to fundamental journalistic values was how actively journalists should become involved in the stories they covered.

Some journalists had come to feel that the issues facing the United States were too important, and the press's influence too great, for them to remain neutral. Rosenthal was quite cognizant of this issue. As he explained in September 1969 memo to Turner Catledge, one of his predecessors as managing editor, "Many of the bright young people who come onto the paper and who will come onto the paper come from an atmosphere in which objectivity is no longer considered a great goal. On the contrary, the things that count for them are advocacy and commitment." An article in the *Wall Street Journal* the following month examined the push among many journalists to become activists or advocates. It contrasted the attitude of Sydney Gruson, a *New York Times* executive and former foreign correspondent, with that of his daughter Kerry, a twenty-one-year-old reporter for the *Raleigh News and Observer*. The elder Gruson said, "I feel very strongly about the purity of the news columns. Pure objectivity might not exist, but you have to strive for it anyway." Kerry Gruson countered, "Objectivity is a myth. There comes a point when you have to take a stand." For her, that point had come with the escalation of the Vietnam War. Like many journalists, she had participated in the nationwide Moratorium Day protests on October 15, 1969.[39]

Tom Wicker had similarly strong feelings about the war in Vietnam. He participated in the "Teach-In" movement on college campuses, in which professors and guest speakers told audiences about the war and how they might help end it. In one particularly fiery speech at Harvard in February 1971, Wicker encouraged protests, civil disobedience, and withholding taxes from the federal government, telling the crowd, "We got one president out and perhaps we can do that again" (referring to Lyndon Johnson's decision not to run for reelection in 1968). *The Boston Globe* printed the complete text of the speech, with the headline reading in part, "New York Times Columnist Goes Activist."[40] Abe Rosenthal, as he often did when Wicker publicly defied the tenets of objectivity, protested to the publisher. In this instance he discussed the issue with Sulzberger in person, but on subsequent occasions he sent impassioned letters. Reacting to Wicker's *Columbia Journalism Review* article later in 1971, in which Wicker called objectivity the press's "biggest weakness," Rosenthal told Sulzberger:

> Here we have a man whose name appears on the masthead telling his readers that what The Times promotes and what is at the base of its existence are not worth having. . . . The editors of The Times struggle to maintain the reputation of its news columns for objectivity and comprehensiveness. It is the most difficult period of struggle in this connection that the Times has ever gone through for the very plain reasons that we are living in a period when more and more young journalists question the principles and when The Times, like all institutions, is buffeted by pressures of unrest and disruption. It seems to me fairly obvious that these people inside the paper who wish us to drop objectivity and comprehensiveness will receive comfort and inspiration from Wicker's article, thus making our job even more difficult than it is or need be.[41]

Despite Rosenthal's pleas, the publisher was reluctant to come down too hard on Wicker. Sulzberger seems to have rebuked Wicker only rarely for making public statements that could damage the *Times*'s reputation.[42] In Wicker's papers and the papers of his *Times* contemporaries, there appear to be only two instances when Sulzberger wrote to Wicker about the issue. In March 1970 Sulzberger sent him a very short memo: "Just a brief note to tell you I have heard a couple of reports regarding your remarks at the Foreign Policy Association as advocating editorializing in the news columns. I believe that this is far from your point of view and I thought I should call it to your attention." (Wicker responded that he had said no such thing.)[43] In 1972, upon learning that Wicker was slated to participate in a convention sponsored by the journalism review and *New York Times* antagonist *[More],* Sulzberger sent him a letter, apparently at Rosenthal's urging. Sulzberger said he was "very distressed to learn" of Wicker's planned participation and reminded him that "as an editor . . . you bring with you the authority of the entire organization." He encouraged Wicker to withdraw from the event, and sent an identical letter to Charlotte Curtis, the *Times* Family / Style editor, who also planned to attend. (Sulzberger later reconsidered his request that Wicker and Curtis withdraw, reasoning that the *Times* would risk even greater embarrassment if people learned that Sulzberger had ordered his editors to stay away from the convention.)[44]

Sulzberger seems not to have evinced the same level of concern that Rosenthal did about Wicker's actions. Knowing how headstrong Wicker was, Sulzberger likely believed that he would continue to say whatever he wished in his *Times* column and in his speeches, regardless of the publisher's scolding. If Sulzberger pushed too hard for Wicker to censor himself, this popular, widely read columnist would likely resign—an embarrassment for Sulzberger and a loss for *Times* readers. In addition, the publisher considered Wicker a close friend; Sulzberger and his wife, Carol, socialized frequently with Wicker and his wife, Neva.[45] So Sulzberger tolerated Wicker's periodic undermining of *Times* standards, to Rosenthal's increasing chagrin.

In a 1974 column Wicker disparaged objectivity *and* seemed to encourage advocacy journalism in the same sentence. Writing that young journalism students were "seeking direct involvement in events," Wicker predicted, "such a student attitude almost certainly portends the death of the press-box mentality—the reporter's persistent myth that he can be a neutral observer rather than an inevitable part of the action."[46] This prompted another missive from Rosenthal to Sulzberger. He noted once again the constant struggle to "keep the paper straight," warning that "if we fail, the nature of this paper and its contribution to American society will suffer. . . . And yet I believe we may indeed fail if we are attacked from within on this principle. This is exactly what happened in Tom Wicker's column." By this time, however, Rosenthal seemed resigned to the fact that Sulzberger would take no action. He acknowledged that as a columnist, Wicker had the right to "say anything he wishes." For his part, Rosenthal said, "I have the right to object and I most certainly do."[47] Beyond that, however, there was little he could do, apart from working even harder to prevent other *Times* journalists from taking Wicker's words to heart.

When it came to advocacy, however, Rosenthal did not have to work particularly hard to gain acceptance for his point of view. While it was not uncommon for journalists at the *New York Times* to grapple with the meaning and practicability of objectivity, they were far less likely to consciously venture into advocacy or activism in their work. Some had been activists in college, but once they began working as professional journalists, most considered it dishonest or unprofessional to advocate a cause or a viewpoint in a news article.[48] Sometimes, however, a journalist's actions might lead to differences of opinion about what constituted advocacy and what did not. For instance, *New York Times* reporter Grace Lichtenstein was a devoted feminist but also firmly devoted to practicing objective journalism.[49] Rosenthal could not shake the impression that she was an advocate for women's causes. In a 1975 Lichtenstein article about changes to rape laws, Rosenthal seized on a line deep in the piece in which she referred to "the movement for a more realistic legal approach to sexual assault crimes."[50] The phrase "more realistic," he claimed, "gives short shrift or no shrift to the opposing point of view, and makes it utterly clear to any reader that the piece strongly advocates the new rape laws." The notion that, as Rosenthal put it, "she has consistently shown an advocacy point of view in her work," limited Lichtenstein's prospects for career advancement and her ability to get the assignments she wanted.[51] When in 1977 she asked to cover the National Women's Conference in Houston, the editors denied her request on the grounds that she was too much of an advocate.[52]

Rosenthal's accusations against Lichtenstein may have stemmed from his wariness of the feminist movement and his personal animosity toward Lichtenstein. In addition to her involvement a gender-discrimination lawsuit that female employees of the *New York Times* filed against the paper, she had in 1972 criticized the *Times* on television for not having enough women or minorities among its leadership—an offense for which Rosenthal bawled her out the next day.[53]

Reporter Grace Lichtenstein in the *New York Times* newsroom in 1971 (in the foreground is George Barrett, an editor on the metropolitan desk). Photograph by Librado Romero, courtesy of Grace Lichtenstein. Used with permission.

Whether or not Lichtenstein engaged in advocacy, the temptation to do so could be hard for journalists to resist when they believed deeply in a cause. For example, when Earl Caldwell traveled through the South to report an article about African-Americans' views on school integration, he was surprised to find many people expressing some nostalgia for the days of Jim Crow schools. He recalled, "One thing they were saying was, 'When we had an all-black school, we had the football coaches, you were the head coach of this—we don't have nobody as a head coach now. We're not even getting any coaching jobs.'" When Caldwell turned in a story with a quote like that, the national editor, Gene Roberts, did not want to publish it. According to Caldwell, Roberts said that some people would seize upon such remarks and use them as justification to stop the process of integration. So the *Times* decided not to run the article.[54]

Viewed one way, Roberts and Caldwell acted responsibly by declining to publish material that would have been distorted and taken out of context in the service of damaging political goals—that was likely the way Roberts and Caldwell saw it. Viewed another way, they failed to be objective by allowing their personal views to influence a news judgment. In retrospect, however, they were drawing a line between the sphere of consensus (the notion that desegregation is just and good) and the sphere of legitimate controversy (desegregation can have good and bad effects).[55] If, as Roberts and Caldwell determined, the views expressed in their story belonged in the sphere of deviance, then there was no need to try to report them objectively.

• • •

AS THAT EXAMPLE SHOWS, it can be hard to pin down the precise meaning and implications of objectivity. Even Abe Rosenthal, probably the fiercest advocate of objectivity in American journalism during his years at the *New York Times,* acknowledged in his journal that the term was tricky. "I'm not going to get hung up on the word," he wrote. "I know what it is and most of us know what it is, even when we struggle with it."[56] Others, however—such as the publisher and editors of the *Los Angeles Times*—were quite hung up on the word. In a 1971 speech, *L.A. Times* publisher Otis Chandler delivered a kind of manifesto outlining the credo in which he and his paper believed, analogous to the message from Rosenthal that the *New York Times* published in 1970. Unlike Rosenthal, however, Chandler felt that striving for objectivity was a fool's errand:

> Probably the most often expressed criticism of the press today is that it has lost its objectivity—that elusive, vague, misunderstood phantom concept called objectivity. . . . Today the press is more honest in its presentation of what it considers to be news, not less honest. You notice I use the word honest rather than objective. I think this is because I detest the word objective. Pursuing the word objective only leads you into a semantic jungle. . . . The entire reporting and editing process involves selectivity, and selection is subjective. . . . [This] does not justify a concept of reporting where the emphasis is on the personal reaction of our reporter, which then leads to advocacy of a specific course of action. . . . The primary function of the press is to provide a large and complete and honest stream of pertinent information, free of personal bias, as much as it is possible to do so.[57]

Beyond stating that there was "no such thing as completely objective reporting"—a statement Abe Rosenthal would have agreed with—Chandler implied that there was no such thing as "the news"; there was only what the press "considers to be news." Nevertheless, he drew a sharp line between accepting your subjectivity as a journalist and indulging in biased coverage or advocacy journalism. He maintained that relying on "the collective best judgment of a great number of experienced professional newsmen" was the optimal way to produce a newspaper.

Many on Chandler's staff felt similarly ambivalent about objectivity. Editor-in-chief Nick Williams rarely gave public speeches, but in 1970 he spoke to an audience at Claremont University, which two of his children had attended. He took the opportunity to "quarrel" with what he called "the basic theory of so-called objective journalism." After pointing out the impossibility of pure objectivity, he argued that even striving for it could be harmful, because that might prevent journalists from interpreting the news in ways that would be useful to their readers.[58]

Williams frequently fielded letters from readers accusing the *Los Angeles Times* of failing to be objective. He took these opportunities to point out the problematic nature of objectivity and to note that it was not, strictly speaking, one of the paper's goals. For instance, one reader in 1970 asked why the *L.A. Times* could not be as objective as the conservative-leaning magazine *U.S. News and World Report*. Williams responded, "The matter of objectivity always is a matter of opinion. It is quite possible to give the appearance of objectivity without, in fact, being all that objective. I suspect you may not agree with this but it is quite true—an article can be completely factual and not be at all objective. This can be achieved by the simple technique of selecting which facts you include in the article."[59] In 1969 Williams told another skeptical conservative reader, "We do try, if not always for objectivity, at least for fairness."[60]

Williams's successor as editor-in-chief, Bill Thomas, made the same distinction. In a 1972 TV interview, Thomas was asked, "Is there such a thing as objectivity, in your judgment, and can an editor expect it of his reporters?" He replied, "No. It's a word that's been tossed around so much that nobody knows what it means anymore. I don't think one can expect pure objectivity of anybody in any field at any time . . . it's probably not humanly possible." However, Thomas quickly indicated that it was mainly the word that was problematic, not the concept. "I think one can expect fairness, and that implies professional standards," he said. "In that regard, looking at objectivity through that definition, then I think you do have a right to expect that."[61]

Beyond the upper echelons of the paper, many reporters and editors at the *Los Angeles Times* preferred concepts like fairness and honesty to the loaded term "objectivity." Tim Rutten, who joined the paper in 1972 at age twenty-three as an editor in the features section and then moved to the editorial pages, recalled frequent debates about the topic. "What we eventually hit on was that it wasn't a matter of objectivity, it was a matter of fairness," Rutten said. "I think most of us ultimately concluded that the word objectivity never should have been used to describe the value we were trying to preserve. We were trying to preserve fairness and even-handedness."[62] Bill Boyarsky, like many newspaper reporters, worked for the Associated Press before landing a job on a major metropolitan daily. The AP had an ironclad insistence on objectivity, because its business model consisted of selling articles to newspapers of all different political orientations. Boyarsky had absorbed that ethos during his time at the AP, but he said that within a few years of joining the *L.A. Times* in 1970, "I realized that objectivity is a bad word. . . . Everybody has opinions and a point of view and is a product of many things, and what you have to do is be aware of your prejudices, your point of view and all that, and if you're doing a news story you have to take that into consideration."[63]

In discussing their reservations about objectivity, these *L.A. Times* journalists do not sound very different from the people who *did* believe in objectivity. Trying to set aside one's prejudices when working on a news story, being fair and evenhanded, refraining from advocacy, eliminating personal bias as much as possible—these were among the main elements of objective journalism as Abe Rosenthal defined it. In many ways the debate was simply a question of semantics. It meant one thing to Rosenthal, but to others it meant something very different. Many journalists equated objectivity with unquestioningly parroting the views of the powerful—failing to challenge Joe McCarthy when he accused people of being communists without any evidence, for example, or printing the U.S. military's claims about how well the war in Vietnam was going without pointing out the dubiousness of the statistics. They thought it meant creating false equivalencies in a misguided attempt at balanced reporting—for example, in a story about an increase in crime, finding a source who believed that crime was decreasing, and giving both sides equal weight regardless of what the evidence might suggest. They associated it with a "just the facts" approach that forbade analysis and forced journalists to obscure the truth. And after November 1969, objectivity in the minds of many meant the kind of reporting Spiro Agnew wanted—something that most journalists, fiercely protective of their independence from government pressure, would never accept.

It is not as if every journalist at the *L.A. Times* disliked the notion of objectivity. There were regular discussions about it in the newsroom or over drinks, with some taking the position that it was worth striving for. In casual conversation and in their correspondence, *Times* editors often used the term to describe what they were trying to achieve.[64] But striving for objectivity was not for them an all-consuming passion, as it was for Abe Rosenthal and others at the *New York Times*. At the *L.A. Times* there was no stream of memos from the editor-in-chief's office raising alarms about editorializing in the news columns. Because Nick Williams was such a strong advocate of interpretive reporting, however, he and other senior editors felt they needed to convey to the staff what was acceptable and what was not. They had several exchanges about that topic in the late 1960s. In a 1970 memo to the three highest-ranking editors under him, Williams explained his position on how to move beyond "so-called objective journalism" without damaging the paper's reputation:

> The judgment of reporters and editors, each from a somewhat different perspective, must be blended to produce the kind of articles that are indeed interpretive but are not—or not quite—pure opinion. We walk a tight rope here. Opinion is the stock-in-trade of drama and music critics and perhaps sports writers, particularly opinion of the personal sort, but I am not persuaded that it should enter decisively into the treatment of the sterner categories of news. . . . Some of the finest writing in The Times in recent years has come very close to this border line of personal opinion. And a few times, I think, it has slipped over the line, occasionally through the use of a single word or phrase.

Slipping over the line was a problem, Williams continued, because the paper's credibility suffered "when any fraction of it seems—to use a readers' frequent phrase—vindictively slanted." After all the "time and sweat" the *Los Angeles Times* had devoted to shedding its image as a shill for the right wing, Williams said, "we have got to be above even the shadow of suspicion that we are ideologues."[65]

This memo was hardly a fulmination against those who would undermine the newspaper's values. By saying he was "not persuaded" that the reporter's opinion should be inserted into news stories, he implied that it was a question on which reasonable people could disagree, and that he had considered the possibility that opinionated news might be acceptable. Writing to a Canadian newspaper editor in 1969 about the absolute necessity of interpretive reporting, Williams pooh-poohed concerns that it might lead to bias. Interpretation "lays us open . . . to the charge, which is getting monotonous, that we are editorializing the news," Williams wrote. "[That] isn't really true and doesn't concern me too much—the charge that we are editorializing is a cliché that means we and the news are disturbing people."[66]

Williams and other *Los Angeles Times* editors worried less than they might have about reporters slanting the news because they had a system in place designed to prevent that. Dennis Britton, who was the paper's Washington editor from 1971 to 1977 before becoming national editor, recalled that an article from Washington might be edited by six different people before making it into print. Each of those people would have a different background and different biases, and each would attempt to remove any bias he or she detected. That process "lent itself to creating copy that was not as biased but that was more neutral," Britton said.[67] Jim Bell, a news editor at the *L.A. Times* from 1965 to 2001, echoed that sentiment. On an important article, he noted, "you had five or six sets of eyes looking at this story . . . and everybody is trying to make sure that it's objective and that we aren't taking some kind of slanted view."[68] Nick Williams made a similar point in a 1969 letter, acknowledging that reporters might sometimes get overzealous and favor one side too strongly, but assuring his correspondent that "editors are supposed to recognize that when it occurs and do a little balancing."[69] Naturally, the *New York Times* had a similar system in place, but Abe Rosenthal was less confident in his

editors' ability to correct for any apparent bias without constant prod-
ding from him. If all six sets of eyes belonged to liberals, after all, they
may not have recognized what conservatives would perceive as biased
reporting.

When it came to safeguarding the *L.A. Times*'s credibility, Nick Williams and his successor, Bill Thomas, did not fixate on a stray word or
phrase slipping past the editors and leading readers to detect some kind
of bias. Their greater concern was that reporters might drift into advocacy. Beginning in the mid-1960s, the paper ventured more and more into
investigative work and interpretive reporting; it could be difficult in such
articles to draw a line between interpretations and exhortations, or between exposés and indictments. (The exhortations and indictments were
meant to be limited to the editorial columns.) Nick Williams sent a memo
on this topic to Otis Chandler in 1968, prompted in part by efforts the
paper had been making to act as an intermediary between the Los Angeles Police Department and leaders of Los Angeles's black community.
Williams wrote, "We do run some psychological risks when our people
begin to think of themselves in any way as 'participants,' even as the re-
layers of messages. For involvement, of any kind or degree, tends to lead
to more involvement." In this same memo, Williams stated that journalists becoming participants was "a highly debatable area," and added,
"uninvolvement when pursuing a socially valuable objective is hard to
maintain" (Chandler wrote "agree" in the margin).[70]

As time went on, however, concerns about the paper's credibility
grew, and it became apparent that the *Times*'s efforts to mediate the relationship between the police and the black community had not been
fruitful. After one ill-fated attempt at mediation in 1969, managing editor
Frank Haven and then-metropolitan editor Bill Thomas each wrote to
Williams. "Reasonable as it sounds to take an active part in solving community problems, our own participation inevitably shapes the news,"
Thomas said. Haven concurred: "I strongly agree we shouldn't be
involved as participants."[71]

The paper's leaders grew ever more convinced that they had to protect their reputation for independence, which meant a stricter policy
against anything that resembled advocacy or conflict of interest. In 1970
Otis Chandler asked Nick Williams and associate editor Bob Donovan

whether they thought he should serve on corporate boards apart from his own (the Times Mirror Company). Donovan said no, because it could create the presumption "of a special relationship between the outside organization and the paper. Even if unjustified, such a presumption could damage the image of independence and objectivity cherished by the paper. This would be doubly unfortunate at a time when the credibility of the press is under widespread challenge." Williams agreed, saying, "The complete and demonstrable, unassailable independence of a newspaper is its greatest asset." He added that journalists should not openly identify as Republicans or Democrats or join any outside organization, even a professional society, if it might cast doubt on their independence.[72]

In a 1978 speech to the Society of Professional Journalists, *L.A. Times* editor-in-chief Bill Thomas argued that the rise of interpretive reporting had made drawing a line between judgment and advocacy more important than ever. "It's ironic that, in a time when journalists have been given unprecedented freedom by their newspapers to make judgment calls on the most explosive issues, the demand has been raised that they be given also the freedom to associate themselves publicly in ways that would call those judgments into question," Thomas said. "We stand or fall individually and as institutions on the issue of credibility. If we are even perceived as lacking it, in any substantial way, we'll fail." Once reporters or editors became identified with one side or another on any issue, Thomas said, "[you] have ruled yourselves out as reliable purveyors of information about that subject, or even related subjects."[73]

When most people thought of advocacy journalism, Thomas noted, they thought of young people pushing for left-wing causes. And without a doubt, the *L.A. Times* was against that. Dennis Britton recalled that when he was Washington editor, he and most of the bureau staff were against the Vietnam War and sympathized with antiwar demonstrators. But if any of them had left the office and joined the protests that were taking place right outside, Britton said, "We would have fired them. . . . We had very strong feelings about becoming part of the news."[74] Thomas felt just as strongly, however, about not advocating for Establishment causes. As he said in his 1978 speech, "I have sat and listened to national leaders of important institutions—fine people, motivated by the highest values—suggest that we not print true stories that tend to create distrust in their areas of interest, because the strength of their institutions is vital to the nation's welfare. What is this? It is advocacy journalism. . . . We must shun it at all costs."[75]

Thomas had clearly taken to heart the complaints that journalists such as Tom Wicker and Nicholas von Hoffman had been making for years: that the press was biased in favor of the Establishment. But at the same time, Thomas knew that many people felt the press was biased *against* the Establishment, and by the mid-1970s this seems to have been his greater concern. During his seventeen-year tenure as *L.A. Times* editor-in-chief, he wrote only one article in the daily paper. Published in March 1975, it was headlined, "The Press: Is It Biased against the Establishment?" His answer, unsurprisingly, was no, but he offered a compelling explanation for the perception of anti-Establishment bias:

> Until about 10 years ago, the press tended to rely almost solely on sources within the so-called establishment institutions. A crime story quoted police spokesmen; an economics story rested on business and industry and chamber of commerce sources; stories about racial problems came from the mouths of government spokesmen and sociology professors. One heard little from black people, the poor, the dissident, the accused criminal, and others who spoke without institutional blessing. To telescope, and perhaps unforgivably simplify, a complex period of recent history, an increasingly sophisticated reading audience became aware that there was more to the story than that.

As a result, Thomas explained, newspapers provided more "nontraditional reporting" (that is, interpretation). Moreover, they began to include more diverse views, so that "where establishment voices alone were heard, others have gained access."[76]

By the time Thomas delivered this speech, in the late 1970s, the peak period of concern about newspapers' credibility and objectivity seemed to have passed. "We are closer than ever before to a position of real and, importantly, *perceived* independence," he told his audience. "We're getting close to a goal that looked unattainable, not so long ago: that of acceptance as a truly independent source of dependable information."[77] This was a far cry from Nick Williams's assessment in the late 1960s and early 1970s. In one speech, citing those on the far right and the far left who were accusing the press of bias, he had declared, "The American press as a whole is facing the most massive assault upon its constitutional freedom that has occurred during my lifetime."[78] In 1968 he had told a reporter for the *Saturday Review,* "We are currently going through a peak period of press abuse." And Williams was far from alone in that belief. The *Saturday Review* article in which he was quoted, headlined "The Press under Assault," noted that Americans of all stripes disliked and distrusted the news media, blaming them for many of the country's problems. "I can't remember anything like the abuse the press is taking today," said the head of United Press International.[79] In 1969 an entire issue of the quarterly newspaper-trade magazine *Seminar* was devoted to the topic, "The Press under Attack."[80]

In the late 1960s and early 1970s, Abe Rosenthal at the *New York Times* was as alarmed as anyone about preserving objectivity and safeguarding his newspaper's credibility. But by 1978 he, too, felt the storm had passed. In the previous three years, the number of memos he had sent about advocacy or editorializing in the news columns had declined sharply. He collected several minor examples of instances "where we may have strayed" and sent them to Punch Sulzberger with the following explanation: "I do think you know that in my own mind there is nothing more important as far as The Times is concerned than the issue of fairness and the level of discourse. My own belief is that in recent years we have gone a hell of a long way to improving it and that whatever excesses that were in the past in American journalism have largely been eliminated as far as The Times is concerned. . . . So I am calling these to your attention not because they indicate a problem but just as a matter of interest."[81] This is a far different tone than Rosenthal had taken five or ten years earlier.

Debates about objectivity, advocacy, bias, and credibility have continued until today—it is hard to imagine that they will ever be resolved, as long as there is a free press. But beginning in the late 1970s those debates reached a kind of stasis. Ever since, critics on the right have leveled the same kinds of charges that Spiro Agnew made: of liberal bias, elitism, arrogance, insularity, and unwarranted power. Those on the left have accused the press of kowtowing to powerful interests while ignoring minorities and the poor. Neither side believed for a moment that the press was actually objective. Yet most news executives and journalists in positions of power continued to insist that they were guided by something like objectivity, even if some preferred not to use that word. At the *New York Times* and the *Los Angeles Times,* journalistic values changed, but only in minimal ways.

Why didn't the challenges to objectivity during the late 1960s and early 1970s have a greater impact? In part because the people in charge believed the challenges had little merit; most of them had been in the newspaper business for decades and had devoted themselves to some variant of objectivity since the beginning of their careers. Some journalists who came of age before the 1960s rejected objectivity, but they were rarely placed in positions of significant editorial responsibility, regardless of how talented they were—Tom Wicker is a prime example (he had been Washington bureau chief, but that was earlier in his career, before his unorthodox views on objectivity developed). Inertia alone, however, cannot account for the press's dogged adherence to its ideals.

Most thoughtful journalists, then as now, occasionally questioned their professional values. Some surely recognized that right-wing critics like Spiro Agnew made valid points; others surely recognized that left-wing critics like Tom Wicker made valid points; many probably felt that each side was right about some things and wrong about some things. But the fact that these critiques were being raised simultaneously made each of them easier to ignore. The leaders of the *New York Times* and the *Los Angeles Times* believed that their newspaper and its coverage should occupy the political center. They said this frequently, both in public remarks and in private correspondence. Accordingly, they viewed it as a positive sign when their behavior angered partisans on both the right and left—that signified that they were exactly where they wanted to be.

In speeches defending the fairness and credibility of the *Los Angeles Times* or of the press in general, Otis Chandler and Nick Williams mentioned, seemingly with pride, that both sides of the political spectrum found fault with them. As Williams said in 1966, "The American press, so vigorously attacked from both the left and the right—described as both the lackeys of capitalism and the dupes of communism— . . . is, I earnestly believe, the *most* responsible of *all* our American institutions."[82] In a 1969 speech about young people's dislike for "the establishment press," Otis

Chandler implied that criticism was a badge of honor, provided that it came from varied sources. "The far right does not like us," said Chandler. "The far left does not like us. . . . Some politicians do not like us. . . . Middle-class establishment adults do not like us." The best way to address that situation, Chandler argued, was for the press to continue doing what it was doing—"to go right on reporting the news as honestly as we can."[83] George Cotliar, who joined the *L.A. Times* in 1957 and became managing editor in 1978, concurred. He recalled that no matter how hard the paper tried to avoid expressing a point of view in its news articles, people on either side of contentious issues like the Vietnam War and racial unrest would accuse the *Times* of favoring the other side. However, Cotliar said, "Maybe that's a positive. If both sides equally think you're doing a crappy job, maybe you're not. Maybe you're doing what you're supposed to do."[84]

This was a common view at many news organizations, including the *New York Times*. Harrison Salisbury, an influential senior editor and reporter, told a friend in 1971 that he was unmoved by criticism of the news media from "the extreme right and the extreme left. . . . It seems to me that this is just the conventional yapping by people who always complain if others do not reflect their opinions. As you know, we get plenty of it here at the Times, and in almost equal measure from radicals who think we are the establishment and reactionaries who think we are the revolution."[85] Seymour Topping, deputy managing editor in the 1970s, recalled, "When I was getting [criticism] from both sides of an issue, there was an indication to me that we were doing our job."[86] Even if editors and executives were liberals, they wanted a centrist newspaper, not a liberal one.

Another source of reassurance that they were doing the right thing in sticking to their traditional ideals came from their newspapers' economic health and prestige. The *Los Angeles Times,* which had been one of the most profitable newspapers in the United States for decades before the 1960s, reached still greater heights of prosperity even as Otis Chandler spent lavishly to improve the paper's quality. Chandler boasted to his biographer, "When I came into management, our pre-tax profit was somewhere around $2 million or $3 million, and I took it to $100 million."[87] Year after year, the *Los Angeles Times* printed more lines of advertising than any other paper in the country; its weekday circulation had gone from 523,000 in 1960, when Otis Chandler became publisher, to more than 1,000,000 in 1970, and it kept growing from there.[88] Moreover, the paper had earned the respect of its peers, something that had always eluded it under Chandler's father and grandfather. It regularly won Pulitzer Prizes, and a spate of magazine articles marveled at the way it had transformed. Observers generally agreed that it was one of the two or three best newspapers in the country. As the Watergate scandal unfolded, the *L.A. Times* ran second only to the *Washington Post* in revealing shocking new developments. With all of these indicators telling Chandler, Williams, Thomas, and the rest of the paper's upper management they were succeeding spectacularly in every way, it would seem like folly to fundamentally change their approach.

The *New York Times* was never a cash cow like its West Coast counterpart, but it was reliably profitable throughout the 1960s and 1970s. The paper's profit margins became dangerously thin in the mid-1970s (1.7 percent in 1975), but that had little to do with its journalistic values or the tone of its coverage. It was a result of the broader economic downturn combined with the fact that many affluent New York City residents—the bread and butter of the *Times* readership—were fleeing to the suburbs. These newly minted suburbanites often gave up the *Times* in favor of one of the much-improved suburban papers, especially Long Island–based *Newsday* (which, incidentally, was purchased by the *L.A. Times*'s parent company in 1970, making Otis Chandler its publisher).

But the business crisis at the *New York Times* lasted very briefly, and by the late 1970s the paper was as financially healthy as it had ever been.[89] Journalistically, it was widely regarded as the greatest newspaper in the country, if not the world, despite increased competition for that title from the *Los Angeles Times* and the *Washington Post*. It scored the biggest scoop of the era with the Pentagon Papers, the military's secret history of the Vietnam War, from which the *Times* published excerpts. And when the Nixon administration sued to halt the publication of articles based on the Pentagon Papers, the *Times* prevailed. The paper's leadership felt confident that the *Times* was financially healthy and fulfilling its core purpose—keeping the public informed and serving as a watchdog for the national interest—more effectively than ever before.

When it came to their fundamental journalistic values, the managers of the two newspapers had the same basic idea: they wanted to keep what was good about objectivity and get rid of what was bad. It was good to be fair, which meant presenting opposing views accurately and respectfully, even if you disagreed with them; it was good to be an observer rather than a participant in the news, and to keep favoritism and personal opinions out of news coverage. It was bad, however, to be a stenographer—to merely report what happened or what was said without providing explanation or interpretation. It was bad to be boring, to write without any color or feeling. The main difference between the *New York Times* and the *Los Angeles Times* on this score was that the former insisted on calling these values "objectivity," while the latter was happy to jettison the word.

Nick Williams believed that "objective reporting" and "interpretive-analytic reporting" were two different approaches to news coverage, but that was a belief he arrived at gradually. During his tenure as editor-in-chief, he and his fellow editors made the decision to embrace the interpretive-analytic approach. In a 1964 memo to Otis Chandler regarding the "general news policies" of the *L.A. Times,* Williams wrote, "Our policy calls for strict objectivity in the selection and placement of news." As for writing, he said, while some explanatory matter should be included, "we definitely do forbid the inclusion of unsupported inferences or insinuations."[90] Over the next several years, however, Williams came to feel that such policies were too simplistic. In a 1970 memo he reflected on the new direction that the paper's news coverage had taken in recent months and years:

> Some time ago . . . we were making a distinction between so-called objective reporting and the kind of interpretive-analytic reporting that we wanted Times reporter / writers to emphasize. Since then, we've moved a long way. . . . In the process, as all of us expected, we have now and then misfired—but hell, we misfired just as frequently when we persevered at "objective" reporting. And I think we have managed with the interpretive approach to come a whopping lot closer to telling our readers what it was all about than we ever could have managed before.[91]

To Williams, objectivity and interpretation were incompatible, and because interpretation was necessary to provide a complete, honest picture of the news, that was the way to go.

At the *New York Times,* Abe Rosenthal and those who shared his views saw no contradiction between interpretation and objectivity.[92] On the contrary, Rosenthal's version of objectivity mandated some degree of interpretation. His favorite kind of article, it seems, was the "news analysis," in which the reporter had far more freedom to provide context and judgments than in a regular news article.[93] In memos to colleagues, Rosenthal referred to the form as "one of the most useful tools that the Times has" and "a very important golden goose."[94] He wanted more of this kind of interpretive reporting, which attempted to explain the meaning behind the news or to predict its potential impact. He also dismissed the notion held by many critics of objectivity, Nick Williams likely among them, that it constrained the writer and led to boring articles. As Rosenthal wrote in his journal in 1971, "Something I keep saying over and over again until I am sure I drive people crazy is that objectivity does not imply dullness or dryness and that indeed dullness and dryness are the opposite of objectivity. Objectivity is an attempt to capture life as it exists, and life is neither dry nor dull."[95] A few years earlier he had tried to explain the same thing to a young reporter who asked if the *Times* had begun to permit personal opinions in news articles: "I said that the Times was far more flexible an instrument of expression than most people realized," Rosenthal recounted to two senior colleagues, "and that a deft reporter could convey not only facts but atmosphere and even emotions of participants in the news simply by adroit use of the language, but I said that nobody . . . was in favor of editorialization of the news."[96]

The differing views on objectivity at the *New York Times* and the *Los Angeles Times* were very much in keeping with the character of the two newspapers and of the men in charge of them. The *L.A. Times* was often referred to as "a writer's paper," which meant that reporters—especially the most talented writers among them—were given great freedom in choosing the topic, angle, style, and length of their articles. Editors would change the copy and remove what they deemed biased or editorialized, but the paper would not ask its writers to strive for an ideal that was difficult to define, impossible to fully achieve, and discredited in the eyes of many journalists. The *New York Times,* on the other hand, had a reputation as "an editor's paper." Articles had to adhere to the paper's standards and house style, and they were often rigorously edited to guarantee that they did so. Some *New York Times* reporters said they dreaded reading their articles in the newspaper, because they would usually find out that the editors had made major changes with which the reporter disagreed.[97]

Personalities also made a difference when it came to each paper's position on objectivity. Nick Williams and Bill Thomas were both easygoing and nonconfrontational, whereas Rosenthal was hard-driving and imperious—stereotypical representations of the difference between the Southern California temperament and the New York City temperament. If Thomas disapproved of something a reporter or a midlevel editor had done, he would direct the person's immediate boss to speak to him or her informally. Rosenthal, in the same situation, would send a biting memo to the offender and his or her boss, or would call them into his office for a tongue-lashing. This difference in management style translated to their position on objectivity. Williams and Thomas thought it was a gray area and issued few directives about it. Rosenthal had a firm definition of objectivity and did everything in his power to ensure that his staff adhered to it.

These variations in the leadership's stance on objectivity were evident in the journalism that the *Los Angeles Times* and the *New York Times* produced, but only in subtle ways. *L.A. Times* news articles tended to state their judgments more plainly than most newspapers, whereas *New York Times* news articles were more circumspect. Nevertheless, the similarities between the two papers stand out far more than the differences. Most of their journalists, and nearly all of their managers, believed that credibility was their most precious asset and that, in order to preserve it, news articles needed to be unbiased and scrupulously fair. They believed that their coverage should originate from the standpoint of the political center, and that for the most part, it did; critics who argued otherwise, they felt, were blinded by their own ideology. They believed that although most of their staff held liberal or left-wing political views, they could put those views aside when reporting or presenting the news.

Having these beliefs called into question so forcefully during the 1960s and 1970s actually helped reinforce them, and journalists became somewhat inured to criticism. This confidence in their core values, along with the immense profitability of their businesses, enabled them to embrace other substantial changes to the news product, from interpretive articles to soft-news sections. The *New York Times* and the *Los Angeles Times*, like most major news organizations, would continue to anger people on the right and the left—particularly those on the right, thanks to their liberal editorial pages and to the rightward shift the country underwent beginning in the 1970s. But they would not need to fundamentally reassess their values and business model again until the Internet revolution of the early twenty-first century.

❈ 4 ❈

The Reader-Oriented Newspaper

A NY BUSINESS, to be successful, must serve its customers effectively. But the press in the first half of the twentieth century was not like just any business. It more closely resembled a utility; most Americans felt they needed a daily newspaper just as they needed heat, electricity, and telephone service. Unlike phone companies and power companies, however, newspapers rarely had local monopolies, so they had to compete with one another—they featured different comic strips, columnists, editorial-page positions, and so on. But when people spoke of newspapers "serving" their readers, they usually referred in high-minded tones to the press's responsibility to foster a well-informed American electorate. The 1947 Hutchins Commission Report on Freedom of the Press, for instance, defined "the service required of the American press by the American people" as providing the means for Americans to make "the fundamental decisions necessary to the direction of their government and of their lives."[1]

By the mid-1960s, the competitive environment was transformed—few American cities supported competing newspapers under separate ownership.[2] Increasing costs for labor and newsprint, combined with stagnant sales, had caused thousands of papers to merge with competitors or shut down. This consolidation was especially apparent in Los Angeles and New York. The *Los Angeles Times* gained a monopoly on L.A.'s morning newspaper market in 1962, when the Hearst Corporation agreed to shutter its second-place morning *Examiner* in exchange for the *Times*'s parent company, Times Mirror, closing its struggling afternoon paper, the *Los Angeles Mirror* (this gave Hearst a monopoly on the afternoon market with its renamed *Herald-Examiner*). New York City boasted four general-interest broadsheet dailies in the early 1960s, but by 1967, after two city-wide newspaper strikes in the space of five years, the *New York Times* was the last one standing.[3]

Despite the winnowed field of big-city dailies, survivors like the *Los Angeles Times* and the *New York Times* faced no shortage of competition. Instead of competing with other metropolitan newspapers, they now had to compete with television, magazines, and smaller suburban papers. With these expanded media options, a growing number of Americans began to consider a daily newspaper superfluous. As *L.A. Times* publisher Otis Chandler wrote in 1966, "Let us face it: many people do not need The Times or any other newspaper."[4] This called for a fundamental rethinking of what newspapers should provide their readers. For over a century, most Americans felt they could not do without a daily newspaper. No longer able to rely on that attitude, editors and news executives would focus on making their product not only indispensable but also enjoyable. In addition to (or instead of) serving the needs of an informed citizenry, as the Hutchins Commission had urged the press to do, it became necessary to serve the desires of distracted consumers.

This shift in the press's role and mission contributed to broader changes in American society and culture. If people were to continue reading newspapers like the *New York Times* and the *Los Angeles Times,* they would do so because they took a personal interest in the material, not because of a sense of civic obligation. The focus on the self grew as the focus on the collective—the community, the nation—waned, both in readers' minds and on newspaper pages. Just as American voters increasingly expected politicians to cater to their desires (for lower taxes, better services, more jobs), American newspaper readers expected editors to cater to *their* desires. They wanted material oriented toward them and their lives; it had to be relevant, entertaining, or useful—preferably all three.

• • •

THE MANAGERS OF SERIOUS-MINDED newspapers like the *New York Times* and the *Los Angeles Times* had always been committed to keeping their readers informed about the major events of the day. They reasoned that people who wished to be entertained by their newspaper, rather than informed, would buy a tabloid. But in the 1950s and 1960s they began to recognize that simply trying to keep readers informed would lead to disaster in their changing business environment. So they moved tentatively—as large, prosperous institutions generally do—toward change. They might consider it beneath their dignity to try to entertain readers, but they could, without compromising their paper's character, try to become more useful. They could cater to their readers without pandering to them, and increasingly that became their goal. The first important step in that direction came in response to the great demographic shift that reshaped American cities in the post–World War II era: the growth of suburbs.

From the 1950s to the 1970s, millions of Americans moved out of city centers and into booming suburban communities.[5] Failing to capture a sizable portion of this market—affluent families whom advertisers wanted desperately to reach—could be disastrous for a metropolitan newspaper. But newly minted suburbanites often had less interest in what was happening downtown than in their own communities, most of which were well served by the small daily or weekly newspapers that sprang up seemingly everywhere in the postwar era. Despite the fact that big-city papers failed in droves, the overall number of newspapers in the United States remained nearly unchanged from 1945 to 1965 because so many suburban and small-town papers were launched.[6] In the country's ten largest metropolitan areas, suburban newspapers saw their circulation jump by 8.5 million between 1945 and 1962, while city papers grew by only 304,000.[7] *Los Angeles Times* editor-in-chief Nick Williams summarized the situation perceptively in a 1970 memo: "The combination of a community newspaper (for the local details) plus a national news magazine—

both of which can be had for less than the cost per week of The Times—
make a formidable circulation competitor. Throw in the rounded picture
that free TV makes available and you begin to know what an editorial
staff must compete successfully against."[8]

The *L.A. Times* made innovative efforts to stave off this "formidable
competitor" for suburban readers. In 1952 it created the first of many
"zoned" editions for residential areas in greater Los Angeles. A small
corps of reporters and editors covered each zone, and their stories
appeared in special sections that came out once or twice a week. In addition to helping maintain or grow the paper's circulation, these zoned
sections also offered an important advertising vehicle: local retailers who
had no need to reach all of the *Times*'s far-flung readers could buy ads in
the zoned sections at lower rates. Newspapers throughout the country
began introducing zoned editions in the 1960s, but the *L.A. Times* was
among the first—not surprising, given the geographically dispersed
character of Los Angeles and the *Times*'s vast pool of capital to invest.[9]
By 1964 the paper had seven zoned editions that generated $1.3 million in
annual profits.[10] In the next decade the number of suburban sections
increased to ten—several of which moved from weekly publication to
daily—and the profits reached nearly $10 million.[11]

The idea for suburban sections came from the advertising department
at the *L.A. Times,* and the editorial side initially showed limited interest.[12]
Experienced reporters and editors had no desire to cover local school
boards and city councils, so the zoned sections were akin to a farm
system—a training ground, where standards and expectations were somewhat lower, for eager young journalists hoping to get promoted to the big
leagues (the main edition).[13] Yet it was impossible to ignore the growing
importance of suburban news to the paper's prosperity. In a 1966 memo
to managing editor Frank Haven, Nick Williams said that Haven's "par-
amount objective" for the coming year should be to coordinate between
the Metropolitan and Suburban staffs in order to get more suburban stories of "high interest" into the main paper. Williams pointed out that "any
major development of ANY sort, no matter in what part of the megalop-
olis it occurs, does interest the entire metropolis."[14] City Hall remained
the most prestigious assignment for a metropolitan reporter, but suburban
sameness meant that a reader in Calabasas might care more about a

report from Pasadena (both affluent suburbs) than the latest mayoral pronouncement.

The clearest statement of the paper's commitment to its suburban operations came in 1968, when the *Los Angeles Times* launched a separate daily edition for Orange County, an area of wealthy, fast-growing communities south of Los Angeles. This edition featured news about Orange County every day, interspersed seamlessly into the main edition's content. Overseen by a respected senior editor, it had its own brand-new printing plant and an editorial staff of thirty-two to start (it eventually grew to more than a hundred).[15] Assistant managing editor George Cotliar, who took over the Orange County edition in 1970, realized that suburban stories potentially had area-wide appeal. He told the staff that he wanted them to write articles that would interest *all* of the paper's readers, not just those in Orange County—he even kept a running tally of how many Orange County stories got published in the main edition.[16]

Whereas the geography of Los Angeles led editors of the *L.A. Times* to take an expansive view of metropolitan and suburban news early on, the *New York Times* had always focused primarily on Manhattan. Its managers assumed that people in the other four boroughs and beyond who wished to be well informed would buy the paper regardless of whether it included news from their home communities. But the shift in wealth from city to suburbs was especially intense in New York. In the 1960s, *Times* managers fretted about their lackluster circulation growth while watching the Long Island–based *Newsday* achieve astounding success. Founded in 1940, *Newsday* had a modest circulation of 52,000 in 1947. As the population of Long Island exploded, so did *Newsday*'s circulation: by 1962 it reached 345,000, and that number had grown to 455,000 by 1970 (the year that Times Mirror, parent company of the *Los Angeles Times,* purchased *Newsday*).[17]

Belatedly recognizing that *Newsday*'s vast readership posed both a threat and an opportunity, in 1966 *New York Times* publisher Arthur Ochs "Punch" Sulzberger appointed a committee to study the possibility of adding separate suburban sections to the Sunday paper. Unlike the free-spending management of the *Los Angeles Times*, Sulzberger wanted to create suburban sections without investing in new staff or production equipment. The committee concluded that doing so would create a "sub-standard" product, "below expected Times quality," that would fail to capture reader interest and would wind up causing the company to lose money—$735,000 a year, by the committee's estimate.[18]

With that dire prediction, the *New York Times* shelved the idea of suburban sections, but not for long. By 1969 the demand by large retail stores for separate suburban sections had become even greater. One of the paper's advertising executives wrote, "We must inevitably satisfy this demand or prepare to do without much of the retail advertising which would otherwise run in The Times."[19] Rather than forego that essential revenue, the *Times* decided to introduce two weekly suburban sections: one for northern New Jersey and one for Brooklyn, Queens, and Long Island.

In preparation for this new venture, several *New York Times* editors and executives traveled to Southern California in 1970 to tour the *L.A. Times*'s Orange County operation.[20] Metropolitan editor Arthur Gelb was not impressed. The zoned sections, he wrote, "are a success as a producer of advertising revenue but a failure in its attempt to maintain respectable journalistic standards." The editors of the *L.A. Times,* according to Gelb, confided to him that the material was "of such poor quality in journalistic terms that the operation was having a negative, embarrassing impact on the whole paper." In Gelb's opinion, the articles "had a gossipy, canned quality—the kind of items that could be found in a folksy small-town paper."[21] This was precisely what Gelb and other editors feared would happen if the *New York Times* created suburban sections—they would not meet the paper's lofty standards and therefore would hurt its reputation.

It was much easier for *New York Times* editors to sneer at someone else's successful product, however, than to create one themselves. To staff their first weekly section, covering Brooklyn, Queens, and Long Island (dubbed BQLI), they hired only four new reporters, using freelancers and an occasional contribution from the metropolitan staff to provide the rest of the content. The section struggled to attract readers, and advertisers complained about the weak response generated by the ads they placed there. BQLI had been running for less than six months when Punch Sulzberger said it needed "a totally brand new look" in order to remain viable.[22] Nevertheless, it limped along for several more years, until management decided to revamp the section entirely, cutting out the New York City boroughs of Brooklyn and Queens and focusing exclusively on suburban Long Island. When Abe Rosenthal asked a colleague, Jack Schwartz, to critique the existing BQLI section in 1975, his comments echoed what Arthur Gelb had said about the *L.A. Times* suburban sections in 1970. "It comes out like a country weekly inside the most sophisticated newspaper in the world," Schwartz wrote. He called it "a mélange of soft features about hobbies, programs, entertainments, etc., most of it written with a certain 4-H club breathiness."[23]

Schwartz's scathing review of BQLI simply confirmed a determination that Rosenthal, Sulzberger, and other editorial decision makers had already made: that they must commit far more resources to suburban coverage. Although the coverage area of the Long Island section was much reduced compared to BQLI, it had a larger staff and nearly twice the budget.[24] In 1976 the *New York Times* added new weekly sections covering the main suburban areas north of the city: Westchester County and Connecticut (Fairfield County).[25] By 1978 the four suburban sections were much improved in quality and on a sounder financial footing, and the paper continued investing more resources in them.[26]

• • •

PROVIDING MORE NEWS about suburban communities was a logical, almost unavoidable choice for metropolitan newspapers, as new competitors siphoned off their readers. However, the desires of affluent readers were changing along with their zip codes. *New York Times* deputy managing editor Seymour Topping said in 1978, "We knew that the attitudes and the lifestyle of our target audiences had changed. Among our potential readers, there was a new emphasis on self as a compelling reader interest. People wanted to learn how to live better, to cope with the growing pressures of their environment, and they wanted more practical guides for a fuller, richer, more satisfying and happier life."[27] In other words, they wanted what journalists call "soft news."

Hard news, the traditional tent pole of newspapers like the *New York Times* and the *Los Angeles Times,* consisted of politics, government, foreign affairs, business, important speeches, reports, statistics. "Soft news" meant the arts, entertainment, literature, society, food, fashion, sports. Some types of articles straddled the two categories: opinion columns, profiles of people in the news, or in-depth features about a trend or development might be considered either hard or soft. But as the labels indicate, hard news commanded respect and prestige, while many journalists looked down on soft news as piddling or insubstantial. Leading newspapers like the *New York Times* and the *Los Angeles Times* prided themselves on providing hard news—it was a central element of their identity. Beefing up suburban coverage did not represent a major change in news values or the allocation of newsroom resources; after all, stories about city government and city life still dominated the metropolitan pages, and reports from Washington and abroad continued to fill page one. Elevating the importance of soft news, on the other hand, demanded a fundamental rethinking of the newspaper's role.

Editors certainly realized prior to the 1960s that there was a great public appetite for soft news, but they did not consider it their duty to feed that appetite until declining readership and competition from other media forced them to do so. Tabloid newspapers treated news as entertainment, and many—such as the New York *Daily News,* whose circulation dwarfed that of the *New York Times*—had achieved enormous success using that formula.[28] At prestigious papers with highly educated, affluent readers, however, most journalists expressed disdain for tabloid-style coverage. Soft news did not offend their sensibilities as much as sensationalism or prurience, but it still smelled like tabloidism, so they came to accept it only gradually. Initially, in the 1950s and early 1960s, they broadened their definition of important news to include what might be called semisoft topics, such as religion, science, and education.[29] In a 1964 speech on "the future of American newspapering," *L.A. Times* publisher Otis Chandler focused mainly on changes that were already under way at top newspapers such as his: he mentioned the need for "detailed reports on the meaning of news" and providing in-depth coverage on a broader range of topics—"water, air pollution, automation, civil rights, schools, freeways." Almost as an afterthought, however, Chandler added, "We must cover special areas of people's interest such as women's news, food, health, drama, fashion, cultural affairs, television, and so on."[30] Such areas soon moved to the forefront of editors' concerns.

At most major metropolitan newspapers, the shift toward soft news occurred in three phases. Traditionally, most soft-news stories had run in the "women's pages," and that is where editors turned their attention first. They revamped sections that had contained bridal photos and news about parties and club meetings to include articles about lifestyle trends and controversial issues such as abortion and divorce. Along the way, many newspapers jettisoned the label "women's pages," which began to look embarrassingly archaic as the feminist movement grew. These name changes helped usher in the second phase, in which editors transformed women's sections to appeal to readers of both sexes. They often moved coverage of entertainment and culture—topics with fairly high readership—to these new sections. The resounding success of the all-encompassing soft-news sections led to the third phase, which began in the mid-1970s. Newspapers created stand-alone sections devoted to any number of discrete soft-news topics, from fashion and food to sports and science.

Throughout this period, the trend that began in newspapers' back pages—catering to readers' needs and desires—migrated toward the front as well. The main news sections still reported on government, politics, and the world at large, but they often placed a greater emphasis on how these issues related personally to the reader.[31] Taken together, these changes reoriented newspapers toward people's everyday lives—their health, their homes, their families, the things they bought, the entertainment they consumed.

Kenneth Jackson, in his landmark work on suburbanization in America, argued that moving to the suburbs caused people to lose their sense of community and their connection with the inner city, as they became more inwardly focused on domestic concerns.[32] This may be true, but it can be easy to exaggerate the extent to which suburbanites severed their ties with the city. As Seymour Topping of the *New York Times* noted in 1978, many suburbanites "wished to retain their link to New York City in cultural terms . . . to know what was going on in the Big Town in the theaters, museums, and restaurants"—the *Times* targeted these readers with its increased soft-news offerings.[33] Reading a metropolitan newspaper could help mitigate the lack of community sentiment. It enabled people to feel like members of two distinct communities: their suburban area (the importance of which the big-city paper validated by devoting a special section to it) and the greater metropolis.[34]

The desirability of suburban life, the emphasis on self, the shift in the average American's role from citizen to consumer, the shrinking of the public sphere and the retreat into private life—the press, as a respected arbiter of cultural values, helped validate these developments. But the journalists who implemented changes at their newspapers expressed little awareness of such long-term societal shifts. They were concerned with attracting readers and, to a lesser extent, advertisers (for where the readers went, the advertisers would likely follow). Some journalists, especially women, also saw the expansion of soft news as an opportunity to bring greater attention and respect to issues that the press had previously slighted. Others, usually men, worried about maintaining their newspaper's reputation for serious, hard news. As the press reoriented itself toward readers in the 1960s and 1970s, these goals sometimes overlapped and sometimes collided.

• • •

IN FEBRUARY 1963 the lead article in the *Bulletin of the American Society of Newspaper Editors* asked what women's pages might look like ten years in the future. There would be less club news, shorter wedding stories, more "sparkle" and less "drabness," predicted the author, *Miami Herald* managing editor George Beebe (who expressed pride in his paper's award-winning women's section). But overall, he said, "There is little likelihood of any drastic change in the years ahead."[35] A companion article in the same issue of the *Bulletin* asked, "Why should the content of women's page news change with the decades? The interims don't bring a different breed of women. Homemakers are interested in the same basic things from one generation to another."[36] It was not only men who expressed such viewpoints. The *Bulletin* had surveyed a number of women's-news editors, all of them female, who made similar predictions about the future of their sections. Maggie Savoy, women's editor of the *Arizona Republic,* said, "The women's pages will always be 'special interest' pages—as are sports, financial, editorial, etc. They will continue to beam toward fashion, food, beauty, child care, society, careers, and homemaking, as they do today."[37]

Five years later, Maggie Savoy was being offered the position of women's editor at the *Los Angeles Times,* and her views had changed drastically.

For one thing, she abhorred the very title "women's editor," although she eventually accepted it.[38] She laid out her vision for the women's section—then called simply Section IV—in a series of memos to editor-in-chief Nick Williams. The paper's female readers in 1968, she said, were "living in a frightening world . . . where almost none of the 'old rules' apply." She mentioned changes in marriage, children, morality, sex, drugs, and religion. Even high culture was no longer a refuge for women: "Art, music, drama, fashion—all in violent flux," Savoy wrote. Under her direction, Savoy proposed, Section IV would tackle this brave new world head-on, providing its readers "guidance" on how to deal with it. Yes, Savoy conceded, the section could still be "bright and beautiful," a "reflection of the best of Los Angeles in fashion, food, society, culture, civic involvement"—it needed to retain the food and fashion advertising, after all. But it should also provide "a daily shot of adrenaline—controversy." Among the topics she suggested were divorce, abortion, capital punishment, open housing, busing, smut, gun laws, and welfare. Williams was impressed, and Savoy took the job.[39]

By this time the *Los Angeles Times* had already shown its dedication to expanding and elevating its soft-news coverage. In 1966 the paper hired Jim Bellows (who happened to be Savoy's husband) as associate editor in charge of soft news—the women's pages, entertainment, travel, real estate, and the Sunday magazines. As editor-in-chief of the much-admired but recently shuttered *New York Herald Tribune,* Bellows had nurtured such writers as Jimmy Breslin and Tom Wolfe, whose vivid storytelling was at the vanguard of what became known as the New Journalism. To hire such a prominent editor expressly for the purpose of soft news demonstrated the commitment that Otis Chandler and Nick Williams wished to make. They wanted innovative stories that would get people talking.

Even before Savoy came on board, Williams showed his desire to make soft news a focal point by addressing contentious, hot-button issues. Early in Bellows's tenure, Williams complimented him on two recent series of articles "of a current sociological nature"—one on the problem of alcoholism and another on attitudes toward premarital sex among college students. "Let's see what we can work up on other such controversial topics," Williams told Bellows. He asked Bellows to have his staff come up with a list of suggestions, reminding him, "I don't mind these being controversial—in fact I don't think they'd be worth a damn if they weren't." Lest Bellows think this smacked of sensationalism—controversy for controversy's sake—Williams assured him, "It's chiefly a matter of the honesty with which they're done, the balance given to them on the pro and con side, and the manner in which they are written."[40] As they expanded the scope of news to include previously taboo topics, Williams and Bellows, mindful of the *L.A. Times* reputation, took care not to cross the line into tabloid-style journalism.

Articles such as these appeared in Section IV of the paper, but the front page also became a showcase for soft news. Beginning in 1968, each day's *Los Angeles Times* featured an in-depth article on the far-left column of page one that readers could get nowhere else—the newsroom called it the non-dupe story, short for nonduplicative.[41] Some of these were hard-news exclusives, but typically they were feature stories with broad appeal— early examples dealt with the ballooning salaries of professional athletes, romantic relationships in communist China, and the endangered habitats of whooping cranes.[42] This became a distinguishing feature of the paper—writers yearned for assignments that might become non-dupe stories, and readers came to anticipate an unexpected and interesting article on the front page each day. It also represented a major investment of resources. A reporter might spend several weeks on a single story and would often have to travel extensively.[43]

Despite such innovations in the main news section, most of the compelling soft-news stories appeared in Section IV, which readers perceived as a women's section. Although it did not bear the label "women's news," its editor was called the "women's editor," and along with the controversial sociological articles that Savoy had championed, it contained such women's-page staples as fashion news, the bridge column, and Dear Abby. So in July 1970, without any fanfare, the *L.A. Times* renamed the section View and began to make it into a general-interest lifestyle and entertainment section. Jean Sharley Taylor, the editor who took over View in 1971 (Maggie Savoy had died of cancer), explained the motivation behind the change: "We were getting about 85 to 87 percent of the women readers," she recalled, but fewer than 10 percent of the men. Her goal was to "hold the women and put in stories that were more humanist to bring in the men, too." The View section, Taylor believed, should say, "This is life as we have it. This is life as some people think it could be."[44]

The evolution of View occurred gradually. The paper did not announce or acknowledge that the section had a new name, and the lead story in the very first View section was hardly revolutionary—it reported on the changing nature of debutante balls.[45] That day's Dear Abby column bore the headline, "She Puts Her Husband First." Despite this inauspicious start for a section trying to break from the traditional women's-page mold, View increasingly left behind parties and weddings. Under Taylor's editorship, it became a showcase for some of the finest writing in the paper—or in any American newspaper, for that matter. Three of the most gifted writers on the staff—Charles T. Powers, Bella Stumbo, and Jim Stingley—all worked primarily for View in the 1970s. Their long, deeply reported features and profiles depicted the struggles and joys of everyday people in fine-grained detail. They employed the techniques of magazine journalism—using narrative, close observation, and revealing quotations gained by spending weeks on end with their subjects—to provide the "humanist" flavor that Taylor sought.[46] The former women's section, once the object of derision in the newsroom, became a section for which reporters clamored to write—it offered them ample space, a broad variety of subject matter, and the opportunity to show off their literary flair (in imitation of the section's stars, Powers, Stumbo, and Stingley).[47] It had also become, by 1975, the most widely read part of the *Los Angeles Times* after the main news section; 80 percent of women and 40 percent of men said they read it every day.[48]

The View section, the *Washington Post*'s Style section (which resembled View but predated it by eighteen months), and others like them were widely praised, but some observers raised objections. Old-fashioned women's pages had been rightly criticized for devaluing women's concerns by lumping them together toward the back of the newspaper. But the new, more prestigious lifestyle sections created a similar problem, argued journalist Lindsy Van Gelder in a 1974 *Ms.* magazine article. Although the content had improved and now included articles on pressing social and political issues, it remained ghettoized. "So we get all the serious news stories about the Equal Rights Amendment, rape-law changes, back-pay lawsuits, and so forth, back among the girdle ads instead of on page one

Reproduced with permission of the copyright owner. Further reproduction prohibited without permission.

A typical front page of the *Los Angeles Times* View section, from June 1973. Photo: Copyright © 1973 Los Angeles Times. Used with permission.

or two or three where they belong," Van Gelder wrote.[49] And in what *Time* magazine labeled the "flight from fluff" among lifestyle sections, newspapers also fled from the unglamorous stories about childrearing and home care upon which many readers of women's pages had depended. "In the rush to make their content 'relevant' to the lifestyles of the 70s," wrote one critic in 1976, "some editors seem to have forgotten that 'liberated' women and men still have the same responsibilities and problems that adults have always had."[50] Even the innovative new content of lifestyle sections was not all it was cracked up to be, said another critic, Zena Beth Guenin. She found that although most people agreed on what the revamped women's sections should cover (for example, the environment, housing, medicine, women's rights), the number of articles about such topics remained very low. Instead, entertainment coverage crowded out nearly everything else (especially in papers such as the *Los Angeles Times*, where arts and entertainment were paired with lifestyle coverage).[51]

Whatever their shortcomings, the new lifestyle sections undeniably became a more central focus of newspapers than women's sections had ever been. Nicholas von Hoffman, a columnist for the *Washington Post*'s Style section, wrote in 1971 that people often asked him whether he resented "being put on the women's page." Not at all, he said, because Style had more readers than the editorial page. He added, "A few months ago [nationally syndicated columnist] Art Buchwald came to the same conclusion and asked to be moved out of the editorial section and back with us."[52] Style, View, and other sections like them represented the newspaper industry's answer to the New Journalism that many leading magazines had adopted to great acclaim in the late 1960s and early 1970s, which allowed writers to tackle unorthodox subjects from unusual angles, to experiment with storytelling techniques, and to blend reporting with opinion. For readers and journalists alike, this was the most exciting development in newspapering in the 1970s—and it had nothing to do with hard news.

• • •

THE *NEW YORK TIMES* women's section in the 1960s carried the heading "Food, Fashions, Family, Furnishings"—the Four F's, as staffers referred to them—and the content rarely strayed from those narrowly defined areas. That is, not until Charlotte Curtis took over as women's-news editor in 1965. A Vassar graduate from a well-to-do Ohio family, Curtis became a society reporter for the *New York Times* in 1963 and enlivened the staid coverage of weddings and charity balls with incisive observations and pithy writing. Two years later, managing editor Clifton Daniel merged the previously separate society and women's-news sections and put Curtis in charge of both.[53] Curtis believed her section should continue to cover fashion, parties, and high society, but she took what many have called a "sociological" view of such news.[54]

In the most famous example of the new sensibility Curtis brought to women's-news coverage, her article about a party thrown by the famous conductor and composer Leonard Bernstein to raise money for the Black Panthers became an opportunity to subtly lampoon rich liberals' infatuation with radical politics. She juxtaposed her observations about the "expensive furnishings, the elaborate flower arrangements, the cocktails and the silver trays of canapés" with choice snippets of conversation: a Panther leader who "attempted to assure a white woman that she would not be killed even if she is a rich member of the middle class with a self-avowed capitalist for a husband"; Leonard Bernstein responding "I dig absolutely" when informed of the Panthers' intention to "take the means of production and put them in the hands of the people."[55] The writer Tom Wolfe, who also attended the party, used it as the basis for his New Journalism classic "Radical Chic."[56]

Curtis also expanded the scope of topics her pages covered. In 1966 she sent a memo to her staff asking, "If you could forget that the page has an FFFF masthead and could write any story you wanted to for a women's news page, what stories would you suggest?" Responses included profiles of women who had achieved great things in the professions, the best college options for young women, and "general subjects like the pill and dope."[57] Those topics and more began appearing in the late 1960s alongside fashion, food, and parties. As a 1969 *New York* magazine profile of Curtis put it, "She simply opened the doors, and there were urban affairs, black models, politics, new lifestyles . . . women doctors and lawyers, housewives who took glamour jobs. Divorced and unwed fathers. Even a shiver of sex."[58] The women's pages under Curtis often pushed the boundaries of what the socially conservative *New York Times* considered good

Charlotte Curtis, who revolutionized "society" coverage as women's news editor of the *New York Times* from 1965 to 1974 (her title changed to Family/Style Editor in 1971). She then became editor of the op-ed page. Photo: Bill Aller / The New York Times / Redux. Reproduction from New York Times Company Records, General Files, MssCol 17802, Box 5, Folder 15. Manuscripts and Archives Division, The New York Public Library, Astor, Lenox and Tilden Foundations.

taste. The stories Curtis assigned reportedly led the paper's publisher, Punch Sulzberger, to exclaim in exasperation (and exaggeration), "My God! You can't get a piece about anybody on the women's pages these days unless she's a black lesbian mother."[59]

Many of the country's leading newspapers overhauled their soft-news sections in the early 1970s. The *Washington Post* discontinued its "For and About Women" section in favor of Style, the *Los Angeles Times* created View, and others followed suit. Sections labeled "women's news" vanished, and new ones took their place, with names like Living, Scene, Portfolio, Accent, and Tempo.[60] The *New York Times* skipped this phase in the evolution of newspaper content. Under Curtis in the mid-1960s, it had begun modernizing its women's pages earlier than nearly any other newspaper. "It may have been the *Post* that did 'Style,' but the spadework of reporting and coverage was [done by] the *Times*," said Marilyn Bender, a reporter on Curtis's staff.[61] Satisfied with a highly regarded section that combined traditional and cutting-edge coverage, the paper eschewed any major alterations to its women's pages in the early 1970s. Its editors conceded that the designation "women's news" had become "progressively more unsatisfactory," but they settled on a barely noticeable name change.[62] The pages inside the newspaper would still be labeled with the Four F's, but beginning in September 1971, the order of the terms would change to Family, Food, Fashions, Furnishings ("family" moving from third position to first). The news index on the front page, instead of listing "Women's News," would say "Family/Style" (and Charlotte Curtis's title would change from Women's-News Editor to Family/Style Editor).[63] A few days before the change occurred, a reader had written in to object to the "insulting classification" of "women's news." Curtis wrote back, informing the reader that the index had just been changed, adding, "Let's hope we never hear from or about 'women's news' again."[64]

While the term "women's news" fell out of favor, its traditional components—food, lifestyles, the home—would become increasingly important at the *New York Times*. In the early 1970s the paper's financial future looked bleak. By 1975, costly union contracts and spiraling expenses, combined with declining circulation and advertising, had nearly pushed the *Times* into the red.[65] This convinced editors and executives to step up their efforts to attract readers and advertising dollars. Their solution was the four-section paper.

Prior to 1976, like most newspapers, the daily *New York Times* was divided into two main sections: the first contained national, international, and business news, along with the opinion pages, while the second had metropolitan news, arts, sports, and everything else (the Sunday paper contained many more individual sections). The four-section *New York Times* kept the first section for news from around the country and the world, and the second section for news from around New York; but that was followed by a third section, the topic of which rotated each day of the week. The first was called Weekend, which appeared on Fridays and covered arts and entertainment. Next came Living (mainly about food), Home, Sports Monday, and Science Times. Business and financial news moved to the fourth section—labeled Business Day and beefed up with columns and feature stories rather than simply breaking-news articles and market data.

This third phase in the development of soft-news coverage—weekday sections dedicated to specialized topics—gave the ailing *New York Times* an enormous boost. The weekday paper had experienced double-digit declines in circulation and advertising lines from 1969 to 1975, but from 1976 (the birth of the four-section paper) to 1982, circulation grew by 12 percent and advertising by 38 percent.[66] Each section produced an immediate bump in sales when introduced, and each, by design, had tremendous appeal to specific groups of advertisers. Living and Home obviously attracted ads for appliances, décor, and so on—the *L.A. Times*'s Home Magazine had long been a huge moneymaker thanks to this category of advertising—but even Science Times became a magnet for specialized advertising with the advent of personal computers. Editors recognized that these new sections served a business purpose as well as a journalistic purpose. Seymour Topping, who as assistant managing editor helped create the four-section paper, recalled that his decision to create a column on computers was guided partly by his knowledge that companies would love to run advertising alongside such a column.[67]

The *Los Angeles Times* was the bulkiest newspaper in America thanks to the enormous volume of advertising it carried, and as a result its news had been printed in four sections since the mid-1950s. In addition to the four regular weekday sections, in 1962 the paper began publishing a Food section every Thursday. This presaged what was to come, but not until the mid-1970s did additional weekday sections appear begin to appear, as the *L.A. Times*, like the *New York Times* and many other big-city newspapers, embarked on what has been dubbed "the sectional revolution."[68] The first volley the *L.A. Times* fired was a magazine insert called *You*, which would appear every Tuesday beginning in October 1976. As the title implied, the goal was to serve readers' interests and desires—the promotional campaign to launch the magazine made this abundantly clear. "'You' will say to the Times reader: this is something that will help you—and give you pleasure," read one brochure. It went on to list the questions that *You* would answer: "Where can I have fun? What's in it for me? How can I find bargains? How can I save money? Where can I go that's different? How can I be more attractive? How can I protect the environment? How can I find a job?"[69] It sounds like a parody of Me Decade self-absorption (the inclusion of a question about protecting the

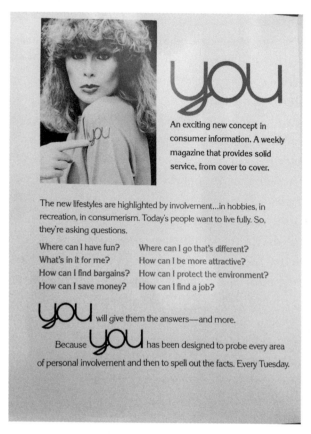

The new lifestyles are highlighted by involvement...in hobbies, in recreation, in consumerism. Today's people want to live fully. So, they're asking questions.

Where can I have fun?   Where can I go that's different?
What's in it for me?   How can I be more attractive?
How can I find bargains?   How can I protect the environment?
How can I save money?   How can I find a job?

Part of a brochure promoting *You,* a weekly magazine devoted to service journalism that the *Los Angeles Times* launched in 1976. Photo: Copyright © Los Angeles Times. Used with permission.

environment seems jarringly out of place), but it represented the *L.A. Times* management's frank assessment—based on reports from their formidable market-research department—of the kind of material the paper needed in order to retain its readers, especially because inflation and rising newsprint costs were forcing them to raise their subscription price.[70]

More new sections followed. Although the *Los Angeles Times* had published fashion supplements periodically in the past, they appeared at long, unpredictable intervals. Beginning in February 1978 a dedicated fashion section came out every Friday. The following year the paper began producing a stand-alone business section every Tuesday—like the *New*

York Times's Business Day, it contained expanded coverage, features, and columns. The final addition to the special-section roster was Focus, which carried features and background stories, heavily illustrated, about national and foreign news. It usually appeared in one or two of the issues later in the week.[71] By 1979, then, the *L.A. Times* included five special weekday sections (Food, You, Fashion, Business, and Focus), just like the *New York Times* (Living, Home, Weekend, Sports Monday, and Science Times).

Different circumstances drove the sectional revolution at these two newspapers. The *New York Times* needed to stop the slow bleed of advertisers and readers that was threatening to push the paper's finances into the red. The *L.A. Times,* by contrast, was operating from a position of strength in the 1970s: apart from the recession year of 1975, each year saw advertising volume and revenues increase significantly, often at double-digit rates. The newspaper division of Times Mirror, the *L.A. Times*'s parent company, reported record profits in 1972, 1973, and 1976–1979. Circulation began to plateau in the late 1970s, but this could be attributed to the frequent price increases necessitated by inflation and rising costs.[72] The *L.A. Times* created the Focus section in 1979 to accommodate overflow advertising—so many business wanted to buy ad space in the paper that there was no room for them all.[73]

Most major newspapers in the 1970s, whether their finances were robust or shaky, moved to add more sections, more features, and more soft news. In other words, they adopted a more liberal attitude toward what merited coverage. But these were not goals in and of themselves. They represented a broader effort to serve readers. In the process, the press began addressing the public more as consumers than as citizens. This trend dovetailed with what was happening in American public life as a whole, a phenomenon that commentators from across the political spectrum remarked upon at the time.[74] As historian Lizabeth Cohen has argued, since the 1970s a more "self-interested" citizenry has begun "judging [government policies] by how well served they feel personally," creating what she calls a consumerized republic.[75] The press, which mediated the people's relationship with government, helped condition them to think this way. Previous generations of *New York Times* and *Los Angeles Times* readers had looked to those newspapers primarily for information they felt they needed to know as educated citizens. Readers in the 1970s still expected that information to be available, but they also expected to find material that would entertain them and that would relate directly to their lives. The managers of the *L.A. Times* promised that *You* magazine would answer the question "What's in it for me?" because they felt, with much justification, that Americans were focused on that question as never before.

• • •

THIS SHIFT IN THE PRESS'S primary purpose, from informing citizens to serving consumers, predated the sectional revolution and permeated the entire paper (not only the portions devoted to soft news). The initial motivating force, as usual, was competition from other media. Although the *Los Angeles Times* was thriving in 1969, editor-in-chief Nick Williams saw storm clouds on the horizon. As he told publisher Otis Chandler, television had changed what a newspaper needed to be:

> TV is so damn easy. Even when it's lousy (much of it is), it's so damned easy to sit there, not excited, mind frequently wandering, but still sitting there. . . . It's even easier to sit there than it is to get up and turn the damned thing off. AND THERE IS OUR PROBLEM. We're never going to turn THAT clock back. But unless we work awfully hard to make the daily newspaper as easy to take as possible, AND as interesting, AND as entertaining, AND as impressive, AND as prestigious . . . we really may have a problem somewhere down the road.[76]

Being impressive and prestigious remained essential, but Williams listed those goals last. The more important goals had to do with being reader-friendly and enjoyable. A few years later, having recently retired, Williams reflected on what he might do differently were he to start from scratch as an editor-in-chief. He mused, "Perhaps we've worked too hard at choosing what our readers ought to know, rather than giving them what may interest them." To that end, instead of filling the front page with the articles that editors deemed most newsworthy, he suggested giving it over to "the most fascinating items" of the day—that might mean a Dear Abby column, a comic strip, or a dispatch from Vietnam.[77]

Williams was clearly being facetious; he meant to provoke self-reflection among editors rather than put forth a serious proposal. Nevertheless, the idea of putting interesting stories on page one, regardless of their hard-news value, is exactly what the *Los Angeles Times* had done with the non-dupe feature it inaugurated in 1968. Such efforts to put the reader's desires first continued for the remainder of Williams's years as editor-in-chief and well into the tenure of his successor, Bill Thomas. Many of the changes were subtle. Since 1961 the paper had provided a summary of each day's major news developments on page two of the front section, grouped under headings such as World, National, State, Metropolitan, and Southland. In December 1968 a new heading appeared: Newsmakers, which featured briefs about celebrities and offbeat, sometimes humorous, human-interest items.[78]

Catering to readers meant more than adjustments to news content, however. As Williams told Otis Chandler in a 1969, "WE WILL HAVE TO MAKE IT EASIER TO READ A NEWSPAPER."[79] That required design changes. Some newspapers in the mid-1960s began experimenting with a six-column page layout instead of eight columns; this reduced eye strain because it required fewer line breaks and hyphens.[80] The *L.A. Times* made the change in 1966, but only for pages without ads—deeper inside the world's biggest newspaper, page after page featured a single skinny column of type hugging the edge of a massive seven-column advertisement. This was a nagging concern for Williams—the inside pages were designed for advertisers, to the detriment of readers. However, he felt that resistance from advertisers and the business department of the *Times* precluded the possibility of change during his editorship (he retired in 1972).[81] Under his successor, Bill Thomas, the rising cost of newsprint provided an excuse for wholesale design changes. In 1974 the paper decided to reduce the overall width of its pages by three-quarters of an inch, which would save more than $4 million a year in newsprint.[82] The narrower page would make it impossible to fit eight columns; six columns became the maximum, which enabled designers to make the pages far more readable and attractive. Thomas enthused about the new look in an article for the *Bulletin of the American Society of Newspaper Editors,* adding that the feared protests from advertisers never materialized.[83]

Improved design was one component of a new concept toward which the *L.A. Times* was moving in the early 1970s: the daily newspaper as a daily news *magazine.* Many of the changes it had adopted were associated with successful general-interest magazines: analytical reporting, varied subject matter, in-depth articles, engaging prose. Nick Williams, Bill Thomas, and Otis Chandler all embraced the term. "If we took our best material, each day, and published it with the finest production techniques, it would be one hell of a daily magazine," Williams wrote to Chandler in 1971.[84] Thomas took this concept and ran with it.[85] In an interview Chandler gave in 1976, he said, "We're primarily what I would describe as a daily news magazine." He explained the two motives behind that approach: "One is to give people every day something that they can't get anyplace else—to make the paper unique and necessary in their lives. Secondly, I think, to give them a break from the hard news. People get pretty discouraged, I think, particularly with what we've been through in the last [ten] years with Vietnam, and the assassinations, and the radicalism. . . . So we try to give them something every day that takes them away from the hard news."[86] Nick Williams had advocated a similar technique in 1969, telling a fellow journalist, "It is our business, as professionals, not ONLY to tell our readers what the hell is happening to their cozy world . . . but we must (I don't think must is too strong) give them something that lifts them, momentarily, from the morass."[87]

Lifting people from the morass, giving them a break from the dreariness of the world—these goals would have sounded ridiculous to serious newspaper editors of the 1940s and 1950s. But in an age when fewer people felt they needed a daily newspaper, it became necessary to make them *want* a daily newspaper. Since World War II, middle-class Americans had been becoming increasingly focused on leisure, entertainment, and self-fulfillment. The trend seemed to reach its zenith in the 1970s, which Tom Wolfe famously labeled the Me Decade (his article appeared just as the *L.A. Times* was announcing *You* magazine).[88] Other forms of media had capitalized on this development—television and magazines most notably, but also radio, which enjoyed a resurgence in the 1960s when the FM band became home to a broad variety of music formats.[89] Newspapers needed to keep pace; they needed to adapt or die.

Change did not come easily at the *New York Times,* however. Whereas the managers of the *Los Angeles Times* embraced the concept of a daily news magazine, many at the *New York Times* recoiled. The traditionalist editorial-page editor, John Oakes, who objected to any feint toward soft news, often complained that Abe Rosenthal was turning the newspaper into a magazine, a charge that Rosenthal angrily rejected. "You jibe at me by calling the newspaper a magazine, and I go home and get mean to my wife," Rosenthal told Oakes in the early 1970s.[90] The *Los Angeles Times* was so loaded with advertising that it needed more editorial material to fill up the pages. At the *New York Times,* by contrast, advertising failed to increase much in the 1970s, and space was at a premium—by the mid-1970s, the paper had to reduce its news hole (the amount of column inches devoted to editorial content) in order to cut costs.[91] So while the *L.A. Times* could plausibly claim that its hard-news coverage remained undiminished even as it began to feature other topics more prominently, the *New York Times* had to cut back somewhere. Rosenthal urged editors to publish fewer transcripts of speeches, to shorten unnecessarily verbose writing, and, when handling a slow-moving story, to resist publishing an article about it every day unless there had been some major development.

For an organization devoted to delivering "all the news that's fit to print" (the motto Adolph Ochs had selected for the *New York Times* in 1897), it was difficult to come to terms with the fact that new kinds of stories were edging some "hard news" out of the paper. In 1962 the powerful, longtime editor of the Sunday *New York Times,* Lester Markel, wrote an article accusing the press of five major sins. First and foremost, he charged, many newspapers had become "media of entertainment rather than of information." Some editors, he lamented, say, "The customer is always right. We must give him what he wants and what he wants is entertainment." Markel disagreed. "Even if the readers want only the kind of pepped-up pablum which is served to them, it is the responsibility of the editors to try to educate them to a better diet," he lectured.[92] Few editors, however, could afford to be contemptuous of their readers' desires, and Markel's admonitions went unheeded.

Markel retired in 1968, but many of his colleagues shared his high-minded concept of what a newspaper should be—including Rosenthal, to some degree, which is why he so resented accusations that he was filling the August *New York Times* with fluff. In his personal journal in 1971, Rosenthal reflected on the changes he had made. Despite the complaints from people like John Oakes, Rosenthal wrote, "The Times remains a hard daily newspaper." He had simply "expanded" the paper's character "by my insistence that no subject is outside of the scope of the paper." He concluded, "I suppose the essential difference between Oakes and myself is that he believes this type of [nontraditional] story does not belong in a daily newspaper, but in a magazine, and I believe most emphatically that any newspaper that confines itself to simply reporting what happened yesterday would wither."[93] This was Rosenthal's most fundamental concern: that the paper remain relevant. What Oakes saw as the high road was actually the road to perdition.

Rosenthal insisted he was not turning the *New York Times* into a magazine, yet many of the ideas he proposed were borrowed from magazines—especially *New York,* the weekly that launched in 1968 under editor Clay Felker and became the hottest magazine of the 1970s. *New York* was best known as a showcase for in-depth features written in the novelistic New Journalism style, but its "secret weapon," Felker said, was its service coverage—useful information about entertainment, food, and shopping.[94] That created loyal readers, and Rosenthal wanted to emulate it. "He was extremely jealous of Clay Felker and his huge success with *New York* magazine," recalled Ed Klein, whom Rosenthal hired as editor of the *New York Times Magazine* in 1976.[95] In March 1970, roughly six months after becoming managing editor, Rosenthal asked several senior editors to bring him ideas about how the *Times* could incorporate the kind of service material that made *New York* so successful.[96] Among his most frequent complaints about Charlotte Curtis's Family / Style section in the early 1970s was that its content sometimes lacked a "service function." In one instance he asked Curtis to look at a service story in *New York* (about children's activities around Easter) and to come up with some similar ideas.[97] And when it came time to hire new staff for the four-section paper, Rosenthal chose former *New York* journalists for two of the most important spots—restaurant critic and editor of Home.[98]

In 1971 Rosenthal made a pitch to the paper's three most senior executives for "a strong program of service information in the field of entertainment," presenting it as a sound business decision. "Readers want and need this kind of information and are attracted to publications that give it to them," Rosenthal wrote, adding that magazines "achieve a kind of intimacy and affection with their readers because through this kind of service, they relate to the happy and upbeat part of their readers' lives."[99] Like Nick Williams and Otis Chandler, he saw value in providing a pleasant diversion from the often-depressing hard news. Rosenthal got his wish in 1972, with a new daily Going Out Guide, which informed readers about noteworthy cultural events in a jaunty, knowledgeable tone.[100]

The idea of providing "service information" could be applied to areas besides just leisure, Rosenthal felt. In 1972 he proposed "a kind of service feature" that would help readers understand the background of a major running news story. Called "Issue and Debate," it would outline the competing views on each side of a given topic.[101] Normally the term "service journalism" applied only to consumer-service material (restaurant listings, shopping guides, doctors' rankings), but Rosenthal used it as a synonym for anything new and potentially useful to readers. The service ethos extended to the business section as well. As a means of attracting young-adult readers, assistant managing editor Seymour Topping wrote in a 1976 memo, the editors wanted to "provide them with a regular service feature . . . dealing with the practical problems of jobs and careers."[102]

The reorientation of the *New York Times* toward service made many editors uneasy. On the one hand, framing the shift as a way to serve readers' needs helped absolve the conscience of self-serious journalists who worried that they were really just pandering to readers' desire for fluff. After all, as the sociologist Daniel Bell and others observed, the country as a whole was transforming into a postindustrial, service-based economy and society, the upper rungs of which would be populated by a growing class of knowledge workers—a demographic group that included journalists and most of their target audience.[103] A service ethos would come to characterize many other professions and workplaces in the following decades. But as Bethany Moreton notes in her study of the service ethos at Walmart, it was a feminized notion with strong Christian undertones.[104] In the fiercely secular, masculine atmosphere of most newsrooms, those elements of service did not resonate. "I kept hearing the phrase, 'We must go after the suburban housewife,'" John Oakes recalled.[105] He held that notion in disdain, preferring to go after the serious man of the world.

Even strong proponents of the four-section approach, such as Rosenthal, Topping, and Arthur Gelb, worried that it might change the "character of the paper," in Rosenthal's words.[106] The first four of the new rotating weekday sections—Weekend, Home, Living, and Sports Monday—had all focused on leisure activities. When in late 1977 it came time to decide on the fifth section, the business department wanted it to cover fashion; Rosenthal insisted it should cover science, and he dug in his heels. As he told an interviewer years later, "I felt three consumer sections in a row—Home, Living, and now Fashion—would tip the paper." It would validate the claims of John Oakes and Lester Markel that "froth" had displaced substance. After a protracted battle with the business side of the paper, Rosenthal got the publisher to side with him and greenlight Science Times—in large part by showing that he could produce the new section without spending any additional money.[107]

Although Abe Rosenthal clearly wanted to emulate Clay Felker's *New York* in many respects, he developed an intense scorn for Felker—perhaps because it pained him to admit that the *New York Times* was becoming more like *New York*. When he read a profile of Felker that the *New York Times Magazine* planned to publish in 1976, Rosenthal's reaction was entirely negative. The article was too admiring, he said, and it failed to note what Rosenthal considered Felker's shallowness. "It isn't so much that he has a news sense, but a circus sense, a circulation sense, and a sense of entertainment," Rosenthal wrote to the editor responsible for the piece.[108] The journalistic crimes for which he condemned Felker—focusing too much on entertainment, shortchanging hard news in an effort to boost circulation—were the same offenses that many critics accused Rosenthal himself of committing. In the end, Rosenthal told the editor to kill the Felker profile.

In a 1978 speech about how the *New York Times* had come back from the brink of financial calamity (thanks in large part to the new soft-news sections), Seymour Topping revealed a great deal about the editors' attitudes toward the new *New York Times*. They realized, he said, that improvements in the paper's coverage of traditional topics would not be enough to increase circulation:

The newspaper must adapt its function to the needs of the changing society. If the reader must be attracted by offering him a more varied smorgasbord of information and service material, there is no reason why the newspaper should not provide it. The important thing is that the news staples should continue on the menu undiminished, that is, the information which the reader needs to perform as an informed good citizen. It is our hope that the reader we bring to The New York Times through Weekend or the Living section or Sports Monday will explore and discover and develop a sophisticated taste for our main course, the hard news.[109]

Economic necessity, Topping admitted, was the mother of this invention. He was somewhat defensive about the new sections, likely anticipating the criticism that they detracted from the paper's seriousness. He insisted that was not the case, but he shared the critics' opinion that soft news was an indulgence—a childish, sugary treat, not the "sophisticated" main course.

Journalists at the *Los Angeles Times* shared this attitude to some extent. Although they were not laden with the baggage of being labeled the country's "paper of record," they had imbibed journalism's conventional wisdom about the hierarchical nature of news: war, government, and politics were at the top—hence their placement on the front page—and other categories of news declined in importance as you moved toward the back of the paper, where "women's news" sections were normally found. The physical layout of the *L.A. Times* offices reflected this viewpoint. The "hard news" staff and the "soft news" or "features" staff worked in separate buildings, with the composing room and a long hallway in between. Tim Rutten, who became an editor on the View section in 1972, noted, "Nobody went from the features side to the news side. . . . They always referred to us as 'that other newspaper.'"[110] Barbara Saltzman, a copy editor for View in the 1970s, recalled, "We were just kind of looked down upon [by the hard-news staff] as stepchildren."[111]

Editor-in-chief Bill Thomas, the man most responsible for making the *L.A. Times* into a daily news magazine, tried to maintain a balance between hard and soft news. He accepted *You* magazine, a business-driven product of questionable journalistic value, but after his retirement, he felt the pendulum had swung too far in the direction of soft news. "We're about to have a section of the paper entitled 'Gee,'" he noted in an unpublished memoir. A newspaper is like a person, he wrote, and during his editorship he envisioned it as "essentially a serious person . . . one with integrity and fairness, literate and possessed of a sense of humor and wide-ranging interests." In 1998, he lamented, with Gee and other features shaped by marketing goals, "the Times is becoming a person who would wear lampshades at parties."[112]

Reporter David Shaw, the *L.A. Times*'s in-house press critic and a favorite of Bill Thomas, was sometimes indelicate in showing his disdain for the soft-news sections of his own paper. When he wrote about former associate editor Jim Bellows becoming editor-in-chief of the *Los Angeles Herald-Examiner*, Shaw commented, "Bellows was in charge of the non-news sections of The Times."[113] Soft news was not simply inferior, Shaw implied, it was not even really news. Speaking to author David Halberstam in the mid-1970s, *L.A. Times* assistant foreign editor Nick Williams Jr. (son of the former editor-in-chief) lamented that "there's less play in the paper for foreign and national news." He explained, "We do our surveys and they tell us to have more features, more Ann Landers, more medical tips, and it's very hard, you know, to deal with the fact that the best things we do bring the least response."[114] To Williams, the "best things" by definition excluded any soft news, even feature stories, arguably the area of the *L.A. Times*'s greatest strength in the 1970s.

The features-side staff absorbed this attitude themselves and sometimes exhibited an inferiority complex. They never challenged the designation of their content as "soft," often referring to it as "software" or "the soft lines."[115] The aura of the much-belittled women's section still lingered. Initially Jean Sharley Taylor had difficulty persuading reporters from others parts of the paper to come write for View. The soft-news sections, including View, had to go to press much earlier than other parts of the newspaper—a necessity, given the need to print more than a million copies of such an enormous paper, but it reinforced the notion that they were a lower priority.

Furthermore, View could be a dumping ground for ads. In the main news sections (national, foreign, and metropolitan), the *Los Angeles Times* had a minimum percentage of editorial content versus advertising

Los Angeles Times associate editor Jean Sharley Taylor (left), who was in charge of View and other soft-news sections, with the paper's film critic, Charles Champlin, and entertainment editor Wayne Warga. Photo: Copyright © Los Angeles Times. Used with permission.

content—usually at least 30 percent editorial content and no more than 70 percent ads. Those restrictions did not apply to View. In 1979 Taylor complained to Bill Thomas, "I am battered from trying to resolve the space thing. . . . It seems wrong to give us 13 percent editorial. The best we ever get is 22 percent. The average is 19 percent."[116] Like the women's pages of old, the soft-news sections lived on sufferance of advertisers. Of course, the existence of the entire newspaper was contingent on ads, but the connection was more explicit with the soft sections. When journalist Marshall Berges interviewed the senior editors of the *Los Angeles Times* in order to write a book about the paper, most made little, if any, mention of advertising. Jean Sharley Taylor, however, spoke about advertising constantly.[117]

Nevertheless, the management of the *Los Angeles Times* recognized the importance of soft news. This was especially evident in the way they promoted the paper. A bumper sticker the company produced in 1978 read: "News Fashion Sports Stocks Travel Humor. It all comes together in The Times."[118] This six-word description of the paper's content conveyed the message that it was, above all, entertaining and useful. That message came through even more clearly in a slogan the *Los Angeles Times* adopted in 1977: "Great Newspaper. Great Usepaper," said the advertisements.[119] When Jim Bellows took over the *Los Angeles Herald-Examiner* in 1978, that paper's gossip column snidely referred to its crosstown rival as "the usepaper."[120]

• • •

MANY *LOS ANGELES TIMES* staffers surely found the "usepaper" moniker silly—even Otis Chandler said he did not care for the slogan.[121] It, and the service-and-soft-news approach more generally, represented a blow to journalists' pride. The Yellow Pages could be useful, and sitcoms could be entertaining, but journalism held itself up as something more—a noble calling, a pillar of American democracy. Traditionalist editors tended to feel this way most strongly. In 1962, before the soft-news revolution had even taken shape, *New York Times* Sunday editor Lester Markel wrote that it might be apt to refer to the press as the "Froth Estate" instead of the Fourth Estate, because it had begun to specialize in entertainment, not information.[122] The ensuing decade and a half did nothing to change his mind.

In a 1976 article Markel lamented the phenomenon of "Gallup editing," by which he meant the use of surveys "to discover what the reader wants and supply it without question." As a result, he said, "the sensational news, gobs of gossip, tons of triviality have been dished out at the cost of significant reporting. Entertainment has been given the play over information; manic efforts have been made to out-TV television." The solution to the press's woes, Markel argued, was simply "to print the news"—that is, to stick to the traditional categories of news (while providing ample interpretation). Only newspapers, he insisted, could "supply the kind of information without which informed public opinion—the *sine qua non* of democracy—cannot exist."[123] *New York Times* columnist John Oakes, the paper's former editorial-page editor, voiced a similar concern in 1978, writing that newspapers, in their attempt to compete with television, had "downgrade[d]" the "traditional mainstays of news, information, and opinion" and were becoming simply "chewing gum for the brain." In doing this, Oakes claimed, "American journalism is weakening its moral if not its legal claim" to special First Amendment protection.[124]

However, Markel and Oakes were retired or nearing retirement in the 1970s, and their protests were drowned out by the defenders of the new, reader-oriented approach. Some argued that the press's dismissive attitude toward soft news had caused it to miss one of the biggest stories of the late 1960s: the consumer revolution, personified by the activist Ralph Nader. In a 1969 issue of the *Bulletin of the American Society of Newspaper Editors,* a former *Washington Post* editor asked, "Why was the 50-year-old story of unsafe automobile design first reported to the public in book form by an obscure young lawyer [Nader]? Why does this same lone man each year dig up more front page stories involving pressing safety matters than all other reporters together?" He answered his own questions by observing that "in all too many newsrooms, major consumer issues are still treated as feature items and relegated to either the women's pages or the wastebasket."[125] Two years later Nicholas von Hoffman made the same point about Nader's revelations putting the press to shame. Summing up, he noted, "American newspapers do their worst job on the topics that are most important to people: food, clothing, shelter, health."[126]

These were valid journalistic justifications for expanding soft-news coverage, and they likely softened the reflexive resistance editors felt when pushed to do something at the behest of the business department. The consumer movement's success undoubtedly gave journalists a new appreciation of the importance of consumer affairs. The *New York Times* began a Consumer Notes column in 1973, and the number of consumer-related stories in the four biggest American newspapers increased tremendously between 1965 and 1975.[127] But the consumer movement also may have changed journalists' outlook on soft news more broadly, by creating an awareness that important stories did not always originate in world capitals or high-level meetings. They could also be lurking in seemingly mundane items like canned food, automobile tires, and children's toys.[128]

New York editor Clay Felker pointed out this blind spot in most journalists' news sense in a 1971 article in the *Bulletin of the American Society of Newspaper Editors.* "Sophisticated journalists tend to become obsessed with major political figures and dramatic events to the exclusion of the mundane but very real problems of everyday existence," Felker said, partly because they write primarily to impress other journalists. But getting "on the side of the reader," according to Felker, could provide an enormous payoff: "The response of readers to consumer journalism, in my experience, has been much stronger than the response to other kinds of articles."[129] Subsequent articles in the *Bulletin,* the premier trade journal for editors, reflect a growing acceptance of soft news's central place in the newspaper and the need to elevate its standing. A 1972 article decried the use of dismissive terms like "soft," "froth," and "frills" to refer to a worthy category of journalism. "Content and substance are not the exclusive property of the hard-news side, and what a tragedy for the newspaper business if they ever should be," the author said.[130]

A 1974 article in the *Bulletin* told editors it was past time for them to reevaluate their attitudes toward hard and soft news. Some press critics, the author noted, derided soft news as "'fluff' or 'features' or 'fillers.' It is properly called information." He continued, "The newspaper's job is to provide useful information which, in this visual age, ought to be presented in an attractive, eye-grabbing form. The information ought to be wide-ranging—from household hints and fashions to editorial page commentary and sports, from comics to financial advice, from investigative stories and summaries of the day's events to crossword puzzles and other entertainments."[131] An article the following year stated, "There is an obvious need to rethink the entire concept of 'news'" and to "redefin[e] the concept of newsworthiness." The author quoted an executive at the Knight Ridder newspaper chain, who said, "What is needed is a new kind of news that prizes utility above all else—how to cook and travel and educate children, what to buy and what to invest in, how to be more successful and better fulfilled in a painfully complicated society."[132]

The journalists writing these articles all agreed that newspapers needed to improve their usefulness, serve the readers, amuse them, and address the issues in their everyday lives. Perhaps the starkest assessment of the situation came in a 1977 *Bulletin* article: "Some, perhaps most, people think newspapers are in the business of providing information. This is simply wrong. Newspapers as well as the rest of the mass media are in the business of providing *entertainment* and those of you who are successful understand this—either consciously or unconsciously. You compete with novels, plays, theater, sports events and soap operas for the attention of the public. You have to meet the wants of your consumers or you'll be out of business or at the very least poorer."[133] The lone voice thundering against service information, entertainment and "froth" in the *Bulletin* was Lester Markel's.[134] To most editors reading the publication, he probably seemed like an out-of-touch relic. Even those who shared his viewpoint on the desirability of hard news versus soft had to acknowledge that given the business environment of the 1970s, newspapers could not model themselves on what the *New York Times* had been during Markel's heyday (the 1940s, 1950s, and early 1960s), as he seemed to suggest.

Whatever qualms journalists had about the shift toward service, entertainment, and soft news, the trend continued in the 1980s and 1990s. By the 2000s, feature stories dominated front pages, and anecdotal or "soft" lead paragraphs had become standard.[135] Television news underwent a similar transformation in the 1970s, 1980s, and 1990s—if anything, the trend was even more pronounced than in newspapers.[136] By the late 1970s, criticism of the Lester Markel variety—that soft news barely belonged in a serious newspaper—had petered out. However, a new variety of criticism arose to take its place. While acknowledging the validity of news about food, lifestyles, and consumer affairs, some critics took issue with how the press covered these topics. The most frequent charge was that they catered exclusively to the wealthy and were more concerned with pleasing advertisers than with serving a journalistic purpose.

An extended critique of the *New York Times* by *Harper's* contributor Earl Shorris in 1977 declared that the new sections were devoted primarily to "gossip and acquisitiveness." He claimed the paper ignored such issues as New York City's exploding rat population and the crumbling of the South Bronx in favor of stories about "goldplated goblets and $90 brass candlesticks"—which he attributed to the fact that "neither Bergdorf Goodman nor Cartier has anything to say to welfare mothers in the South Bronx."[137] The authors of a 1983 profile of Abe Rosenthal in the *Washington Journalism Review* noted, "The Times never catered to the poor, but it never excluded the poor, either." That began to change when the four-section paper was introduced: "With the Home and Living sections,

Abe Rosenthal has drawn a line, and most New Yorkers are on the other side."[138]

Similar accusations could be leveled, and were, against the *Los Angeles Times.* The paper's obsession with "affluent, mostly white readers coveted by advertisers" had caused it to skimp on coverage of racial minorities and their communities, said a 1979 article in the *Columbia Journalism Review.*[139] An article published a few months later said, "The public opinion reflected in the *Times* for too many years has been that of the city's white, middle-to-upper classes."[140] Critics had been making similar charges about the priorities and motivations of the paper for years. In a thoroughly researched, 600-page book about the *L.A. Times* published in 1977, Robert Gottlieb and Irene Wolt charged that Otis Chandler's paper was essentially unchanged from the paper his grandfather Harrison Gray Otis had published—a tool for the Southern California elite to enhance their power and wealth. "The soft news feature approach of the new, mid-seventies, *Times* . . . complemented the soft mood throughout the paper," they wrote. "*Times* staff and *Times* editors became the contented link to an establishment world the paper had done much to create. Soft news at the *Times* was good news for the Chandlers and their friends."[141]

Editors showed little compunction, however, about targeting affluent readers at the expense of others. In terms of possible side effects from the shift toward service and soft news, this ranked well below the concern that triviality or shallowness might seep into the paper. The success of serious broadsheets like the *New York Times* and the *Los Angeles Times* had always depended on their ability to attract wealthy readers and, by extension, the advertisers who wished to reach them. This business strategy, they reasoned, enabled them to be financially sound, which in turn enabled them to fulfill their public-service role in American democracy: acting as a guardian of the public interest, and providing accurate reports on developments in the nation and the world. A newspaper would be no good to anyone if it could not pay its bills or its reporters' salaries.

Concerns about profitability outweighed any desire to reach readers from varied demographic or socioeconomic groups. Editors discussed this consideration matter-of-factly. In a 1971 memo about why the *New York Times* must include more "service information," Abe Rosenthal emphasized that such information "relates directly to the readers who mean most to us—and to advertisers—the young and the affluent."[142] The *New York Times* director of marketing in a private 1977 letter explained that his strategy was to target an "upscale" audience, "people of influence and affluence." He stated rather proudly his awareness that this was "an elitist and classist marketing approach."[143] Similarly Nick Williams, in his private communications in the late 1960s, observed that the "basic audience" and "major market" for the *L.A. Times* was "the white middle class."[144] Speaking to David Halberstam in the 1970s, he noted, "We don't sell any papers in Watts."[145]

This intentional orientation of the newspaper toward affluent readers—which usually equated to white readers—was no secret. In a 1978 speech about the difficulties facing metropolitan newspapers, *New York Times* deputy managing editor Seymour Topping explained why his paper needed to expand its circulation in the suburbs in order to survive. "Television is the principal information medium of lower-income blacks and Spanish-speaking people who have replaced many of the middle-income classes in the central cities," he said.[146] The audience the *Times* was after had moved to the suburbs, and the paper pursued them there. Topping tactfully avoided noting the demographic profile of those suburban readers, but clearly the vast majority were white and wealthy. *L.A. Times* publisher Otis Chandler was not always so careful. In a 1978 television interview, he acknowledged that his paper was "failing" in its coverage of minority communities, but he justified that failure by blaming it on financial considerations. Covering those communities in an effort to attract the readers who lived there, Chandler said, would "cost us millions of dollars." He explained, "We couldn't get the advertising to support that, because the mass black audience and the Chicano audience do not have the purchasing power that our stores require to spend additional money in the *Times*."[147]

Although journalism is a business, journalists at most prestigious news organizations tend to distrust the profit motive and weigh it against the ideals of truth, justice, and an informed citizenry. This conflict between business goals and journalistic goals came to a head in the 1970s as the reader-oriented newspaper took shape. Journalists reconciled themselves to the newspaper's new focus by altering their concept of news. The concept had begun evolving in the 1960s. In 1970, when Abe Rosenthal outlined the mission of the *New York Times,* he defined news as "not simply what people say and do but what they think, what motivates them, their styles of living, the movements, trends and forces acting upon society."[148] It is difficult to quarrel with that definition, and it can encompass most of the changes in news content that occurred in the 1970s. The sectional revolution and the rise of soft news changed the nature of newspapers more than any other development in the 1960s and 1970s; yet compared to other changes in the era, this one went smoothly.

≋ 5 ≋

Minorities and Women in the Newsroom

A Two-Pronged Struggle

P OWERFUL, established institutions generally reflect and reinforce the
dominant attitudes of the broader culture. The mainstream press in
the mid-twentieth century, like most of corporate America, practiced rampant discrimination against minorities and women, both in employment
practices and in news coverage. At the *New York Times* and the *Los Angeles Times* in the early 1960s, most African-Americans were employed
as elevator operators, mail clerks, or janitors, apart from a few token black
reporters or copy editors (this was the case at nearly all large daily newspapers). Most women, if they were not secretaries or switchboard operators, toiled on the family or society pages, regardless of whether they
wished to cover other types of news. The product these newspapers put
out reflected the makeup of the staff and the assumptions of the white-
male-dominated society of the era. While the *New York Times* and *Los
Angeles Times* ably covered the civil rights movement in the South, minority communities in their own cities received scant attention. On the
rare occasions when women appeared in the main news sections, they
were generally depicted in stereotypical or demeaning ways.

Throughout the 1960s and 1970s the press wrestled with race and
gender on two fronts: first, the question of employment opportunities and

discrimination in the newsroom, and second, whether and how to change news coverage. For most female journalists and journalists of color, these issues were urgent and interrelated. The white men responsible for staffing and coverage decisions, however, sometimes disagreed. Furthermore, the men running these newspapers wished to implement changes gradually and to seek a middle ground between opposing points of view. But incrementalism and accommodation were unacceptable to many supporters of the women's-rights movement and the black freedom struggle—especially by the 1970s, as they grew increasingly frustrated by the slow pace of progress. The result, predictably, was conflict.

Initially, news organizations' responses to allegations of discrimination, whether based on race or on gender, proceeded in the same way. They grudgingly accepted that existing practices must change, hired more reporters from the previously excluded group, and expanded coverage of that group's concerns. By the late 1970s, however, the two paths were diverging. Efforts to improve the representation of minorities in the newsroom stalled, especially when it came to appointing minority journalists to supervisory positions (as editors rather than reporters). Coverage of minority communities and issues they cared about became less prominent than it had been in the late 1960s and early 1970s. Women, on the other hand, while still facing employment discrimination, steadily increased their representation on staff, including in positions of editorial responsibility. Many of the deficiencies in coverage to which women had objected in the 1960s were vanishing. Naturally, changes in employment practices influenced changes in coverage: women, with a greater presence in the newsroom, could advocate more effectively for the changes they wanted than could minorities. But the most important driver of change was the desire to give readers what they wanted.

• • •

WHILE EDITORS at the *New York Times* and the *Los Angeles Times* overwhelmingly supported the movement to end racial segregation in the South, they showed few misgivings about the de facto segregation that reigned in their own newsrooms in the early 1960s. The *New York Times* employed three black reporters and the *L.A. Times* one Latino reporter, but otherwise both staffs were all-white.[1] This sometimes hindered news-gathering efforts. In 1964, *New York Times* chief of correspondents Harrison Salisbury discussed with a colleague the possibility of assigning a major exposé in which a reporter would pose as a migrant farmworker in Florida. "It goes without saying that he must be a Negro; all the migrants in the East Coast stream are," one memo said. But with so few black reporters, Salisbury noted, "we just don't have anyone meeting the necessary qualifications this year." The *Times* discarded the story idea.[2]

The *New York Times* and the *Los Angeles Times* were hardly exceptional in their dearth of minority reporters. Industry-wide, in 1968 African-Americans accounted for only about 1 percent of all newsroom jobs.[3] The civil rights movement had made some editors feel guilty about their failure to integrate the newsroom. The black journalist Tom Johnson, who would join the *New York Times* in 1966, recalled being hired at *Newsday* three years earlier, his first job in the white press. The editor-in-chief told him, "We keep writing in this paper about integration and all that and I looked around and we ain't got a single Negro reporter—and we never had one."[4] Like many editors, he seemed to think it was sufficient to have *one*—a form of tokenism that was little better than exclusion. That began to change with the wave of urban riots that swept through the nation from 1964 to 1968. Two of the earliest outbreaks came in the home territories of the *New York Times* and the *L.A. Times:* Harlem in July 1964, and Watts in August 1965.

It quickly became obvious that white journalists could not effectively cover riots such as these. During the Harlem riot, a group of teenagers jumped a *New York Times* photographer and beat him so badly that he nearly lost an eye.[5] When the Watts riot broke out, the *L.A. Times* did not have a single black reporter on staff, and any white person entering the area during the unrest was likely to be attacked. On the second night of rioting, a twenty-four-year-old African-American messenger from the classified-ad department, Robert Richardson, walked into the city room. He lived in Watts and offered to phone in reports from the scene, despite the risk to his safety. The resulting dispatches earned him a series of front-page bylines.[6] The paper's overall coverage, despite relying on mostly white journalists and a few black stringers, won the Pulitzer Prize for local news spot reporting. The *New York Times,* by contrast, had no black journalists on its national staff to send into Watts, and as a result, national editor Claude Sitton recalled, "The coverage read as if it were written from a distance, from outside the ghetto looking in."[7]

The shock of Watts sent nearly every prestigious big-city newspaper scrambling to hire at least a couple of black reporters, if only to avoid the embarrassment of appearing hypocritical—advocating integration in editorials that were written by an all-white staff. But editors often complained that "qualified" black journalists were hard to find. The January 1966 issue of the *Bulletin of the American Society of Newspaper Editors* contained a survey of newspapers' efforts to diversify their staffs, published under the headline "Where Are All the Competent Newsmen Who Happen to be Negroes?"[8] When a reporter asked *New York Times* metropolitan editor Abe Rosenthal in 1965 why he had only one black reporter on his staff, Rosenthal replied, "Looks terrible. I know it. You know it. But what the hell is there to do when for all these years Negroes have not been getting the training or the education that you have to have, white or black, to be a reporter on the *Times*? There just isn't any big pool of Negro talent out there waiting, or if there is, I haven't been able to find it."[9]

Rosenthal and other editors may have sincerely believed that their good-faith efforts to hire black journalists were being stymied by an insufficient supply, but two factors likely led to that mistaken perception. First, a qualified black reporter's credentials might have been different from those of a qualified white reporter. Elite newspapers like the *New York Times* sought to hire people who had attended top universities and who had already worked at other prestigious news organizations. However, few African-Americans were able to attend top universities or get hired at prestigious news organizations in those days. Second, few white newspapers made any significant attempt to go out and find black journalists. They expected to recruit new hires through the usual channels: referrals from colleagues and friends, and bylines they saw in other publications. Of course, when all the colleagues and friends were white, and all the other publications staffed almost entirely by whites, this process did not bring in any black prospects.

Later in the 1960s, leading news organizations stepped up their recruitment of black journalists—often raiding the African-American press for talent. Racial turmoil was one of the biggest stories in the nation, and editors recognized that their lack of minority staff impeded their ability to cover that story fully. Riots were an obvious example of the problem, but the ongoing stories of urban unrest, poverty, and the Black Power movement presented equally important challenges. Sources for such stories mistrusted white reporters and often refused to speak to them (indeed, they also mistrusted black reporters working for the "white press"). According to Earl Caldwell, an African-American reporter hired at the *New York Times* in 1967, at meetings of black militants the participants would often begin by declaring, "Reporters out!" "We would tell these people, 'We understand this story, we can report this story and bring a dimension to it that doesn't exist,'" he recalled. "They began to alter that [statement]. It became, 'white reporters out!'" The white reporters who were removed (sometimes bodily) might protest to their editors that the black reporters should have left in solidarity with them, but the editors sided with Caldwell and the black reporters—the most important thing was to get the story.[10]

Such considerations underscored the need for more minority journalists at metropolitan newspapers, as did the constant desire to protect the paper's image. In 1968 the National Advisory Commission on Civil Disorders (better known as the Kerner Commission), which President Lyndon Johnson had established to examine the causes of the recent riots, issued a blistering condemnation of the news media, both for its poor coverage of black life in America and for its dismal record of employing African-Americans.[11] "The plaint is 'we can't find qualified Negroes,'" the Kerner Commission wrote. "But this rings hollow from an industry where, only yesterday, jobs were scarce and promotion unthinkable for a man whose skin was black."[12] Journalists may have disliked hearing this from a government commission, but many had begun to arrive at similar realizations themselves—indeed, the nation's leading editorial pages had high praise for the report, including its sections on the media.[13]

Newspapers began hiring more black journalists in the late 1960s, but the process was slow and haphazard. The American Society of Newspaper Editors (ASNE), the industry's leading professional association, barely addressed the question of diversifying newsrooms until 1972, when it formed a Minority Employment Committee. That committee disbanded two years later after failing to effect any change in ASNE policies.[14]

Moreover, the few black journalists who got hired at white newspapers often found an unhospitable environment. Robert Richardson, the *L.A. Times* messenger who provided crucial eyewitness accounts of the Watts riots, got promoted to reporter afterward. But he had no professional training, and he started at the lowest rung, on what was referred to as the "disaster desk." Essentially the job consisted of sitting in a bar with other reporters all night, waiting for a fire to break out and then rushing to the scene. Feeling isolated and overwhelmed, Richardson became an alcoholic and was fired within a year; he eventually wound up homeless on Skid Row.[15] Other black journalists at the *Los Angeles Times* in the 1960s sometimes got cues that they did not belong. Ray Rogers, the first experienced black reporter the paper hired (in 1965), once found that someone had left a campaign button for George Wallace, the virulently racist Alabama governor, on his desk.[16] Bill Drummond, an African-American reporter who had been working in Louisville, was hired sight-unseen by the *L.A. Times* in 1967, and the editors who hired him were apparently unaware of his race. When he showed up in the newsroom and introduced himself, the metropolitan editor appeared flummoxed and perhaps disappointed.[17]

At the *New York Times*, according to two black reporters who worked there in the late 1960s, company security guards (who were white) singled out African-Americans for racist humiliations. After boarding a crowded elevator to go up to the newsroom, Earl Caldwell recalled, he would sometimes be pulled off just before the door closed; the guard would say something like, "O.K., come on out of there. Where do you think you're going?" C. Gerald Fraser remembered leaving the office once with an armful of books—free copies from publishers that a senior colleague had given him. A security guard so doggedly persisted in suggesting that Fraser had stolen the books that Fraser, exasperated, handed the whole stack over to the man. The guards performed a variety of duties. When the newsroom got too crowded, as it did on election nights, they would come in to remove people who were not reporters. On one such night, according to Earl Caldwell, "one of the guards comes over to me and says, 'O.K., it's time to leave, get out.' I said, 'I work here.' The guard said, 'No, you don't, and it's time for you to leave.' I'm standing with a group of other reporters. They have to tell him—not tell him—they have to *convince* him that I belong there, I have reason to be there."[18]

Among newsroom colleagues, however, such overt racism was rare. The unexamined assumptions of white journalists were far more pernicious to black reporters' ability to do their jobs. As historian Pamela Newkirk has noted, "The unspoken expectation was for blacks and other minorities to fit into an established culture that was not expected to bend to accommodate them." What they needed, according to Newkirk, was "space to assert their unique cultural values and norms, and also the freedom to reflect ideas and attitudes that could contest mainstream—meaning white—thought."[19] This boiled down to how minority reporters would cover the news. Most of them bristled at the press's insistence on objectivity, because objectivity as generally practiced, they felt, meant favoring the perspective of the white middle-class over all others.[20]

Journalism was not the only profession to struggle with incorporating minorities into its ranks after the Civil Rights Act of 1964 ended the era of legally sanctioned discrimination. Nearly all high-status, high-paying occupations had excluded nonwhites. Consider the proportion of African-Americans (the only nonwhite race counted in the census) in three other professions. African-Americans constituted 0.5 percent of engineers in 1960, 1.1 percent in 1970, and 2.5 percent in 1980. As for lawyers and judges, 1.2 percent were black in 1960, 1.3 percent in 1970, and 2.8 percent in 1980. African-Americans were slightly better represented among social scientists: 2.0 percent in 1960, 3.1 percent in 1970, 5.5 percent in 1980.[21] The number of minorities holding newsroom jobs, by comparison, increased fourfold between 1968 and 1978—from less than 1 percent of the total to a still meager 3.9 percent.[22] That percentage might have been expected to rise even faster, however, because newspapers generally expected no specialized training or education beyond a bachelor's degree (unlike in engineering, law, or social science). Although progress was slow, the era of racial exclusion in the press ended in the 1960s; the struggle over changing coverage of race was just beginning.

• • •

FROM THE TIME of the Montgomery bus boycott in 1955 to the March on Washington in 1963, there was no bigger domestic news story than the fight against Jim Crow in the South. The *New York Times* and many other leading news organizations covered the movement admirably, despite facing intense hostility from southern authorities and, sometimes, mobs.[23] The *Los Angeles Times,* with only three national correspondents in the early 1960s, had no reporters stationed in the South and relied mainly on wire service articles for its coverage, although in 1965 the paper hired Pulitzer Prize winner Jack Nelson away from the *Atlanta Constitution* to open a new Atlanta bureau. But whatever the difficulties of covering the civil rights movement in the South, handling racial problems in Northern and Western cities (like New York and Los Angeles) proved far more vexing.

Newspapers like the *New York Times* and the *Los Angeles Times,* with their white, middle-to-upper-class audiences, had generally ignored the situation in their cities' ghettoes. But they realized in the early 1960s, as civil rights activists began shifting their focus to the North, that the growing social unrest demanded attention. At the urging of managing editor Frank McCullough, in February 1963 the *L.A. Times* ran a six-part series on Mexican-Americans in Los Angeles, followed by a four-part series on African-Americans in June 1963. The series on Mexican-Americans focused mainly on questions of culture and assimilation. The author, Ruben Salazar, addressed the problems of alienation, criminality, and disease in the Latino community, but he made little effort to explore their causes. There was no mention of discrimination in housing and employment, and no mention of complaints about unfair treatment from police and the courts.[24]

Even this tame series, however, caused consternation at the paper. Years later McCullough recalled that a group calling themselves the East Los Angeles Chamber of Commerce threatened to boycott the *Times* in response to the articles. Salazar investigated and discovered that the group consisted of "about two people," according to McCullough, but nevertheless, "it scared the hell out the *Times,* this protest. [Editor-in-chief] Nick [Williams] said to me, 'Hey, you're not doing any more?' I said, 'Yeah, we're doing two more, blacks and Jews.' He said, 'No, you're not.'"[25]

Despite Williams's opposition, the series on L.A.'s African-Americans, written by a white civil rights reporter named Paul Weeks, went ahead. It might not have, except that the black community forced the paper's hand on June 6, 1963, when a coalition of civil rights groups led by the NAACP announced plans for a campaign of boycotts, sit-ins, and mass demonstrations to fight segregation and discrimination in Los Angeles County.[26] Compared to Salazar's series on Latinos, Weeks's series on African-Americans featured grievances more prominently—largely because African-American leaders and their allies were better organized and had existing relationships with the mainstream press. However, the series seems to have been scaled back from what McCullough initially envisioned. There were four articles instead of six, and they were shorter than the articles about Mexican-Americans. Moreover, none of the four appeared on the front page, whereas all six articles in the earlier series had page-one placement.[27] (The planned series on the Jews of Los Angeles, for whatever reason, did not appear.)[28]

In 1963 the *New York Times* also decided to take a long, hard look at its home city's racial problems. The paper assigned one of its three black reporters, Layhmond Robinson, to assess the mood of New York's black community. His insightful, deeply reported article, published on page one, might have served as a wakeup call to many *Times* readers. The article's subheadline, which summarized it accurately, read, "Years of Resentment Find Outlet in Wave of Protests—'Now-or-Never' Feeling Sweeping Moderation Aside."[29] However, the paper undermined the article's impact by pairing it with another the following day, this one exploring white New Yorkers' responses to blacks' increasing demands for equality. The prevailing view, this article implied, held that protests had "gone too far" and that "the new militancy . . . is doing the cause of Negro rights more harm than good." The reporter, Charles Grutzner, dwelled on whites' complaints of reverse discrimination, mentioning, for instance, the "humorous" activities of a group called SPONGE—Society for the Prevention of Negroes Getting Everything.[30] Publishing these articles as a two-part series framed the issue of civil rights as one that affected blacks and whites equally; it created a rough—and false—equivalency between antiblack discrimination and alleged antiwhite bias.

But whatever the impact of isolated bits of reportage like the stories by Layhmond Robinson, Ruben Salazar, and Paul Weeks, they remained just that: isolated bits. The routine stories about minority communities focused on crime, gangs, and bloodshed. In many newspapers, crime stories identified nonwhite suspects by race, while adding no racial designation for white suspects—a practice that continued into the 1970s (although not at the *New York Times* or the *L.A. Times*).[31] Newspapers reported on civil rights groups' activities, but often with little context about their grievances, and often with a disproportionate focus on extreme groups such as the Black Muslims. The 1968 Kerner Commission report highlighted the press's failure to cover "the story of race relations in America . . . with the wisdom, sensitivity, and expertise it demands." "They have not shown an understanding or appreciation of—and thus have not communicated—a sense of Negro culture, thought, or history," the report charged. "Far too often, the press acts and talks about Negroes as if Negroes do not read the newspapers or watch television, give birth, marry, die, and go to PTA meetings."[32]

This kind of criticism stung; it convinced many white journalists that they must improve their coverage of black America.[33] Shortly after publication of the Kerner Report, *New York Times* assistant managing editor Theodore Bernstein wrote a memo to the publisher and five senior editors, lamenting that "by far the largest number of news items concerning Negroes relate to . . . the black-white confrontation." To remedy this, Bernstein advocated publishing positive stories about the black community in order to "make the Negroes feel that they are part of the community in general and that we are paying attention to them." He even suggested that the *Times* "relax its standards" of newsworthiness when it came to publishing such articles.[34] The editors rejected the notion of altering news standards, but they did begin to "search harder for those meaningful stories," according to metropolitan editor Arthur Gelb.[35] On February 1, 1969, for example, the entire page of the "second front"—the first page of the second section, showcasing metropolitan news—was given over to a pair of positive articles about minority neighborhoods. In case readers failed to get the message, a box on the page read:

> From Watts in Los Angeles to Roxbury in Boston, communities in trouble are often viewed by outsiders as uniform in the economic, racial, and ethnic problems that give these communities their adverse images. But such general images tell only part of the story. In New York City, for example—in the predominantly black Bedford-Stuyvesant district of Brooklyn and in the largely Puerto Rican Mott

Haven area of the Bronx—there are positive aspects of urban living often lost in blanket generalizations.

As an attempt to win over readers dissatisfied with the treatment of minority neighborhoods in the *New York Times*, however, this effort was pathetically clumsy. The only "positive aspects," these articles suggested, were enclaves of well-kept townhouses in otherwise decrepit areas. The article about an unexpectedly attractive street in Mott Haven noted that "the street's residents are still mostly white," and the concluding quote came from an Irish-American man who said, "Anyone who's lived with Puerto Ricans knows the advances they've made. You either live with them or you keep running, and you can't run forever."[36] It may have been unintentional, but the piece conveyed the message that the best neighborhood was the neighborhood with the most whites.

Coverage of local minority communities in the *New York Times* began to improve dramatically in 1970, when Arthur Gelb asked Charlayne Hunter, a young black reporter who had been hired two years earlier, to establish a Harlem bureau. Hunter gladly accepted, viewing it as an opportunity to write "about people, not problems."[37] She had no trouble fulfilling that goal, turning in features about, for instance, a collector who had amassed 7,000 books on black literature and history, a Harlem radio host dedicated to improving her community, and the annual arrival of a convoy of trucks from Georgia to sell soul food on street corners.[38]

The *Los Angeles Times* compiled a similarly uneven record of covering the news from L.A.'s minority communities. Publisher Otis Chandler said in a 1969 interview, "We are going into the black community and doing enterprise stories, and trying to tell . . . the fact that there are people who are doing fine things in that community"—as examples, he mentioned stories about "a black dress shop in Watts, a foster mother in East Los Angeles."[39] Such articles could often come off as patronizing, however. A prominently placed story from September 1967 described how a twenty-three-year-old white housewife and model from Orange County, Harriet Goslins, was training eight young African-American women from Watts to become dental assistants. A worthy story, perhaps, but it reinforced the stereotype that undereducated inner-city residents needed help from benevolent white outsiders. It was accompanied by a large photo of Goslins, in a chic sleeveless dress, holding up a model of the mouth as seven African-American girls in white nurses' uniforms dutifully look on.[40]

It may have been tricky for white journalists to write human-interest stories about people and communities of color, but covering the growing political militancy of minority groups presented an even greater challenge. The decision makers at the *New York Times* and the *Los Angeles Times* held the typical view of most affluent, moderate-to-liberal whites: their enthusiasm for the early, integrationist phase of the civil rights movement turned to bewilderment and dismay as disenchanted young people embraced cultural nationalism, radical politics, and sometimes violence. Nothing brought out that bewilderment and dismay quite like the Black Power movement.

Although Black Power advocates had many goals—improving conditions in inner-city communities, instilling a sense of cultural pride in African-Americans, ending racial discrimination in housing, education, and employment—for most white audiences their violent rhetoric drowned out all other aspects of their message. As newspapers like the *New York Times* and the *Los Angeles Times* reported, the militant leader Stokely Carmichael called for "armed struggle" by blacks in America, urging them to "pick up guns" and to "turn out and tear up the city."[41] Carmichael's successor as head of the Student Nonviolent Coordinating Committee (SNCC—renamed the Student National Coordinating Committee in 1969), H. Rap Brown, repeatedly encouraged African-Americans to arm themselves and to "burn the country down."[42]

Such remarks convinced *Los Angeles Times* editor-in-chief Nick Williams that the likes of Carmichael and Brown were too extreme to even bother engaging. In a 1968 memo to publisher Otis Chandler, he wrote, "We are NOT going to 'save' or cool the hysterically committed black—the Panthers, who WANT anarchy and WANT civil war. They're crazy, and before it's all over (long before) they're either going to get killed or get terrified by the killing. God knows I don't want that, even for people who say they instinctively hate me, BUT if they are determined on anarchy and mau-mau-ism they're going to get it."[43]

Williams, who had grown up in Virginia and Tennessee, admitted to a colleague in 1967 that earlier in life, "I was the complete product of my Southern background. . . . I intended to keep the White-Black stratification complete, as it had been since Negroes first became American slaves."[44] His outlook had changed dramatically from that time, but he still believed that major alterations in American society—like major alterations at the *L.A. Times*—must occur gradually, and that radicalism was unacceptable. As he wrote to the paper's top editors in 1969, "I am by *no* means opposed to any *useful modifications* of the 'white, middle-class capitalistic' structure of our society—*but* I am damned strongly opposed to any terroristic revolutionary progress to *destroy* it." With that in mind, Williams said, the *L.A. Times* should be "very explicit" about the threat posed by the Black Panthers and similar groups, suggesting that the staff's liberal sympathies had caused them to go soft on these radicals. "In our zeal to heal the racial breech [*sic*]—a zeal I share—we may on occasion have omitted some of the nastier bits about the Black Panthers, SNCC, BSU [Black Student Union], and so on."[45]

But Williams alone could not shape the paper's coverage, and the views of other decision makers differed from his. National editor Ed Guthman, a former aide to Robert F. Kennedy, was keenly interested in the grievances of African-Americans, as was publisher Otis Chandler. The man most responsible for day-to-day coverage of black radicalism was metropolitan editor Bill Thomas, who laid out his views on the topic in a 1968 speech to a group of mostly white college students. With the advent of "the black revolution," he said,

> arrogance and lack of reasonableness—and racism—will be coming more and more, now, from black to white, and it's going to be tougher and tougher to take it. But one must stop and think how long the black man has been taking it, and how unreasonable it would be to expect him not to dish it out for a change. One must also stop and think, that while he has made progress in the last decade or so, the Negro still has a long way to go. And despair and frustration quite humanly give way to rage when slight progress and continued promises bring the goal tantalizingly near, yet it never seems quite reachable.[46]

Clearly, Thomas disliked black radicalism and considered it misguided, but he wanted to rationalize and comprehend it, instead of simply assail it as baseless crazy talk.

This attitude was apparent in some of the *Los Angeles Times* coverage. In late 1968 one of the paper's few African-American reporters, William Drummond, managed to obtain a series of interviews with the essayist and Black Panther leader Eldridge Cleaver. The resulting profile of Cleaver appeared in the coveted "non-dupe" spot on the front page.[47] While Drummond acknowledged Cleaver's past as a rapist and quoted some of his incitements to violence, the article was relatively sympathetic; it attempted to explain Cleaver and his ideas rather than judge them. Drummond's observations convey a deeper understanding of Black Power than readers could get from a brief story about the latest inflammatory speech. "So much of what Cleaver does in public is designed for effect," Drummond wrote. The "fearsome Black Panther" persona was simply Cleaver's means of appealing to young African-Americans and drawing attention to his ultimate cause—"improving the conditions of his people."[48]

This disconnect between rhetoric and reality among black radicals also struck some journalists at the *New York Times*. In 1968 metropolitan editor Abe Rosenthal and national editor Claude Sitton assigned a white reporter named Douglas Kneeland to speak with various journalists and experts about "problems in our racial coverage." Kneeland reported back that the main criticism, of the *New York Times* and other news organizations, concerned their failure to put events into perspective. "Too often, I am told, we confuse the symbol with the substance. Most people in the field agree, for instance, that we have done a disservice in the past by making it appear that the likes of Stokely, Rap, and the Black Panthers had the power to do the things they were threatening instead of making it clear that they were more a manifestation of a disorganized anger that certainly exists among black youth."[49] Shortly thereafter, Earl Caldwell began writing a series of deeply reported pieces about the Black Panthers and their activities in New York and California.[50] Caldwell developed such good sources on the Panthers, in fact, that the FBI tried to pressure him to become an informant.[51]

However, higher-ups at the *New York Times* and the *Los Angeles Times* had reservations about giving prominent, meaningful coverage to the Black Power movement. Initially they worried about the impact their coverage might have on society. Following the series of riots that marked the "long hot summer" of 1967, Senator Hugh Scott (a Pennsylvania Republican) suggested that TV networks bore some blame for the violence, because they had broadcast snippets of inflammatory speeches from "such individuals as H. Rap Brown and Stokely Carmichael."[52] Editors at the *New York Times* believed this was a valid concern for newspapers as well, but as assistant managing editor Harrison Salisbury told executive editor Turner Catledge, "To fail to give due and objective attention to the demagogue, the agitator, the angry men, young and old, who are tossed up by the deep conflicts in our society is to evade a prime responsibility of the press." He continued, "The fact that Stokely Carmichael's ideas and those of The New York Times may be leagues apart does not relieve us of the responsibility for reporting what the Carmichaels, the Rap Browns and their ilk have to say and what effect it has on the community."[53] This belief—that on issues of great importance, the press's duty to inform the public outweighs all other concerns—was widely held at prestige papers such as the *New York Times* and the *L.A. Times,* and invoking it was a sure way to prevail in any argument.

Although civic responsibility was a prime concern, it was hardly the only one. As always, newspaper managers had to consider readers' perceptions. In 1973 *New York Times* columnist and executive James "Scotty" Reston sent a memo to publisher Punch Sulzberger in which he expressed concern about the direction of the paper. "Obviously the problems of the city, the noisy minorities with their problems and criticisms of contemporary society, are news, but I wonder if we don't over-cover them and give the impression that *The Times* is primarily interested in these all-out characters," Reston wrote. "Sometimes I think we are in danger of making [1972 Democratic presidential candidate] George McGovern's mistake. He didn't mean to get himself identified with the hairy young, abortion, amnesty, and the legalization of marijuana, but a helluva lot of people got the impression that these were his primary interests."[54] Clearly Reston worried about fueling the accusation of liberal bias. Readers who already harbored suspicions about the paper's ideological slant might find it guilty by association if it devoted too much coverage to "radical" ideas—after all, Spiro Agnew had criticized the media for "elevating" people like Stokely Carmichael with copious coverage.

The *New York Times* had already fielded complaints that it was too interested in, or too sympathetic toward, what Reston dismissively called "the noisy minorities." A 1970 article about the black radical Angela Davis noted that she had been friends with the four girls killed in the infamous 1963 bombing of an African-American church in Birmingham, Alabama, which, as the *Times* reporter said, "helped shock the nation into realizing that blacks historically had been the victims of almost continuous violence. Seven years later the blacks were fighting back, and Angela Davis was with them."[55] Upon reading this article, the editor and publisher of the *Tulsa Tribune* wrote to *New York Times* associate editor Clifton Daniel deploring what he considered a lack of "balance"; he made a veiled threat to stop subscribing to the New York Times News Service (a major revenue stream for the *Times*) if this type of reporting continued.[56] After consulting with other editors, Daniel defended the story, but complaints such as these likely had an impact. If nothing else, they allowed editors to feel they were occupying the middle ground between white reactionaries and black radicals—precisely where they wanted to be.

Like Scotty Reston, the two top editors of the *L.A. Times* in the late 1960s worried they might "overdo" the issue of racial unrest and protest. Nick Williams, in a 1968 memo to associate editor Jim Bellows about what kind of coverage he wanted in the paper's feature section, said, "I think we have certainly done enough about [the racial or integration theme] in that section and have probably overdone [it] to some extent."[57] In a separate memo to Bellows a few months earlier, Williams had warned him not to have too many articles on "racial issues" in *West,* the paper's Sunday magazine.[58] Managing editor Frank Haven, one of the more conservative figures in the newsroom, felt even more strongly. In a memo addressed to "the publisher's advisory committee," he named as his number-one concern the "direction [and] thrust" of the paper, saying, "We must be cognizant of the growing number of readers we turn off" with "the social and political moralizing some of them charge we do to excess in the national area." Specifically, Haven wrote, he feared that "the miles of words we have published on Southern segregation, the Negro problem in our area, the Mexican-Americans, the poor, to name a few well-beaten subjects, in all sections of The Times, haven't been read by quite a few of our readers, and that many resist reading one more story on the subject."[59]

Throughout the 1970s the managers of the *Los Angeles Times,* the *New York Times,* and other major newspapers struggled to find the proper balance in their coverage of race-related topics. One year they might agree with Haven and Reston that such topics were getting too much coverage, and the next year they might bemoan the lack of stories on such pressing problems. They also worried about the balance between negative and positive stories concerning communities of color. Much of the difficulty stemmed from the fact that newspaper managers remained overwhelmingly white. The number of black journalists in newsrooms had increased dramatically since the mid-1960s, but nearly all were reporters, not editors. The author of a 1979 *Columbia Journalism Review* article about minorities in American newspapers exaggerated only slightly when he wrote, "Nonwhites who hold newsroom jobs of real influence and authority can be ticked off on both hands, with several fingers left over."[60] The *L.A. Times* in particular was a laggard in promoting minority journalists to decision-making roles. An internal report noted that as of March 1978 the paper had zero minorities employed as "officials or managers in the editorial department."[61] The *New York Times* in the late 1970s was only marginally better, with one African-American, Paul Delaney, holding an editor's job.[62] (Others had declined offers to move from writing to editing positions.)[63]

As a result, the overall outlook and policies of newspapers changed little. As *New York Times* reporter Tom Johnson put it in a 1972 interview, "The *Times* generally still reflects the attitudes of the successful white American, and these attitudes are quite often unresponsive or even antagonistic towards the needs and aspirations of minorities."[64] Even as the contingent of black reporters at the *New York Times* grew, this sentiment remained. As reporter Gerald Fraser said bluntly in a 1979 interview, "When you view the hiring, the assignments, the promotions, and the product, there is a clear indication that the people who run the paper do not intend to acknowledge any sort of significant minority presence. . . . Essentially, they don't want us around here, and they don't want our viewpoints."[65]

In 1974 a group of *New York Times* employees sued the paper for racial discrimination, but the plaintiffs all came from departments outside the newsroom. As the suit dragged on, however, nearly all of the black journalists at the *Times* lined up against their employer. Even Roger Wilkins, a highly paid editorial writer who had close personal relationships with

C. Gerald Fraser, who worked as a reporter for the *New York Times* from 1967 to 1991. Photo: August 23, 1975, File Photo. Reginald Stuart / © The New York Times / Redux.

editor-in-chief Abe Rosenthal and publisher Punch Sulzberger, "got into the discrimination suit with fervor," he later wrote, testifying about "deficiencies in [the paper's] coverage of minority issues, its treatment of me and its handling of black talent."[66] The case was settled out of court in 1980, with the *Times* paying $685,000 and agreeing to implement an affirmative action plan.

In 1990 the *Los Angeles Times* published a four-part series by media reporter David Shaw on minorities and the press. "No matter how enlightened and well-meaning white editors may be," Shaw wrote, "the press will not change its fundamental approach to covering minorities and routinely include them in the mainstream of the daily news flow until there are many minority editors participating significantly in the decision-making process."[67] Shaw acknowledged that his own newspaper had performed worse than most when it came diversifying its corps of senior editors. "The Times still has no high-ranking minority editor with any major decision-making power in the daily news operation," he noted.[68]

Not only did minorities' advancement in the newsroom stall after the mid-1970s, so did the drive to improve and expand coverage of minority communities. It did not necessarily go backward, but newspaper managers seemed to feel that the improvements they made in the 1960s and early 1970s were sufficient. Earl Caldwell, who covered race relations for the *New York Times* from 1967 to 1974, noted that when he joined the paper, "the story of race was exploding into the biggest story of all." In the months after the assassination of Martin Luther King Jr., he recalled, "there was a period when I had more front-page stories in the newspaper than anybody."[69] By the late 1970s, however, stories about race had become a much lower priority. As *New York Times* reporter Gerald Fraser told the *Columbia Journalism Review* in 1979, "No one can succeed here as a reporter of black affairs because there is no interest in that subject."[70]

A 1979 article about the shortcomings of the *L.A. Times* focused largely on its lackluster coverage of minorities and their concerns. "The minority coverage here stinks," said Austin Scott, one of the paper's few black reporters. According to the editor of the *Los Angeles Sentinel,* an African-American weekly, "People in the black community say the *Los Angeles Times* doesn't give a damn about them."[71] Few cases illustrated this perception better than the story of Eula Love, a black woman killed by police in her front yard in January 1979. A gas company employee said she assaulted him when he came to collect on an unpaid bill, and when the gasman returned with two police officers, Love was wielding a kitchen knife. The officers each emptied their revolvers, striking Love eight times. While the *Los Angeles Herald-Examiner* played the story as major news, the biggest story of the day, it warranted only a one-paragraph brief in the *Times.*[72] The paper's apparent disregard of the Eula Love story captured national attention, with the journalist Richard Reeves delivering a stern condemnation in *Esquire:* "The *Times* probably didn't give a damn one way or the other about Eula Love, and assumed its readers didn't either," he charged.[73]

Reeves's assessment may have been harsh, but he was onto something. When a TV interviewer suggested to *L.A. Times* publisher Otis Chandler in 1978 that his paper did a poor job of covering minorities, Chandler responded, "I think that's fair," then admitted that he did not intend to address that shortcoming. Minority communities, he said, lacked the purchasing power to make them desirable to *Times* advertisers, and besides, "It's not their kind of newspaper. It's too big, it's too stuffy, if you will, it's too complicated."[74] These remarks, suggesting that people of color were not smart or serious enough to read the *Times,* provoked a flood of angry letters accusing Chandler of racism. In his form-letter response, Chandler denied the charge of racism but stood by his statement.[75]

The *New York Times* expanded its coverage in several ways in the mid- to late 1970s, but none of them would likely increase its appeal in minority communities. The new lifestyle sections that the paper introduced targeted affluent, mainly white suburbanites.[76] So did the new "regional weeklies," Sunday supplements with news about the well-to-do suburbs around New York City. The paper's original suburban section, launched in 1971, was BQLI, covering Brooklyn, Queens, and Long Island. In 1975 the editors decided to drop the more racially and socioeconomically diverse communities of Brooklyn and Queens and focus exclusively on Long Island. In 1977 the *New York Times* created new Sunday sections devoted to Westchester County, New York, and Fairfield County, Connecticut, wealthy areas north of the city. The paper explicitly targeted "upscale" readers, conducting surveys to discover what interested them and what did not. The report about what to cover in Bridgeport, Connecticut, which contained a "very desirable shopping plaza" and an "undesirable industrial" area, is instructive: "Bridgeport shopping is important news; the rest of Bridgeport is not."[77]

At the *New York Times* and the *Los Angeles Times* alike, financial considerations led management to scale back minority coverage in the 1970s. The need to cater to readers—in particular, affluent suburbanites— outweighed all other concerns, and editors believed that their target audience did not care to read about police killings in the inner city or about the goings-on in "undesirable" parts of town. They had not necessarily believed this a decade earlier. In 1968 Nick Williams had acknowledged that the white middle class constituted his paper's main audience, but he argued that "we are serving the interests of that middle class when we tell them precisely what the Negroes and the Mexican-Americans think and are doing."[78]

In part this logic implies that minorities matter only in that they might pose a threat to white-dominated social order. But interpreted another way, it implies that all Americans, regardless of their race, should care about the race story because it was simply so important. By the late 1970s few editors at major newspapers shared that conviction. White liberals' enthusiasm for fundamental social change had waned; suburbanites, their numbers having increased due to white flight, could ignore the turmoil in the depressed inner city; the charismatic, headline-grabbing leaders of the 1960s and early 1970s (such as Martin Luther King Jr., Huey Newton, and Angela Davis) had died or faded from the scene.[79] The priority that newspapers placed on coverage of inner-city minority communities shifted accordingly. The downgrading of minority coverage was primarily a business decision—perhaps an inevitable one for papers that were shedding readers and advertisers, like the *New York Times*—but that did not mitigate the disappointment of those who hoped for more complete, prominent coverage of the country's most intractable social problem.

● ● ●

THE RACISM OF MOST NEWSROOMS prior to the 1960s was essentially passive. There was little animosity toward minority journalists or minority communities; managers simply did not hire those journalists or cover those communities. By contrast, the sexism of the press was active. Newspapers hired women, but those who managed to avoid the secretarial pool were generally restricted to working on the women's pages, covering topics in which most male journalists had no interest, like homemaking, fashion, and parties. The main news pages, produced almost entirely by men, reflected the reigning societal assumption of male superiority. Women rarely appeared, and when they did, they were depicted in demeaning, stereotypical ways.[80]

The *New York Times* may have been slightly better than most news organizations in its treatment of women. One female journalist, Anne O'Hare McCormick, earned the chance to be a foreign correspondent for the paper in the 1920s and proved herself a tremendous talent; she became a foreign-affairs columnist, won the Pulitzer Prize, and got appointed to the *New York Times* editorial board (the only woman to do so until the 1970s). McCormick's experience was the exception to the rule, however. Until the 1960s men held nearly every other job outside of the women's-news department.

Befitting the *Los Angeles Times*'s reputation before 1960 as one of the country's most reactionary papers, its newsroom atmosphere was especially misogynistic. Nick Williams's predecessor as editor-in-chief, L. D. Hotchkiss, "vowed that a woman reporter would never sit at his city desk, but at the same time a female clerk or typist could not pass through the newsroom without being fondled," according to author Dennis McDougal.[81] Even as Williams and Otis Chandler began transforming the *Times* into a top-quality newspaper in the early 1960s, the reporting staff (apart from the women's pages) remained exclusively male. The gender barrier in the city room did not fall until 1964, when Dorothy Townsend got transferred from the women's section to local news after years of persistent requests.[82]

The Civil Rights Act of 1964 prohibited employment discrimination on the basis of sex as well as race, but while editors scrambled to address their lack of black reporters, there was no equivalent move to hire women or to allow them an alternative to the women's-section ghetto. A 1965 memo from *New York Times* assistant managing editor Harrison Salisbury to his boss exemplifies management's attitude toward female hiring. In a conversation with the paper's photo editor, Salisbury wrote, "I asked whether he'd ever considered a gal fotog. He said no. I said why not have one, equipt with tight-belted trenchcoat, long blonde hair and a scooter and three floppy cameras hung around the neck. He seemed rather dazzled by the notion. I don't see what special good this gal would be, but I see no reason why we should not explore the field and see if there might not be a plus for us there."[83] This passed for forward thinking at the time (but it did not result in the hiring of any female photographers).

The following year the *Bulletin of the American Society of Newspaper Editors* published a survey of editors on the question of why they had so few women in their newsrooms. In contrast to the embarrassment and regret Abe Rosenthal expressed in 1965 when asked about his staff's lack of black reporters, these editors brushed off the question of women's underrepresentation with unapologetic sexism. One editor attributed his paper's "troubles with women" to their menstrual phases. Another wrote that the only women generally found in his newsroom were summer interns, "but these lovelies are gone before our men . . . have a chance to ask them what time they get off and what they are doing this evening." A third griped that most women journalists "shudder when you suggest they might want to work on pages designed for them" (the women's pages). The *Bulletin* also included a box labeled "Ten Commandments for Dealing with Women Employees," which reminded newspapermen that women are insecure, fearful, temperamental, vindictive, and in need of constant praise.[84] There was little danger that women might read this material and take issue with it, because the membership of the American Society of Newspaper Editors remained almost exclusively male.[85]

The number of female reporters working outside of women's pages began to creep up in the late 1960s as the feminist movement gained strength. By the end of the decade the *New York Times* had women writing for every section of the paper, including prestigious assignments like Washington and Saigon. The *Los Angeles Times* in 1967 hired for its metropolitan staff Linda Mathews, who had been the first female managing editor of the *Harvard Crimson,* and she began writing major, substantive stories almost immediately. In 1969 Marlene Cimons became the first woman reporter in the paper's Washington bureau.

But despite these superficial indications of progress, sexism remained firmly entrenched. Neither paper had any female editors outside of the women's section; the *New York Times* reportedly had an explicit policy in the 1960s that no woman would ever become an editor.[86] Women at both papers often got passed over for choice assignments and pigeonholed into covering "soft" stories. Marlene Cimons, for instance, wanted to write "substantive, serious" articles from Washington, but her brief was to cover social life. She managed to write about other topics occasionally, and showed her aptitude for it, but despite repeated requests, it took ten years for her to get transferred off the party beat.[87] Black reporters often found themselves in similar situations in the 1960s, assigned only to race-related stories. Explaining why he quit the *New York Times* in 1965, Theodore Jones wrote that he had "decided that there was little chance of becoming anything more than a black reporter covering black-oriented events for the newspaper."[88]

Like minorities, women journalists engaged in two parallel struggles: they fought job discrimination in the newsroom and sexism in news coverage. In the 1970s they regularly challenged their bosses on both fronts. By this time the feminist movement had raised the consciousness of many newswomen: they were more aware of sexism and more aware of their ability to fight it, especially after female staffers at *Newsweek* sued their employers for discrimination in 1970.[89] Moreover, their numbers had increased to constitute a critical mass—they could band together and demand that management address their grievances.

According to the United States census, women accounted for 36.5 percent of reporters and editors in 1960, 40.4 percent in 1970, and 49.0 percent in 1980. These are far greater numbers than for female engineers (0.8 percent in 1960, 1.7 percent in 1970, 4.6 percent in 1980), female lawyers and judges (3.4 percent in 1960, 4.8 percent in 1970, 13.8 percent in 1980), or female social scientists (24.9 percent in 1960, 18.6 percent in 1970, 37.2 percent in 1980).[90] The census figures can be misleading, however, because they include editors and reporters at magazines (many of which were special-interest women's magazines) and those in newspapers' women's sections. A survey of fifteen daily newspapers of varying circulation in 1979 found that their newsrooms were 36.2 percent female, on average—compared to 29.3 percent in 1974.[91] But it is harder to measure the more consequential shift: the increasing number of women working outside of the fashion, family, or society pages. Although the shift began in the mid-1960s, it was a slow process that failed to meet the expectations of most female journalists.

The frustrations of women at the *New York Times* had been simmering for years. In a July 1969 announcement about several upper-level promotions at the paper, Punch Sulzberger gushed about the "wealth of young talent" on staff, "younger men" with the capacity to lead the organization into the future. Grace Glueck, an art reporter, found the lack of any mention of women upsetting, and she wrote a short letter to Sulzberger telling him so.[92] The publisher responded the next day, informing Glueck that her point was well taken and that he would consult with "key management executives" about it.[93] Two and a half years passed, however, and there was no follow-up from Sulzberger or anyone else.

Several women in the newsroom secretly organized a caucus, and in May 1972 they sent a five-page letter to Sulzberger and other top company executives. Noting the lack of female editors and executives, the group wrote, "We feel the *Times* is and always has been remiss in seeing that women employees reach positions in the vital decision-making areas of the paper." They also noted that women were generally paid less than men with similar credentials doing similar work, and that "in the area of job expectations, men are encouraged to think in terms of larger goals by virtue of the better assignments and promises of promotion given to many. We feel that few executives seriously entertain the idea that women should have access to the varied experiences that would equip them for executive responsibilities." In closing, they urged the *Times* to adopt an affirmative action policy that would rectify inequities in pay, hiring, and promotion.[94]

Several meetings between *New York Times* management and the women's caucus followed, but management, while conceding the validity of the caucus's points and promising to improve the situation of women at the paper, refused to commit to any specific steps. In a January 1973 memo to all company employees, Punch Sulzberger wrote, "I wish now to state our strong conviction that women must be treated as well as men at every level of The Times."[95] Those words did not translate into action, however. As one of the caucus leaders, foreign desk copy editor Betsy Wade, recalled, there was "plenty of sweet talk to our faces and carrying on just the same behind our backs."[96] The company resisted providing figures about male-female salary differentials, but the bits of data that the caucus's lawyers managed to wring out hinted at gross inequities. In November 1974 they took their case to U.S. District Court.[97]

A bitter legal battle raged for the next four years. Abe Rosenthal accused the plaintiffs of being biased, mentally unstable, or simply poor journalists (the latter accusation would justify their lower pay and lack or promotion). The women's caucus dredged up embarrassing memos in which male editors made demeaning references to female employees' looks and spoke frankly about their discriminatory practices ("What does she look like?" asked one editor about a prospective female hire. "Twiggy? Lynn Redgrave? Perhaps you ought to send over her vital statistics, or picture in a bikini"; one woman's supervisor wrote on her personnel evaluation, "I would make her my first assistant if she were a man").[98] The case was settled in 1978, with the *Times* agreeing to pay $350,000 and to carry out, under court decree, an aggressive affirmative action plan.[99]

The women's drive for equal treatment in the newsroom occurred as they simultaneously pushed to eliminate sexism in news coverage. In

June 1972, a month after the women's caucus's initial letter to Sulzberger, Betsy Wade sent a three-page memo to Abe Rosenthal with recommendations for how to avoid sexist language (examples: do not refer to adult women as "girls"; do not treat women "as livestock" by focusing on their physical attractiveness; if a woman is a physician or a Ph.D., call her "Dr.," not "Miss" or "Mrs.").[100] Rosenthal had been hearing similar messages from outside the paper. Also in June 1972, he met with a group from the National Organization for Women (NOW), which presented him with a forty-page report on how to achieve "better representation of women in *The New York Times.*" It emphasized the same points as Wade's memo, along with many others, all supported by clippings from the *Times* with the objectionable passages underlined in red.[101]

The NOW report opened Rosenthal's eyes to the pervasiveness of antifeminist language in the paper. Although he had previously acknowledged that sexist passages occasionally made it into print, he considered them regrettable but rare missteps.[102] Being presented with such comprehensive evidence of sexism forced him to concede that a systemic problem existed. He sent a copy of the report to all the senior editors, asking them to "please make notes of those usages and customs in The Times that you agree should be changed." In a memo to three other news executives, Rosenthal admitted that he was "surprised" by NOW's findings and was moved to find "methods of eliminating some of the distasteful usages that this study reveals."[103]

Two weeks later Rosenthal noticed that an article about the Wimbledon tennis tournament referred to "America's three top-ranked girls." He sent a note to the sports editor: "I don't belong to NOW but I do think they have some significant points and that writers, including and perhaps particularly in sports, tend to downgrade women by the words they use. Those weren't girls, they were women. Please get the word around."[104] Rosenthal's sensitivity to sexism went only so far, however. He objected to the world "girls" being applied to professional athletes but made no comment on the article's very next sentence, which said the defending Wimbledon champion Evonne Goolagong was "as unconcerned as if she were skipping rope" while she mounted a comeback in her quarterfinal match—a subtly infantilizing, gendered description.[105]

After Rosenthal's "fascinating discussion" with NOW he told one letter writer, "We have changed many of our usages and, hopefully, become more attentive to the whole subject" of "the dignity of women."[106] On several occasions between 1972 and 1974, he directed senior editors to eliminate sexist usages when they came to his attention.[107] He wrote to a feminist critic in 1974, "My consciousness has indeed risen about feminism, and privately and publicly I give full credit to the people I know in the feminist movement and to the movement itself."[108] There were strict limits to Rosenthal's feminism, however, and his battle with the women's caucus seemingly hardened his views. In August 1973 ten female staffers, among them several leaders of the caucus, posted an open letter to Rosenthal on an office bulletin board protesting a *Times* article about women traffic cops that they deemed "a totally offensive put-down of women."[109] Although the article's sexism is fairly blatant, Rosenthal decided not to reply to the letter; he viewed any public badmouthing of the *Times* as a personal insult and a sign of disloyalty.[110]

Rosenthal was at his most unyielding when it came to the term "Ms.," which he refused to allow in the pages of the *New York Times*. The paper's policy dictated that if a man named John Jones was quoted or described, he would be referred to initially by his full name, then as "Mr. Jones" in any subsequent mentions. But Jane Jones would be identified as either "Miss Jones" or "Mrs. Jones" on the second mention. This required reporters to ask women about their marital status although in most cases it was irrelevant to the article. If a woman asked to be referred to as Ms., the *Times* would not honor that request. In a letter to one such woman (a lawyer involved in a case about which the paper had written), Rosenthal explained the reasoning behind this policy. If the *Times* used Ms. for women who preferred that term, he said, "we would be duty bound to refer to everybody by any honorific he or she chose," which would quickly "reach the point of absurdity."[111]

Rosenthal's dubious logic regarding the use of Ms. did not convince most feminists. In fact, the paper's position on honorifics helped fuel the women's caucus. As Grace Glueck later wrote, "How [the caucus] got started was that in 1972 Grace Lichtenstein was kvetching about the fact that the *Times* would not permit the use of the title Ms. in the paper. Several of us . . . got to thinking that this style rigidity was symptomatic of more basic problems."[112] Others felt even more strongly. In March 1974 a coalition of women's groups picketed the *New York Times* building to protest the paper's "refusal to respect women by using the designation Ms. when requested."[113] In his stand against Ms., Rosenthal had a strong ally in *Times* publisher Punch Sulzberger. Responding in 1974 to one of the many letters calling for his paper to allow the use of Ms., Sulzberger wrote, "Mr., Mrs., and Miss, old-fashioned, if you will, are, in our judgment, terms of respect that civilized people across the world understand. We feel no need to scrap them in favor of Ms." As if to underline his contempt, Sulzberger addressed his correspondent as "Miss Martinez" although her letter to him had been signed "Ms. Barbara Fultz Martinez."[114] That same day, Sulzberger sent a memo to his staff reminding them not to use Ms. when addressing their outgoing mail. "It is NOT repeat NOT The New York Times style," he wrote.[115] In the face of such obstinacy, complaints continued for years to come, until Rosenthal in 1986 finally relented and allowed the use of Ms., explaining in a note to readers that it had, in his judgment, "passed sufficiently into the language to be accepted as common usage."[116]

News organizations throughout the country wrestled with the question of honorifics in the 1970s. Many dropped them altogether; others allowed Miss, Mrs., or Ms. depending on the person's preference; and others, like the *New York Times,* continued to insist on Miss or Mrs. The *Los Angeles Times* went back and forth. The editors stopped using honorifics in 1975 but reinstated them a year later. According to managing editor Frank Haven, when a woman killed in a car crash was referred to by last name only, "there was a feeling it was improper."[117] There was no ban on the term "Ms.," however, and by the early 1980s most courtesy titles had once again disappeared from the paper.[118] In contrast to the heated debates that occurred at the *New York Times,* Haven claimed to be unaware of any complaints stemming from the *L.A. Times* decision to reinstate honorifics in the mid-1970s.[119] Nor did the issue gain much traction in the newsroom. Barbara Saltzman, one of two female copy editors for the View section in the 1970s, recalled telling her male colleagues that the paper should stop referring to women as Mrs. or Miss; they dismissed the idea and, as a joke, began referring to her as "Saltzperson."[120]

This flyer for a 1974 demonstration raises some of the grievances that feminists held against the *New York Times*. Photo: Manuscripts and Archives Division, The New York Public Library, Astor, Lenox and Tilden Foundations.

Nevertheless, women at the *L.A. Times* were determined to be taken seriously. In 1972 a group of the paper's female journalists joined with NOW to file a complaint with the Fair Employment Practices Commission (FEPC) of California, arguing that the *Times* discriminated against women and nonwhites in hiring, promotion, and pay.[121] As the FEPC investigated, women in the newsroom organized a caucus to negotiate with management. They met with editor-in-chief Bill Thomas and other executives several times in 1974, pairing their grievances about employment discrimination with their objections to discriminatory treatment of women in news coverage. The *L.A. Times,* they charged, was run like an old-boys club, with male editors promoting and giving raises to their friends while passing over the talented women with whom they did not have close relationships. Hoping to end that practice, the women's caucus demanded that job openings be posted publicly so that all company employees would have a shot at them. They also wanted to see salary figures to determine whether or not women were being paid less than men in similar positions.[122]

Los Angeles Times management took the women's caucus seriously, wishing to avoid the kind of lawsuits that had shaken and embarrassed *Newsweek,* the *New York Times,* and several other major news organizations. They promised that future job openings would be posted on bulletin boards in all *L.A. Times* offices, and after some foot-dragging they agreed to share certain data on salaries.[123] Management found its position bolstered in May 1975 when the FEPC issued its report. The investigation found no evidence of gender discrimination in salaries and stated that the paper had made great strides in hiring women since 1971. "I am confident that the *Los Angeles Times* is sincere in its desire to cooperate with the Women's Caucus and in its desire to expand employment opportunities for females in the Editorial Department," wrote the FEPC's affirmative action administrator.[124] The women's caucus fizzled out shortly thereafter, partly because some members feared their involvement might hurt their careers at a time when many newspapers were cutting jobs.[125]

• • •

THE PRESS'S TRADITIONALLY dismal treatment of minorities and women in employment improved considerably in the 1960s and 1970s, but it still fell well short of equality. Although newspaper managers acknowledged the need to integrate women and minorities more fully into their staffs, they conceived of these two groups differently. They considered the lack of minorities serious and difficult to rectify, while they considered the lack of women trivial and far easier to address. As a result, they mishandled both groups. Because they believed integrating minorities to be so difficult, they often treated them as the "other" and made them feel unwanted. Because they failed to recognize the extent of the discrimination women faced, they did not go far enough to root it out. The *New York Times* provides a prime example of this dynamic.

A pair of memos Abe Rosenthal sent in the early 1970s illustrate how his views on minority journalists diverged from his views on women journalists. In 1971 he wrote to Scotty Reston, "By hook or by crook we are going to get more blacks on the paper because we need them. . . . There are not many first-rate ones around yet because this business was for so long exclusionary."[126] The following year he had a tepid response to a proposed affirmative action plan for women at the *New York Times*. The plan focused on areas "where we are already doing fairly well," he said, and he took issue with a suggestion that the paper step up its efforts to find qualified women reporters. "If we were able to hire as many reporters as we wanted, believe me, we would find no problem at all in getting totally qualified women in virtually every field. The country is full of them."[127] Talented black journalists, in this view, were rarities to be sought out actively, whereas talented female journalists abounded and would eventually succeed without any special measures being taken by management.

Many newspapers created special training programs for minority journalists to address the perceived lack of qualified candidates. The *New York Times* in 1972 discussed taking two or three black employees who worked outside the newsroom and training them to become copy editors.[128] The *Los Angeles Times* in 1983 created a Minority Editorial Training Program (METPRO), in which minority college students and recent graduates spent a year at the paper taking courses and learning the basics of reporting; this training was intended to prepare them for a job at the *L.A. Times* or other leading news organizations.[129] Programs such as these, well intentioned though they might be, smacked of paternalism and conveyed the impression that minorities were not naturally fit for the newsroom. As a 1979 article about race in journalism stated, "Minority reporters are especially sensitive to the implication that all of them, irrespective of talent or experience, need special handling in order to compete."[130] Indeed, some white journalists intimated that their black colleagues had been hired because of their race and not their ability. Gerald Boyd, who joined the *New York Times* Washington bureau in 1981, recalled one senior editor welcoming him by saying, "I really enjoyed your clips. They're so well-written. Did you write them yourself or did someone write them for you?"[131]

Women might also find their abilities questioned, but their grievances were more likely to be dismissed as overblown. The glacial progress in promoting women to editorial decision-making positions demonstrated management's belief that there was no systemic problem and that the imbalance would fix itself over time. Despite the slew of gender-discrimination lawsuits against news organizations, in 1975 the newspaper industry's premier trade publication still found it acceptable to ridicule women seeking equal opportunity in journalism. That year the *Bulletin of the American Society of Newspaper Editors* had a male journalist contribute a dispatch from an event billed as the National Conference on Women in the Media. He concluded his tongue-in-cheek article by writing, "It is my solemn and onerous duty to report that it looks as if the good times are over. The day is coming, if it is not already here, when it may be impossible for a hiring editor to look at a chick just out of journalism school and only see a pair of boobs."[132]

By the end of the 1970s, women and minorities alike continued to face unequal treatment in the newsroom, but women were on their way to far greater integration and influence. In large part that was a result of simple demographics. The *L.A. Times* 1973 affirmative-action policy stated that the *Times* wished "to achieve a level of minority and female employment in parity with the work force in the combined Los Angeles and Orange County area."[133] Most other newspapers had similar goals, and pursuing them ensured that women would constitute a far greater proportion of newsroom staff than minorities; their perspective would become impossible to ignore, and they would be less likely to feel alienated from the rest of the staff.[134]

By the end of the 1970s women would have far fewer complaints about news coverage than they had at the beginning of the decade. The most frequent complaint concerned story placement: articles about the women's movement and individual women's achievements sometimes appeared in lifestyle sections rather than in "hard news" sections, like main news and business.[135] This was a valid point, especially as it applied to strictly political stories, such as a report on the National Women's Conference that appeared, as one reader put it, "juxtaposed between the blithering Bianca

Jagger and a dippy bunch of 'tennis mothers.'"[136] But articles pertaining to women appeared throughout the paper, rather than being strictly confined to one section as in the past. Moreover, stories generally got better display and more space in the View section of the *Los Angeles Times* or the Family/Style section of the *New York Times* than they would get on an inner page of the main news section.[137] As the View editor Jean Sharley Taylor wrote to one disgruntled reader in 1979, "View has not been a social section for a long, long time, and its coverage of human and economic trends—of interest to both men and women—has consistently been ahead of the best in the country."[138] Responding to a fellow journalist who objected to an article about prominent women writers appearing on the Family/Style page, Abe Rosenthal explained that if the Family/Style page were to present "important stories on important subjects," it would have to include stories that could fit just as easily into other sections of the paper. To limit the page "news of the home and fashion" would be "to go backward journalistically," he said.[139]

With this explanation Rosenthal implied that a double standard still existed for judging a new story's importance: while some news related to women went in the main news sections and some in the renamed, revamped women's section, *all* news related to men went in the main news sections. Compared to the sexist practices of earlier years, however, that double standard was relatively benign. In an indication of how much had changed since the press's mocking treatment of the 1968 Miss America protests a decade earlier, NOW cofounder Betty Friedan wrote to Abe Rosenthal to praise the *New York Times*'s coverage of the 1978 Equal Rights Amendment campaign. She voiced her approval that "it started on the front page and continued on the news page[s] every single day—just like serious political news about men."[140]

Providing quality coverage of issues that male editors had previously ignored or consigned to the women's pages came easily. After all, that fit in with the goals of making news coverage relevant to readers' daily lives and focusing on "soft" topics such as lifestyle trends, the family, health, ideas, and profiles. Providing quality coverage of poor, inner-city communities, on the other hand—something about which many minority journalists felt strongly—was much harder. Given the crisis facing most major cities in the 1970s, stories about crime, hopelessness, and despair stood out, resulting in an overwhelmingly negative portrayal of communities of color.[141] This troubled black journalists such as Robert Maynard, who had worked at the *Washington Post* and later became editor and publisher of the *Oakland Tribune*. "What we now seek is portrayals of our communities as places inhabited by real people, not pathological fragments," he explained in 1979.[142]

The foremost example of a "pathological fragment" came in 1980, when the *Washington Post* published a front-page article, titled "Jimmy's World," about an eight-year-old heroin addict living in southeast Washington, D.C. It was full of stereotypical depictions of black pathology: a world of absent fathers, rape, despair, and nihilism, in which Jimmy's mother didn't even care to give him a name when he was born. "Drugs and black people been together a long time," she is quoted as saying to rationalize her son's heroin habit.[143] Some in the *Post* newsroom doubted the story's veracity, especially after a seventeen-day search by the Washington police—in response to the public outcry the article caused—failed to locate Jimmy. But the paper stood by its reporter, a young African-American woman named Janet Cooke, who had been hired less than a year earlier. The following spring, "Jimmy's World" won the Pulitzer Prize for feature writing. The prize announcement, however, brought renewed scrutiny to Cooke and her article, and her editors began to doubt her truthfulness after realizing she had lied on her résumé about her educational background. Under intense questioning, she eventually admitted that "Jimmy" did not exist. She gave back her Pulitzer Prize and resigned from the *Post*.[144]

The "Jimmy's World" debacle illustrated some of the shortcomings of the mainstream press's efforts at becoming more racially integrated. Editors often claimed to want stories that showed the richness and variety of life outside their own white, upper-middle-class world; but what they really wanted, many black journalists sensed, were stereotypical depictions of black pathology. The *Washington Post*, the 300 other papers that reprinted Cooke's story, and the Pulitzer Prize committee confirmed this.[145] Additionally, the reaction to Cooke's downfall revealed the suspicion with which many white journalists viewed their black colleagues. Several articles, including the *Post*'s ombudsman's report, suggested that Cooke had received special treatment because of her race; some claimed she had sullied the reputation of all black journalists.[146]

Leaping to conclusions about favoritism and affirmative action run amok showed a misunderstanding of the facts in the case. Cooke lied on her résumé because she knew that her unexceptional qualifications (bachelor's degree from the University of Toledo, a few years' experience on the *Toledo Blade*) never would have landed her an interview at the *Post,* regardless of her race. As she said years later in her only interview about the scandal, "My goal was to create Supernigger."[147] Upon being hired, Cooke did not join the main news staff. Instead she was assigned to the Weeklies section—"the *Post*'s boot camp, peopled with interns and probationers, most of them minority or female." Her primary motivation for fabricating the Jimmy story, according to the former colleague who interviewed her, was to escape the "ghetto" of the Weeklies.[148]

The "Jimmy's World" scandal notwithstanding, the efforts of women and minorities in the 1960s and 1970s led to major improvements in the press by 1980. Most newspapers became more inclusive in their employment practices and more sophisticated, empathetic, and fair in their coverage of groups and issues they had previously ignored or belittled. A month before the *Washington Post* published "Jimmy's World," the *Los Angeles Times* published an exhaustively reported, three-week-long series on life in Watts, fifteen years after the deadly riots that made it a household word. The articles discussed the neighborhood's problems with frankness and sensitivity, while also calling attention to some hopeful developments. It was an ambitious and impressively executed project, reported and written by black, white, and Latino journalists.[149]

Although these articles went unrecognized by the Pulitzer Prize committee, they outshine by any measure the 1965 *Los Angeles Times* series on Watts after the riots, which earned the paper a Pulitzer. The fact that the 1965 series won a Pulitzer while the 1980 series was not even a finalist indicates the extent to which newspaper journalism in general, and reporting on race and poverty in particular, had improved during those fifteen years. But the changes in attitudes toward women and minorities did not occur in isolation. As Chapter 6 will show, they were linked to broader changes in journalists' political beliefs and in the relationship between the press and the country's most powerful institutions.

❆ 6 ❆

The Press and the Powerful

From Allies to Adversaries

"WE ARE LIVING in a time of revolution," *Los Angeles Times* publisher Otis Chandler told a conference of his company's executives in May 1969. "You can go right down the list," he said: race, student unrest, riots, crime, pollution, wars, poverty, corruption. "It is a very difficult time to be in this business of reporting news, because people do not tend to agree with what you are saying to them. They don't want to hear the bad news."[1]

But it was not simply the tumultuous events of the day that made reporting so difficult; changes in journalists' practices and beliefs created a host of challenges that the press had not faced in previous generations. The first set of changes predated the "revolution" that Otis Chandler mentioned. During the early to mid-1960s, interpretive reporting became a central component of news coverage, transforming the reporter from stenographer to analyst. News articles would increasingly include the reporter's judgments about controversial issues, in addition to quotes and background information.[2] The second set of changes resulted from the revolutionary climate of the late 1960s and early 1970s. Even those journalists who remained wary of the era's radical movements recognized some truth in their critiques: the injustice of the Vietnam War, the systemic nature of racism and poverty, the self-interest and sometimes corruption of America's corporate and political class. These realizations led to a more skeptical, adversarial approach to news coverage.

Moreover, many journalists were swept up in the movements to remake American society, and their passion helped pull the entire profession to the left. News professionals following the precepts of objectivity tend to seek out a centrist position.[3] But in a newsroom where the main ideological division was between Cold War liberals and adherents of the New Left, the center could appear significantly to the left of what the country at large would consider the middle of the road. Journalists understood, of course, that the newsroom was not a microcosm of the nation, but even if they tried to correct for their own and their colleagues' political leanings, the views of the Silent Majority rarely merited the same respect as the views of the left. For one thing, leftist views seemed more newsworthy: calls for reshaping American society from colorful provocateurs made for better copy than calls for law and order or lower taxes from local chambers of commerce. (This would begin to change in the late 1970s, as the New Right adopted more effective media tactics.) Plus, newspapers worried greatly about failing to attract young readers, and because they believed the educated youth to be overwhelmingly left-wing, they wished to treat such ideas respectfully.

Vice President Spiro Agnew, in his speeches denouncing the news media in 1969 and 1970, suggested that journalists had adopted the anti-establishment attitude of the era. He had a point. They were more likely than in previous decades to challenge the White House, to write critically about powerful institutions, and to publicize the views of dissenters. They were, in some ways, imbued with the spirit of 1968, a year of protests, upheaval, and idealism. But to label this attitudinal shift "liberal bias," as Agnew did and as many others have done, oversimplifies the issue. It suggests that journalists are driven by a partisan agenda—that they treat conservatives and their causes harshly while treating liberals and their causes gently, with the goal (whether conscious or unconscious) of advancing the liberal causes. On certain social issues, such as abortion or gay rights, journalists often do allow their personal sympathies for the liberal position to influence their coverage. The *New York Times*'s first ombudsman, Daniel Okrent, acknowledged as much in a 2004 column.[4]

Author Eric Alterman, in a book devoted to the proposition that liberal media bias is a myth, also conceded that reporting on many social issues reflects reporters' liberal sympathies. But as Alterman argues convincingly, that rarely occurs in other areas of the news, especially not in national politics and elections.[5]

In his memoir, the prominent Washington columnist and pundit David Broder brushed off the accusation of left-wing ideological bias in the newsroom, saying, "There just isn't enough ideology in the average reporter to fill a thimble."[6] That depends on how one defines ideology. Certainly, few journalists were devoted followers of Karl Marx or Ayn Rand, but as a group, they were far more likely than the population at large to share certain ideological values. Those values included a sympathy for the perceived underdog, a distrust of concentrated power, and a belief in government's responsibility to address social and economic ills. Sociologist Herbert Gans, in his study of journalists' practices, concluded that their "enduring values are very much like the values of the Progressive movement of the early twentieth century."[7] Gans classified that movement as neither liberal nor conservative, but in its attitude toward government and big business, it was undoubtedly liberal by contemporary standards.[8] Mainstream journalists generally did not set out to take down Richard Nixon or to undermine U.S. efforts in Vietnam, as Agnew and other alleged, but their professional ideals did change profoundly during the late 1960s and early 1970s. As these changing attitudes seeped into journalism from the broader culture, the Nixon administration expedited the process.

• • •

THE AMERICAN PRESS had a long tradition of claiming an adversarial role in its dealings with government, but during the early Cold War period most newspapers merely paid lip service to it. They might oppose the government in strongly worded editorials, but news coverage rarely challenged official statements, and investigative reporting on Washington, the statehouse, or city hall was a rarity. The mainstream press and other powerful institutions in the 1950s and early 1960s were associates, not adversaries. The *New York Times,* wrote journalist Richard Rovere in 1962, was "the official Establishment daily."[9] The *Los Angeles Times* was essentially a vehicle for the interests of Southern California business, and by the admission of its future editor-in-chief, "a propaganda organism . . . of the Republican Party."[10] Some journalists recognized that they may have become too cozy with the powerful. As *New York Times* managing editor Clifton Daniel said in a 1960 speech, "There was a time when newspapermen seemed to be more outspoken than they are today, more contemptuous of authority, more defiant of restraints on their freedom." That attitude had diminished, Daniel said, because "we are engaged in a desperate competition with world communism," but he suggested that the press would benefit from an injection of that lost verve.[11]

The idea of being outspoken, defiant, and contemptuous of authority sounded fine in the abstract, but the *New York Times* applied it unevenly in the early 1960s—especially when questions of America's national interest and the "competition with world communism" were at stake. In April 1961 the paper had a potentially explosive story about the CIA training Cuban anticommunist guerrillas for an imminent invasion of the island at a location known as the Bay of Pigs. Publisher Orvil Dryfoos and Washington bureau chief James "Scotty" Reston, however, worried that running the article as planned—under a large, two-column headline on the front page—could jeopardize the operation and damage national security. As a result, the paper removed any references to the imminence of the invasion and to the CIA's role in training the guerrillas. While the article remained on page one, the headline was toned down, and much smaller.[12] On other occasions, the paper did not comply with government requests to alter their coverage in deference to national security, as when, in 1963, President Kennedy pressured publisher Arthur Ochs "Punch" Sulzberger to reassign reporter David Halberstam from the Saigon bureau. (Kennedy objected to Halberstam's pessimistic reports about the U.S. military's efforts in Vietnam.) Sulzberger refused, and Halberstam was told to postpone a planned vacation so it would not appear that the *Times* was wavering; Halberstam's articles later won the Pulitzer Prize.[13] Yet the fact that Kennedy felt comfortable making such a request testifies to the nature of the relationship.

Rarely do profound shifts in attitude occur at a precise moment, but 1965 marked a key tipping point. The first major student uprising (the Free Speech Movement at Berkeley) had recently begun and the first mass protests against the Vietnam war took place—unmistakable signs that dissent and radicalism were on the rise, especially among the young. As civil rights leaders turned their attention to the North, and as the Watts riots in August 1965 eclipsed the previous summer's inner-city disturbances, it became clear that racial discord was intensifying, despite the passage of two landmark civil rights bills. In truth, the phenomena that most people associate with "the sixties"—mass protests, campus radicalism, social change, the rise of the counterculture—characterized the decade from 1965 to 1974 more than the decade from 1960 to 1969.[14]

Similarly, the professional norms of journalism changed around 1965. Journalists no longer felt a responsibility to protect politicians or to take them at their word when they invoked the national interest. Examining the attitudes and behavior of top *New York Times* editors in 1964 versus 1966, the contrast is striking. In 1964 managing editor Clifton Daniel wrote to a colleague that he had "heard several people remark" about how President Lyndon Johnson could be "extraordinarily demanding and abusive" toward his staff. However, he continued, "this is a very delicate matter and one that I don't think we should mention in the paper unless it comes in some way to public notice."[15] By 1966 such judgments no longer went unquestioned. When national editor Claude Sitton removed a passage from an article about Israeli general Moshe Dayan because he felt it "would inevitably call into question the general's reputation," Washington editor Tom Wicker was appalled. "I do not understand our business to be the protection of reputations," he told Sitton. "I had always thought . . . that our business is to get as nearly at the facts and publish as much of the truth as we can. Therefore, I am at a loss to understand why we did not publish the Dayan story."[16]

Other news outlets showed less restraint than the *New York Times* concerning stories that might embarrass the powerful. While Clifton Daniel in 1964 had advised against reporting how "abusive" Lyndon Johnson was toward his staff, in 1966 *Parade* magazine (which came bundled inside hundreds of Sunday newspapers across the country) devoted an entire article to the topic. The piece began, "Not since slavery was abolished has the nation known a tougher taskmaster than Lyndon B. Johnson. He drives his staff 12 to 16 hours a day, scourges them with a whiplash tongue, intrudes on their private lives without apology, demands their total loyalty and utmost devotion."[17] Johnson wanted the press to make him look good, as they had done so often for his predecessor, Kennedy. The press rarely obliged. This stemmed in part from the stark contrast between the two men's personalities: the smooth, refined JFK versus the brash, crude LBJ. Johnson tried to win over influential journalists by entertaining them at his ranch in Texas, but this tactic often backfired. Instead of complimentary stories, the *New York Times* wrote about how Johnson drove his Lincoln Continental maniacally through a cow pasture, startling the animals with a bullhorn for no apparent reason.[18] The *Los Angeles Times* described how the president used his ranch to try to manipulate the press and to exert complete control over government information.[19] This frustrated Johnson to no end. As one White House reporter said in 1965, "He just can't understand how a reporter can write a critical story after he's been down on the ranch."[20]

But the newly critical tone of Washington reporting owed more to changes in the press than to a change of presidents. Clifton Daniel, who advised extreme deference toward the White House in 1964, had moderated his views by 1966. That June he gave a speech condemning his paper's handling of the Bay of Pigs story five years earlier, saying that if the *Times* and other newspapers "had been more diligent in the performance of their duty," the disastrous invasion might have been averted. "It is our duty as journalists and citizens to be constantly questioning our leaders and our policy, and to be constantly informing the people," said Daniel. In addition to publishing a news article about Daniel's speech, the *Times* also printed copious excerpts from it, taking up nearly an entire page in the main news section—an indication that his *mea culpa* represented the new position of the paper as a whole.[21] Assessing the state of the *New York Times* in 1965, journalist Roger Kahn wrote:

> The *Times* is trying to redefine the nature of its reporting. How much and how often should it break from its traditional policy of printing only what is announced? How can it best respond to the threatening field of news management? How can it contend with the efforts of politicians, lawyers, the medical lobby, civil-rights groups, police, to create and manipulate "news" for selfish ends? To what extent should the *Times* embark on the dangerous business of

investigative reporting, of looking for things that are not announced, even denied?[22]

In the ensuing decade, the *New York Times* would step decisively away from the practice of printing only what is announced and would begin, gradually, to move into the investigative field. This effort was already under way when Kahn's article appeared in October 1965. A team of reporters was preparing a five-part exposé about the CIA that would question whether the agency was out of control and its activities were detrimental to American interests. The series, published in April 1966, revealed the vast scale of CIA activities and the fact that the agency operated with little oversight from Congress or the White House.[23] Certainly the agency and many others in Washington would have preferred not to see these articles published. However, the series was not especially critical of the CIA. Its main conclusions were that more formal oversight would be counterproductive, and that for the agency to function properly, all it needed was a responsible director and a U.S. president willing to exercise close supervision (both of these conditions had been met, the articles implied, since the wakeup call delivered by the Bay of Pigs fiasco). Moreover, prior to publishing any of its articles about the CIA, the *New York Times* invited former CIA director John McCone to read the entire series and push back on anything he considered inaccurate, unfair, or a threat to national security.[24]

The *New York Times* and the government had been allies for much of the 1940s and 1950s, but by the mid-1970s they would become adversaries. The CIA series in 1966 kicked off the period of transition; produced in consultation with the agency, it raised probing questions but no alarms. Another *New York Times* investigation of the CIA, published in December 1974, illustrates the extent of the change. Written by Seymour Hersh, its lead sentence declared, "The Central Intelligence Agency, directly violating its charter, conducted a massive, illegal domestic intelligence operation during the Nixon Administration against the antiwar movement and other dissident groups in the United States, according to well-placed government sources."[25] No CIA director, it is safe to assume, was invited to vet that article prior to publication. The *Los Angeles Times* and most other news organizations underwent a similar transformation in their attitude toward government and toward concentrated power more generally. This transformation likely would have occurred regardless of the national political situation, but two factors made it occur quickly and decisively: Vietnam and Nixon.

• • •

DURING THE HEIGHT of U.S. involvement in Vietnam, from 1965 to 1973, the war was an omnipresent concern for most Americans, and for nearly all journalists. Of particular interest for journalists, however, was the so-called credibility gap: the fact that much of what the U.S. government was saying about the war—and therefore much of what the media reported—bore little relation to the truth.[26] Journalists who had worked in Vietnam felt especially angry about the government's obfuscations and its attempts to manipulate the press, because the coverage of the war, based on official sources, contradicted their firsthand knowledge. But eventually, as troop levels, bombing raids, and antiwar protests grew in tandem, it affected every working journalist, as a professional and as a citizen.

By the time the antiwar movement reached its zenith, in 1969–1970, few journalists could remain detached. Dennis Britton, then news editor of the *Los Angeles Times* Washington bureau, recalled the nationwide "moratorium day" protests in the fall of 1969, which called for a moratorium on U.S. bombing in Vietnam. "Most of us, if not all of us, were anti-war," said Britton. "We looked out on these demonstrators, and it was really inspiring and emotional." As a result, he said, some of the coverage was "overly sympathetic to the demonstrators. And pulling it back was hard for me and the other editors in the bureau, because we were sympathetic to the demonstrators. I hope that what came out was fair and balanced, but I don't know if I'd bet on that."[27] Other newspapers experienced similar issues. "We had a problem containing some of the reporters' personal feelings about the moratorium," *New York Times* Washington bureau chief Max Frankel wrote to Abe Rosenthal.[28] When a group of reporters at the *Wall Street Journal* decided to march in the protests, all that their bosses could do was insist that they not carry a sign reading "Wall Street Journalist for the Moratorium" (they worried that people who saw it might question the paper's objectivity).[29] At the magazine publisher Time Inc., employees not only joined the demonstrators, they circulated a petition calling for an "immediate and unilateral" U.S. withdrawal from Vietnam, standing in front of Time headquarters in midtown Manhattan to solicit signatures from passersby.[30]

The ongoing trauma of Vietnam established a baseline level of antagonism between the press and the government. That antagonism increased with each passing year, but several specific occurrences caused it to spike. Three of the most famous moments in twentieth-century American journalism occurred in the brief span from 1969 to 1973: the revelation of the My Lai Massacre, the publication of the Pentagon Papers, and the investigation into Watergate. All three had profound effects on the development of an adversarial press.

In September 1969 a U.S. Army public information officer in Georgia released the information that Lieutenant William Calley Jr. was being court-martialed for the murder of "an unspecified number of civilians in Vietnam." Tipped off to the significance of the case by a Pentagon source, Seymour Hersh, then a young freelance journalist, went after the story with great energy. After interviewing Calley and several soldiers under his command, Hersh wrote in shocking detail about the massacre of several hundred people, many of them women and children, at a hamlet called My Lai. Hersh believed that if he approached any major newspaper with the article, they would insist on rechecking all the facts "and then write their own story." So instead he offered it to two leading magazines, *Life* and *Look,* both of which turned him down. Hersh wound up selling the story to an upstart news agency called Dispatch News Service, which got it published in about thirty papers across the country on November 13, 1969.[31] One week later, as follow-up articles about My Lai began to appear, so did a series of graphic images taken by an army photographer, Ronald Haeberle, who was present at the massacre; one of them, on the cover of the *Cleveland Plain Dealer,* showed the bodies of more than a dozen women, children, and babies piled on a dirt road—this amplified the impact of the story enormously, as did subsequent television interviews with members of Calley's company.[32]

Journalists, like most Americans, reacted to the news about My Lai with shock and revulsion. Public opinion had already begun to turn against the war by this time, and My Lai surely caused many people to move from ambivalence to opposition. As Hersh himself noted shortly after he broke the story, "We're doing exactly the things we went into the war to stop."[33] But many journalists felt an additional pang when they saw the byline "Seymour M. Hersh, Dispatch News Service" under the biggest investigative story of the entire conflict. How did an unknown freelancer scoop the major news organizations that, collectively, had hundreds of experienced reporters covering Vietnam and the Pentagon?[34] Few of the men running those organizations had any ready answers. The head of United Press International (one of the two major wire services), while admitting his "embarrassment" at being scooped by Hersh, noted that because no reporters were on the scene at My Lai, the press was "at the considerable mercy of military information officers"—a particularly weak excuse, given that a military information officer released the information about Calley's arrest.[35] *Los Angeles Times* editor-in-chief Nick Williams simply said that his paper was "a little too deliberate in pursuing our own independent investigation" of My Lai; they declined to buy Hersh's piece, he explained, because they would not have the option of "checking out the details" themselves before publishing it.[36]

Many journalists likely agreed with the explanation from the *Village Voice,* the left-wing weekly that was unrelentingly critical of the mainstream press. "Editors of the country's major newspapers live in dread of stories which will be considered irresponsible," wrote Judith Coburn and Geoffrey Cowan. "In their view, although many of them would deny it, the press is the fourth branch of government: information source, confidant, friendly critic." Because they were too prone to self-censorship, too wary of challenging the government, they lacked the "independence or imagination to track down" stories such as My Lai.[37] Hersh himself pointed to "self-censorship by the reporters" as a major reason the mainstream press failed to beat him to the My Lai story.[38]

The same day that Seymour Hersh's first report on My Lai appeared, Vice President Spiro Agnew gave his first speech about the news media, in which he accused television newscasters of injecting a left-wing bias into their reports and undermining the nation's efforts in Vietnam.[39] One week later, on November 20, 1969, photographs of the carnage at My Lai surfaced and newspapers ran the most shocking stories to date about the massacre, based on soldiers' firsthand accounts. Despite meeting no resistance, the company killed more than a hundred civilians in a casual, "business-like" manner—"women and children and old men mostly."[40] That night Agnew gave his second speech attacking the news media. This time he focused his ire on the printed press, especially the *New York Times* and the *Washington Post,* which he accused of slanting their news coverage to denigrate the Nixon administration, particularly on Vietnam. The timing was coincidental, but the confluence of Agnew's verbal assaults and the My Lai disclosures sent an unmistakable message to many journalists. The press's hesitancy to report a story that would anger the government nearly caused it to miss one of the most momentous revelations of the war. Simultaneously, the Nixon administration was trying to intimidate journalists, insulting their professionalism, and undermining their credibility with the public. Given these facts, journalists might logically conclude, the only proper position was an adversarial one.

A crucial test of this adversarial ethos came in 1971 when Daniel Ellsberg, a former Pentagon contractor who had worked on a top-secret history of U.S. involvement in Vietnam, decided to go public with the report's findings—to expose decades' worth of the government's bad decisions and lies. Ellsberg chose to leak what became known as the Pentagon Papers—roughly 7,000 pages—to the *New York Times,* entrusting them to Neil Sheehan, a reporter he had never met but whose work on Vietnam he admired.[41] Publishing reams of confidential military information would expose the paper to major legal repercussions and cause many Americans to question its patriotism, and the decision to do so came only after an intense back-and-forth between the paper's editors, lawyers, and publisher, with whom the responsibility ultimately lay. The company's law firm told Sulzberger that the government would sue the *Times* and win, but he disregarded that advice and sided with Scotty Reston, managing editor Abe Rosenthal, and in-house counsel James Goodale, who argued that the *Times* had a responsibility to share this information with the public regardless of the consequences.[42] Conscious of the adversarial mood in the newsroom, Rosenthal told Sulzberger that if they chose not to publish, "it would make a mockery of everything we ever told reporters, because how could we possibly ask them to go out in search for the truth when at a time when the ultimate truth, the biggest story ever presented to The Times, had been placed in our laps and we turned away from it out of fear of the consequences of publication."[43] The first installment of the Pentagon Papers series appeared on June 13, 1971.

Although the Pentagon Papers said nothing about the Nixon administration's conduct in Vietnam (the study concluded in 1967), the White House was furious about the leak. When Sulzberger refused Attorney General John Mitchell's request that he cease publication of the series, the government obtained a temporary injunction against the *New York Times* to prevent the release of any additional material. But Ellsberg, anticipating this possibility, had more copies on hand, portions of which he distributed to the *Washington Post,* the *Boston Globe,* and several other newspapers. Despite entreaties and warnings from the government, those papers, too, published articles based on the Pentagon Papers, and they too became the targets of injunctions. With the administration suing the country's leading newspapers in an effort to restrict their most cherished right—the right to publish what they wished—what journalist would deny that they were adversaries? The Supreme Court put an end to this escalating battle between the administration and the press on June 30, 1971. In a 6–3 decision, the justices ruled that the government could impose "prior restraint"—that is, dictate in advance what cannot be printed—only when publication posed a "grave and irreparable danger" to the nation. The Pentagon Papers, the court said, did not meet that standard. During the Pentagon Papers furor, the *Washington Post* published an article discussing the press's adversarial relationship with the government throughout U.S. history. The reporter brought up many examples, but tellingly, the Pentagon Papers was the first since World War II.[44]

By the time the Watergate scandal broke in 1972, few journalists required additional convincing that they should adopt an adversarial posture toward the government. But Watergate gave them greater confidence in that belief, as nearly every aspect of the affair seemed to validate the notion of adversarial journalism. In the early stages of the story, few newspapers apart from the *Washington Post* pursued it doggedly, wary of appearing to target Nixon unfairly in an election year, and dubious that the White House could have masterminded so crude and brazen a scheme as to break into Democratic Party headquarters, steal files, and plant listening devices. Eventually, thanks to Bob Woodward and Carl Bernstein's reporting, other news organizations—especially the *New York Times* and the *Los Angeles Times*—realized they had been too cautious, not adversarial enough, and they scrambled to catch up. The *New York Times* had recently hired Seymour Hersh, whom they assigned to Watergate, and sent investigative reporter Nicholas Gage from New York to Washington to dig up some exclusives; the *Los Angeles Times* shifted many of its Washington resources to Watergate, with the bureau's news editor, Dennis Britton, admonishing the reporters to "get off your ass and knock on doors."[45]

Nixon's aides famously compiled several lists of the president's perceived opponents, intending to "use the available federal machinery to screw our political enemies." While the Nixon enemies came from various fields—politics, business, labor, entertainment, academia—the largest contingent came from the media.[46] When the U.S. Senate's investigation revealed the Nixon "enemies list" in June 1973, it came as no surprise to the Washington bureau of the *L.A. Times;* they had recently realized that all six reporters and editors working on the Watergate story were being audited by the IRS; none had ever been audited previously. "Once we figured that out, it was very difficult not to be really pissed," Dennis Britton recalled.[47]

The push for a more adversarial press came mainly from reporters and midlevel editors, but it filtered upward. In early 1970, when a group of disgruntled *New York Times* journalists came together to challenge Abe Rosenthal's direction of the newsroom, they had a hard time agreeing on a specific set of grievances.[48] But when they eventually met with Rosenthal and his assistant to hash out their differences, "they questioned whether The Times was doing enough in its role of adversary to the government"—that was the first issue they raised, according to Rosenthal's assistant's summary of the meeting.[49] The most prominent people in journalism—columnists, editors-in-chief, publishers—maintained cordial personal relationships with the people and institutions their papers challenged or investigated, but the mutual trust had dissipated. In an earlier era Scotty Reston had been the exemplar of access journalism—he cozied up to the Washington elite in order to present an insider's view of politics. But by 1972 even Reston had embraced adversarialism, as he demonstrated in a speech to the American Society of Newspaper Editors:

[Spiro Agnew] prefers the reporting of the last generation, and I have to admit that it was a lot chummier then than now. . . . We were in those days far too close to the men in power, and therefore, far too inclined to let our sympathy or affection for them get in the way of our work. . . . Conflict between the government and the press is unavoidable and even desirable. . . . If I have to come out plain against our profession, my complaint is, not that it has been too tough and skeptical, but too easy and too trustful.[50]

Some might attribute the increasingly adversarial relationship between the press and the government solely to journalists' antipathy toward the Nixon administration and the passions inflamed by the Vietnam War. To be sure, this was a major factor. Many, perhaps most, journalists felt an intense loathing for Nixon—they considered him a liar, a sleaze, and an enemy of press freedom.[51] The feeling of contempt was mutual. With the notable exception of Henry Kissinger, who formed strategically friendly relationships with many journalists, the Nixon team never envisioned anything but an adversarial relationship with the press. They occasionally had cordial exchanges when the administration received favorable coverage, but neither side expected that to be the norm. In December 1968 the president-elect told his cabinet appointees, "Always remember, the men and women of the news media approach this as an adversary relationship."[52] As the White House's clashes with the news media became increasingly public, members of the administration explained away the controversies by saying that adversarialism was desirable. The relationship between the media and government should be "adversary, probing, and suspicious," Spiro Agnew said in 1971. In a 1972 op-ed in the *New York Times,* Nixon's communications director, Herb Klein, wrote that "the adversary relationship between government and the press . . . is healthy and necessary."[53] As if to underscore the point and infuriate journalists, he added, "so certainly is an adversary relationship in some ways between the public and the press."[54]

As the Nixon administration increased the bombing in Vietnam and expanded the raids into Cambodia and Laos, the indignation of antiwar journalists grew. Reporting on the prevailing attitude of reporters toward Nixonites at the 1972 Republican National Convention, journalist Richard

Reeves quoted a *New York Times* reporter who said, "I can't even speak to them without remembering that I hate them." This reporter was no New Left activist but a middle-aged "Clark Kent" type "noted for his fairness." Reeves added, "I picked him at random—at least half the reporters I met were saying the same thing several times a day."[55]

•   •   •

THE INCREASE IN ADVERSARIAL journalism was not merely a reflection of anti-Nixon sentiment; if that had been the case, the phenomenon would have been restricted mainly to national politics. In fact, the press's approach to nearly every topic became more adversarial. The shift began with the coverage of government, but not only at the national level. In New York and Los Angeles, the relationship between the city's leading newspaper and the municipal power structure changed dramatically in the 1960s and early 1970s.

The story of *Los Angeles Times* reporter Ruben Salazar helps illustrate the broader transformation of the paper. Born in Juarez, Mexico, Salazar grew up just across the border in El Paso, Texas, eventually becoming a reporter for the *El Paso Herald-Post* before moving to California and getting a job with the *L.A. Times* in 1959.[56] He married an Anglo woman who worked in the paper's classified ads department, and they made a home in conservative, lily-white Orange County. Salazar was a talented, tenacious reporter, but not a boat-rocker. As his daughter later said, "My father led a completely Anglo life. He was a professional. He was part of the Establishment."[57] His 1963 series on Mexican-Americans in Los Angeles (discussed in Chapter 5) raised hackles among some conservative Chandler family members but was "tame by later standards," as Chandler biographer Dennis McDougal puts it.[58]

In 1965 Salazar began a year-long assignment in Vietnam, and his writing began to show an increasing tendency to challenge those in power. He infuriated his military minders when he wrote that the Viet Cong was openly selling a communist propaganda magazine "right under GI noses," in a town where more than 15,000 U.S. soldiers were based.[59] When Los Angeles mayor Sam Yorty traveled to South Vietnam in December 1965, Salazar wrote dismissively about the visit, questioning the value of such "whirlwind trips" by American dignitaries; he noted that Yorty

Ruben Salazar, who experienced a political awakening as a *Los Angeles Times* reporter and columnist before being killed while covering a protest in 1970. Photo: Copyright © 1970 Los Angeles Times. Used with permission.

had accidentally misplaced $430 worth of traveler's checks at a cocktail party and that he had sustained a "war wound" when he bumped his head on the low-slung roof of a field hospital.[60] Yorty accused Salazar of "distortions and lies" and called the paper's coverage "very wrong and very evil."[61]

By the time he returned to Los Angeles in 1968, Salazar had experienced something of a political awakening and identified strongly with the Chicano movement, which demanded greater rights and respect for Latinos.[62] His dispatches for the *Times* in 1969 included front-page articles about students protesting for the right to speak Spanish and about the impact of U.S. drug interdiction efforts on everyday people in Mexican border towns.[63] When Salazar decided to give up daily newspaper reporting to become the news director of a local Spanish-language TV station, the *Times* offered him a part-time position as a columnist, writing about Latino affairs. As *Newsweek* observed, "Salazar regularly turns in hard-hitting weekly columns attacking 'Anglo' racism and voicing serious Mexican-American grievances."[64] He also questioned police tactics in dealing with minority communities (in his column and on TV), much to the LAPD's annoyance. Officers visited Salazar and urged him to tone down his criticism, lest he rile up the Latino community; instead, Salazar wrote in his column about the officers' attempt to pressure him, further embarrassing the department.[65]

On August 29, 1970, Salazar was covering an antiwar demonstration in East Los Angeles dubbed Chicano Moratorium Day. When it began to turn violent, he and his TV crew temporarily retreated into a bar for safety. A few minutes later a sheriff's deputy fired a tear-gas projectile into the bar, allegedly on the belief that a man with a gun was inside. The projectile struck Salazar in the head and killed him instantly. Although no charges were brought, many of Salazar's friends in the journalism community and in the Chicano community suspected foul play on the part of law enforcement.[66] Salazar had begun his career at the *L.A. Times* as a member in good standing of Southern California's conservative establishment. A decade later, he had become so great an antagonist to that establishment that it was not farfetched to think that municipal authorities might have had him killed.

Prior to the 1960s the *L.A. Times* editor in charge of covering city hall, Carlton Williams, was mainly interested in influencing policies, not in ferreting out the truth for his paper's readers. Williams reputedly roamed the city council chambers and instructed members on how they should vote. One councilman who opposed the *L.A. Times* quipped that Williams "ought to wear a ringmaster's uniform and carry a whip."[67] The paper could be scathing in its treatment of mayoral candidates it opposed, but that was just politics—once the campaign passed, they sought a mutually beneficial relationship with city hall. So in 1961, when Democrat Sam Yorty challenged the *Times*-backed incumbent, Republican Norris Poulson, the paper inveighed against Yorty in its editorials and played up Poulson's accusations that his opponent was corrupt. Yorty, in response, called Poulson a puppet of the *L.A. Times* and questioned his close relationship with Carlton Williams.[68] After Yorty defeated Poulson, however, he and the *Times* reconciled, and the paper's editorial page supported his bid for reelection in 1965. But Carlton Williams had retired by that time, and the journalistic ethos at the *Times* had changed—Yorty would not receive any favorable treatment in the news columns. Indeed, he repeatedly complained to Otis Chandler that the paper's coverage of him was too tough.[69]

Yorty was a pugnacious character, and after he won reelection with the *L.A. Times*'s support, he and the paper became bitter enemies. When Otis

Chandler remarked at a 1966 awards reception that Yorty had not dealt effectively with the question of race since the previous summer's riots, Yorty called a press conference at which he challenged Chandler to a public debate "before any audience in the city." He noted that 20 percent of the municipal workforce was African-American, adding pointedly, "I wonder what percentage of the employees of the *Times* are Negro. How many Negroes are on the board of directors of the Times Mirror Company?"[70] (The answer to the latter question, of course, was zero.)

Whereas in previous decades the *Los Angeles Times* might have been content to snipe at Yorty in editorials and publicize the accusations of his opponents, by the 1960s it was becoming an investigative newspaper. In 1967 the paper published two major exposés revealing corruption in the city administration—first on the zoning board, and then on the Harbor Commission. One member of the zoning board resigned over the scandal, and four members of the Harbor Commission were indicted on bribery and perjury charges. Two of the four were convicted and served prison terms, and the *Times* investigation won a Pulitzer Prize.[71] Yorty denounced the exposés as politically motivated and later alleged that "the publisher of this great paper owns the district attorney, and the two of them appear to be in a conspiracy to try and get the mayor."[72] The *Times*-Yorty feud reached a new height in 1968 when the mayor sued the newspaper for libel over an editorial cartoon implying that he was insane (Yorty sought $2 million in damages; a judge promptly dismissed the case).[73]

The *L.A. Times* relationship with the Los Angeles Police Department, once characterized by beat reporters sharing drinks with cops who gave them access to crime scenes, also changed, as Ruben Salazar's story demonstrates vividly. The paper's conservative business manager, Robert Nelson, felt the situation had become so dire that he must intervene to help patch up the relationship between the *L.A. Times* and the LAPD. Nelson arranged for police chief Ed Davis to meet with the *Times* city editor and managing editor. However, when editor-in-chief Nick Williams got wind of this, he was furious. "I told [Nelson] that under no account would they ever go to a meeting like that, they were not to attend," Williams recalled.[74] Williams was no liberal, but he recognized that the norms of journalistic practice had changed. The disgruntled Chief Davis, Williams likely presumed, would use such an informal meeting to either

"I've got to go now. . . . I've been appointed Secretary of
Defense and the Secret Service men are here!"

Los Angeles Times editorial cartoonist Paul Conrad, widely considered one of the
two best cartoonists in the nation, often provoked strong reactions, especially
from conservative readers. This Conrad cartoon of Sam Yorty prompted the Los
Angeles mayor to (unsuccessfully) sue the *Times* for libel. Photo: Used with
permission of the Conrad Estate.

intimidate the editors or try to ingratiate himself with them. Nevertheless, the paper remained wary of criticizing the police. When a reporter
on the scene of a campus protest at UCLA in May 1970 witnessed instances of police brutality, his editor initially insisted that the information be cut from the story, on the grounds that it could not be verified. Only
after the university chancellor expressed concern about excessive force
were the reporter's observations included (in a follow-up story).[75]

Then again, *L.A. Times* editors had reason to fear the police department's wrath. When the UCLA chancellor claimed to have been
misquoted regarding police brutality, Chief Davis labeled metropolitan editor Bill Thomas "public enemy number one" for stirring up an-

tagonism against the police. Although Davis relented after Thomas convinced him the chancellor had indeed been quoted accurately, relations between the paper and the police continued to deteriorate.[76] As a 1977 monograph about the *L.A. Times* noted, "*Times* reporters, often caught in the middle of conflicts between the police and the black, brown, and student communities, more and more began to view clashes involving the LAPD from the point of view of the victim."[77]

In a front-page article in March 1975, editor-in-chief Bill Thomas acknowledged that a major change had occurred. "Until about 10 years ago," he wrote, crime reporting relied solely on police sources, and "one heard little from . . . the accused criminal." As a result of broader societal changes, "the newspaper today reflects far more diverse views," Thomas explained. "And to some policemen who see themselves accused by those they view as society's enemies, the newspaper is anti-cop." But in truth, according to Thomas, news coverage had simply become fairer and more complete.[78]

Chief Davis disagreed. Five months later he sent a letter to publisher Otis Chandler canceling his subscription. He requested that it be printed in full, and the *Times* complied. "In your 1975 war on me, almost every reporter who has had any part of reporting anything I have said has engaged in repeated, slanted reporting and downright lies," Davis wrote. He called the *Times* "a journalistic liar," adding, "the soul of your paper is sick."[79] Looking back at the feud with Davis years later, Thomas seemed unperturbed by it, saying the chief's attacks were "tongue in cheek," meant to bolster police morale. "When he made his case against the *Times,* which he did frequently, I always thought I saw a twinkle," Thomas wrote in an unpublished memoir.[80] Like most leading newspaper editors, Thomas believed in an adversarial press and he believed in the importance of staking out a middle ground. With many critics assailing the *Times* for its cozy relationship with the downtown establishment, the paper could cite its feud with Chief Davis to show that it was not afraid to challenge powerful public officials.[81]

The *New York Times,* too, developed a more adversarial relationship with its local government in the late 1960s. Like many newspapers, for decades it had a tacit understanding with the police force: the paper got special treatment and news tips, and the police got sympathetic coverage.

When press cars were parked illegally or *New York Times* delivery trucks blocked traffic as they were being loaded with papers, officers looked the other way (or accepted payoffs).[82] Reporters did special favors for beat cops and police officials, hoping to be rewarded with news scoops later on.[83] As late as 1968, *New York Times* management received advance notice when the police planned to evict student protesters from several administration buildings at Columbia.[84] *Times* journalists knew that corruption was rampant in the NYPD, but for years they declined to report on it. While researching a story about drug addiction in Greenwich Village in 1964, reporter Martin Arnold learned that police officers frequently extorted money from drug dealers instead of arresting them; sometimes the cops even confiscated contraband and resold it themselves. Arnold's editor, Arthur Gelb, recalled, "We were unable, however, to print the accusations because those who made them would not stand behind them."[85] That excuse rings hollow. If the paper wished to expose this corruption, it could have devoted additional resources to the story and could have granted its sources anonymity.

The *New York Times*'s refusal to report critically on the police bothered some editors. In March 1966, as the paper was reporting on a series of inconsequential bureaucratic clashes between the police department and the mayor's office, assistant managing editor Harrison Salisbury vented his frustration to managing editor Clifton Daniel. "No one is talking about reality," Salisbury said in a memo. He explained:

> The reality of the police is this: The New York department has been run for years by what is called variously the Irish Mafia or the Brotherhood, an all-for-one-one-for-all group which protects each other and, also, and this is very very important, divides on a reasonable businesslike basis the cut from protection—the 10 bucks or $100 that *every* bar in the city pays off, the smaller payoffs of every local businessman who doesn't want his store windows kicked in, the much bigger payoffs of Con Ed, the truckers, the retailers, the 7th Avenue boys, etc. . . . Now, in addition to what might be called the "legitimate" take of the police from business there is also the criminal take from the bookies, the numbers, the dope runners, the prostitutes, the shakedown lads, the crooks of all kinds.[86]

The bureaucratic clashes and personnel changes, Salisbury explained, could jeopardize this arrangement. "That's what the police story is about," he concluded. "I'd like to see a whiff of it in the paper."[87]

No such whiff would appear, despite the fact that a top *New York Times* editor had detailed knowledge of criminal activity by the police. Several years passed before the *Times* blew the whistle on police corruption. As *Times* editor Arthur Gelb recounted in his memoir, things began to change in late 1967 when he hired David Burnham, who had previously worked for the President's Commission on Law Enforcement and Administration of Justice, to cover the police beat. Like any good police reporter, Burnham cultivated sources inside the department; unlike most, he did not shy away from critical stories. In December 1968 he revealed that police officers routinely slept on the job during their overnight shifts instead of patrolling the streets—a practice known in police slang as "cooping." When Burnham described the story to an assistant editor, he was advised to drop it,—"the *Times* was not interested in 'crusading' stories." That ethos had begun to change, however, and Gelb successfully pushed for Burnham's article to appear on page one.[88]

This and other stories by Burnham convinced two cops who were disgusted with their colleagues' corruption that the *New York Times* might help them expose the scandal. The cops, Frank Serpico and David Durk, collaborated with Burnham on a six-month investigation. Burnham's stories hit the front page in April 1970, describing in vivid detail the endemic corruption that Harrison Salisbury had painted in broad strokes in his internal memo four years earlier.[89] The police commissioner and his deputy resigned in the aftermath of the exposé, and Mayor John Lindsay appointed a commission to investigate police corruption. The *New York Times* would no longer be able to count on friendly treatment from the police, but the adversarial approach yielded a series that burnished the paper's reputation immeasurably. (Serpico's story formed the basis for the acclaimed 1973 film *Serpico,* starring Al Pacino.)

When John Lindsay launched his successful campaign for mayor of New York in 1965, the *Times,* like much of the national press and intelligentsia, was infatuated with him. A handsome, charming, liberal Republican reformer, Lindsay received blanket coverage in the news pages and sympathetic treatment in editorials.[90] "It was difficult not to be dazzled by his star quality," admitted Arthur Gelb, recalling a lunch that he and Abe Rosenthal had with Lindsay in 1965.[91] On election night, when Lindsay came away with a narrow victory, Rosenthal and Gelb reputedly rejoiced in the newsroom and yelled, "We won!" After the new mayor took office, Rosenthal socialized with Lindsay's campaign manager turned deputy mayor, Robert Price, who would show up in the newsroom and try to chat with reporters or sneak a glance at the stories they were working on.[92]

Even prior to the 1960s most *New York Times* journalists would have disapproved of such a chummy relationship between the editors responsible for covering city hall and a deputy mayor. But in the late 1960s most considered it appalling, and it could not last—especially not after Lindsay began failing to live up to his promise. Galled by Rosenthal's friendship with Price and by their paper's kid-glove treatment of Lindsay, the reporters had an "urge to stick their fingers in someone's eye," according to one of the paper's correspondents.[93] In 1968 and early 1969 the *Times* published several investigative stories that revealed waste and corruption in the Lindsay administration, infuriating the mayor and damaging his public image.[94] Still, the reporters remained on the lookout for any sign that the editors were going easy on the mayor. In August 1969, when the *Times* delayed publishing a story about Lindsay taking free trips on a corporate jet, it caused an uproar in the newsroom. As one of Rosenthal's deputies informed him, "Feelings on the staff ran *very* strong. . . . Our non-publication of [this] piece was seen as nothing less than a cover-up for Lindsay."[95]

• • •

ADVERSARIALISM DEVELOPED first in the coverage of politics and public affairs, but in the 1970s it began to take hold in what had been one of the most sedate newspaper sections: business. Traditionally the business section had consisted mainly of data on financial markets, summaries of major companies' earnings reports, and puff pieces on successful executives and new product launches. The *Los Angeles Times* in the 1950s would sometimes take corporate press releases and simply print them as news, without changing a word.[96]

As late as 1967 the corporate-booster ethos remained dominant, judging by a package of stories that the *Bulletin of the American Society of News-*

paper Editors published under the heading "Examining Bus-Fin [Business-Financial] Coverage." Fawning treatment was the norm. The editor of the *Chicago Daily News,* touting his business section's innovations, noted that they sought out local companies and rising executives to profile. An executive with the Gannett newspaper chain offered that at two of his company's papers, "one of the most popular features on the business section cover . . . is a daily photo of a pretty girl in local business." The editor of the *Buffalo Evening News* noted the difficulty of finding space to write about all the releases of new car models. Evidently he felt these should be covered as news, which in effect amounted to free advertisements: "Pictures and descriptions of new cars are offered to our readers in such profusion," he observed.[97] As a result of this complaisance on the part of business journalists, several major revelations about product safety and unethical business practices were exposed in the 1960s not by traditional reporters but by consumer advocates such as Ralph Nader— causing great embarrassment to the press.[98] By the mid-1970s, however, the dynamic had changed dramatically, especially at elite newspapers like the *New York Times* and the *Los Angeles Times.*

Before Otis Chandler took over the *L.A. Times* in 1960, the paper's publishers had been closely allied with the Merchants and Manufacturers Association, a pro-business lobby. By the mid-1970s, according to *L.A. Times* labor reporter Harry Bernstein, the group's members could not get Chandler or editor-in-chief Bill Thomas to even return their phone calls. So instead they called up a reporter and said, "rather plaintively, 'Is there any way you can get some coverage into the paper? Our annual meeting is coming up and we can't get a line into the *Times*.'"[99]

Bill Thomas was unmoved by complaints that his paper was biased against corporate interests, whether those complaints came from within the paper or from outside. On multiple occasions *L.A. Times* business manager Robert Nelson objected to articles by the syndicated columnist Mike Royko that criticized advertisers. When Royko in 1974 rebutted a suggestion from the head of General Motors that consumers should buy new, more fuel-efficient cars not only to boost the economy but also to support conservation, Nelson was beside himself. He told Otis Chandler that he could not believe "any editor would be stupid enough to publish such an article," referring to it as "industry assassination." Thomas

Bill Thomas, editor-in-chief of the *Los Angeles Times* from 1972 to 1989. Photo: Copyright © 1989 Los Angeles Times. Used with permission.

defended the article as a valid expression of opinion and argued that "the degree to which the piece dovetails with our advertisers' interests" should not factor into publication decisions.[100] When in 1975 the *L.A. Times* published a front-page story about the Los Angeles–based defense contractor Northrop treating legislators to all-expenses-paid hunting trips, one local chamber of commerce charged the paper with being "anti-business" and "intentionally trying to damage Northrop at a very critical time." Thomas responded, "To suggest . . . that we withhold legitimate news because its timing may be harmful to a particular business concern is to badly misread our obligations to all our readers."[101]

Many business leaders in the 1970s simply assumed the press was out to get them. They "often complain that many reporters are biased against the profit system," said CBS News president Arthur Taylor in 1975.[102] In 1977 an insurance executive matter-of-factly wrote to Abe Rosenthal about "the tendency of the business sections of the Times and other national newspapers to emphasize the 'bad news' side in reporting on financial and business matters."[103] In 1978 the former head of Time Inc., Louis Banks, warned that business leaders "have a growing contempt for mass journalism, and it is visceral, pervading." His article was headlined "Memo to the Press: They Hate You Out There."[104] *New York Times* publisher Punch Sulzberger summed up the most frequent complaints in a 1977 speech titled "Is the Press Anti-Business": "A great many businessmen suggest that a new tone is creeping into journalism. They find that the big corporation is *too* often portrayed as the villain, and the consumer movement as the hero. That bad news is reported with glee and good corporate news relayed grudgingly. That the profit motive is *derogated* by writers who seem to prefer more government control."[105]

The news executives trying to explain this antagonism all cited a change in journalistic practices and attitudes. Sulzberger told his corporate audience, "A more analytical—a more skeptical, sometimes more critical—approach is being taken. And this is not only true with business reporting. Government, education, the courts, and the press itself are subject to this new scrutiny." Before concluding, Sulzberger added that there should be a "healthy tension" between business and the press—"a relationship not quite so adversary as that which exists between press and government."[106] Two years earlier CBS's Arthur Taylor made an almost identical argument. "Recent years have seen . . . an increasing questioning of established institutions and established ways of doing things," he said. "Government has been questioned, as have religion, education, and journalism. Much of that heat has been directed at business as well." The "business-press relationship," Taylor argued, should be a "healthy adversarial relationship."[107]

Sulzberger adopted this viewpoint about business journalism after considerable soul-searching and hand-wringing. In 1974 he requested that each of his two top editors—managing editor Abe Rosenthal and Sunday editor Max Frankel—write an essay discussing the fairness of *Times* coverage and the perception among the business community that the paper was "too left" or "anticapitalist."[108] Frankel's memo exemplifies the new attitude that had developed in the late 1960s and early 1970s:

> Who is elected to run our major businesses, how they make their decisions and how they use their power and wealth to influence political life are all central issues in the news. In pursuing that news, major news organizations are no more "anti-business" than we are

"anti-government" when we ask the same questions of City Hall or the White House. If anything, as our more vigorous critics on the left have often contended, we have been more naturally and too easily "pro-business" and "pro-government" in our many routine and unquestioning reports of how politicians and corporate leaders define themselves and their works. . . . So if fairness is taken to mean that we report business the way it sees itself, we are going to disappoint the complainants.[109]

Most others in the *New York Times* newsroom likely shared these beliefs—the notion that big business was a "central issue" and not a specialized topic, that the press's attitudes toward business and government should be similarly adversarial, and that coverage needed to be re-centered after years of having been too soft. Sulzberger, were he to reject Frankel's viewpoint, would have been severely out of step with his staff.

Despite Sulzberger's acceptance of the new norms of adversarial reporting on business, he worried that his paper was antagonizing the business community unnecessarily—especially with its editorial page, which under the direction of John Oakes gained a reputation as hostile to big business. Although Oakes claimed not to be "anti-business," Sulzberger felt that his editorials gave a different impression—"We were undoubtedly perceived to be against big business," Sulzberger recalled.[110] An August 1976 *BusinessWeek* article about the *New York Times* called it "stridently anti-business in tone," and Sulzberger seems to have agreed—as did other members of the New York Times Company board of directors, who objected to Oakes's positions on governmental regulation and the environment.[111] Earlier that year Sulzberger had forced Oakes into an early retirement. In part, bureaucratic considerations drove the move: Sulzberger was consolidating the daily and Sunday operations of the paper under Abe Rosenthal, and he wanted to provide Sunday editor Frankel, whose job was being eliminated, with a top-level position so that he would not resign (Frankel became editorial-page editor and eventually succeeded Rosenthal as executive editor). But Sulzberger's frustration with the paper's reputation as antibusiness—much of which derived from the editorial page—was also a major factor.[112] As Frankel recalled, Sulzberger felt "that there was just a constant whipping in tone against the business community under Oakes. And he felt that the business community deserved to be treated a little more respectfully, even when we disagreed with what they were doing."[113]

• • •

IN A 1972 essay the conservative intellectual Irving Kristol argued that journalists prior to the 1960s were craftsmen putting out a fairly homogenized product: quotation-laden articles organized in the inverted pyramid style, with a sprinkling of uncontroversial background information. By the 1970s their education levels and their ambitions had risen dramatically, and they aspired to much more—journalism had become a calling rather than simply a craft. Summarizing the results of this shift, Kristol wrote, "Whereas journalism was always distrustful of all *public officials,* it is now distrustful of all *public authority:* the corrupt official has been replaced by the corrupt institution as journalism's natural enemy." Many journalists, he continued, saw themselves as "engaged in a perpetual confrontation with the social and political order (the 'establishment,' as they say)."[114] Kristol was engaging in a bit of hyperbole. Major news organizations were still part of the Establishment, and journalists sought mainly to hold powerful institutions accountable, not to discredit or subvert them. But many journalists had a natural inclination to distrust and challenge sources of authority, and developments in the late 1960s and early 1970s validated that inclination. Investigative journalists became the heroes of the profession—some, like Bob Woodward and Carl Bernstein, even became canonized in major Hollywood movies.[115] Journalists who had defied the government by writing skeptically about official claims that the United States was winning the Vietnam War in the early 1960s saw their reputations soar.[116]

Irving Kristol returned to the theme of journalists' newfound adversarialism in 1975, but this time he asserted that it was related to left-wing advocacy. "Most journalists today . . . are 'liberals' who believe in large and powerful government," he wrote. "They believe the United States government must help feed the world, defend and promote civil liberties throughout the world, mediate conflicts among the peoples of the world, redistribute income in favor of the poor and the unlucky, regulate the activities of the large corporations." These beliefs, Kristol argued, led journalists to the contradictory position of pushing for "more powerful and more extensive government" while simultaneously undermining public confidence in government with their adversarial reporting.[117] But in reality such beliefs—if indeed most journalists held them—were peripheral to most day-to-day reporting. Far more important was the belief in challenging the powerful, regardless of the political implications. That is why, as Kristol noted (undermining his own argument), "trade union leaders and university presidents, the political left as well as the political right" had become frustrated with journalism's adversary posture.[118] It is why Jimmy Carter received no more favorable coverage than Gerald Ford.[119]

The best evidence to show that the shift toward adversarialism had more to do with journalistic values than political ones can be found in the unlikeliest part of the newspaper: the sports section. When launching the Sports Monday section of the *New York Times* in 1977, deputy managing editor Arthur Gelb recalled that he wanted it cover sports "just the way city reporters wrote about politics or government," with "hard-hitting interviews" and frank analysis.[120] Sports reporters and their subjects had always been allies, to a far greater extent than metro reporters or Washington correspondents. By the late 1970s, however, most major news organizations advocated a more adversarial approach. As the sports editor of the Associated Press, Wick Temple, observed in 1977, "something has happened to the good old American sportswriter." Sports reporters were becoming indistinguishable from reporters on other sections of the paper, he noted. They were writing interpretive stories, sociological stories, and investigative stories, often incurring the wrath of their subjects in the process.

Temple wrote disparagingly of the old style of sportswriter who gave the profession "a bad name": "He takes free trips at the expense of the team, writes stories for team programs and is paid for them, scatters free tickets among his friends. . . . He is the darling of the sports establishment because he is a mouthpiece for the organization he is supposed to be covering. He sells tickets and protects the management point of view. . . . Fortunately, from the courthouse to the press box, the breed is vanishing."[121] Journalism's professional norms had changed to such an extent that a reporter would be ostracized for having a hand-in-glove relationship with his or her news subjects—even in sports, where such a relationship with the hometown team might be considered harmless.

• • •

EDITORS AND NEWS EXECUTIVES accepted the need to take a more adversarial approach because they believed the relationship between the press and the powerful was out of balance, too collusive. Even a critic of adversarial journalism like Irving Kristol conceded that before 1965, "most major newspapers . . . were 'co-opted' into the political establishment."[122] But by the mid- to late 1970s, many thought the pendulum had swung too far in the opposite direction. The press, said Otis Chandler in a 1975 interview, "[has] gone bananas following Watergate. We seem to have lost our sense of balance, our sense of proportion. . . . We seem to each day delight in jumping all over any new possible participant in some alleged illegal or unethical or unpopular act." Instead, they needed occasionally "to tell our readers that all is not lost, that much is good that is happening at city hall and on the campuses and in the state capitals and in Washington and even in the White House."[123]

In an interview with David Halberstam during the same time period, Chandler said that his national editor, Ed Guthman, had taken the adversarial approach too far. Guthman had been perceived as a potential successor to Nick Williams when he joined the *Los Angeles Times* in 1964, but over the years his star faded, and he left the paper in 1977.[124] He had "a different idea of journalism than we do," Chandler told Halberstam. "Ed really thinks that we should be looking under carpets and rocks all day long, at all levels of government, that there's nothing there but bad guys and we should be turning them over. And we don't really feel that. He is in a way more aggressive and assertive than we were."[125]

Chandler was not alone in suggesting that the investigative impulse sometimes needed to be restrained. In a 1976 column the liberal commentator Tom Braden noted that the *Washington Post* was "taking a verbal beating" for being too adversarial. He cited three recent stories as examples: one about a senator's son using food stamps, one about former vice president Hubert Humphrey being treated for a bladder ailment, and one about Secretary of State Henry Kissinger, years earlier, having tried to help his fiancée's brother get a government job. "What people are saying about The Post is that 'It's out to get,' that its tone is accusatory, that it sees cabals in chance encounters, plots in coincidences, and cover-ups in privacy," Braden wrote. He observed that "at the same time that investigative journalism is the rage . . . there seems to be a backlash developing against investigative journalism."[126]

There was also a backlash against overly aggressive business coverage. Writing in the mid-1970s, the onetime *Fortune* editor Louis Banks noted, "Most ranking editors of mass media see business as suspect until proven innocent. At the attitudinal level this means a greatly overweighted coverage of anti-business pronouncements." He added that "the latest vogue in business reporting," consumerism, "is attitudinally anti-business by definition, and the media is coming to have something of a vested interest in pushing coverage which, on net, provides a distorted view of reality."[127]

Banks reassessed the situation in a follow-up article in 1980. He used the metaphor of a staircase to describe the state of business reporting. In the mid-1970s, he argued, most business coverage had been stuck on "step one" of the staircase, a place where journalists see big business as "worth a story only when its pinstriped executives are hauled before some government agency. Coverage is usually by general assignment people whose instincts are political, rather than economic, and whose principal sources are usually adversaries of business." But by 1980, Banks wrote, many newspapers had ascended to step three. "The attitude [toward business] is one not of automatic hostility but of sophisticated curiosity. . . . The ultimate test of Step Three work is that business and labor people aren't entirely comfortable with the coverage of their own activities, but as readers they read with respect to learn what the rest of the business world is really up to."[128]

The shift that Banks detected in press coverage of business mirrored the shift in the attitude toward business in society at large. Alarmed by the consumer movement, the anticapitalist left, and the increase in government regulation, business leaders in the 1970s made concerted efforts to turn the tide of public opinion—and more importantly, legislation—back in their favor. New groups such as the Business Roundtable, along with revitalized old groups such as the Chamber of Commerce, mounted formidable lobbying and public relations campaigns.[129] Even on college campuses the image of corporate America had been rehabilitated by

1980—business was by far the most popular undergraduate major in the country, and organizations such as Students in Free Enterprise found a receptive audience for their message that a career in business was fun, exciting, and noble.[130]

As usual, the political climate of the country influenced journalists' ideas about the proper balance of coverage. Louis Banks, a pillar of the journalistic establishment, exemplified the attitude of many top editors.[131] He disparaged the old style of business journalism, "where corporate activities are accepted as news virtually at the handout level" and the editors "are friendly fixtures at Rotary or Chamber of Commerce meetings." The changes of the 1960s and 1970s brought some much-needed toughness, skepticism, and professionalism, he felt, but some over-eager journalists—products of "the turbulent sixties," in his words—had gotten carried away.[132] To achieve a new, more desirable balance, Banks implied, journalists had to stake out a middle ground, acting as neither toadies nor crusaders. When people on both sides of an issue were equally dissatisfied with the coverage, that indicated a job well done.

This notion of striking the right balance typified many journalists' thinking not only about business reporting but also about news coverage more generally. Abe Rosenthal recalled that he felt the *New York Times* had been "pulled off course and to the left in the late 60s and early 70s" but that by the 1980s it was back in the center, as it should be.[133] One might expect that sentiment from Rosenthal, who was more conservative than most *New York Times* journalists, but *Washington Post* reporter William Greider, who went on to work for the left-wing publications *Rolling Stone* and *The Nation,* felt the same way. Prior to the Nixon era, he told David Halberstam, the *Post* and other newspapers like it had "an almost institutional bias in favor of the White House and government and the established order." Then "the turbulence of the late 60s" had "jarred" the news media, which became overtaken by "irreverence" for orthodox society and authority. Looking back on the changes from the perspective of the late 1970s, he felt the press's antagonism toward the established order was "excessive," saying, "We were printing too much media theater, you know, kids chaining themselves to the Statue of Liberty."[134]

Otis Chandler stated a similar opinion even more bluntly in a 1976 speech. The news media, he said, "are going through a period of temporary insanity." He elaborated: "In our zeal to print the truth about everything and everyone, we have lost our perspective about our more traditional and certainly more sensible role of keeping the people informed. . . . I think the media have become too shrill, too unthinking, too uncaring, too bloodthirsty." This did not mean, however, that Chandler believed the press should revert to the journalistic practices of the 1950s. Because he was speaking to a group of advertising executives, he addressed the "conflict" between business and the media, but he did not apologize for the press's conduct or accept the accusation that it was anti-business. "Both sides are natural adversaries," he said, reminding his audience, "We are not boosters of business or industry; that is not our function."[135]

What *was* the press's function, then? In part, according to Chandler, to "open our pages to new voices that are speaking out for new causes. They are often the voices of protest, of alienation, and of militancy." And while the "traditional establishment beat" remained important, he said, they had begun "covering it in a different way." Echoing the points in Bill Thomas's 1975 article about the press and antiestablishment bias, Chandler noted:

> We no longer ask just the white psychologist to analyze the causes of a ghetto riot. We also ask the black rioter. We no longer accept without question the assurance of a utility company engineer that a nuclear power plant site is geologically safe. We also ask an expert representing environmentalists. And we certainly did not accept the word of a president, who had our endorsement every time he ran for public office, that he was innocent of all wrongdoing. We demanded his impeachment.[136]

Chandler's position represented the mainstream thinking in many newsrooms at the time. He acknowledged the backlash against adversarialism and conceded that the press had become overzealous. But he believed firmly that the changes in journalistic practice of the previous decade—a more adversarial posture, a broader definition of news, an openness to dissenting voices—had been necessary and salutary. Only a slight adjustment was required to achieve the proper balance.

Some newspaper journalists had reservations about the fundamental changes in their product, even before those changes became entrenched in the 1970s. Nick Williams wrote to a Canadian newspaper editor in 1969, "It is almost with relief that I find, now and then, an old-fashioned sex or crime scandal on the front page of The Times. Or an account of an incredibly heroic struggle against nature. Anything, damned near, to break the monotony of the Great Issues"—by which he meant "student dissent, permissiveness in the arts, racial confrontation."[137] *New York Times* correspondent John Corry, writing a memoir two decades later, expressed a similar lament: "Man bites dog would once have been a story, but it might not be now, unless it touched on racism, sexism, gay rights, or the rain forest."[138]

These expressions of nostalgia for the pre-1965 days of journalism do not indicate that Williams, Corry, or other journalists regretted the changes that had taken place or wished to turn back the clock. On the contrary, Williams himself had decided that the *Los Angeles Times* should downplay "old-fashioned sex or crime scandal" stories in favor of more substantive, analytical news. But with new journalistic values firmly in place, skeptical coverage of the fissures and shortcomings in the American system had become an accepted, central feature of the newspaper package. There was no chance of leading newspapers like the *New York Times* and the *L.A. Times* returning to simpler "man bites dog" journalism, which made it easy to romanticize that era as less complicated and more fun.

Although few journalists sincerely pined for the days before adversarial coverage became the norm, many politicians, business leaders, police chiefs, and other figures in the news most certainly did. They believed the press had begun treating them unfairly and exhibiting bias in its coverage, and they said so publicly. The statements of such influential people reinforced the view among the general population that the press was biased or untrustworthy. But suspicion and cynicism were on the rise throughout American society, and if the press had refrained from adversarialism, it might have sunk even lower in public esteem. Between 1966 and 1976, the Harris Survey reported a steep decline in the percentage of American expressing "a great deal of confidence" in leaders of the country's key institutions. Confidence in Congress dwindled from 42 percent to 9 percent, in the White House from 41 to 11, in major companies from 55 to 16, in higher education from 61 to 31, and in medicine from 72 to 42. The press, whose skeptical reporting helped drive those declines in confidence, saw a relatively modest decline—from 29 percent to 20 percent—in those expressing "a great deal of confidence" in its leaders.[139] Nearly all of those confidence figures would continue to trend downward in subsequent decades, as an adversarial press and a cynical populace became fixtures on the American scene.[140]

A decline in trust did not translate to a decline in profits, however. Just as Americans who disapproved of Congress as an institution continued to vote for *their* incumbent representative, Americans who disapproved of the press as an institution continued to buy *their* newspaper. Members of Congress tried to deliver what a majority of the voters in their district wanted, and newspapers tried to deliver what a majority of the readers in their circulation area wanted. Inevitably, voters and readers would occasionally disapprove of something their congressperson or their newspaper did or said. But they could overlook those instances, because on balance they were satisfied, and, crucially, there were few alternatives. A viable challenger to a strong congressional incumbent might come along only two or three times per decade. And prior to the Internet age, if people wished to remain deeply informed about local, national, and foreign news, they simply had to read a high-quality daily newspaper.

Despite their concerns about credibility and competition from other media, therefore, leading metropolitan newspapers like the *New York Times* and the *Los Angeles Times* had every reason to be confident about their prospects as the 1970s drew to a close. Their product had improved in myriad ways since the early 1960s—it had become bolder, broader, better written, more entertaining, more visually appealing, more relevant to readers' lives. And indeed, thanks to the groundwork laid in the 1960s and 1970s, the 1980s and 1990s would be banner decades for the *New York Times,* the *Los Angeles Times,* and the press as a whole, both journalistically and financially. As a result, the values and goals that guided them in the 1970s became even more deeply embedded in the journalism profession.

American Journalism and Its Values, 1980–2018

Validation, Devastation, Alteration

CHANGE OFTEN COMES in waves—a period of upheaval followed by a period of relative calm. The mainstream American press in the 1980s and 1990s experienced one such period of calm. There was still conflict, and there was still change, but the industry generally continued along the course its leaders had plotted in the 1960s and 1970s: more interpretation, a liberal definition of newsworthiness (including more soft news), a continued commitment to adversarial journalism, and a continued devotion to nonpartisan news coverage that allowed for judgments but not opinions. The question at hand for most journalists shifted from "What should our ideals and practices be?" to "How should we implement the ideals and practices upon which most of us agree?"

The distinguishing feature of this era, in retrospect, is the remarkable financial stability of the news business. With money rolling in, there was no convincing justification for making fundamental changes. Success in the 1980s and 1990s validated the ideals and practices that emerged from the 1960s and 1970s. Indeed, the only new wrinkle in the debate about journalism in this era arose from the concern that media organizations were *too* profitable. As large corporations bought up news outlets, some academics and journalists argued, those outlets increasingly shifted their focus from producing good journalism to producing ever-growing profits. "Corporate media giants" were constantly getting "wealthier and more powerful," Robert McChesney argued in a 1999 book. The problem, he said, was that "this concentration accentuates the core tendencies of a profit-driven, advertising-supported media system: hypercommercialism and denigration of journalism and public service."[1]

Ten years later, such concerns would seem quaint. The digital revolution upended the traditional business model of most news organizations, which responded by slashing their budgets to avoid going belly-up. It was a period of devastation, with journalists being laid off by the thousands and venerable publications folding. The devastation started gradually in the early 2000s, as audiences and advertising dollars began migrating online, but it accelerated rapidly after the 2008 economic crash. From 1985 to 2007, the total number of newspaper journalists in the United States had fluctuated between 53,000 and 57,000. In 2010 it was 41,500, and by 2015 the figure had declined to 32,900 (at that point, the American Society of Newspaper Editors stopped keeping track).[2] Yet most of what became known as the "legacy" media continued to hold fast to the values that had guided them since the 1970s—even though their upstart competitors were embracing different values and thriving. Some online-only news organizations were unabashedly partisan, some focused narrowly on one topic area, and some dropped the notion of adversarial reporting.

In the lead-up to the 2016 election, however, established news organizations and journalists began to subtly alter their values—especially their emphasis on "down the middle" reporting that would not appear partisan. They did so in response to two separate but related developments: the political polarization of online news audiences and the rise of Donald Trump. Throughout the 1980s, 1990s, and 2000s, journalists had never stopped questioning objectivity, but they focused mainly on the same shortcomings that left-wing critics had identified in the 1960s and 1970s: that objectivity was dishonest, that it forced reporters to withhold information from the public, that it inevitably privileged the perspectives of the powerful.

In the mid-2010s two other, more fundamental concerns led the case against objectivity. First, it made less sense from a business perspective.

Newspapers in the twentieth century strove to be impartial largely because they wished to appeal to the broadest possible audience. But in the twenty-first century it became increasingly difficult to attract a broad audience from across the ideological spectrum. Very few backers of Donald Trump would choose to spend their money to support what Trump labeled the "fake news media" and declared to be "the enemy of the American people." Second, many journalists held the same concern that drove a previous generation to alter the definition of objectivity: that it was responsible for bolstering a demagogue.

Journalists felt the same way about Donald Trump in the 2010s as journalists had about Joe McCarthy in the 1950s: he exploited their norms to get saturation coverage, and he represented an extraordinary threat to the republic. Many journalists attributed the unexpected rise of each man to the tremendous volume of coverage he received.[3] Like McCarthy, Trump understood how to dominate each news cycle with inflammatory statements and attacks. During the primary campaign season, Trump received $2 billion worth of free media coverage—roughly six times more than any of his Republican rivals.[4] The press boosted Trump, just as it had boosted McCarthy, despite the widespread belief among journalists that both men were liars and charlatans who threatened to undermine American democracy.[5]

In the 2000s, when the established press began trying to fend off new competitors siphoning away their audience, they did so by doubling down on their old values. They emphasized objectivity, comprehensiveness, and seriousness, in the hope of distinguishing themselves from online news that was partisan, narrow, and often light-hearted or cheeky. But in the 2010s the values of the legacy media and the online upstarts began to converge. Apart from some partisan right-wing outlets, hardly any news organization, new or old, tried to mask its distaste for Donald Trump. The online upstarts began broadening their coverage, and the legacy media (as many began calling news organizations that had been around before the 1990s) began adopting a breezier tone. A new consensus regarding journalism's values and practices began to emerge. There were three phases that led to this point: validation, devastation, and alteration.

Validation: 1980–2005

The 1980s and 1990s were a good time to work in journalism. At most major news organizations, the pay was good, the perks (especially for executives and star reporters) were even better, and layoffs were a rarity.[6] To be sure, there were some worrisome signs for the newspaper business as a whole. The U.S. population kept growing, but overall newspaper circulation remained stagnant, and an ever-dwindling percentage of people—especially young people—developed a newspaper habit.[7] And during the 1990–1991 recession, total newspaper advertising revenue declined drastically, from approximately $60 billion to $50 billion.[8] Nevertheless, the financial outlook for individual newspapers was generally rosy, because there were not as many of them as there had been a few decades earlier. Most papers enjoyed a monopoly position in their hometowns; in 1997, of the 1,500 daily newspapers in the United States, 99 percent were the *only* daily newspaper in their city.[9] So although the pie was not growing, fewer competitors were vying for a slice.

In this environment, the typical newspaper produced reliable profit margins of 20 percent or higher, year after year. TV networks and mass-circulation magazines were similarly flush with cash. Naturally this made media companies attractive takeover targets, both for larger media companies and for huge conglomerates whose core businesses had little to do with media. For example, the manufacturing company Westinghouse purchased CBS (its news and entertainment divisions) in 1995 for $5.4 billion. In 1993 the New York Times Company purchased the *Boston Globe* (and several smaller Massachusetts newspapers) for $1.1 billion. The concentration of media ownership, a long-standing worry for many journalists and observers, accelerated tremendously in the 1980s and 1990s. In 1983 the journalist-scholar Ben Bagdikian published *The Media Monopoly,* which warned that fifty large corporations owned the vast majority of the country's media outlets (newspapers, magazines, book publishers, radio and TV stations, movie studios, record companies). By the time Bagdikian wrote a seventh edition of the book, in the early twenty-first century, those fifty corporations had shrunk to five.[10]

Many journalists, like Bagdikian, had serious concerns about this state of affairs—but their concerns did not center on the industry's economic outlook. Given the robust profits media outlets were earning, their surging stock prices, and the eye-popping sums paid to acquire them, the business model appeared sound. As the well-known CBS News reporter turned academic Marvin Kalb argued in 1999, corporatization (along with the rise of cable news) had led to "a revolutionary transformation of the news business from a public service to a predominantly commercial enterprise, where profit tends to trump service at nearly every bend in the road."[11]

Of course, American journalism had been "a predominantly commercial enterprise" since at least the 1830s, but in previous decades most owners of news organizations (especially newspaper publishers) had spent their lives in the news business and had some respect for journalistic norms and values. Prior to the 1960s no major newspaper was part of a publicly traded company. Many journalists saw their organizations as public trusts, to be cherished and honored for their contributions to democracy and civil society. Publishers like Punch Sulzberger (at the *New York Times*) and Otis Chandler (at the *Los Angeles Times*) had indulged that view. But in an age of corporate media, news organizations often got treated as simply one of many business units, to be scrutinized for their contributions to the parent company's profits.

Not even the *Los Angeles Times* was immune from this trend. In 1995, as the paper's profits shrank and many of its associated companies were losing money, a new boss came on board: former General Mills executive Mark Willes. Nicknamed the Cereal Killer (a jibe at his non-news background), Willes laid off 150 journalists at the *L.A. Times* and shuttered ailing properties such as *New York Newsday* and the *Baltimore Evening Sun*.[12] It caused even more consternation in the newsroom when Willes announced that he wanted to tear down the metaphorical wall between the advertising department and the news department that most publications considered sacrosanct—"I'll use a bazooka, if necessary," he said. To accomplish that goal, Willes paired the editor of each section of the paper with an advertising sales manager.[13]

In 1999 Willes and his deputy took their philosophy too far. The paper produced a special edition of the *Los Angeles Times Magazine* about the opening of a new sports arena, the Staples Center—but although it was presented as editorial content, they produced it in collaboration with the arena's owners, who took a cut of the profits.[14] This unethical fiasco horrified journalists, and it hurt the paper's credibility with readers, too.[15] All this was occurring at a time (the mid- to late 1990s) when the *L.A. Times,* like most newspapers, was still reliably profitable—in fact, the company's stock price nearly tripled in the first two years of Mark Willes's tenure.[16] The economic outlook for the business appeared stable. The main problem at the *L.A. Times* and elsewhere, many journalists concluded, was greedy corporate owners trampling on the cherished ideals of independence and public service. So instead of seeking new values and practices to guide them, journalists focused on implementing the old ones, and on protecting them from the demands of upper management.

Profits, Principles, and Politics

Corporate owners enthusiastically accepted some of the journalistic practices that emerged from the 1960s and 1970s—soft news, naturally, was an easy sell. It was uncontroversial, relatively cheap to produce, and a reliable revenue driver. Some journalists grumbled about the increased focus on entertainment, food, and shopping, as they had in the 1970s. But it had become a perfunctory complaint, something to be included in any laundry list of modern journalism's shortcomings. Journalist James Fallows, in his 1996 book *Breaking the News* (a thorough critique of the news media), devotes only a couple of pages to the problem of "news as spectacle" and "the convergence of 'news' and 'entertainment.'"[17]

Journalists and media executives had more common ground on the issue of interpretive reporting, which had become increasingly central to most newspapers beginning in the 1950s. A major rationale for the practice was that readers wanted it, and that newspapers needed to provide it if they wished to compete with TV news, radio, and magazines. Journalists liked interpretation, too. To analyze the news rather than simply transmit it was more fun, more challenging, and more likely to earn respect from colleagues; they considered it part of journalism's public service mission, to help the public develop a deeper understanding of their world.[18]

As had happened with the nightly TV news in the 1960s, a new form of competition in the 1980s compelled newspapers to focus on interpretive reporting. The creation of the twenty-four-hour news network CNN in 1980 dealt yet another blow to newspapers' ability to break news; many readers were already familiar with the day's top stories by the time they picked up their morning newspaper. The Pulitzer Prize board in 1984 put its stamp of approval on interpretation by creating a new category for "explanatory journalism." The head of the Pulitzer board made the same argument that advocates of interpretive reporting had been making since the 1940s: "In the increasingly complex age in which we live, the task of illuminating and explaining intricate and seemingly abstruse issues and concerns has become one of the major responsibilities of journalism."[19] By 1996 two additional cable-news networks were on the air (Fox News and MSNBC), and an increasing number of Americans could get news updates around the clock from the Internet. Commentators began referring to a "24-hour news cycle."[20]

For newspaper reporters, especially those who covered national news, the twenty-four-hour news cycle further diminished the importance of articles that merely told what happened rather than explaining *why* it happened. This change in values was apparent to political operatives as well as journalists. Regardless of their political affiliation, they lamented it. In 1996 the press representatives for the rival presidential campaigns of Bill Clinton and Bob Dole expressed remarkably similar complaints about news coverage. Clinton's press secretary, Mike McCurry, remarked to journalist Ken Auletta that "the hard-news lead and story have been replaced by the analytical story," with "context" displacing straightforward reports of what the candidate said or did. That same day Dole's communications director, John Buckley, told Auletta, "The margins have widened for political coverage. The way it should work is: Cover what he did, what he said, but don't lead with the context and the interpretation."[21]

Even the old-fashioned scoop—breaking an important story before any competitors—no longer counted for much, because the scoop would not remain an exclusive for long. As *Washington Post* political reporter Paul Taylor said in 1996, "The era of the pure scoop is long gone. To the extent that there is a competitive nature to this business, it's trying to arrange the known facts in the most intelligent, prescient way." Taylor was quoted in a *Columbia Journalism Review* article about reporters' new

focus on getting a "conceptual scoop"—that is, coming up with an original interpretive angle on the news. In addition to earning journalists the
admiration of their colleagues (at the *Los Angeles Times,* political reporter
Ronald Brownstein was nicknamed the Great Analyzer), conceptual
scoops could lead to TV appearances and book deals.[22]

Journalists did not pursue interpretive reporting solely out of self-
interest, however. Most of them believed, as the Pulitzer Prize chair said,
that "illuminating and explaining" was "one of the major responsibilities
of journalism." James Fallows agreed in his 1996 book, asserting that
"journalism exists to answer questions like, 'What is really going on?' and
'Why is this happening?'"[23] That belief, which had been somewhat
controversial in the early 1960s, prevailed in most newsrooms by the
1970s; by the 1990s it had become journalistic dogma. However, Fallows
argued, many journalists in the 1990s were taking it too far. They had
become so focused on interpreting the news that they often skipped
over the substance of it. They held the attitude, in Fallows's words, that
"what you are writing about doesn't matter, really"—only your analysis of
it matters.[24]

In other ways, too, Fallows showed, journalists sometimes went to extremes in their embrace of the values that emerged from the 1960s and
1970s—especially objectivity. Fallows began his first chapter (titled "Why
We Hate the Media") by describing a 1987 TV program about ethical di-
lemmas, featuring the famous broadcast journalists Mike Wallace and
Peter Jennings. If they were covering a war and learned that enemy forces
had laid an ambush for U.S. soldiers, the newscasters were asked, would
they warn the Americans or would they let the ambush unfold and
record the story as neutral, objective observers? Jennings initially
said he would try to alert the American troops, but after Wallace brow-
beat him about the journalist's duty to remain independent and detached, Jennings retracted his answer and agreed with Wallace that the
"ethical" decision would be to allow their country's soldiers to be am-
bushed and, in all likelihood, slaughtered. The military men on the
program with Wallace and Jennings considered this a disgraceful, arro-
gant response; most viewers surely did too.[25]

Such rigid, heedless devotion to objectivity as Mike Wallace espoused
was far from the norm. The objectivity ideal remained a topic of intense

debate in journalism circles throughout the 1980s and 1990s. But the framework of that debate remained the same as it had been in the 1960s and 1970s. Critics on the right argued that objectivity was a ruse to mask the press's liberal agenda; critics on the left argued that it led journalists to censor themselves and reinforce the status quo; media eminences acknowledged the drawbacks of objectivity but suggested that it was better than the alternatives.

Not until Donald Trump would a national Republican leader launch so vitriolic an attack on the media as Spiro Agnew had done—mostly because it wasn't necessary. As a 1984 *Newsweek* article observed, "The assumption of a liberal bias in the press is now dogma for many conservatives."[26] Conservative politicians and intellectuals maintained a steady drumbeat of criticism that drove home the message effectively. Senator Jesse Helms in 1985, borrowing almost word for word from Agnew's speeches a decade and a half earlier, accused the "elite media" of "liberal bias." Network television in particular, Helms said, was "produced by men and women, who, if they do not hate American virtues, they certainly have a smug contempt for American ideals and principles."[27] On a TV news program that same year, *National Review* publisher William Rusher said, "I charge that the major media in the United States are a bunch of slanted liberals who have deliberately, systematically, over a long period of time delivered the liberal line."[28]

Articles in conservative journals in the 1990s wrote about liberal bias in matter-of-fact tones—they dutifully marshalled evidence to show that it existed, but they were more interested in whether journalists were still claiming to be objective, or whether liberal bias contributed to the public's unfavorable view of the media.[29] And with the rise of conservative talk radio in the 1990s, Republican politicians didn't need to channel Agnew, because they had extremely effective surrogates doing just that. Rush Limbaugh and other right-wing radio hosts amassed enormous audiences and devoted countless hours to bashing the mainstream media as elitist and slanted.

The right-wing critique of objectivity was passionate and sustained, but it lacked originality. Conservatives in the 1980s and 1990s called out the media for the same sins that Agnew and others—such as Edith Efron and Reed Irvine—emphasized in the late 1960s and early 1970s. "The blatant left-wing agenda [of the press] has made a mockery of the term 'objective journalism,'" said L. Brent Bozell III, head of the conservative Media Research Center, in a 1996 speech at the National Press Club. Bozell claimed that the media was engaged in a "nonstop onslaught against the conservative movement."[30] The conservative radio host Mike Rosen in 1996 argued that "liberals in the media" were "lobbying" for Bill Clinton's ideas; their professed "objectivity and even-handedness" was merely a "self-serving distortion."[31] In a 1998 editorial about public distrust of the mainstream media, *Investor's Business Daily* chalked it up to bias, saying, "They offer a liberal slant, cloaked in the guise of objectivity."[32]

However, journalists still had to contend with a critique of objectivity from the opposite side of the political spectrum. Adherents of the New Left in the 1960s roiled newsrooms with the argument that objectivity favored the powerful and reinforced the status quo, because it failed to question bourgeois assumptions and privileged the views of politicians, business owners, and influential institutions. By the 1980s, partly as a result of that critique, the press became more adversarial and began to include a broader range of views in its coverage. Yet the increasing corporatization and homogenization of the mass media gave additional ammunition to those alleging conservative bias. Whereas the left-wing critique came from within the profession in the 1960s and 1970s (from the likes of Tom Wicker and Nicholas Von Hoffman), in the 1980s and 1990s it came mainly from academia. Although the views of Ben Bagdikian, Noam Chomsky, and Robert McChesney differ significantly, all wrote influential books in the 1980s and 1990s arguing that journalism was serving its corporate masters rather than the public good, and that under such circumstances objectivity was a sham.[33]

Others wondered if the decades of conservative complaints about liberal bias had caused journalists to overcorrect in the name of objectivity. Mark Hertsgaard titled his 1989 book about the press and Ronald Reagan *On Bended Knee,* alluding to the posture that reporters adopted toward the president. On the book's very first page, Hertsgaard quoted *Washington Post* executive editor Ben Bradlee, who said that his staff had been too soft on Reagan for fear of being accused of bias. Since the *Post* had the reputation of being "great liberals," and Reagan was "a really true conservative," the thinking in the newsroom was: "We've got to really behave ourselves here. . . . And we did this. I think in the process that this paper and probably a good deal of the press gave Reagan not a free ride, but they didn't use the same standards on him that they used on Carter and on Nixon."[34]

Despite Bradlee's apparent contrition about failing to subject Reagan to tough scrutiny, left-wing commentators detected the same dynamic at work in press coverage of the two subsequent Republican presidents. In a *New York Times* op-ed just after the 1988 election, Mark Crispin Miller argued that TV news displayed an "anti-liberal bias," with harsh coverage of Democratic candidate Michael Dukakis and generous coverage of George H. W. Bush and Dan Quayle. Because TV journalists tended to be liberal in their personal beliefs, Miller wrote, "reporters bend over backwards to seem not at all critical of Republicans. Eager to evince his 'objectivity,' the edgy liberal reporter ends up just as useful to the right as any ultra-rightist hack."[35] *New York Times* columnist Paul Krugman offered a similar analysis of President George W. Bush and his adminis- tration. The "tyranny of even-handedness," Krugman wrote in 2004, caused moderate and liberal journalists to "bend over backward to say nice things about conservatives," because they were "desperate to dif- ferentiate themselves from 'irrational Bush haters.'"[36]

By the 1990s few journalists embraced objectivity as wholeheartedly as Abe Rosenthal had done in the 1960s. The ideal had been poked and prodded from so many angles for so many years that nearly everyone could see some holes in it. But for all of objectivity's shortcomings, the news in- dustry's leaders did not reject it completely. Winston Churchill suppos- edly said, "Democracy is the worst form of government except for all those other forms that have been tried from time to time"—many journalists adopted a similar attitude toward objectivity. As Mark Hertsgaard wrote in *On Bended Knee*, most journalists covering Reagan embraced "refined versions of the doctrine of objectivity. If it was impossible to avoid a point of view entirely, they would do their best to minimize it. . . . They would strive for 'fairness' and 'balance' (the two buzzwords that had arisen to replace 'objectivity' in the journalistic lexicon). They would, above all, remain politically neutral."[37] The term "objectivity," as Hertsgaard noted, had become unfashionable—in a 1992 column *Washington Post* ombudsman Joann Byrd called objectivity "a pretentious fantasy that turned reporters into stenographers and produced irresponsible journalism." But the ideal behind the term had staying power. In her column the following week, Byrd backtracked, writing, "It would be an overstatement to say that objectivity is dead." She explained that she preferred an updated version of objectivity that journalism professor Edmund Lambeth laid out in a 1986 textbook: "objective interpretation."[38]

Within the journalism industry's leading professional association, there was a similarly ambivalent attitude toward objectivity. Since its founding in 1909, the Society of Professional Journalists (SPJ; originally called Sigma Delta Chi) had been devoted to the objectivity ideal.[39] When the group revised its code of ethics in 1973 and 1987, each time it contained a line calling for "objectivity in reporting the news." But when the code was revised again, in 1996, the reference to objectivity dropped out.[40] Instead the revised code urged journalists to "distinguish between advocacy and news reporting," and to label analysis and commentary. But according to one account, the SPJ did not intend to reject objectivity as a value—they simply wanted to allow journalists who worked for ideological magazines to feel included.[41] Two years later the president of the SPJ, *Denver Post* reporter and editor Fred Brown, implied that the organization erred in dropping objectivity from its ethics code. In a column offering advice to young journalists, his first counsel was, "Try objectivity." Brown acknowledged that journalists are "constantly making judgments" (meaning they cannot be completely objective), but he argued that they must try to make those judgments based on evidence, and "uninfluenced by emotion, surmise, or personal opinion."[42]

Given that partisans on both sides of the ideological spectrum continued to accuse the press of bias, news industry leaders could continue to believe that they were achieving their goal of "straight-down-the-middle" reporting. As CBS News executive Don Hewitt put it during a 1985 debate about press credibility, "The problem really is that the left wing thought we were all fascists, and now the conservatives think we're all communists. They're both wrong."[43] The press's own research reinforced the perception that accusations of bias cut both ways. In 1997 the American Society of Newspaper Editors (ASNE) commissioned an in-depth study called the Journalism Credibility Project. As part of an effort to gauge the public's perception of bias, the study asked people whether, compared to themselves, newspapers were "more politically liberal" or "more politically conservative." While roughly 66 percent of respondents older than forty-five said "more liberal," 48 percent of people aged twenty-five to forty-four said "more conservative," as did a majority of those younger than twenty-five (a demographic that the industry desperately wanted to win over, given that they were the least likely to read a newspaper).[44]

Figures such as these validated the belief that the press was successfully occupying a political middle ground, and that partisan gripes were just that—partisan gripes. The two great media success stories of the 1980s provided further validation for the goal of political centrism. Few ambitious new ventures were launched in that era, because the barriers to entry were extremely high—starting a major publication or cable-news network required tens of millions of dollars—but two newcomers managed to succeed in the crowded media landscape: CNN, launched in 1980, and *USA Today,* launched in 1982. Although they lost money for their first several years of operation, by the late 1980s each had established a large, loyal audience and was reaping enormous profits. At both CNN and *USA Today,* objectivity and nonpartisanship were central components of the winning formula. When the conservative media mogul Rupert Murdoch and the Republican strategist Roger Ailes created Fox News Channel in 1996, they too professed a devotion to objectivity—despite scoffs from left-leaning journalists—adopting the slogan "fair and balanced."

Sexism, Racism, and Liberalism

If anything caused more tension in the newsrooms of the 1960s and 1970s than objectivity, it was the twin issues of gender and race. As with objectivity, gender and race remained points of contention in the 1980s and 1990s, but the trajectory that had been established in the previous years did not change. Women continued to battle discrimination and made slow but steady progress toward equality, while minorities traveled a bumpier road.

At the *Los Angeles Times* a gender-discrimination complaint advanced by an informal women's caucus stalled in the mid-1970s, but the paper's female journalists continued to feel that the senior editors favored men.

In 1987, forty-seven female *L.A. Times* staffers sent a letter to publisher Tom Johnson, telling him, "Most women at the *Times* work as assistants and deputies to men and wonder if there is any opportunity for advancement." There were no women, they noted, among the senior editors who determined the makeup of the front page at the daily news conference. In addition, the requirement that job opportunities be posted had become meaningless, the women's letter charged—sometimes editors flagrantly ignored it, and sometimes they posted the job only after they had picked a candidate privately.[45] Six of the letter's signers met with editor-in-chief Bill Thomas a few weeks later to discuss their concerns. Although the complaints about hiring and promotion echoed those of the previous decade, this time there was no mention of pay inequities or demeaning references to women in the news pages; nor was there any reference to attorneys or the possibility of a lawsuit, as there had been in 1974.[46]

At the *New York Times,* too, allegations of sexism continued well into the 1980s. As part of the 1978 settlement of the gender-discrimination lawsuit *Times* women had brought, the company committed to achieving certain hiring goals for women. But as of 1984 it was nowhere close.[47] When Max Frankel succeeded Abe Rosenthal as executive editor in 1986, the paper still had no women as news executives or as editors of the main news desks (metro, foreign, national, and business). Women's ascension into the editor ranks had been so slow that "none were even in line" to head those desks, according to Frankel.[48] And there were still gender-based disparities in pay, as reporter Leslie Bennetts learned in 1987 after she became engaged to one of her colleagues on the culture desk. Although she had more experience and seniority than her fiancé, his salary was 25 percent higher. When the paper refused to increase her pay to match his, she quit to accept a (much better-paying) job writing for *Vanity Fair.*[49] Punch Sulzberger's son, Arthur Ochs Sulzberger Jr., remarked in the mid-1980s that the *Times* was "just miserable to women," something he was determined to change when he became publisher in 1993.[50]

Sulzberger Jr. followed through on that goal to some extent—in 2003 the paper got its first female managing editor, Jill Abramson, and in 2004 the New York Times Company got its first female CEO, Janet Robinson. But Robinson was abruptly fired in 2011, for unclear reasons.[51] Earlier that year Sulzberger promoted Abramson to executive editor—another first for a woman at the *New York Times*—but he fired her in 2014, in a move that seemed tinged with sexism.[52] The paper's official statements cited Abramson's management style as the primary reason for her removal, calling her too autocratic and brusque. However, as the *New Yorker*'s Ken Auletta wrote, some women at the *Times* questioned "whether a man with similar behavior would be viewed the same way."[53] Indeed, Abe Rosenthal often behaved like a tyrant, but it did not cost him his job. Moreover, Abramson had learned several weeks before her firing that Bill Keller, who preceded her as executive editor, had received significantly better pay and benefits; she complained about it to company leadership and consulted a lawyer.[54]

In the newspaper industry as a whole, employment figures for women rose throughout the 1980s and 1990s, although they started from a very low baseline in the 1970s. In 1979 women constituted fewer than 4 percent of ASNE members (drawn from upper ranks of editorial staffs). That number increased to 10 percent by 1992, and to 19 percent in 2001.[55] The imbalance was smaller when it came to overall staffing, but it persisted over the years. A 1979 survey found that anywhere from 30 to 39 percent of newsroom employees were female.[56] In 1998, the first year they were included in the ASNE annual diversity census, women made up 37 percent of newsroom employees. However, women did hold more leadership positions, accounting for 34 percent of supervisors.[57] Women's advancement in hiring plateaued at that point, even though there were far more women earning college degrees in journalism than men. According to the annual ASNE survey, the proportion of women in America's newsrooms has never exceeded 38 percent, and the proportion of female supervisors has never exceeded 36 percent.[58] Moreover, women remained grossly underrepresented in high-visibility positions such as columnists and Washington reporters.[59]

Equal employment opportunity was just half the battle for women in the press. They also wanted to rid news coverage of sexism—the tendency to emphasize women's physical appearance or marital status, to belittle their achievements, to put articles that primarily concerned women in a "soft news" section or toward the back of the paper. Examples of sexism in news coverage still abound, but they are the exception rather than rule, as they had been in the early 1970s. Sexist headlines and leads often provoke a backlash on social media, which raises journalists' awareness of the need to avoid them.[60] But most of the time press coverage reflects values and assumptions that liberal feminism helped to make mainstream in the 1970s: acknowledging the fact that women face discrimination, assuming that women can perform the same roles in society as men, and most controversially, evincing support for women's right to choose to have an abortion.[61]

Although the press in the 1960s and 1970s expressed greater concern over its lack of racial diversity than its lack of gender diversity, that concern rarely resulted in more nonwhites advancing through the newsroom ranks. The situation did not change much in the 1980s and 1990s, despite increased efforts to recruit and promote minority journalists at newspapers such as the *New York Times* and the *Los Angeles Times*. Minorities remained underrepresented, especially at the senior levels.

In 1978, a decade after the Kerner Commission issued its report excoriating the press for its failure to hire minorities or include minority perspectives in its coverage, there had been embarrassingly little progress: only 4 percent of professional newsroom employees were nonwhite. That year, prodded by African-American journalists and some white editors (especially editors of southern newspapers), the American Society of Newspaper Editors announced an ambitious goal: by 2000, the percentage of minorities in daily newspaper newsrooms would match the percentage of minorities in the general population.[62] The ASNE vote was unanimous, and many prominent publications made a real commitment to increasing their diversity—although in the end they fell short of their diversity targets.

In 1983 the *Los Angeles Times* created a Minority Editorial Training Program (METPRO), which selected promising young nonwhites for an eleven-month traineeship during which they would learn the reporting trade and eventually write articles, mainly for the suburban editions. METPRO, according to metropolitan editor Noel Greenwood, was "created out of frustration" at the *L.A. Times*'s failure to increase the diversity of its staff. Although it involved a significant monetary investment— a budget of $150,000 in 1984, $281,000 in 1985, and $326,000 in 1986— the paper considered it a rousing success.[63] The trainees earned high praise from their bosses, and nearly all of them got jobs at large metropolitan newspapers (many received multiple offers). The biggest problem with the program, Noel Greenwood reported to editor-in-chief Bill Thomas, was that its graduates were going off to work for competing newspapers. He suggested the program be recast as a feeder system exclusively for Times Mirror papers.[64] Although the company did not institute that recommendation, it expanded METPRO: it began training people to be editors as well as reporters, and *Newsday* (a Times Mirror property) began a METPRO of its own. By 1989 the program's projected budget was nearly $1 million.[65] METPRO continued into the twenty-first century, even after the Tribune Company purchased Times Mirror.

The *New York Times* did not have an extensive training program like METPRO, but it also tried to increase minority representation on its staff. In 1989 executive editor Max Frankel recalled Paul Delaney from Europe, where he had been the Madrid bureau chief, and appointed him "senior editor for newsroom administration." Delaney's job, as he later put it, "was to help change the color of the staff" (the *New York Times* initially hired Delaney as a reporter in 1969, and he became the paper's first black editor—a deputy editor on the national desk—in 1977).[66] The effort resulted in many more African-Americans, Latinos, and Asians entering the newsroom, Delaney said, especially after Arthur Ochs Sulzberger Jr. became publisher in 1992—although Delaney added, "There was no question, women fared much better than minorities at the paper and in the profession."[67] For a time Frankel even instituted a "one-for-one" policy, meaning that the *Times* had to hire one nonwhite reporter for every white one. However, many editors strongly opposed this, and eventually Frankel dropped the policy.[68]

As with women, the number of minorities in American newsrooms plateaued in the late 1990s and the 2000s, at around 12 or 13 percent of the total.[69] In the late 1990s, ASNE recognized that its commitment to having minority representation in the newsroom equal that of the population could not be achieved by the year 2000 as planned—so the goalpost was moved to 2025.[70] And as with women, African-Americans rarely became seniors editors or executives with responsibility for important policy and coverage decisions. In a 1990 article on minorities in the journalism profession, *L.A. Times* media reporter David Shaw found that nonwhites constituted "only 1% to 2% (at most) of the nation's executive editors, editors-in-chief, and managing editors."[71] In 2014 the *New York Times* appointed its first-ever African-American executive editor, Dean Baquet. But despite Baquet's presence at the top of the newsroom hierarchy, there remained a "blinding whiteness" among the staff as a whole, according to public editor Liz Spayd, who pointed out that the lack of minorities was especially notable in the most coveted positions: Washington reporters, sports, cultural critics, opinion writers, the Styles section.[72]

Many advocates of newsroom diversity assumed that it would lead to more nuanced, sensitive coverage of minority communities. In the 1980s and 1990s, however, progress on that front was uneven. The *Los Angeles Times* provoked an outcry in 1981 when it published a story headlined "Marauders from Inner City Prey on L.A.'s Suburbs," complete with an illustration showing "large arrows leaping like Panzer divisions from South Central Los Angeles to predominantly white suburbs" (in David Shaw's words). Just three years later, however, the paper won a Pulitzer Prize for a series on Latinos in Los Angeles that was reported by Latino, black, and white journalists.[73]

Just as it remained possible to find many examples of sexism in news coverage from the 1980s and 1990s, damaging racial stereotypes and assumptions continued to appear. As the subheadline of a 1990 David Shaw article on race and the media stated, "By focusing on crime, poverty and aberrant behavior, newspapers fail to give a complete portrait of ethnic minorities."[74] A 1997 article in the reporters' trade magazine *Quill* found that African-Americans held the same grievances against the mainstream press that they had nursed for decades. As one source put it, "Good things happen in the black community, but you never see it. You only hear about us when we have a disturbance."[75] Pamela Newkirk, in her definitive book about race in the mainstream media, found no shortage of objectionable news coverage from the 1980s and 1990s.[76]

Despite frequent lapses, the press was making a conscious effort to grapple with the issue of race in nuanced, nonstereotypical ways, and to acknowledge the shortcomings of its usual coverage. David Shaw's four-part series on race and the media in the *L.A. Times* in 1990—in which he took his own paper to task—provides one example. The New Orleans

Times-Picayune went even further, with a seven-month series that presented a frank portrayal of the city's (and the newspaper's) history of racism, and its enduring legacy. The series won accolades but also created tremendous controversy and bitterness among the *Times-Picayune*'s staff and readers; it was edged out for the Pulitzer Prize by *another* newspaper's examination of racial tensions in the local community (the *Akron Beacon-Journal*).[77] In addition to one-off reports such as those, some newspapers tried to include people of color as part of their routine coverage. *USA Today,* for instance, had a policy stating that of the four photographs featured above the fold on page one each day, at least one must show a member of an ethnic minority.[78]

The press often failed to live up to its ideals regarding race, but by the 1990s the ideals were clearly established. Most major news organizations endorsed the use of affirmative action to increase their staff's racial diversity; they recognized the persistence of racism in American society and in their own industry; and they wanted to provide multidimensional coverage of minority communities rather than fall back on stereotypes about crime and pathology. These are essentially liberal ideals—they are based on assumptions that the modern conservative movement does not share. Predictably, they inspired a conservative backlash. The right-wing journalist William McGowan devoted an entire book, published in 2000, to criticizing the news media's "liberal" attitude toward race (and to a lesser extent, gender).[79]

More recently, right-wing news outlets such as Fox News and Breitbart.com have taken an approach opposite to that of the legacy media. They often play up stories about crimes committed by people of color, in particular undocumented immigrants—despite the fact that immigrants are statistically less likely to commit crimes than are native-born citizens.[80] Breitbart frequently promoted stories, some of them misleading or fabricated, in which Muslims or African-Americans were accused of violent acts. The site labeled some stories with the tag "black crime"—a tag it removed in 2017 after many observers called it racist.[81] In 2017–2018, when the #MeToo movement received blanket coverage from most media organizations, Fox News focused on cases of sexual abuse with female perpetrators while downplaying accusations against prominent men—unless the alleged abuser was a Democrat.[82]

Devastation: 2005–2015

Ever since total newspaper circulation in the United States began to stagnate, in the 1960s, journalists and news executives felt anxiety about the future of their business. But with individual publications earning solid profits and advertising revenue continually increasing (albeit with occasional dips during times of recession), the press's day of reckoning seemed to lie in the distant future. The Internet, however, hastened that day's arrival. Classified advertising, which had provided more than one-third of the revenue at some newspapers in the 1990s, withered away as people realized they could sell things and hire people more easily on sites such as Craigslist and Monster.com, which required little or no payment from users. And with so much high-quality news available for free online—from web portals like Google and Yahoo!, from individual newspaper websites, and from news aggregators like Digg and the Huffington Post—audiences and the advertisers who sought to reach them began migrating away from print publications. The trend lines in circulation and advertising quickly changed from stable to slipping. As journalism chronicler Alex S. Jones noted, "In 2006, the newspaper industry went into a collective panic."[83]

The panic deepened when the Great Recession hit in 2008. What had been a slow leak of troubles turned into a gusher. Nearly all print publications hemorrhaged jobs and slashed costs—some news organizations went out of business, and others became skeletal operations that employed few, if any, full-time reporters.[84] The numbers were stark. Nationwide there were 42 percent fewer newspaper journalists in 2015 than in 2001,[85] and the decline in advertising revenue was even sharper: from an all-time high of $63.5 billion in 2000, it shrank to $23 billion in 2013.[86] An article in the *Atlantic* in early 2009 predicted in all seriousness that the *New York Times* could go out of business later that year.[87]

Clearly, the press faced an existential crisis more severe than that of the 1970s. Back then newspapers altered their practices to retain the audience they might otherwise lose to competing media or to a basic lack of interest in the newspaper product. To compete with TV and weekly newsmagazines, newspapers provided more interpretation and investigations; to compete with city magazines and community weeklies, newspapers offered more service material aimed at consumers, and more local news from suburban areas; to broaden their audience and attract younger readers, they increased the emphasis on entertainment and soft news.

In the period from 2005 to 2015, however, the newspaper press made few adjustments to its fundamental values. To be sure, newspapers adapted their practices to the demands of online audiences. One might even say that they adopted a new set of Internet-age values. Professor of media and public affairs Nikki Usher, who spent five months embedded in the *New York Times* newsroom in 2010, argues based on her observations that "three core values of online journalism"—immediacy, interactivity, and participation—guided the paper as it adapted to the digital age. She acknowledges, however, these "new news values" did not displace the old ones; they were simply layered on top.[88] Even as blogs, aggregators, and niche-oriented news sites became increasingly popular, the *New York Times* and other legacy media imitated them only in superficial ways (launching in-house blogs, for instance). But for the most part, legacy media companies held fast to the values and practices they had established in the 1970s.

In a way they had no choice. Print newspapers had large staffs (even after substantial cutbacks) and existing revenue streams that they could not abandon. Online media startups were able to succeed, in part, because they could operate on a shoestring budget. Yet it was also a journalistic choice for newspapers to reject the values and practices of their online competitors. For decades newspapers had endeavored to reach the largest possible audience by covering every topic of general interest and by providing what they felt was impartial, independent, in-depth news coverage. Online-only news organizations did not pursue that strategy. Most focused on a specific niche in their coverage—TMZ and celebrities, Politico and national politics, Mashable and digital media. Some mainly rewrote headlines and linked to other news stories with brief introductory comments (the Drudge Report, Andrew Sullivan's Daily Dish, the Huffington Post in its early days). And almost none of the online-only outlets that discussed politics or national affairs claimed to be impartial. On the contrary, they tried to be opinionated and provocative—that was a central part of their appeal.

From the beginning of the digital age, many mainstream journalists were contemptuous of their upstart competitors. They depicted bloggers as amateurs opining from their basements (or perhaps their parents' basements) while wearing pajamas, not doing the serious work of journalism. Old-media eminences disparaged blogs and news aggregators as "parasites," feeding off the content produced by traditional reporters.[89] By the 2010s legacy media were taking online media more seriously (the "pajamas" remarks became much scarcer), but the two sides still had divergent values. Traditional media retained a serious tone, especially in headlines, and they relied on their editors' judgment to determine coverage priorities and the newsworthiness of different stories (unlike many online news organizations, which relied on web-search data and sought out topics that were trending on social media). Moreover, traditional media—led by the *New York Times*—insisted on maintaining their commitment to objectivity, even as many bloggers and new-media organizations lambasted the ideal and proclaimed their model of journalism with a point of view to be superior.

In many ways the debate mirrored the controversy over objectivity in the late 1960s and early 1970s. Voices on the right ridiculed it as a smokescreen, while voices on the left condemned it as a straitjacket—and both sides attributed the mainstream media's decline in credibility (and by extension its economic troubles) to its claims of impartiality. The left-wing blogger Markos Moulitsas articulated that belief at a 2010 panel discussion about the potential demise of the *New York Times:* "A lot of the decline in these traditional media outlets is because people have lost faith that those publications don't have ulterior motives or agendas," Moulitsas said. "People like me, I have an agenda, and I'm very clear about it. But the *New York Times,* they try to be something better than that."[90]

In 2013 the left-wing journalist-activist Glenn Greenwald had a lengthy online exchange with *New York Times* executive editor turned columnist Bill Keller. Greenwald charged that journalists who try to be objective are "dishonest" for concealing their true feelings and cowardly in their "glaring subservience to political power" (as an example, he cited reporters' reluctance to state plainly when a government official is lying). Keller countered that journalists should provide enough information to enable the reader to decide whether or not someone is lying. As professionals, Keller argued, journalists can set aside their personal opinions—and they must, in order to maintain their credibility and get "closer to the truth." Like Otis Chandler four decades earlier, Keller rejected the word "objective"—it "suggests a mythical state of perfect truth," he wrote—but defended the principles it implies.[91] It was essentially the same argument that Abe Rosenthal might have had with a New Left acolyte forty years earlier.

When *New York Times* public editor Margaret Sullivan in 2014 told a group of young journalists what values she considered most important, they were the same values that the paper had promoted since the 1970s. Journalists should "not [be] afraid to be adversarial when needed," Sullivan said. They should "serve the public," not any personal, partisan, or commercial interest. And they must maintain a commitment to "truth and fairness."[92] Sullivan tiptoed around the question of objectivity, but in a column the year before, she suggested she was all for it, provided reporters did not confuse it with the pitfall of false equivalence (which she defined as "an even split between opposing beliefs in every article," regardless of what the facts suggest). "Getting at the truth can require setting aside personal views to evaluate evidence fairly," Sullivan wrote. "If that's impartiality, it remains not only worthwhile but crucially necessary." The paper's associate managing editor for standards, Philip Corbett, felt even more strongly. He told Sullivan, "I flatly reject the notion that there is no such thing as impartial, objective journalism—that it's some kind of pretense or charade, and we should just give it up, come clean and lay out our biases." Corbett argued that abandoning those ideals would "erode our credibility and feed the false notion that there are no real facts, no impartial reporting or analysis—just spin and polemic."[93] The objectivity debate raged as fiercely as it had since the 1970s, but for the time being, the traditionalists retained the upper hand.

Alteration: 2015–Present

In the early twenty-first century, old-media values and new-media values were starkly opposed on the questions of impartiality, tone of coverage, scope of coverage, and intended audience. Since around 2015, however, they have begun to converge. The press is undergoing the greatest change in its ideals and practices—indeed, the first major change—since the 1970s. Partly this convergence results from online-only news organizations broadening the scope of their coverage and their intended audience, in order to grow. For example, Buzzfeed added in-depth political reporting to its core offerings of listicles and personality quizzes. BusinessInsider transformed from a specialized news site into a general-interest one. The Huffington Post added sections on everything from parenting to food to religion. But the primary reason for the convergence is that legacy media companies are subtly altering their values.

As editors and executives at print publications came to terms with the devastation that the digital age brought, they were not sure how to respond—the business was changing so quickly, and there seemed to be no winning formula. Should news organizations force online audiences to pay for their content or should they provide it free of charge? Should they try to distribute information on their own platforms or should they partner with others? Should they imitate some of the practices of their online-only competitors or try to differentiate themselves? Headlines in the *American Editor* (a newspaper-industry journal) reflected this extreme uncertainty about the path forward. A 2006 article about how to respond to the digital challenge was titled "The Answer Is: Nobody Knows." A headline from 2008 asked, "Is There Still a Winning Strategy?"[94] The digital-media theorist Clay Shirky, in a 2009 blog post, posed the question of who will cover the news when traditional newspapers drastically cut their staffs. "I don't know. Nobody knows," wrote Shirky, who is generally not shy about making predictions. "It's easier to see what's broken than what will replace it."[95]

By 2015 much of that uncertainty had been replaced by indisputable facts. Income from online advertising could not, on its own, support an ambitious news-gathering operation—online subscriptions or other revenue streams must supplement it. Social media would be the primary driver of traffic to news sites. Most people prefer news that reinforces their existing ideological views. Those facts led to two inevitable conclusions. First, news organizations had to focus on producing content that people would share on social media. Second, they had to find ways to make people pay for their online news despite being accustomed to getting it for free. As a means of increasing subscription revenue, most newspapers settled on the "metered paywall" model: users could view a certain number of articles each month (usually five or ten) without being asked to pay, then they would be required to subscribe in order to view more.[96] The *New York Times* instituted a metered paywall in 2011, and most other leading papers followed suit (the *Los Angeles Times* in 2012, the *Washington Post* in 2013, the *Boston Globe* in 2014, the *Chicago Tribune* in 2016).

Because it is relatively easy to get around a metered paywall, and because the Internet remains awash in free news, providing coverage that people want to read is not enough to build up a solid subscriber base. Instead, news organizations have concluded that they can employ three primary strategies to gain subscribers. First, they can provide information that is not available for free anywhere else (this may be a viable model for organizations covering specialized topics or local news, but it does not work well for national, general-interest publications). Second, they can try to gain an enormous audience and make their content so irresistible that a small portion of those people will subscribe. Third, they can foster feelings of loyalty among a core audience—that core audience, even though they know they could skirt the paywall or get similar coverage elsewhere, would then be inspired to pay for a subscription in order to support the publication's mission.

The logical solution for most publications targeting a national audience is to strive for some combination of those latter two strategies: make people want to click and make people feel loyal. One area in which online-only publications excel, of course, is making people want to click. So naturally, many legacy news outlets have begun imitating the practices of their online competitors. This has caused some hand-wringing among journalists and media observers about whether journalists should change their coverage practices (or lower their standards, depending on one's viewpoint) in pursuit of eyeballs. It echoes the debate over soft news and "fluffy" lifestyle coverage in the 1970s: then as now, the traditionalists deplored what they saw as pandering, low-brow content, while the pragmatists cared more about reversing the downturn in profits that threatened to put some publications out of business.

If in the 2000s one could sum up old-media disdain for new media with the word "pajamas" (as in bloggers' supposed apparel of choice), in the 2010s the preferred put-downs became "cat videos" and "clickbait." Those were the genres of content most likely to "go viral" on social media, according to the conventional wisdom. But most journalists did not enter their profession in order to promote misleading headlines or videos of adorable pets. Online publications devoted to creating shareable content, such as Buzzfeed and Upworthy, earned sneers the same way that the Huffington Post and the Drudge Report had a decade earlier. In spite of that attitude, however, the country's most venerable newspapers have imitated certain elements of the Buzzfeed-Upworthy model.

The *Washington Post,* after its sale to billionaire Amazon founder Jeff Bezos in 2013, began to alter its coverage goals. As its managing editor for digital, Emilio Garcia-Ruiz, noted in 2015, "I've seen us go from one very simple strategy, which was to own Washington, to now a strategy of owning the world."[97] The key to that strategy is to build what the *Post*'s managers call a "customer engagement funnel." Using social media, they aim to bring as many people as possible to washingtonpost.com (the top of the funnel) in the hope that some will find the content so engaging that they are pulled deeper into the funnel, where they decide to subscribe.[98] To get people into the funnel—to increase the number of visitors to the website—traditional front-page stories, presented in a traditional way, are not sufficient. Instead, the *Post* and other newspapers are turning to clickbait-style headlines and articles that people are likely to share on social media.

The classic clickbait format misleads readers by making a vague promise on which the story does not deliver (the headlines declares, "You won't believe what happened next," when in fact what happens next is entirely predictable or mundane). While few news organizations stoop to that level, many use a less objectionable version that Upworthy perfected: the "curiosity gap" headline—a two-sentence headline that withholds key information, making readers click through in order to satisfy their curiosity (an example from the *Washington Post:* "This Woman's Labored Breathing Alarmed Her Friends. Doctors Were Startled to Find the Cause").[99] Beyond headlines, newspapers increasingly began imitating their online-only competitors by emphasizing what the *New York Times* termed "disposable web journalism" that is "focused on the viral at the expense of the substantive."[100] *Washington Post* watchers have no trouble citing stories that might fall into that category: an examination of the hidden dangers of the Elf on a Shelf doll; articles derived from viral videos (of a dancing cop or of Pope Francis kissing a sick child); a narrative headlined "This is what happened when I drove my Mercedes to pick up food stamps."[101] All of these happen to be substantive stories, but they are all stories that just as easily could have appeared on Buzzfeed.

The *New York Times* is pursuing a slightly different strategy than the *Washington Post*. As a major internal report on the company's future stated in 2017, "We are not trying to maximize clicks and sell low-margin advertising against them. We are not trying to win a pageviews arms race."[102] This sounds like an implicit jab at the *Post,* which had recently surpassed the *New York Times* in monthly pageviews (it does not accurately describe the *Post*'s strategy, however, which is to maximize clicks in order drive paid subscriptions—not in order to sell online advertising). But the *Times* report also downplayed the importance of viral content, in contrast to the approach of the *Washington Post* and most other news organizations. Viral content, according to the report, does not inspire enough loyalty to compel people to subscribe: "A story that receives 100,000 or 200,000 pageviews and makes readers feel as if they're getting reporting and insight that they can't find anywhere else is more valuable to The Times than a fun piece that goes viral and yet woos few if any new subscribers." The report added that the *New York Times* should distinguish itself from online competitors by resisting "the lures of clickbait"— which it was doing successfully, according to the authors.[103]

The *New York Times* has certainly resisted clickbait in its most misleading or sensationalized forms. But inevitably it has adopted some of the practices of successful online-news ventures, especially when it comes to headlines. Unlike in the print newspaper, articles published online have no constraints on how short or long their headlines must be. Therefore the *New York Times* (like the *Washington Post* and other newspapers) assigns a different headline to the online version of a print story. They often try out multiple headlines simultaneously, then use real-time data to determine which headline is more effective (this is called A/B testing).[104] During one week in February 2017 the following two headlines shot to the top of the paper's "trending" list: "A Jewish Reporter Got to Ask Trump a Question. It Didn't Go Well" and "I Ignored Trump News for a Week. Here's What I Learned."[105] Such headlines—using the curiosity-gap formula that Buzzfeed and Upworthy employ so successfully—would not have appeared in the *New York Times* in 2010 (in either the print edition or the online version).

The changes are not limited to headlines. The *New York Times* has a box positioned prominently on the right side of its homepage where users can scroll through recently posted articles. Although the articles come from nearly all sections of the newspaper—world news, national, obituaries, entertainment, business, science, health—the common thread between them is that they have some potential to be widely shared on social media. Among the article topics featured there on a randomly selected day: a newly discovered "mucus-shooting worm-snail"; a father who got in trouble for pulling his daughter out of school for a trip to Disney World; the nutritional value of the human body for ancient cannibals; and the phenomenon of students getting accepted into all eight Ivy League colleges.[106] But while the material is highly shareable, the presentation is sedate: rather than a sensationalized or curiosity-stoking headline, there is a thumbnail image alongside a one- or two-sentence summary of the article.

• • •

FUN, SHAREABLE ARTICLES can increase a news organization's online traffic, and they can induce casual visitors to linger rather than quickly click away to another destination. But people are unlikely to pull out their credit cards and subscribe unless they feel a deeper allegiance to a publication. In an age of extreme partisanship and tribalism based on political affiliation, that allegiance is only likely to come when readers feel that a publication shares their general political outlook. The "down the middle" approach to news coverage that most newspapers had endorsed since the 1960s was based partly on a sense of journalistic propriety, but it was also a pragmatic business decision. Newspapers wanted to appeal to the broadest possible audience—they did not want to alienate any potential subscribers with news articles that seemed biased. From the 1960s to the 1990s, when people who wanted in-depth local and national news coverage had only one or two options—and when their options did not include a free product—that logic made sense.

By the early 2000s the environment was radically different. Among Republicans, distrust and contempt for the mainstream media had grown steadily since the 1970s. Several Gallup polls between 2004 and 2015 asked how much trust and confidence Americans had in the news media to report full, fairly, and accurately; each time, roughly two-thirds of Republicans said "not very much" or "none at all." In 2016 the figure shot up even higher, with roughly 86 percent of Republicans declaring their mistrust of the mass media.[107] And that small subset of Republicans who expressed some degree of trust may have been equating "the mass media" with local TV news, their local newspaper, or talk radio, rather than the network newscasts and national publications that are more frequently accused of liberal bias.

From a business standpoint, it would be reasonable to write off this portion of the population as a lost cause. Better, perhaps, to focus on retaining the loyalty of left-wing partisans who might be lured away by more ideological sites—after all, newspapers had been stewing for years about the tendency of "parasitic" partisan blogs to cut into their traffic by piggybacking on traditional reporting (summarizing the contents of a newspaper article and slapping a more provocative headline on it). However, no sea change in the tone or viewpoint of political news coverage occurred between 2004 and 2015. Economic concerns alone were not reason enough for news organizations to alter their deep-seated ideals about impartiality and objectivity. As in the 1950s with the rise of interpretive reporting, economic concerns had to be coupled with a journalistic or public-service justification. And as in the 1950s, with Joseph McCarthy, that justification came from a politician who violated established norms of conduct.

Journalists tend to subconsciously sort things into categories. The political theorist Daniel Hallin has argued that certain ideas reside in a sphere of consensus, while others are in the sphere of legitimate controversy, and others are in the sphere of deviance—that is, beyond the pale of acceptable discourse.[108] From the beginning of Donald Trump's campaign and up through his inauguration, he made statements that mainstream journalists considered in the sphere of deviance: saying all Muslims should be banned from entering the country, endorsing the use of torture, refusing to promise he would accept the election results as legitimate (just to name a few). It was not only left-leaning journalists who considered such ideas deviant. Both living Republican ex-presidents, and the two previous Republican candidates for president, refused to endorse Trump. The leading conservative opinion journal, *National Review*, devoted an entire issue to making the case against Trump; the two most prominent right-wing intellectuals in the country, George Will and Bill Kristol, also announced their staunch opposition to the GOP candidate. Writing in the *Columbia Journalism Review* in the midst of the campaign, David T. Z. Mindich took note of these extraordinary conditions and said they might lead to a "Murrow moment" in which journalists veer away from objectivity and challenge a powerful figure the way CBS News's Edward R. Murrow had challenged Joe McCarthy in 1954.[109]

The *New York Times*'s Jim Rutenberg assessed the situation similarly in his weekly media column in August 2016: "If you're a working journalist and you believe that Donald J. Trump is a demagogue playing to the nation's worst racist and nationalistic tendencies, that he cozies up to anti-American dictators and that he would be dangerous with control of the United States nuclear codes, how the heck are you supposed to cover him?" The answer, Rutenberg implied, was not to strive for objectivity, but to let the reporting reflect the "potentially dangerous" nature of a Trump presidency. "It is journalism's job," he wrote, "to be true to the readers and viewers, and true to the facts, in a way that will stand up to history's judgment."[110]

For the most part journalists heeded Rutenberg's advice. They emphasized the ways in which Trump deviated from the norms of American democracy, they contradicted the falsehoods he spouted, and they talked about the bigotry that his campaign unleashed. On Twitter, political reporters for major news organizations—not opinion writers—showed their disdain for Trump rather clearly (although the disdain from Trump and his allies toward the press was much harsher). As media critic Jack Shafer wrote the day after the election, "The press succeeded in exposing Trump for what he was. Voters just decided they didn't care."[111]

After Trump's election, the press's adversarial posture toward him intensified. Almost immediately a debate broke out in journalism circles about whether or not the press should "normalize" Trump and his presidency.[112] Should they treat him as they would have treated Marco Rubio or John Kasich (traditional Republican politicians) as president, or should they continue to emphasize Trump's dangerous abnormalities—in par-

ticular, his seeming unpreparedness for the job and his authoritarian tendencies? The overwhelming consensus was that the press should not
normalize Trump—that the conventions of journalism must be altered.[113]

As in the 1960s, when objectivity received an update in the dual interests of democracy and news-industry profits, the current alteration of professional norms has an economic basis too. Many publications got a large
influx of new subscribers after the election—most of them, presumably,
aghast at the outcome (the "Trump Bump," some called it).[114] To keep that
momentum going, news organizations experimented with new slogans
and marketing campaigns that left little doubt as to where they stood.
"Slate won't normalize Donald Trump. Help us hold him accountable,"
read a subscription appeal on the Slate.com homepage in November 2016.[115]
The *Washington Post* in February 2017 added the slogan "Democracy
Dies in Darkness" to the front page of its print edition and to every page
on its website. Although the paper's management denied that this was a
reference to the Trump administration, it seems likely that most readers
would interpret it as such.[116] The *New York Times* launched a high-profile
ad campaign (including a television spot during the 2017 Oscars broadcast) highlighting its commitment to truth in the context of several of the
Trump administration's controversial policies and statements.[117]

Strategies such as these suggest that major news organizations are
giving up on a large percentage of the population. They imply that
everyone in the target audience views Trump's presidency with great trep-
idation. Some observers have recognized the magnitude of the shift that
seems to be under way. The media analyst Jeff Jarvis predicted in February 2017 that the Trump administration would bring about the end of
the mass media—large news organizations would still exist, he argued,
but they would no longer be "mass" media because they would not speak
to the entire public. Jarvis based this belief on his assumption that major
newspapers and networks would "bring down" Donald Trump with investigative and adversarial journalism (not because of a partisan vendetta
but because Trump is hopelessly corrupt and incompetent). At that point,
"any last, small hope that anyone on the right would ever again trust, listen to,
and be informed by the press will disappear," Jarvis wrote. "The press
that survives, the liberal press, will end up with more prizes and subscriptions, oh joy, but with little hope of guiding or informing the nation's

conversation."[118] That may be an overstatement, but Jarvis's basic point is valid. Whereas the market for news used to be segmented in terms of geography and socioeconomic class, the main dividing line now is ideology.

Donald Trump and many of his surrogates have claimed that news organizations such as the *New York Times,* the *Washington Post,* and CNN fabricate stories to harm the Trump administration, with no regard for truth and fairness. That is nonsense, but it is true that most news organizations cover Trump differently than they covered previous presidents—even George W. Bush, who had few admirers in the press corps.[119] Trump's adviser Kellyanne Conway described the dynamic fairly well. "I think there's something called presumptive negativity," Conway said in February 2017. "It's, 'What is he saying, what are his advisers saying, what are they doing today? There must be something wrong or something negative.'"[120] If Trump were a normal president, a journalist striving for objectivity would try to keep those presumptions in check. But many journalists have determined that Trump is not normal, and that to normalize him would be dishonest and cowardly.

The former *New York Times* executive editor Bill Keller, in his 2013 exchange with activist journalist Glenn Greenwald, opposed the idea of making judgment calls on controversial political topics. If a politician says something untrue, Greenwald suggested, call it a lie; when discussing waterboarding, call it torture. Keller, for his part, advocated "telling [readers] what they need to know to decide for themselves" rather than "telling them what they ought to think."[121] This, however, was a pre–Donald Trump statement. When Trump was a candidate and president-elect, his mendacity went far beyond the normal parameters of politics—the exaggerations, prevarications, and misrepresentations from which politicians usually retreat when they are shown to be untrue. Trump routinely made outrageous, baseless statements (for example, claiming Muslims in New Jersey were cheering on 9/11, that millions of undocumented immigrants voted illegally for Hillary Clinton, and that his modest electoral-college victory was a "massive landslide"), and he refused to budge despite overwhelming evidence that he was wrong.

Given that brazen level of commitment to spreading falsehoods, the *New York Times* decided that it would be appropriate to use the word "lie" to describe what Trump was doing. The paper even used it in headlines in the news section on multiple occasions.[122] The *New York Times* opinion section in June 2017 devoted a full page to a "definitive list" of lies Trump had told since taking office.[123] The *Washington Post*'s "Fact Checker" section maintains a similar list, but it refers to "false and misleading claims" rather than lies. News articles in the *Post,* as in many other news organizations, tend not to call Trump's statements lies, but most stories make clear (usually in the headline) when Trump has said something demonstrably false.[124] Even the news agency Reuters—which still has a compelling business reason to strive for objectivity, because it sells stories to publications of all ideological stripes—acknowledged the challenge that Trump presents. In a statement published shortly after Trump's inauguration, Reuters editor-in-chief Steven Adler wrote about the "attacks" that could be expected to come from the White House; he compared the task of covering the Trump administration to covering the news in authoritarian countries with no free press.[125]

New York Times executive editor Dean Baquet has been asked multiple times about Donald Trump's impact on journalism, and he acknowledges that it is tremendous. Trump "forced us . . . to get comfortable with saying something is false," Baquet noted in October 2016. "He will have changed journalism."[126] Two months later, responding to complaints that the *Times* and others were drawing conclusions in their coverage of Trump rather than letting readers decide for themselves, Baquet made a comparison with coverage of the civil rights movement. Journalists "used very powerful language" in news articles, Baquet said. "And I think had they obfuscated in the face of what they were witnessing, that would have been cowardly."[127] Baquet quickly specified that he was not equating the Trump administration with segregationists, but his clear implication was that the country is facing a similar moment in its history and that traditional journalistic objectivity will not do.

Trump has much in common with the American press's greatest twentieth-century antagonists. Like Senator Joseph McCarthy, Trump has a tendency to make shocking, often unsubstantiated claims that allow him to dominate the news cycle. Like Richard Nixon and Spiro Agnew, Trump accuses the news media of being untrustworthy and biased against him. In fact, many of Trump's claims are far more easily disproved than

McCarthy's were, and his attacks on the news media are far more vituperative than Agnew's. The press responded to McCarthy's rise with more interpretive reporting, and to Nixon's and Agnew's attacks with more adversarial journalism. When the careers of each of those politicians ended in disgrace (McCarthy censured by the Senate, Nixon and Agnew resigning their offices) while the news media continued to thrive, journalists could feel vindication about the decision to alter their professional values. But although the press won those battles, the war raged on.

In 1976 *New York Times* executive editor Abe Rosenthal offered a pointed assessment of Nixon and Agnew's crusade against the news media. Substitute the name "Trump" for Nixon and Agnew, and the same could be said in 2018. As Rosenthal saw it, the Nixon administration's goal was "to break the press—or rather those journals and broadcasters that Nixon-Agnew felt threatened the control of the American mind that the administration believed was its prerogative." To that end, Rosenthal continued, they launched "a political and propagandistic attack aimed at convincing the country that the press was biased and represented interests antagonistic to the interests of the public—that the government and the people were 'we' and the press was 'they.'"[128] News organizations that cede the moral high ground of impartiality make it easier for politicians to depict the press as "they." Five decades ago, when America's leading newspapers faced enormous political and economic pressure from many sides, they continued to report doggedly on public affairs while trying to remain apolitical. That approach served the press remarkably well at the time, and it can provide a model still.

Notes

Acknowledgments

Index

Notes

Abbreviations

BASNE	*Bulletin of the American Society of Newspaper Editors*
Curtis Papers	Charlotte Curtis Papers, Schlesinger Library, Radcliffe Institute, Harvard University
Halberstam Collection	David Halberstam Collection, Howard Gotlieb Archival Research Center, Boston University
LATR	Los Angeles Times Records, Huntington Library, San Marino, California
Oakes Papers	John B. Oakes Papers, Rare Book and Manuscript Library, Columbia University Library
Reston Papers	James B. Reston Papers, New York Times Company Records, Manuscripts and Archives Division, New York Public Library
Rosenthal Papers	A. M. Rosenthal Papers, New York Times Company Records, Manuscripts and Archives Division, New York Public Library
Salisbury Papers	Harrison E. Salisbury Papers, Rare Book and Manuscript Library, Columbia University Library
Wicker Papers	New York Times Company Records, Manuscripts and Archives Division, New York Public Library
Women's Caucus Papers	New York Times Women's Caucus Papers, Schlesinger Library, Radcliffe Institute, Harvard University

Introduction: Liberal Values, Not Liberal Bias

1. "Stormy Curtiss-Wright Meeting Told of Plane Test," *New York Times,* April 21, 1960, 41.

2. Phyllis Lee Levin, "From Tweeds to Tiaras, British Fashions Have a Ball," *New York Times,* April 21, 1960, 26.

3. I chose this date to compare because, like April 21, 1960, it was the third Thursday in April. Because newspaper advertising, and thus the amount of editorial content, varies considerably with the days of the week, this is a more valid comparison than with April 21, 1980 (a Sunday).

4. Craig R. Whitney, "News of Olympic Boycott Move Puzzles Ordinary Soviet Citizens," *New York Times,* April 17, 1980.

5. David A. Andelman, "M.T.A.'s Head Now Sees No Early Productivity Saving," *New York Times,* April 17, 1980.

6. Linda Greenhouse, "High Court Limits Localities' Defense in Civil Rights Suits," *New York Times,* April 17, 1980.

7. Drew Middleton, "Mining Iran: Free of Risk?," *New York Times,* April 17, 1980, A12; Adam Clymer, "Endorsements: Pursuing Will-o'-the Wisps," *New York Times,* April 17, 1980, D17.

8. Anthony Austin, "In Gorky Exile, Sakharov Fate Is Still Unclear," *New York Times,* April 17, 1980, A7.

9. Jim Naughton, "An Off-Base Campaign," *New York Times,* April 17, 1980, B26.

10. Karen W. Arenson, "Hunts Cited in Effort on Silver Curb," *New York Times,* April 17, 1980, D1.

11. The total number of pages in the April 17, 1980, edition was 168.

12. Deborah Rankin, "The 'Green Card' and Housekeepers," *New York Times,* April 17, 1980; Suzanne Slesin, "Traveling the Circuit of Spring House Tours," *New York Times,* April 17, 1980; Helen Lawrenson, "Kitty Miller's Last Party: Mementos of an Elegant Life," *New York Times,* April 17, 1980.

13. Claudia Luther, "A Little Blue Plymouth Has Brown Seeing Red," *Los Angeles Times,* April 17, 1980, 1.

14. Penny Girard, "Safe Deposit Boxes—No Vacancies at Banks," *Los Angeles Times,* April 17, 1980, 1.

15. Headlines included "DAR Warns President of Perils at Summit," giving prominent coverage to the annual meeting of the right-wing Daughters of the American Revolution, and "Herter Lashes Out at Communists," accompanying a large photo on page 3 of Secretary of State Christian Herter delivering a speech.

16. "Anarchy Protects No One," *Los Angeles Times,* April 21, 1960.

17. A comparison between each newspaper's coverage on a random day in 1940 and a random day in 1960 reveals very few significant changes. The same goes for a comparison between 1980 and 2000.

18. John L. Hulteng, "Some Questions for the Future of Newspapers," *Nieman Reports,* April 1961, 25.

19. Prominent examples include Daniel Bell, *The End of Ideology: On the Exhaustion of Political Ideas in the Fifties* (New York: Free Press, 1960); and Geoffrey Hodgson, *America in Our Time: From World War II to Nixon—What Happened and Why* (Princeton, NJ: Princeton University Press, 1976).

20. Draft text of Sigma Delta Chi Foundation Lecture by Turner Catledge, University of Kansas, December 2, 1965, Harrison E. Salisbury Papers, box 535, folder 75, Columbia University Library. As Catledge's choice of pronoun indicates, he envisioned the typical reader as male, as did most of his colleagues.

21. Charlotte Curtis, memorandum to the staff, June 7, 1966, Charlotte Curtis Papers, box 7, folder 15, Schlesinger Library, Radcliffe Institute, Harvard University (hereafter cited as Curtis Papers).

22. Daniel Bell, *The Coming of Post-Industrial Society: A Venture in Social Forecasting* (New York: Basic Books, 1973), 15, 17.

23. Charles E. Scripps, "The Magazine Competition," *Nieman Reports,* July 1959, 17–19.

24. When one *Los Angeles Times* reader canceled his subscription because he believed its coverage resembled communist propaganda, executives forwarded the letter to one another with notes making fun of his over-the-top criticisms and his suggestion that they "clear out the publisher and editor." When L.A.'s police chief canceled his subscription, the publisher forwarded the letter to the circulation director with a note saying, "Sorry I couldn't hold onto this sub for us—but the Chief has apparently gone bananas." At the *New York Times*, when a subscriber's cancellation letter accused the paper of "biasing and coloring the news," the publisher used it as fodder for a running joke with his cousin, the editorial page editor, ribbing him for his liberal editorials. William D. Weed to Norman Chandler, October 3, 1964, with attached notes, Los Angeles Times Records (hereafter cited as LATR), box 292, folder 1, Huntington Library, San Marino, CA. Edward M. Davis to Otis Chandler, August 19, 1975, with attached note from Otis Chandler to Bert Tiffany, LATR, box 440, folder 5. Arthur Ochs Sulzberger to John B. Oakes, July 10, 1973, and July 24, 1973, John B. Oakes Papers, box 14, folder "Arthur Ochs Sulzberger: General Memos, 1963–73," Columbia University Library.

25. A few of the many examples: Robert O. Self, *All in the Family: The Realignment of American Democracy since the 1960s* (New York: Macmillan, 2012); Lisa McGirr, *Suburban Warriors: The Origins of the New American Right* (Princeton, NJ: Princeton University Press, 2001); Thomas Frank, *What's the Matter with Kansas: How Conservatives Won the Heart of America* (New York: Macmillan, 2004); Eugene Robinson, "Ben Carson and the Conservative Culture of Victimization," *Washington Post,* November 9, 2015.

26. See Bruce J. Schulman, *The Seventies: The Great Shift in American Culture, Society, and Politics* (New York: Free Press, 2001), xv; Howard Brick, *Age of Contradiction: American Thought and Culture in the 1960s* (New York: Twayne, 1998), xv; Michael J. Lacey and Francis Oakley, eds., *The Crisis of Authority in Catholic Modernity* (New York: Oxford University Press, 2011); "Record Lows in Public Confidence," Harris Survey Press Release, October 6, 1975, available at http://media.theharrispoll.com /documents/Harris-Interactive-Poll-Research-RECORD-LOWS-IN-PUBLIC -CONFIDENCE-1975-10.pdf, accessed January 29, 2016.

27. See Eli Pariser, *The Filter Bubble: How the New Personalized Web Is Changing What We Read and How We Think* (New York: Penguin, 2011); and Cass R. Sunstein, *Infotopia: How Many Minds Create Knowledge* (New York: Oxford University Press, 2006), 9–11, 97–102.

28. Promotional brochure for *You* magazine, n.d., LATR, box 608, folder 17.

29. Kevin Kruse, *White Flight: Atlanta and the Making of Modern Conservatism* (Princeton, NJ: Princeton University Press, 2005), 234. See also Thomas Byrne Edsall and Mary D. Edsall, *Chain Reaction: The Impact of Race, Rights, and Taxes on American Politics* (New York: W. W. Norton, 1992), 227–229.

30. Nick Kotz, "The Minority Struggle for a Place in the Newsroom," *Columbia Journalism Review,* March/April 1979, 28.

31. Arthur Ochs Sulzberger, "View from the 14th Floor," *Times Talk,* December 1967, 4, pamphlets, box 41, folder 2, New York Times Company Records, Manuscripts and Archives Division, New York Public Library.

32. The full quotation takes a more cynical view of journalism. It comes from Finley Peter Dunne's fictional Irish bartender Mr. Dooley, sketches of whom appeared in newspapers across the United States in the 1890s and 1900s. In a sketch from around 1902, Mr. Dooley says (in his exaggerated Irish dialect), "Th' newspaper does ivrything f'r us. It runs th' polis foorce an' th' banks, commands th' milishy, conthrols th' ligislachure, baptizes th' young, marries th' foolish, comforts th' afflicted, afflicts th' comfortable, buries th' dead an' roasts thim aftherward." Finley Peter Dunne (uncredited), *Observations by Mr. Dooley* (New York: Harper and Brothers, 1902), 240.

33. Text of Otis Chandler speech at the University of Kansas, April 30, 1975, LATR, box 234, folder 10.

34. Irving Kristol, "Is the Press Misusing Its Power?," *Chicago Tribune,* January 11, 1975.

35. Gay Talese, *The Kingdom and the Power: Behind the Scenes at the New York Times, the Institution That Influences the World* (New York: Random House, 1969).

36. Table titled "Circulation, New York City Newspapers," Curtis Papers, box 8, folder 8.

37. E. C. Daniel, "Rising Above the Noise and Turmoil," *BASNE,* October 1, 1960, 1.

38. Turner Catledge, *My Life and the Times* (New York: Harper and Row, 1971), 195.

39. Unlike most prominent *New York Times* journalists from this era, Rosenthal did not publish a memoir. The only biography of him, by Joseph C. Goulden, is thoroughly researched but tainted by the author's unremittingly negative interpretation of Rosenthal as a person and a journalist (Joseph C. Goulden, *Fit to Print: A. M. Rosenthal and His Times* [Secaucus, NJ: Lyle Stuart, 1988]). More nuanced accounts of Rosenthal and of the *New York Times* during his editorship can be found in: Talese, *The Kingdom and the Power;* Edwin Diamond, *Behind the Times: Inside the New New York Times* (New York: Villard Books, 1994); Susan E. Tifft and Alex S. Jones, *The Trust: The Private and Powerful Family behind the New York Times* (Boston: Little, Brown, 1999); Harrison E. Salisbury, *Without Fear or Favor: The New York Times and Its Times* (New York: Times Books, 1980); and Arthur Gelb, *City Room* (New York: Marian Wood/G. P. Putnam's Sons, 2003).

40. The most informative works about the *New York Times* during the 1970s are Diamond, *Behind the Times,* and Gelb, *City Room.*

41. Jack Hart, "The Information Empire: A History of the Los Angeles Times from the Era of Personal Journalism to the Advent of the Multi-Media Communications Cor-

poration" (Ph.D. diss., University of Wisconsin–Madison, 1975), 271; David Halberstam, *The Powers That Be* (New York: Laurel/Dell paperback, 1986), 146 (orig. pub. 1979).

42. L. D. Hotchkiss, Times Editorial Department Report, 1952, LATR, box 608, folder 7.

43. Nick Williams to Mrs. William Colhoun, August 15, 1968, LATR, box 464, folder 12.

44. There are several histories of the *Los Angeles Times* and its individual publishers. The most thorough and useful are: Dennis McDougal, *Privileged Son: Otis Chandler and the Rise and Fall of the L.A. Times Dynasty* (Cambridge, MA: Perseus, 2001); Halberstam, *The Powers That Be;* Robert Gottlieb and Irene Wolt, *Thinking Big: The Story of the Los Angeles Times, Its Publishers, and Their Influence on Southern California* (New York: G. P. Putnam's Sons, 1977); and Hart, "The Information Empire." A good, brief overview, heavily illustrated, can be found in Bill Boyarsky, *Inventing L.A.: The Chandlers and Their Times* (Los Angeles: Angel City Press, 2009). The authorized history of the *L.A. Times,* commissioned by the paper, covers much the same ground as the others but glosses over most of the controversial issues: Marshall Berges, *The Life and* Times *of Los Angeles: A Newspaper, A Family, and a City* (New York: Atheneum, 1984).

45. Campbell Watson, "Los Angeles Times News Staff Doubled (to 516) in 10 Years," *Editor & Publisher,* February 6, 1971, 18–19; Hart, "The Information, Empire," 179; Gottlieb and Wolt, *Thinking Big,* 445–446; John Corry, "The Los Angeles Times," *Harper's,* December 1969, 76.

46. Corry, "The Los Angeles Times," 81; Times Mirror Company annual report, 1964, LATR, box 118, folder 14; Times Mirror Company annual report 1969, LATR, box 199, folder 4. The 1960 and 1970 annual reports list only the revenues for the newspaper division as a whole (which in 1960 also included the *Los Angeles Mirror* and in 1970 included the *Dallas Times Herald, Newsday,* and the *Orange Coast Daily Pilot*), but the 1964 annual report contains a bar graph listing the *Los Angeles Times*'s revenues for each of the previous five years, and the 1969 annual report mentions *L.A. Times* total revenue in its summary of the newspaper's performance.

47. Nick Williams to Dorothy B. Chandler, January 25, 1973, LATR, box 448, folder 13.

48. Times Mirror Company Annual Reports, 1960–1971, LATR, box 118, folders 10–15, and box 119, folders 1–6. Because the *Los Angeles Times* was part of a conglomerate that owned several other newspapers, the annual reports do not always specify the amount of revenue or profits from the *L.A. Times* alone. The 1969 annual report mentions that the *L.A. Times* had revenues of $158 million. The 1974 annual report says that *L.A. Times* revenues exceeded $200 million for the first time in its history. The 1971 report says only that revenues for the entire newspaper publishing division (which also included the *Orange Coast Daily Pilot* and *Newsday*) were $244.8 million.

49. McDougal, *Privileged Son,* 214. Even *L.A. Times* staffers agreed; according to journalist Molly Ivins, who visited the *L.A. Times* as a *New York Times* reporter in 1979, "the reporters admitted the L.A. Times is 'edited with a shovel.'" Molly Ivins to David R. Jones, April 1979, Seymour Topping Papers, box 16, folder 1, New York

Times Company Records, Manuscripts and Archives Division, New York Public Library.

50. Barbara Saltzman, interview with author, August 28, 2014; Dennis Britton, interview with author, September 26, 2014.

51. Leslie Bennetts, interview with author February 1, 2016.

1. Opening the Door to Interpretation

1. Louis M. Lyons, "A Glance Backward at the Press," *Nieman Reports,* January 1959, 7.

2. Christopher B. Daly, *Covering America: A Narrative History of a Nation's Journalism* (Amherst: University of Massachusetts Press, 2012), 213.

3. Michael Schudson, *Discovering the News: A Social History of American Newspaper* (New York: Basic Books, 1978), 146–148. See also Kathy Roberts Forde, "Discovering the Explanatory Report in American Journalism," *Journalism Practice* 1, no. 2 (May 2007): 227–244.

4. See Schudson, *Discovering the News,* 121–144.

5. Walter Lippmann, *Public Opinion* (New York: Harcourt Brace, 1922), 358.

6. The Commission on Freedom of the Press, *A Free and Responsible Press* (University of Chicago Press, 1947), 1–22, emphasis in original. Quotations at 1, 21, 22.

7. Quoted in Hillier Krieghbaum, "Straight News Is Not Enough," *Nieman Reports,* October 1955.

8. Gay Talese, *The Kingdom and the Power: Behind the Scenes at the* New York Times, *the Institution That Influences the World* (New York: Random House, 2007), 262–263 (orig. pub. 1969).

9. Fox Butterfield, interview with author, August 12, 2014; Michael Schudson, *The Rise of the Right to Know: Politics and the Culture of Transparency, 1945–1975* (Cambridge, MA: Belknap Press of Harvard University Press, 2015), 157.

10. "Better Reporting Held Modern Need," *New York Times,* August 27, 1952.

11. Turner Catledge in his memoir recalls that, along with Reston, economics correspondent Russell Porter wrote some of the earliest news analysis articles: Turner Catledge, *My Life and the Times* (New York: Harper and Row, 1971), 211. A search of the *New York Times* database on ProQuest, however, does not return any news-analysis articles by Porter between 1946 and 1960 comparable to the articles by Reston and Baldwin.

12. See, for example, Hanson W. Baldwin, "New Naval Concept: An Analysis of the Fleet's Air Arm and the Role of Carriers in Future Strategy," *New York Times,* December 3, 1954; Baldwin, "Soviet Marshals' Power: An Appraisal of the Increased Power of Army Displayed in Current Events," *New York Times,* February 10, 1955; James Reston, "Power in Absentia: An Analysis of the President's Influence on Plans and Policies of Capitol Hill," *New York Times,* January 4, 1956.

13. For early examples of the "News Analysis" box, see Hanson W. Baldwin, "The Pentagon Program: President's Reorganizing Plans Viewed as Unsuitable to Congress and Military," *New York Times,* April 7, 1958; James Reston, "A Change in Strategy:

Attorney General Leaves No Doubt This Time on Plans for Little Rock," *New York Times,* September 11, 1958.

14. Katherine Fink and Michael Schudson, "The Rise of Contextual Journalism, 1950s–2000s," *Journalism* 15, no. 1 (January 2014): 3–20.

15. Kevin G. Barnhurst and Diana Mutz, "American Journalism and the Decline in Event-Centered Reporting," *Journal of Communication* 47, no. 4 (Autumn 1997): 27–52.

16. Thomas E. Patterson, *Out of Order* (New York: Knopf, 1993), 82. The percentage of interpretive stories continued to grow after 1976; the most dramatic shift was between 1968 and 1972.

17. As Edwin Bayley has shown, a few newspapers treated McCarthy's accusations skeptically and gave in-depth coverage to those who rebutted him (Bayley mentions the *Washington Post* in particular), but most of the press—especially the wire services—inadvertently served his purposes. Edwin R. Bayley, *Joe McCarthy and the Press* (Madison: University of Wisconsin Press, 1981), 66–76, 148–149.

18. Ibid., 75–76. Two of the earliest and most prominent commentators were Richard Strout of the *Christian Science Monitor* and Douglass Cater, founding editor of the *Reporter.*

19. Elmer Davis, *But We Were Born Free* (Indianapolis: Bobbs-Merrill, 1954), 176. Davis was paraphrasing University of Oregon School of Journalism dean Gordon Sabine.

20. Ibid., 148, 160.

21. Bayley, *Joe McCarthy and the Press,* 85.

22. Ernest H. Linford, "The Full Dimensions of the News," *Nieman Reports,* October 1955. This was the text of a speech Linford had delivered in January 1955.

23. Krieghbaum, "Straight News," 15.

24. Davis, *But We Were Born Free,* 175.

25. Barry Bingham, "Newspapers in Crisis," *Nieman Reports,* October 1959.

26. James Reston to A. H. Sulzberger (addressed "Dear Mr. Gus"), n.d., circa 1952, James B. Reston Papers, University of Illinois Archives, available at http://imagesearchnew.library .illinois.edu/cdm/compoundobject/collection/reston/id/932/rec/2.

27. Nick Williams to Otis Chandler, June 15, 1966, Los Angeles Times Records (hereafter cited as LATR), box 228, folder 1, Huntington Library, San Marino, CA.

28. Otis Chandler to Norman Chandler and Al Casey, January 5, 1966, LATR, box 220, folder 32.

29. David Murray to A. M. Rosenthal, July 27, 1968, A. M. Rosenthal Papers, box 14, folder 14, New York Times Company Records, Manuscripts and Archives Division, New York Public Library (hereafter cited as Rosenthal Papers).

30. Charles E. Scripps, "The Magazine Competition," *Nieman Reports,* July 1959.

31. J. Edward Murray, "The Crisis of Meaning," *Editor & Publisher,* February 4, 1961, 7.

32. See for example Ernest H. Linford, "The Full Dimensions of the News," *Nieman Reports,* October 1955; Krieghbaum, "Straight News"; [Adamantios] Polyzoides, "Complicated Situation Facing U.S.," *Los Angeles Times,* February 23, 1956, 8;

Murray Illson, "Complex Era Put to Young Editors," *New York Times,* March 14, 1958, 18.

33. Catledge, *My Life and The Times,* 211.

34. "A.P. Reports Rise in News Analysis," *New York Times,* April 6, 1962, 54.

35. Schudson, *Rise of the Right to Know,* 168.

36. Max Frankel, *The Times of My Life and My Life with the Times* (New York: Delta trade edition, 2000 [1999]), 106.

37. Richard F. Pourade to Nick Williams, August 17, 1960, and n.d., with enclosures, LATR, box 459, folder 2.

38. Text of Nick Williams speech to California Newspaper Publishers Association, June 20, 1961, LATR, box 468, folder 15.

39. Irving Kristol, "The Underdeveloped Profession," *The Public Interest,* Winter 1967, 50–51.

40. John B. Oakes to A. O. Sulzberger, October 9, 1963, and A. O. Sulzberger to John Oakes, October 15, 1963, John Oakes Papers, box 13, folder "Arthur Ochs Sulzberger: Memos Re Content of News / News V. Editorial," Columbia University Library (hereafter cited as Oakes Papers).

41. Bayley, *Joe McCarthy and the Press,* 127.

42. James S. Pope, "Interpretation—Or Shabby Reporting?," *Columbia Journalism Review,* Fall 1961.

43. Ibid.

44. David Starr, "The Quiet Revolution," *BASNE,* April 1963, 2.

45. Ibid.

46. Draft text of Turner Catledge speech for Sigma Delta Chi Foundation Lecture, Lawrence, KS, December 2, 1965, Harrison E. Salisbury Papers, box 535, folder 75, Rare Book and Manuscript Library, Columbia University Library (hereafter cited as Salisbury Papers).

47. Murray, "The Crisis of Meaning," 7.

48. Text of Otis Chandler remarks on "The Future of American Newspapering" at ASNE Panel Discussion, April 17, 1964, LATR, box 228, folder 43.

49. Barnhurst and Mutz, "Decline," 32; Stepp, "Then and Now," 64. Barnhurst has described the changes in news coverage that began in the 1960s as "the new long journalism," which focused less on events and more on the meanings of events. See Kevin G. Barnhurst, *Seeing the Newspaper* (New York: St. Martin's Press, 1994), 14–15.

50. David Halberstam, *The Powers That Be* (New York: Laurel / Dell, 1986), 485 (orig. pub. 1979).

51. Stephen Hess's 1978 survey of Washington reporters found that 93 percent had a college degree. Roughly 95 percent of those aged forty-nine or younger were college graduates, compared to only 85 percent of those fifty and older, giving an indication of the trend toward higher education levels. The personnel files of *New York Times* reporters in the 1960s and 1970s show that the younger ones were much more likely to have gone to elite universities and to have excelled academically. Stephen Hess, *The Washington Reporters: Newswork* (Washington, DC: Brookings Institution, 1981), 162, 165.

52. Nick Williams to Otis Chandler, n.d. (circa November 1962), LATR, box 451, folder 2.

53. John L. Hulteng, "Some Questions for the Future of Newspapers," *Nieman Reports,* April 1961.

54. Irving Kristol, "The Underdeveloped Profession," *The Public Interest* (Winter 1967); George Lichtheim, "'All the News That's Fit to Print': Reflections on the *New York Times,*" *Commentary,* September 1965, 33–46.

55. The most prominent hire was Robert J. Donovan, the highly respected Washington bureau chief of the *New York Herald-Tribune,* who joined the *L.A. Times* in 1962; but the *L.A. Times* in the early 1960s also hired journalists away from such publications as *Time,* the *Wall Street Journal, BusinessWeek,* and the *Atlanta Journal-Constitution.*

56. Text of Nick Williams speech to Fresno State chapter of Sigma Delta Chi, February 1963, LATR, box 468, folder 17.

57. Otis Chandler to Nick Williams, June 23, 1966, LATR, box 228, folder 1.

58. John Corry, "The Los Angeles Times," *Harper's,* December 1969, 81.

59. David Halberstam, typed notes from first interview with Bob Donovan, n.d. (circa 1976), from the David Halberstam Collection, box 193, folder 3, Howard Gotlieb Archival Research Center, Boston University.

60. Harrison Salisbury to James Reston, May 1, 1968, Salisbury Papers, box 541, folder 38.

61. A. M. Rosenthal, summary of News Committee meeting, September 25, 1968, Salisbury Papers, box 167, folder 6.

62. A. M. Rosenthal, summary of News Committee meeting, November 25, 1968, Salisbury Papers, box 167, folder 6.

63. *New York Times,* house advertisement, "If Everybody Screams, Nobody Hears," March 20, 1970, 42.

64. Joe Lelyveld, interview with author, September 5, 2014.

65. John Oakes to Arthur Ochs Sulzberger, January 3, 1968, Oakes Papers, box 13, folder "Arthur Ochs Sulzberger: Memos Re Content of News / News V. Editorial."

66. Arthur Ochs Sulzberger to James Reston, September 18, 1969, Melvin Cook to Gene Roberts, November 26, 1969, and A. M. Rosenthal to Arthur Ochs Sulzberger, November 28, 1969, all Rosenthal Papers, box 92, folder 14.

67. M. L. Stein, "Everything Changes—Even the Newsroom," *Saturday Review,* July 10, 1971, 45–50.

68. Ibid., 50.

69. Bill Thomas to Otis Chandler, April 25, 1973, LATR, box 395, folder 9.

70. Talese, *Kingdom and the Power,* 56.

71. David R. Jones, interview with author, October 7, 2014. On the shift of power from the bullpen to reporters-turned-editors like Rosenthal, see also Susan E. Tifft and Alex S. Jones, *The Trust: The Private and Powerful Family behind the New York Times* (Boston: Little, Brown, 1999), 455; and Chris Argyris, *Behind the Front Page* (San Francisco: Jossey-Bass, 1974), 35.

2. Objectivity and the Right: A Worthy Ideal Abandoned

1. Willard Edwards, "Republicans Usher in New Political Era," *Chicago Tribune*, July 19, 1964; Tom Wicker, *On Press* (New York: Viking, 1978), 1–2.

2. As one *New York Times* editor wrote to the managing editor about covering Goldwater in 1964, "Questions arose about what he really meant and whether the reporter should report what he said or what he meant"; Harold Faber to Turner Catledge, November 24, 1964, Clifton Daniel Papers, box 14, folder 7, New York Times Company Records, Manuscripts and Archives Division, New York Public Library. Robert Alan Goldberg, *Barry Goldwater* (New Haven, CT: Yale University Press, 1995), 224; "An Editorial: The Attack on the Press," *Columbia Journalism Review* 3, no. 3 (Fall 1964): 10; Robert J. Donovan, "Goldwater Leaning to Television in Campaign," *Los Angeles Times*, August 12, 1964, 6; "The Press Viewed Differently by Goldwater and Rep. Reuss," *New York Times*, August 11, 1964, 23.

3. "Transcript of Goldwater's Concession and News Conference in Phoenix, Ariz.," *New York Times*, November 5, 1964, 20.

4. "Helping Hands," *National Review*, April 5, 1966, 302; "The Voice of the Times, Is Not, Laus Tibi Domine, the Voice of Asia," *National Review*, July 26, 1966, 714; "Speak Up, Everybody," *National Review*, March 24, 1964, 222.

5. Although Kristol was not as conservative in 1967 as he would later become, he was firmly opposed to 1960s liberalism; Peter Steinfels, *The Neoconservatives: The Men Who Are Changing America's Politics* (New York: Simon and Schuster, 1979), 87.

6. Irving Kristol, "The Underdeveloped Profession," *The Public Interest*, Winter 1967.

7. "Peril to Conservatives," *Los Angeles Times*, March 12, 1961. The investigative series, by Gene Blake, ran in five installments, March 5–9, 1961.

8. David Halberstam interview notes for *The Powers That Be*, second interview with Bob Donovan, from the David Halberstam Collection, box 193, folder 3, Howard Gotlieb Archival Research Center, Boston University (hereafter cited as Halberstam Collection).

9. David Halberstam, *The Powers That Be* (New York: Laurel/Dell, 1986), 490 (orig. pub. 1979).

10. The day before the election, Brown had asked his supporters to elect "good Democratic senators like Tommy Kuchel"—a *Republican* senator from California—before correcting himself and saying he meant Kuchel's opponent. The *L.A. Times* defended the omission of this remark from its news coverage by saying, "The Times reported no campaign charges and countercharges on the last day before the election." "AP Reported Flubs by Nixon and Brown" (AP), *Washington Post*, November 9, 1962, 2; "Nixon Bitterly Assails Press in Bowing Out," *Los Angeles Times*, November 8, 1962, 1.

11. "Transcript of Nixon's News Conference on His Defeat by Brown in Race for Governor of California," *New York Times*, November 8, 1962, 18.

12. Otis Chandler letter to J. D. Middleton, May 6, 1964, Los Angeles Times Records (hereafter cited as LATR), box 448, folder 15, Huntington Library, San Marino, CA. Charles Mohr, "Attacks Provoke Goldwater Camp, *New York Times*, May 30, 1964, 6.

13. Max Frankel, "Agnew: A Broad Attack on TV and the Press," *New York Times*, November 23, 1969, sec. 4, 1.

14. Transcript of speech from John R. Coyne, *The Impudent Snobs: Agnew vs. the Intellectual Establishment* (New Rochelle, NY: Arlington House, 1972), 266–268.

15. Ibid., 267–269.

16. John Anthony Maltese, *Spin Control: The White House Office of Communications and the Management of Presidential News* (Chapel Hill: University of North Carolina Press, 1994), 54–57; Justin P. Coffey, *Spiro Agnew and the Rise of the Republican Right* (Santa Barbara, CA: Praeger, 2015), 99.

17. Transcript of speech from Coyne, *Impudent Snobs*, 271–272.

18. Jules Witcover, *White Knight: The Rise of Spiro Agnew* (New York: Random House, 1972), 322.

19. John Oakes to James Reston, December 1, 1969, John Oakes Papers, box 12, folder "James Reston," Rare Book and Manuscript Library, Columbia University Library (hereafter cited as Oakes Papers). William Greider, "Public Backs Agnew Blast at Networks," *Washington Post,* November 15, 1969; "Most Callers Supported Agnew," *Washington Post,* November 22, 1969.

20. Coffey, *Spiro Agnew,* 106.

21. Contrary to popular belief, Agnew did not call journalists "nattering nabobs of negativism"—that insult was directed at his opponents in Congress. His other most famous erudite-sounding insult, "an effete corps of impudent snobs," was aimed at radical college students and their sympathizers. See Norman P. Lewis, "The Myth of Spiro Agnew's 'Nattering Nabobs of Negativism,'" *American Journalism* 27, no. 1 (Winter 2010): 89–115.

22. Transcript of speech in Houston on May 22, 1970, printed in Coyne, *Impudent Snobs,* 332–334.

23. Ibid.

24. "Mitchell Assails Veracity of Media" (UPI), *New York Times,* May 1, 1971.

25. Quoted in Coffey, *Spiro Agnew,* 99.

26. As David Greenberg notes, the Republican National Committee had begun emphasizing the theme of media bias in its newsletter, and "with polls showing that most people believed the press was sometimes biased, the president knew his adversaries were vulnerable." David Greenberg, *Nixon's Shadow: The History of an Image* (New York: W. W. Norton, 2003), 146–147.

27. Mark Feldstein, *Poisoning the Press: Richard Nixon, Jack Anderson, and the Rise of Washington's Scandal Culture* (New York: Farrar, Straus and Giroux, 2010), 129.

28. Witcover, *White Knight,* 314; Greenberg, *Nixon's Shadow,* 147–150.

29. Witcover, *White Knight,* 315, 320.

30. Halberstam, *The Powers That Be,* 908–916.

31. Max Frankel, interview with author, September 9, 2014.

32. See Chapter 6 for more on the rise of adversarial journalism.

33. Transcripts in Coyne, *Impudent Snobs,* 267, 272. Incidentally, the decision to equate the civil rights pioneer Carmichael with the neo-Nazi Rockwell speaks volumes about the Nixon administration's view of the Black Power movement.

34. Transcript in Coyne, *Impudent Snobs,* 259.

35. James Reston, "Washington: The Voices of the Silent Majority," *New York Times,* November 28, 1969.

36. "The Perils of Spiro," *Washington Post,* September 25, 1968.

37. Richard Homan, "No Formula for Peace, Agnew Says," *Washington Post,* September 23, 1968; "Agnew Explains 'Polack' and 'Jap,'" *New York Times,* September 24, 1968, 37; Witcover, *White Knight,* 253–261.

38. A. M. Rosenthal memorandum for the file, January 23, 1970, A. M. Rosenthal Papers, box 1, folder 13, New York Times Company Records, Manuscripts and Archives Division, New York Public Library (hereafter cited as Rosenthal Papers); Arthur Ochs Sulzberger letter to Spiro Agnew, January 28, 1970, Rosenthal Papers, box 1, folder 14; exchange of memos between A. O. Sulzberger and John Oakes, January 1970, Oakes Papers, box 14.

39. Seymour Topping memo to A. M. Rosenthal, December 4, 1969, Rosenthal Papers, box 1, folder 14.

40. Spiro Agnew letter to A. M. Rosenthal, January 30, 1970, and A. M. Rosenthal letter to Spiro Agnew, February 3, 1970, Rosenthal Papers, box 1, folder 14.

41. Richard Nixon to Alden Whitman, January 19, 1970, Rosenthal Papers, box 31, folder 27.

42. Alden Whitman, "Nixon's Inner Circle Here Remains Close to Him," *New York Times,* January 17, 1970.

43. James M. Naughton, "Agnew Ends Visit to Vietnam, Hailing U.S. Policy as Right," *New York Times,* January 2, 1970.

44. Sulzberger memo to Raskin, Rosenthal, and Schwartz, November 21, 1969, Oakes Papers, box 14.

45. Theodore Bernstein to A. O. Sulzberger, December 12, 1969, Rosenthal Papers, box 70, folder 2.

46. A. H. Raskin memo to A. O. Sulzberger, n.d., and A. H. Raskin memo to Sydney Gruson, April 5, 1971, Oakes Papers, box 12, folder "A. H. Raskin."

47. Transcript of "A Chat with Otis Chandler," "News Conference," KNBC-TV, November 29, 1969, LATR, box 232, folder 10.

48. "Agnew vs. Press: Round Two," *Los Angeles Times,* November 23, 1969.

49. Nick Williams to E. J. Bataille, November 26, 1969, LATR, box 447, folder 9; Nick Williams to Saul David, December 2, 1969, LATR, box 449, folder 9; Nick Williams to C. J. Ammann, June 2, 1970, LATR, box 466, folder 1; Nick Williams to Herbert R. Murphy, June 29, 1970, LATR, box 457, folder 4.

50. "Response to Vice President's Attack," *New York Times,* November 21, 1969, 22; Frank Stanton address to International Radio and Television Society, New York, November 25, 1969, LATR, box 231, folder 14.

51. The Harris Survey, "Public Confidence in Institutions Remains Low," press release, November 13, 1972. www.harrisinteractive.com/vault/Harris-Interactive-Poll-Research-PUBLIC-CONFIDENCE-IN-INSTITUTIONS-REMAINS-LOW-1972-11.pdf. As the title of the press release indicates, confidence in nearly all American institutions declined in the 1960s, but that was little consolation to newspaper managers.

52. Nick Williams memo to Otis Chandler, August 24, 1966, LATR, box 230, folder 2.

53. Transcript of Otis Chandler speech at Claremont Men's College Public Affairs Forum, November 2, 1967, LATR, box 230, folder 13.

54. Nick Williams to Stu Loory, July 23, 1971, LATR, box 454, folder 9.

55. Bill Thomas speech to Management Conference Installation Banquet, June 1972, LATR, box 408, folder 4.

56. Memorandum from "I. V." (Ivan Veit) to Mr. Sulzberger, March 27, 1973, Oakes Papers, box 15, folder "Ivan Veit."

57. James Reston memo, March 12, 1969, Charlotte Curtis Papers, box 8, folder 2, Schlesinger Library, Radcliffe Institute, Harvard University (hereafter cited as Curtis Papers).

58. Oakes to Sulzberger, October 9, 1963; Oakes to Sulzberger, October 6, 1964; Oakes to Sulzberger, October 21, 1964; Oakes to Sulzberger, October 23, 1964; Oakes to Daniel Schwarz, January 16, 1968; Oakes to Sulzberger, June 13, 1974; all in Oakes Papers, box 13.

59. George Cotliar, interview with author, September 16, 2014.

60. Nick Williams speech to California Newspaper Publishers Association, June 1961, LATR, box 468, folder 15.

61. A. M. Rosenthal memo to Gene Roberts and Arthur Gelb, November 7, 1969, Rosenthal Papers, box 70, folder 2.

62. Exchange of memos between A. O. Sulzberger and A. M. Rosenthal, May 13, 1970, Curtis Papers, box 8, folder 3. Sulzberger seems to have sent the memo to Rosenthal at the suggestion of *Times* family/style editor Charlotte Curtis.

63. A. M. Rosenthal memo to Joan Whitman, June 19, 1974, Rosenthal Papers, box 69, folder 13; Lacey Fosburgh, "Lonely and Full of Hate, She Joined the Nazi Party—She's Less Lonely Now," *New York Times,* June 6, 1974, 42.

64. Text of Otis Chandler speech at the University of Maryland Distinguished Lecture Series, April 17, 1969, LATR, box 232, folder 1.

65. Transcript of "News Conference," KNBC-TV, November 29, 1969, LATR, box 232, folder 10.

66. Clay S. Felker, "Guerrilla Tactics for Consumer Journalism," *BASNE,* July–August 1971, 6; Timothy Crouse, *The Boys on the Bus* (New York: Random House, 1972).

67. Herbert J. Gans, *Deciding What's News: A Study of CBS Evening News, NBC Nightly News, Newsweek, and Time* (New York: Vintage Books, 1980), 52–62.

68. Bill Boyarsky, interview with author, July 31, 2014.

69. A. H. Raskin memo for A.O.S., n.d., Oakes Papers, box 12, folder "A. H. Raskin." All of these suggested changes would tend to increase the number of pages that Raskin and his boss, John Oakes, would oversee.

70. On the creation of the *New York Times* op-ed page, see Susan E. Tifft and Alex S. Jones, *The Trust: The Private and Powerful Family behind the New York Times* (Boston: Little, Brown, 1999), 463–464; Edwin Diamond, *Behind the Times: Inside the New New York Times* (New York: Villard Books, 1994), 292–295.

71. A. O. Sulzberger memo to John Oakes, December 5, 1969, Oakes Papers, box 14.

72. Seymour Topping to A. M. Rosenthal, December 4, 1969, Rosenthal Papers, box 1, folder 14.

73. Journal entry, March 13, 1971, A. M. Rosenthal Papers (personal papers), box 4, Manuscripts and Archives Division, New York Public Library.

74. Rosenthal to Sulzberger, December 8, 1969, Rosenthal Papers, box 70, folder 2.

75. See Chapter 6 for more detail on Oakes's ouster.

76. Max Frankel, interview with author, September 9, 2014.

77. On the transformation of the *L.A. Times* in the early 1960s, see Halberstam, *The Powers That Be,* 547–563.

78. Nick Williams form letter response to reader complaints, n.d. (circa 1964), LATR, box 448, folder 15.

79. Otis Chandler to J. D. "Tex" Middleton, May 6, 1964, LATR, box 448, folder 15.

80. Jim Bassett, "Some Random Notes on the 'Image' Report," May 15, 1964, LATR, box 292, folder 1. The memo is dated "5/15" and does not give the year, but the "image report" to which it refers was conducted in early 1964—see LATR, box 448, folder 15, materials related to "Opinion Setters Media Image Survey."

81. Nick Williams to Robert U. Brown, August 21, 1969, LATR, box 449, folder 15.

82. Eugene H. Dyer to James Bassett, July 23, 1970, LATR, box 294, folder 10.

83. James Bassett to Eugene H. Dyer, August 3, 1970, LATR, box 294, folder 10.

84. Bill Thomas to Otis Chandler and Robert D. Nelson, January 5, 1972, LATR, box 395, folder 10.

85. Nick Williams to Gust W. George, March 3, 1970, LATR, box 466, folder 6.

86. "Get Out of Vietnam NOW," *Los Angeles Times,* June 7, 1970; Nick Williams to S. N. Spry, June 22, 1970, LATR, box 466, folder 9.

87. See, for example, "In Defense of Business," *Los Angeles Times,* February 2, 1975; "Business Beleaguered," *Los Angeles Times,* May 20, 1975; "Labor Ignores the Greater Good," *Los Angeles Times,* February 14, 1971; "Labor Takes a Walk," *Los Angeles Times,* March 24, 1972.

88. Dennis McDougal, *Privileged Son: Otis Chandler and the Rise and Fall of the L.A. Times Dynasty* (Cambridge, MA: Perseus, 2001), 480n3.

89. The paper reversed this policy in 2008. See Scott Martelle, "The Times Endorses Obama and McCain," *Los Angeles Times,* February 2, 2008, http://articles.latimes.com/2008/feb/02/nation/na-endorse2.

90. "Some Changes in the Editorial Pages," *Los Angeles Times,* September 23, 1973.

91. Seymour Topping to A. O. Sulzberger, March 17, 1971, Seymour Topping Papers, box 2, folder 11, New York Times Company Records, Manuscripts and Archives Division, New York Public Library.

92. Otis Chandler to "Times Employees and Their Families," September 9, 1976, LATR, box 170, folder 5; memo to Otis Chandler, author unknown, August 24, 1972, LATR, box 607, folder 12.

93. "Some Changes in the Editorial Pages," *Los Angeles Times,* September 23, 1973.

94. David Shaw, "Political Columnists: What Became of the Liberals?," *Los Angeles Times,* April 9, 1984.

95. Media Matters for America, "Black and White and Re(a)d All Over: The Conservative Advantage in Syndicated Op-Ed Columns," September 2007, cloudfront.mediamatters.org/static/pdf/oped_report.pdf.

96. Nicole Hemmer, *Messengers of the Right: Conservative Media and the Transformation of American Politics* (Philadelphia: University of Pennsylvania Press, 2016), 220–226.

97. This remains the dominant right-wing critique of the news media today, although the demands for less interpretive reporting have fallen off—an indication of how entrenched and accepted interpretive reporting has become.

98. Freddie Miller to Otis Chandler, February 16, 1967, LATR, box 224, folder 45.

99. Halberstam, *The Powers That Be*, 408. Although Chandler surely sympathized with the young, black, and poor, it seems hard to believe that, as a fabulously wealthy white forty-one-year-old, he would have shown such a profound lack of self-awareness. It is possible that Halberstam's source (a CBS journalist) misheard or misremembered Chandler's comment: see David Halberstam, notes for *The Powers That Be*, Halberstam Collection, box 193, folder 3.

100. Pamphlet with text of Otis Chandler address before Colorado Press Association Convention, February 21, 1969, LATR, box 231, folder 17.

101. Transcript of Otis Chandler speech at Claremont Graduate School, May 20, 1978, LATR, box 235, folder 24.

102. David Halberstam interview with Phil Kerby, n.d., notes for *The Powers That Be*, Halberstam Collection, box 193, folder 15.

103. Robert Scheer, "Jimmy, We Hardly Knew Y'All," *Playboy*, November 1976.

104. Bob Gottlieb and Irene Wolt, "The Changing of the Guard—and the Future—at the Times," *Los Angeles*, December 1977, 336–337. See also transcript of Marshall Berges interview with Robert Scheer, September 28, 1979, LATR, box 583, folder 2.

105. Gottlieb and Wolt, "Changing of the Guard," 336–337.

106. Nick Williams to Saul David, December 2, 1969, LATR, box 449, folder 9.

107. For one survey of reporters' political views in the 1930s, see Leo C. Rosten, *The Washington Correspondents* (New York: Harcourt Brace, 1937), 340–349.

108. Nick Williams to Dorothy B. Chandler, January 25, 1973, LATR, box 448, folder 13.

109. Bill Thomas to Otis Chandler, April 25, 1973, LATR, box 395, folder 9.

110. Roger Rappaport, "A Young Journalist Puts His Typewriter Where His Mouth Is," *BASNE*, July–August 1971, 3–5.

111. A. M. Rosenthal to James Reston, March 25, 1971, James B. Reston Papers, box 2, folder 8, New York Times Company Records, Manuscripts and Archives Division, New York Public Library.

112. A. M. Rosenthal to James Reston, August 4, 1968, Rosenthal Papers, box 70, folder 2.

113. Peter Millones to A. M. Rosenthal, n.d., and James Greenfield to A. M. Rosenthal, January 31, 1973, Rosenthal Papers, box 6, folder 11.

114. Paul Beck to Steven V. Roberts, August 20, 1970, Rosenthal Papers, box 35, folder 32; Steven V. Roberts, "Crackdown in California," *Change* 2, no. 4 (July–August 1970): 3–6. Roberts's earlier dispute with the editors in New York—Abe Rosenthal in particular—came in 1968, after he wrote about the student uprising at Columbia in the *Village Voice:* see Chapter 3.

115. Seymour Topping to Gene Roberts, August 27, 1970, Rosenthal Papers, box 35, folder 32.

116. Steve Roberts, interview with author, October 3, 2014.

117. John D. Lofton Jr. to A. O. Sulzberger, January 27, 1974, and A. M. Rosenthal to A. O. Sulzberger, February 12, 1974, Rosenthal Papers, box 69, folder 13.

118. A. M. Rosenthal to A. O. Sulzberger, February 12, 1974, Rosenthal Papers, box 69, folder 13.

119. Thomas E. Patterson, *Out of Order* (New York: Knopf, 1993), 79.

120. Paul Taylor, *See How They Run: Electing the President in an Age of Mediaocracy* (New York: Knopf, 1990), 23, cited in Patterson, *Out of Order,* 19.

121. Irving Kristol, "Crisis for Journalism: The Missing Elite," in *Press, Politics and Popular Government,* ed. George F. Will (Washington, DC: American Enterprise Institute, 1972), 43–44. Kristol's essay in this volume was adapted from a speech he gave in 1971.

122. Patterson, *Out of Order,* 114.

123. Robert L. Bartley, "The Press: Adversary, Surrogate Sovereign, or Both?," in Will, *Press, Politics and Popular Government,* 10–14, quotation at 11.

3. Objectivity and the Left: An Ideal Worth Abandoning

1. Advertisement, *New York Times,* March 20, 1970, 41.

2. The other two beliefs were "that every accused man or institution should have the immediate right of reply" and "that we should not use a typewriter to stick our fingers in people's eyes just because we have the power to do so." A. M. Rosenthal memorandum for the staff, October 7, 1969, A. M. Rosenthal Papers, box 70, folder 2, New York Times Company Records, Manuscripts and Archives Division, New York Public Library (hereafter cited as Rosenthal Papers).

3. Rosenthal to James Reston, August 4, 1968, Rosenthal Papers, box 70, folder 2.

4. "Attack on Objectivity Increases from Within," *Editor & Publisher,* June 13, 1970, 24.

5. Stanford Sesser, "Journalists: Objectivity and Activism," *Wall Street Journal,* October 21, 1969.

6. Ted Boyle to A. M. Rosenthal, January 12, 1970, and Charles Bailey to A. M. Rosenthal, December 4, 1969, Rosenthal Papers, box 70 folder 2; see also box 92, folders 12 and 13.

7. Herbert Brucker, "What's Wrong with Objectivity?," *Saturday Review,* October 11, 1969.

8. Transcript of remarks by John H. Colburn at the annual meeting of the Blue Pencil Club of Ohio, May 17, 1970, Los Angeles Times Records (hereafter cited as LATR), box 232, folder 14, Huntington Library, San Marino, CA.

9. Hunter S. Thompson, *Fear and Loathing: On the Campaign Trail '72* (New York: Grand Central, 2006), 33 (orig. pub. 1973).

10. Robert D. McFadden, "Campus Activism Fades, Style of 1950's Prevails," *New York Times,* April 23, 1973.

11. A. M. Rosenthal to Arthur Gelb and Mitchel Levitas, April 24, 1973, Rosenthal Papers, box 70, folder 1.

12. John W. Finney, "Absenteeism in Senate," *New York Times,* April 1, 1972.

13. A. M. Rosenthal to John Finney, Max Frankel, and Robert Phelps, April 3, 1972, Rosenthal Papers, box 70, folder 1.

14. Arthur Krock, "The Democrats: Deja Vu," *New York Times,* July 10, 1972, 21.

15. A. M. Rosenthal memo to Lawrence Hauck and David R. Jones, July 10, 1972, Rosenthal Papers, box 70, folder 1.

16. A. M. Rosenthal, "Combat and Compassion at Columbia," *New York Times,* May 1, 1968.

17. Steven V. Roberts, interview with author, October 3, 2014.

18. Steven V. Roberts, "The University That Refused to Learn," *Village Voice,* May 9, 1968, 2.

19. A. M. Rosenthal memorandum for files, May 22, 1968, Rosenthal Papers, box 35, folder 32.

20. Steven V. Roberts, interview with author, October 3, 2014.

21. Daniel C. Hallin, *The "Uncensored War": The Media in Vietnam* (New York: Oxford University Press, 1986), 116–117.

22. C. Gerald Fraser, interview with author, October 24, 2014.

23. Ibid.; Earl Caldwell, interview with author, October 3, 2014.

24. Earl Caldwell, interview with author, October 3, 2014.

25. C. Gerald Fraser, interview with author, October 24, 2014.

26. Author interviews.

27. Donald Barker to John Oakes, April 11, 1972, Harrison Salisbury Papers, box 8, folder "John Oakes," Rare Book and Manuscript Library, Columbia University Library (hereafter cited as Salisbury Papers).

28. Nicholas von Hoffman, "Newspaper Objectivity," *Washington Post,* June 29, 1970.

29. Tom Wicker, "The Greening of the Press," *Columbia Journalism Review,* May/June 1971, 7–12.

30. Ibid.; transcript of lecture by Tom Wicker at the University of California, Riverside, February 29, 1972, Tom Wicker Papers, box 18 folder 5, New York Times Company Records, Manuscripts and Archives Division, New York Public Library (hereafter cited as Wicker Papers).

31. Leslie R. Colitt, "The Mask of Objectivity," *The Nation,* June 17, 1968, 789–791; David Deitch, "Case for Advocacy Journalism," *The Nation,* November 17, 1969, 530–532; Edwin Diamond, "'Reporter Power' Takes Root," *Columbia Journalism Review,* Summer 1970, 12–18.

32. Milton Viorst, "Le Monde: Very Serious, Very Successful," *Columbia Journalism Review,* September/October 1974, 44–48.

33. Arthur Gelb, *City Room* (New York: Marian Wood/G. P. Putnam's Sons, 2003), 536.

34. David Schneiderman to A. M. Rosenthal, January 26, 1972; Rosenthal to Schneiderman, January 27, 1972; Rosenthal to Harrison Salisbury, January 28, 1972; all in Salisbury Papers, box 167, folder 12.

35. Edwin Diamond, "The Cabal at the New York Times: Which Way to the Revolution?," *New York,* May 18, 1970; Gelb, *City Room,* 533–537.

36. Joseph Lelyveld, interview with author, September 5, 2014.

37. Journal entry, January 29, 1971, A. M. Rosenthal Papers (personal papers), box 4, New York Public Library (hereafter cited as Rosenthal Papers [personal]).

38. *[More],* May 1971, 2.

39. Stanford Sesser, "Journalists: Objectivity and Activism," *Wall Street Journal,* October 21, 1969, 22.

40. "Tom Wicker Turns on Harvard Teach-In," *Boston Globe,* February 25, 1971.

41. A. M. Rosenthal to Arthur Ochs Sulzberger, May 26, 1971, Rosenthal Papers, box 70, folder 1.

42. The Arthur Ochs Sulzberger papers, at the New York Public Library, are closed to researchers until 2035.

43. Arthur Ochs Sulzberger to Tom Wicker, March 16, 1970, and Wicker to Sulzberger, March 17, 1970, Wicker Papers, box 7, folder 11.

44. A. M. Rosenthal to Arthur Ochs Sulzberger, March 15, 1972, and Arthur Ochs Sulzberger to Charlotte Curtis, March 16, 1972, Rosenthal Papers, box 87, folder 8. Arthur Ochs Sulzberger to Charlotte Curtis, April 4, 1972, Charlotte Curtis Papers, box 8, folder 6, Schlesinger Library, Radcliffe Institute, Harvard University.

45. Susan E. Tifft and Alex S. Jones, *The Trust: The Private and Powerful Family behind the New York Times* (Boston: Little Brown, 1999), 422–424.

46. Tom Wicker, "Seeking an Impact on Events," *New York Times,* October 15, 1974.

47. A. M. Rosenthal to Arthur Ochs Sulzberger, October 17, 1974, Rosenthal Papers, box 69, folder 13.

48. Author interviews.

49. Grace Lichtenstein, interview with author, August 29, 2014.

50. Grace Lichtenstein, "Rape Laws Undergoing Changes to Aid Victims," *New York Times,* June 4, 1975, 1.

51. A. M. Rosenthal to David R. Jones, Hedrick Smith, and John Herbers, June 4, 1975, Rosenthal Papers, box 27, folder 2.

52. Grace Lichtenstein, interview with author, August 29, 2014.

53. Transcript of *Behind the Lines,* WNET/Channel 13, February 21, 1972, Rosenthal Papers (personal), box 15, folder 1; Grace Lichtenstein interview with author, August 29, 2014; Nan Robertson, *The Girls in the Balcony: Women, Men, and the New York Times* (New York: Random House, 1992), 143; Joseph C. Goulden, *Fit to Print: A. M. Rosenthal and His Times* (Secaucus, NJ: Lyle Stuart, 1988), 374–375.

54. Earl Caldwell, interview with author, October 3, 2014.

55. See Hallin, *The "Uncensored War,"* 116–117.

56. Journal entry, January 29, 1971, Rosenthal Papers (personal), box 4.

57. Chandler delivered the same remarks in other speeches as well. Transcript of Otis Chandler speech at UCLA, May 21, 1971, LATR, box 233, folder 8; transcript of Otis Chandler speech at Temple Beth Am, January 12, 1971, LATR, box 233, folder 1.

58. Text of Nick Williams speech to Claremont University Club, circa 1970, LATR, box 469, folder 1.

59. Nick Williams to George Garton, June 16, 1970, LATR, box 466, folder 9.

60. Nick Williams to Richard L. Bean, June 19, 1969, LATR, box 447, folder 9.

61. Transcript of "News Conference," May 13, 1972, KNBC-TV Los Angeles, LATR, box 409, folder 7.

62. Tim Rutten, interview with author, August 2, 2014.

63. Bill Boyarsky, interview with author, July 31, 2014.

64. Dennis A. Britton, interview with author, September 26, 2014. Jim Bell, interview with author, August 28, 2014. Gene Blake letter to Southwest District Courts Associa-

tion, March 8, 1971, LATR, box 448, folder 1. In a 1968 memo to Otis Chandler, Williams noted, "We have to be damn careful of our objectivity"; Williams to Chandler, September 13, 1968, LATR, box 448, folder 15. To a reader in 1970, he said the *Times* was written "objectively"; Williams to Woodruff De Silva, October 16, 1970, LATR, box 449, folder 9.

65. Williams to Frank Haven, Jim Bellows, and Jim Bassett, March 20, 1970, LATR, box 466, folder 6. In other memos, Williams wrote that the *L.A. Times* must be "like Caesar's wife"—that is, above suspicion.

66. Nick Williams to Jack Nightscales, October 15, 1969, LATR, box 466, folder 1.

67. Dennis A. Britton, interview with author, September 26, 2014.

68. Jim Bell, interview with author, August 28, 2014.

69. Nick Williams to Richard L. Bean, June 19, 1969, LATR, box 447, folder 9.

70. Nick Williams to Otis Chandler, September 13, 1968, LATR, box 448, folder 15.

71. Thomas to Williams, March 18, 1969, and Haven to Williams, n.d., LATR, box 461, folder 10.

72. Robert J. Donovan to Otis Chandler, September 9, 1970, and Nick Williams to Otis Chandler, September 14, 1970, LATR, box 220, folder 32.

73. Text of Bill Thomas speech before 1978 Region 11 SPJ-SDX Conference, Costa Mesa, California, April 22, 1978, LATR, box 408, folder 7.

74. Dennis A. Britton, interview with author, September 26, 2014.

75. Text of Thomas speech before SPJ-SDX Conference, April 22, 1978.

76. Bill Thomas, "The Press: Is It Biased against the Establishment," *Los Angeles Times,* March 30, 1975.

77. Text of Thomas speech before SPJ-SDX Conference, April 22, 1978 (emphasis in original).

78. Text of Nick Williams speech to Fourth Annual Current Affairs Seminar, n.d., LATR, box 469, folder 5.

79. M. L. Stein, "The Press under Assault," *Saturday Review,* October 12, 1968.

80. *Seminar: A Quarterly Review for Newspapermen,* September 1969.

81. A. M. Rosenthal to Arthur Ochs Sulzberger, January 23, 1978, Rosenthal Papers, box 92, folder 11.

82. Text of Nick Williams speech to Theta Sigma Phi, Denver, April 17, 1966, LATR, box 468, folder 20 (emphasis in original); text of unlabeled Nick Williams speech, n.d., LATR, box 468, folder 19.

83. Text of Otis Chandler speech to the Colorado Press Association Convention, February 21, 1969, LATR, box 231, folder 17.

84. George Cotliar, interview with author, September 16, 2014.

85. Harrison Salisbury to Earl J. Johnson, December 3, 1971, Salisbury Papers, box 6, unlabeled folder.

86. Seymour Topping, interview with author, May 5, 2013.

87. Dennis McDougal, *Privileged Son: Otis Chandler and the Rise and Fall of the L.A. Times Dynasty* (Cambridge, MA: Perseus, 2001), 358.

88. See Chapter 4 for a more detailed discussion of the business and financial state of the *L.A. Times* during this era.

89. "Behind the Profit Squeeze at the New York Times," *BusinessWeek,* August 30, 1976. See Chapter 4 for a more detailed discussion of the business and financial state of the *New York Times* during this era.

90. Nick Williams to Otis Chandler, April 8, 1964, LATR, box 448, folder 15.

91. Williams to Frank Haven, Jim Bellows, and Jim Bassett, March 20, 1970, LATR, box 466, folder 6.

92. Although this chapter mainly emphasizes Rosenthal's views, he spoke for many of the paper's senior editors. Two of his three predecessors as the top editor even asked for his help in formulating their own views on objectivity. See A. M. Rosenthal to James Reston, September 4, 1968, and Turner Catledge to A. M. Rosenthal, September 4, 1969, Rosenthal Papers, box 70, folder 2.

93. See Chapter 1 for more on the "news analysis" form.

94. A. M. Rosenthal memo to senior editors and Bullpen, July 24, 1973, and A. M. Rosenthal memo to Clifton Daniel, David R. Jones, and Robert Semple, December 12, 1973, Rosenthal Papers, box 92, folder 8.

95. Journal entry, January 29, 1971, Rosenthal Papers (personal), box 4.

96. A. M. Rosenthal to Clifton Daniel and James Reston, August 29, 1968, Rosenthal Papers, box 70, folder 2.

97. Fox Butterfield, interview with author, August 12, 2014; C. Gerald Fraser, interview with author, October 24, 2014; Mickey Carroll, interview with author, August 28, 2014.

4. The Reader-Oriented Newspaper

1. The Commission on Freedom of the Press, *A Free and Responsible Press* (Chicago: University of Chicago Press, 1947), 29.

2. David R. Davies, *The Postwar Decline of American Newspapers, 1945–1965* (Westport, CT: Praeger, 2006), 117.

3. The broadsheets that folded between 1960 and 1967 were the *Journal-American,* the *World Telegram & Sun,* and the *Herald Tribune.* One major tabloid, the *Mirror,* also folded, but the *Daily News* and the *Post,* both tabloids, continued to publish, as did the business newspaper the *Wall Street Journal.*

4. Otis Chandler to Norman Chandler and Al Casey, January 5, 1966, Los Angeles Times Records, box 220, folder 32, Huntington Library, San Marino, CA (hereafter cited as LATR).

5. As Kenneth Jackson notes, the suburban population in the United States grew from 36 million in 1950 to 74 million in 1970; in the 1970 census, suburbanites outnumbered city dwellers and rural residents for the first time. Between 1950 and 1980, population declined in 18 of the 25 largest U.S. cities. Kenneth T. Jackson, *Crabgrass Frontier: The Suburbanization of the United States* (New York: Oxford University Press, 1985), 283–284.

6. Davies, *Postwar Decline,* 112–114.

7. "Suburb and City," *Columbia Journalism Review,* Summer 1963.

8. Nick Williams, memo titled "Editorial Outlook," April 7, 1970, LATR, box 452, folder 5.

9. On other newspapers adopting zoned sections, see William B. Dickinson, "Wooing the Suburban Reader with Zoned Editions," *BASNE,* March 1, 1965.

10. Vance Stickell to Robert D. Nelson, memo titled "Suburban Section Report," December 1966, and map titled "Los Angeles Times Suburban Sections" (1964), LATR, box 80, folder 8.

11. Memo from Robert D. Nelson, April 9, 1973, LATR, box 80, folder 9; map titled "Los Angeles Times Suburban Sections" (1972), LATR, box 80, folder 9; table titled "Suburban Section Financial Performance 1979," LATR, box 85, folder 7.

12. Vance Stickell to Phil Magwood and Bob Christy, January 14, 1977, LATR, box 71, folder 6.

13. Claudia Luther, interview with author, September 12, 2014. Arthur Gelb to A. M. Rosenthal (discussing visit to *L.A. Times*), September 21, 1970, A. M. Rosenthal Papers, box 85, folder 4, New York Times Company Records, Manuscripts and Archives Division, New York Public Library (hereafter cited as Rosenthal Papers).

14. Nick Williams to Frank Haven, December 29, 1966, LATR, box 444, folder 4.

15. "The Press: Launching a Satellite," *Time,* March 29, 1968, 45; George Cotliar, interview with author, September 16, 2014.

16. George Cotliar, interview with author, September 16, 2014.

17. "Suburb and City"; "Times Mirror to Buy Balance of Newsday," *Los Angeles Times,* October 27, 1970.

18. Report of Publisher's Special Committee, "Sectional Runs: Evaluation of Minimum Cost Product," October 1966, Rosenthal Papers, box 110, folder 7.

19. Andy Fisher to Max Falk, Charles Guthrie, Walter Mattson, Abe Rosenthal, Mark Senigo, and Warren Wolfe, October 27, 1969, Rosenthal Papers, box 110, folder 7.

20. Lee Smith, "The Battle for Sunday," *New York,* October 25, 1971. Memo from Robert D. Nelson (subject: Los Angeles Times tour by New York Times management group), September 1, 1970, LATR, box 76, folder 6.

21. Arthur Gelb to A. M. Rosenthal, September 21, 1970, Rosenthal Papers, box 85, folder 4.

22. Arthur Ochs Sulzberger to Clifton Daniel, December 8, 1971, and J. W. Campbell to Max Falk, September 14, 1972, Rosenthal Papers, box 62, folder 2.

23. Jack Schwartz to A. M. Rosenthal, August 6, 1975, Rosenthal Papers, box 62, folder 2.

24. Peter Millones to A. M. Rosenthal, August 8, 1975, Rosenthal Papers, box 62, folder 2.

25. This brought the total number of suburban weeklies to four—the New Jersey section had launched in 1972, shortly after BQLI—where it remained for decades.

26. James Greenfield to A. M. Rosenthal and Seymour Topping, February 23, 1978, and Peter Millones to A. M. Rosenthal, n.d. (circa 1978), Rosenthal Papers, box 108, folder 1.

27. Text of Seymour Topping speech at University of Pennsylvania, January 1978, Rosenthal Papers, box 44, folder 8.

28. In 1960 the *Daily News* had a circulation of over 2 million and a Sunday circulation of over 3.4 million, compared to 686,246 (daily) and 1,371,939 (Sunday) for the *Times.*

"Facts and Figures for Managers and Supervisors—The New York Times," February 7–8, 1973, Charlottes Curtis Papers, box 8, folder 8, Schlesinger Library, Radcliffe Institute, Harvard University (hereafter cited as Curtis Papers).

29. See Chapter 1 for a discussion of this shift.

30. Text of Otis Chandler remarks at American Society of Newspaper Editors panel discussion, April 17, 1964, LATR, box 228, folder 43.

31. For example, consider this opening paragraph about the 1968 crisis in the global monetary system: "With the experts on every hand proclaiming loudly that the week's gold panic threatens nothing less than the destruction of the international financial system, the average American who is struggling to understand why is also asking himself another, more urgent, question. What does the panic mean to me?" (The article proceeded to answer that question.) Eileen Shanahan, "What It Means to U.S.," *New York Times,* March 17, 1968.

32. Jackson, *Crabgrass Frontier,* 272–282.

33. Text of Seymour Topping speech at University of Pennsylvania, January 1978, Rosenthal Papers, box 44, folder 8.

34. As Benedict Anderson famously argued, newspapers create an "imagined community" among their readership. See Benedict Anderson, *Imagined Communities: Reflections on the Origin and Spread of Nationalism* (London: Verso, 1983).

35. George Beebe, "Women's Pages in 1973," *BASNE,* February 1963.

36. Thomas J. Berrigan, "Why *Should* Content Change with the Decades?," *BASNE,* February 1963.

37. "The Metropolitan Point of View," *BASNE,* February 1963.

38. Savoy's husband, Jim Bellows, recalled in his memoir that she "balked at the label 'society editor'" but "put up with it for a while" until she got the more fitting title "women's editor." In her memo to Nick Williams, however, Savoy wrote, "Definitely interested in taking the job (and the title, if you insist) of SOCIETY EDITOR of the Los Angeles Times. . . . THIS SHOULD BE CLEARLY UNDERSTOOD: I do not want, now or at any time, to be Woman's [*sic*] Editor. Positively." Jim Bellows, *The Last Editor: How I Saved the New York Times, the Washington Post, and the Los Angeles Times from Dullness and Complacency* (Kansas City: Andrews McMeel, 2002), 144. Maggie Savoy to Nick Williams, "Thoughts about Section IV," n.d., with Williams handwritten note to "OC," LATR, box 433, folder 6.

39. Maggie Savoy to Nick Williams, "Thoughts about Section IV," n.d., with Williams handwritten note to "OC," LATR, box 433, folder 6.

40. Nick Williams to Jim Bellows, August 21, 1968, LATR, box 464, folder 12.

41. It was also known as the Column One story, because the position in which it appeared was page one, column one.

42. Frank Haven memorandum, April 2, 1969, LATR, box 444, folder 4. Ross Newhan, "The Idol Rich," *Los Angeles Times,* November 12, 1968; Robert S. Elegant, "Problem of Young Love Boggling the Thoughts of Mao," *Los Angeles Times,* February 21, 1969; Nicholas C. Chriss, "Dredgers, Oil Drilling Peril Rare Whooper," *Los Angeles Times,* March 19, 1969.

43. Claudia Luther, interview with author, September 12, 2014.

44. Transcript of Jean Sharley Taylor interview with Marshall Berges, September 13, 1979, 38–39, LATR, box 583, folder 13.

45. Marylou Luther, "Today's Debutante: Vanishing Institution?," *Los Angeles Times,* July 26, 1970, E1.

46. For example, some of Powers's early articles for View were about the retirement of a shipping clerk at Firestone, a couple trying to live normal lives as they recovered from heroin addiction, and the experiences of drivers and passengers on one of L.A.'s most crime-ridden bus routes. Charles T. Powers, "Retirement: The Icing on a 26-Year Cake," *Los Angeles Times,* October 8, 1972; Powers, "That Nice Young Couple Next Door—They're Junkies," *Los Angeles Times,* February, 18, 1973; Powers, "A Ride on Line 92: RTD's Rough Route," *Los Angeles Times,* November 14, 1973. For more on the philosophy behind View, see Robert Gottlieb and Irene Wolt, *Thinking Big: The Story of the Los Angeles Times, Its Publishers, and Their Influence on Southern California* (New York: G. P. Putnam's Sons, 1977), 471–472.

47. Jean Sharley Taylor interview, News service, KNBC-TV Los Angeles, December 26, 1974, transcript in LATR, box 627, folder 14; Tim Rutten, interview with author, August 2, 2014; Barbara Saltzman, interview with author, August 28, 2014.

48. Table titled "Readership Figures," July 1975, LATR, box 91, folder 5.

49. Lindsy Van Gelder, "Women's Pages: You Can't Make News out of a Silk Purse," *Ms.,* November 1974; Mills, *A Place in the News,* 118. Dustin Harp also noted that lifestyle sections often hampered the "integration of content about women" into all sections of the newspapers: Dustin Harp, *Desperately Seeking Women Readers: U.S. Newspapers and the Construction of a Female Readership* (Lanham, MD: Lexington Books, 2007), 44.

50. Susan H. Miller, "Changes in Women's / Lifestyle Sections," *Journalism Quarterly* 53, no. 4 (Winter 1976): 646–647; "Flight from Fluff," *Time,* March 20, 1972, 48.

51. Zena Beth Guenin, "Women's Pages in American Newspapers: Missing Out on Contemporary Content," *Journalism Quarterly* 52, no. 1 (Spring 1975): 66–69, 75.

52. Nicholas von Hoffman, "Women's Pages: An Irreverent View," *Columbia Journalism Review,* July / August 1971, 52–54.

53. Marilyn S. Greenwald, *A Woman of the Times: Journalism, Feminism, and the Career of Charlotte Curtis* (Athens, OH: Ohio University Press, 1999), 84.

54. See, for instance: "Sociologist on the Society Beat," *Time,* February 19, 1965; Robert D. McFadden, "Charlotte Curtis, a Columnist for the Times, Is Dead at 58," *New York Times,* April 17, 1987; Mills, *A Place in the News,* 120–121.

55. Charlotte Curtis, "Black Panther Philosophy Is Debated at the Bernsteins'," *New York Times,* January 15, 1970.

56. Tom Wolfe, "Radical Chic: That Party at Lenny's . . . ," *New York,* June 8, 1970; and Tom Wolfe, *Radical Chic and Mau-Mauing the Flak Catchers* (New York: Farrar, Straus and Giroux, 1970). See also Michael Lewis, "How Tom Wolfe Became . . . Tom Wolfe," *Vanity Fair,* November 2015, http://www.vanityfair.com/culture/2015/10/how-tom-wolfe-became-tom-wolfe.

57. Charlotte Curtis memo to staff, with responses, June 17, 1966, Curtis Papers, box 7, folder 15.

58. Julie Baumgold, "Charlotte, Star Reporter," *New York,* October 6, 1969.

59. Nan Robertson, *The Girls in the Balcony: Women, Men and the* New York Times (New York: Random House, 1992), 123.

60. Van Gelder, "Women's Pages"; Mills, *A Place in the News,* 118.

61. Mills, *A Place in the News,* 121.

62. Seymour Topping to A. M. Rosenthal, January 27, 1971, Curtis Papers, box 8, folder 4.

63. Memo from Seymour Topping to senior editorial and production staff, September 17, 1971, Curtis Papers, box 8, folder 4.

64. Ann Sawyer, letter to the editor, September 11, 1971, and Charlotte Curtis to Ann Sawyer, September 16, 1971, Curtis Papers, box 8, folder 4.

65. "Behind the Profit Squeeze at the New York Times," *BusinessWeek,* August 30, 1976, 42.

66. Gerald Lanson and Mitchell Stephens, "Abe Rosenthal: The Man and His *Times,*" *Washington Journalism Review,* July / August 1983, 24–25.

67. Seymour Topping, interview with author, May 5, 2013. The personal-computer column, written by Erik Sandberg Diment, began in June 1982.

68. A play on the term "sexual revolution," a frequent topic of discussion in the 1960s and 1970s. For the term "sectional revolution," see, for example, Edwin Diamond, *Behind the Times: Inside the New New York Times* (New York: Villard Books, 1994), 146–147; Leo Bogart, "Newspapers in Transition," in Douglas Gomery, ed., *Media in America: The Wilson Quarterly Reader* (Washington, DC: Woodrow Wilson Center Press, 1998), 72–73; Jim Willis, *The Age of Multimedia and Turbonews* (Westport, CT: Praeger, 1994), 111.

69. Folder of promotional materials for *You* magazine, n.d., circa 1976, LATR, box 608, folder 17.

70. "You Debuts in the Times," *Among Ourselves* (*Los Angeles Times* internal newsletter), October 1976, LATR, box 607, folder 2. Transcript of Jean Sharley Taylor interview with Marshall Berges, September 13, 1979, 28, LATR, box 583, folder 13.

71. Memo from Craig St. Clair to Carolyn Hom about history of L.A. *Times* supplements, February 25, 1991, LATR, box 608, folder 8.

72. Times Mirror Company annual reports, 1971–1979, LATR, box 119, folders 6–10, and box 120, folders 1–4.

73. Memo from Craig St. Clair to Carolyn Hom about history of L.A. *Times* supplements, February 25, 1991, LATR, box 608, folder 8.

74. Lawrence B. Glickman, *Buying Power: A History of Consumer Activism in America* (Chicago: University of Chicago Press, 2009), ix–xiii. Although these commentators lamented the shift from citizen to consumer, associating it with civic disengagement and apathy, Glickman argues that "the American political tradition of consumer activism" is a time-honored form of active citizenship and an indicator of a robust democratic system (1 and passim).

75. Lizabeth Cohen, *A Consumers' Republic: The Politics of Mass Consumption in Postwar America* (New York: Alfred A. Knopf, 2003), 9.

76. Nick Williams to Otis Chandler, July 10, 1969, LATR, box 448, folder 15.

77. Nick Williams, "Is Our Concept of Editing a Paper Wrong?," *BASNE*, May–June 1973.

78. For instance, the second installment of Newsmakers, on December 12, 1968, included items about: an Australian beauty queen temporarily prevented from boarding a flight to the United States because she did not have a visa (a photo of her ran alongside the item); a blind man who had made free long-distance calls by whistling a perfect imitation of the signal used by the phone company; and a college student who stripped naked during a performance-art piece at a Detroit theater.

79. Nick Williams to Otis Chandler, July 10, 1969, LATR, box 448, folder 15. All-capitals in original.

80. Norman E. Isaacs, "Roses for the Six-Column Look," *BASNE*, March 1965, 6–8.

81. Nick Williams to Otis Chandler, July 10, 1969, LATR, box 448, folder 15; Nick Williams to Otis Chandler, March 3, 1971, LATR, box 395, folder 9.

82. Otis Chandler, Los Angeles Times Employee Bulletin, October 21, 1974, LATR, box 170, folder 4.

83. William Thomas, "New Page Width at the Los Angeles Times: More Plusses than Minuses," *BASNE*, April 1975, 12–15. The *New York Times* made the switch from eight columns to six in 1976.

84. Nick Williams to Otis Chandler, March 3, 1971, LATR, box 395, folder 9.

85. Nick Williams mentioned Thomas advocating the daily magazine concept in a memo to Otis Chandler on February 23, 1971 (LATR, box 448, folder 15). Tim Rutten, who worked closely with Thomas for years, recalled Thomas's belief that "successful newspapers were going to be the ones that most resembled a daily magazine." Tim Rutten, interview with author, August 2, 2014. See also David Halberstam notes of interviews with Jim Bassett and Frank McCullough, David Halberstam Collection, box 192, folder 6, and box 193, folder 19, Howard Gotlieb Archival Research Center, Boston University (hereafter cited as Halberstam Collection).

86. Transcript of unidentified interview with Otis Chandler, circa 1976, LATR, box 228 folder 25.

87. Nick Williams to Jack Nightscales, October 15, 1969, LATR, box 466, folder 1.

88. Tom Wolfe, "The 'Me' Decade and the Third Great Awakening," *New York*, August 23, 1976. The first issue of *You* appeared on October 5, 1976.

89. Michele Hilmes, *Only Connect: A Cultural History of Broadcasting in the United States*, 4th ed. (Boston: Wadsworth/Cengage Learning, 2014), 247–248.

90. Chris Argyris, *Behind the Front Page* (San Francisco: Jossey-Bass, 1974), 163, 167. Argyris used the code name R for Rosenthal and code names T and Q for Oakes in a failed attempt to preserve the anonymity of the *New York Times* in his book. See also David M. Rubin, "Behind the Front Page," *[More]* magazine, November 1974.

91. For discussions about reducing the news hole, see Rosenthal Papers, box 92, folder 9.

92. Lester Markel, "The Real Sins of the Press," *Harper's Magazine*, December 1962, 85–93.

93. A. M. Rosenthal, journal entry, January 29, 1971, A. M. Rosenthal Papers (personal papers), box 4, Manuscripts and Archives Division, New York Public Library (hereafter cited as Rosenthal Papers [personal]).

94. Deirdre Carmody, "Clay Felker, Magazine Pioneer, Dies at 82," *New York Times,* July 2, 2008.

95. Ed Klein, interview with author, May 15, 2013.

96. Memo from A. M. Rosenthal, March 17, 1970, Curtis Papers, box 8, folder 3.

97. Greenwald, *A Woman of the Times,* 133.

98. They were Mimi Sheraton and Nancy Newhouse. Diamond, *Behind the Times,* 150.

99. A. M. Rosenthal to Ivan Veit, Arthur Ochs Sulzberger, and James Reston, September 20, 1971, copy in A. M. Rosenthal personal journal, 1971, Rosenthal Papers (personal), box 4.

100. The feature, written by Richard Shepard, debuted on February 28, 1972.

101. Memo from A. M. Rosenthal, November 27, 1972, Curtis Papers, box 8, folder 6. The first "Issue and Debate" piece appeared a mere five days after Rosenthal sent this memo: Leonard Buder, "Issue and Debate: The Boycott of Schools in East Harlem," *New York Times,* December 2, 1972. It remained a regular feature throughout Rosenthal's editorship.

102. Seymour Topping to David Jones, John Lee, and Mitchel Levitas, September 16, 1976, Seymour Topping Papers, box 16, folder 3, New York Times Company Records, Manuscripts and Archives Division, New York Public Library. This feature became the Careers column, which appeared on Wednesdays starting November 17, 1976, written by Elizabeth Fowler.

103. Daniel Bell, *The Coming of Post-Industrial Society: A Venture in Social Forecasting* (New York: Basic Books, 1973).

104. Bethany Moreton, *To Serve God and Wal-Mart: The Making of Christian Free Enterprise* (Cambridge, MA: Harvard University Press, 2009).

105. Diamond, *Behind the Times,* 119.

106. Ibid., 155.

107. Ibid., 158–160.

108. A. M. Rosenthal to Jack Rosenthal, September 15, 1976, and October 15, 1976, Rosenthal Papers, box 13, folder 18. Jack Rosenthal (no relation to Abe Rosenthal) was editor of the *New York Times Magazine.*

109. Text of Seymour Topping speech at University of Pennsylvania, January 1978, Rosenthal Papers, box 44, folder 8.

110. Tim Rutten, interview with author, August 2, 2014.

111. Barbara Saltzman, interview with author, August 28, 2014.

112. Bill Thomas, "A Concise Biography of William F. Thomas," unpublished memoir, 126–127. Provided courtesy of Michael Thomas.

113. David Shaw, "Paper's Plan for Revival—Be Local, Be Lively," *Los Angeles Times,* April 21, 1978.

114. David Halberstam, notes on interview with Nick Williams Jr., n.d. (circa 1976), Halberstam Collection, box 194, folder 13.

115. I dislike using the term "soft news" because of the value judgment it implies, but I do not believe there is a better alternative to use in this chapter.

116. Jean Sharley Taylor to Bill Thomas, n.d. (circa May 1979), LATR, box 440, folder 6.

117. See LATR, Marshall Berges interviews with Jean Sharley Taylor (box 583, folder 13), Robert Gibson (box 580, folder 3), John Lawrence (box 581, folder 5), Mark Murphy (box 582, folder 3), and Bill Shirley (box 583, folder 6).

118. Robert H. Flannes, Los Angeles Times Employee Bulletin, May 5, 1978 (with enclosed bumper sticker), LATR, box 170, folder 7.

119. Peter Benjaminson, *Death in the Afternoon: America's Newspaper Giants Struggle for Survival* (Kansas City: Andrews, McMeel, and Parker, 1984), 175; "Update," *Los Angeles Times* San Fernando Valley section, October 16, 1977, 1.

120. Larry Kramer, "James Bellows May Have the Toughest Job of All," *Washington Post*, March 5, 1978.

121. Transcript of Otis Chandler interview with Michael Jackson for KCET-Los Angeles, March 23, 1978, LATR, box 235, folder 22.

122. Markel, "The Real Sins."

123. Lester Markel, "The Remedy Is to Print a NEWSpaper," *BASNE*, October 1976, 3–6.

124. John B. Oakes, "Dwindling Faith in the Press," *New York Times*, May 24, 1978.

125. Arthur E. Rowse, "Consumer News Coverage," *BASNE*, August 1969, 1–4.

126. Nicholas von Hoffman, "Women's Pages: An Irreverent View," *Columbia Journalism Review*, July–August 1971, 52.

127. The Consumer Notes column in the *New York Times*, written by Gerald Gold, first appeared on June 30, 1973. The four newspapers were the *New York Times*, the *Washington Post*, the *Chicago Tribune*, and the *Los Angeles Times:* Susan H. Miller, "Changes in Women's/Lifestyle Sections," *Journalism Quarterly* 53, no. 4 (Winter 1976): 643–644.

128. On the consumer movement's impact, see Glickman, *Buying Power,* and Robert N. Mayer, *The Consumer Movement: Guardians of the Marketplace* (Boston: G. K. Hall, 1989).

129. Clay S. Felker, "Guerrilla Tactics for Consumer Journalism," *BASNE*, July–August 1971, 6–11.

130. Mort Pesky, "Soft News: Ever Harder," *BASNE*, April 1972, 1, 8–9.

131. Robert J. Cochnar, "The Establishment Conspiracy and Other Crimes by the Press Critics," *BASNE*, October 1974, 3–7.

132. Susan H. Miller, "Women and the News," *BASNE*, October 1975, 10–15.

133. Michael C. Jensen, "The Sorry State of News Reporting and Why It Won't Be Changed," *BASNE*, April 1977, 16–17.

134. Lester Markel, "Lester Markel: So What's New?," *BASNE*, January 1972; Lester Markel, "The Remedy."

135. Michele Weldon, *Everyman News: The Changing American Front Page* (Columbia: University of Missouri Press, 2008).

136. James T. Hamilton, "The Market and the Media," in Geneva Overholser and Kathleen Hall Jamieson, eds., *The Press* (New York: Oxford University Press, 2005), 351–371.

137. Earl Shorris, "Cutting Velvet at the New York Times," *Harper's,* October 1977, 102–110.

138. Gerald Lanson and Mitchell Stephens, "Abe Rosenthal: The Man and His *Times,*" *Washington Journalism Review,* July–August 1983, 24–28.

139. Felix Gutierrez and Clint C. Wilson II, "The Demographic Dilemma," *Columbia Journalism Review,* January–February 1979, 53–55. See also Richard Reeves, "Mr. Otis Regrets," *Esquire,* April 10, 1979.

140. Michele Willens, "The Los Angeles Times: Catching Up with the Times," *California Journal,* April 1979, clipping in LATR, box 594, folder 16.

141. Gottlieb and Wolt, *Thinking Big,* 477.

142. A. M. Rosenthal to Ivan Veit, Arthur Ochs Sulzberger, and James Reston, September 20, 1971, copy in A. M. Rosenthal personal journal, 1971, Rosenthal Papers (personal), box 4.

143. Donald A. Nizen to David Shaw, March 24, 1977, LATR, box 431, folder 2.

144. Nick Williams to Otis Chandler (OC), n.d., circa March 1969, LATR, box 461, folder 10.

145. David Halberstam notes on first interview with Nick Williams, circa 1976, Halberstam Collection, box 194, folder 13.

146. Text of Seymour Topping speech at University of Pennsylvania, January 1978, Rosenthal Papers, box 44, folder 8.

147. Transcript of Otis Chandler interview with Michael Jackson for KCET-Los Angeles, March 23, 1978, LATR, box 235, folder 22. The folder also contains many angry letters regarding Chandler's comments.

148. Advertisement, *New York Times,* March 20, 1970, 41.

5. Minorities and Women in the Newsroom: A Two-Pronged Struggle

1. The three black reporters at the *New York Times* were Layhmond Robinson, Junius Griffin, and Theodore Jones. By 1966 all had left the paper. When Tom Johnson was hired in February of that year, he became the only black reporter in the newsroom; see Arthur Gelb, *City Room* (New York: Marian Wood/Putnam, 2003), 381, 400. The one Latino reporter at the *Los Angeles Times* was Ruben Salazar—see Chapter 6 for a discussion of Salazar's life and career.

2. John Pomfret to Harrison Salisbury, April 15, 1964, and Harrison Salisbury to John Pomfret, April 27, 1964, Harrison E. Salisbury Papers, box 536, folder 20, Rare Book and Manuscript Library, Columbia University Library (hereafter cited as Salisbury Papers). This story proposal may have been inspired by Edward R. Murrow's famous CBS News documentary about migrant farmworkers, *Harvest of Shame,* which aired in 1960.

3. Pamela Newkirk, *Within the Veil: Black Journalists, White Media* (New York: NYU Press, 2000), 4. Figures showing newsroom employment of other racial minorities in the 1960s are not available.

4. Thomas A. Johnson, "Essay: A Graduate of the Black Press," Robert C. Maynard Institute for Journalism Education, http://mije.org/historyproject/Essay-AGraduateof TheBlackPress.

5. Arthur Gelb, *City Room* (New York: Marian Wood/G. P. Putnam's Sons, 2003), 390.

6. See four articles by Robert Richardson in the *Los Angeles Times:* "Eyewitness Account: Get Whitey, Scream Blood-Hungry Mobs," August 14, 1965; "'Burn Baby

Burn' Slogan Used as Firebugs Put Area to Torch," August 15, 1965; "Childhood Vanishes in Embers during Fearful Curfew Hours," August 16, 1965; "A Taste of What It's Like," August 22, 1965. Although the first article identified him as "an advertising salesman for The Times," he was in fact a messenger. Daina Beth Solomon and Dexter Thomas, "Urban Legend about Times Reporting during Watts Riot Conceals a Sadder Truth," *Los Angeles Times*, August 14, 2015, http://www.latimes.com /local/wattsriots/la-me-watts-richardson-20150814-story.html.

7. Gene Roberts and Hank Klibanoff, *The Race Beat: The Press, the Civil Rights Struggle, and the Awakening of a Nation* (New York: Alfred A. Knopf, 2006), 396.

8. "Where Are All the Competent Newsmen Who Happen to Be Negroes," *BASNE*, January 1966.

9. Roger Kahn, "The House of Adolph Ochs," *Saturday Evening Post*, October 9, 1965, 58.

10. Earl Caldwell, interview with author, October 3, 2014.

11. *Report of the National Advisory Commission on Social Disorders* (Washington, DC: U.S. Government Printing Office, 1968), 210–212.

12. Ibid., 211.

13. "Imbalance Found in Riot Stories; Editorial Reaction," *Boston Globe*, March 3, 1968, 23; "On Reading the Riot Report," *New York Times*, March 21, 1968, 46; "The Survival of a Nation," *Los Angeles Times*, March 3, 1968, G6. Some newspapers, however, felt the report went too far in its call for the press to communicate to its (white) audience "a sense of the degradation, misery, and hopelessness of life in the ghetto." The *Chicago Tribune* considered this "a call to propagandize." "Urban Grievances and the Press," *Chicago Tribune*, March 4, 1968, 20.

14. Gwyneth Mellinger, *Chasing Newsroom Diversity: From Jim Crow to Affirmative Action* (Urbana: University of Illinois Press, 2013), 46–47.

15. Solomon and Thomas, "Urban Legend."

16. Robert Gottlieb and Irene Wolt, *Thinking Big: The Story of the Los Angeles Times, Its Publishers, and Their Influence on Southern California* (New York: G. P. Putnam's Sons, 1977), 394.

17. Outtake of Bill Drummond interview for the film *Ruben Salazar: Man in the Middle* (dir. Phillip Rodriguez, Public Broadcasting Service, 2014). Available at https://www .youtube.com/watch?v=ztq_-JjOylo.

18. Earl Caldwell, interview with author, October 3, 2014; C. Gerald Fraser, interview with author, October 24, 2014.

19. Newkirk, *Within the Veil*, 72, 80.

20. See Chapter 3 for more on objectivity and the objections that minorities and other groups raised about it.

21. U.S. Bureau of the Census, *Census of Population: 1960. Subject Reports: Occupational Characteristics* (Washington, DC: U.S. Government Printing Office, 1963), 21–22; U.S. Bureau of the Census, *Census of Population: 1970. Subject Reports: Occupation by Industry Final Report* (Washington, DC: U.S. Government Printing Office, 1972), 1, 3, 97, 99; U.S. Bureau of the Census, *Census of Population: 1980. Subject Reports: Occupation by Industry* (Washington, DC: U.S. Government Printing Office, 1984), 1.

22. Newkirk, *Within the Veil,* 78. That figure includes all minorities, not just African-Americans. Census data do not include the percentage of African-Americans working as newspaper reporters and editors in 1970 or 1980.

23. See Roberts and Klibanoff, *The Race Beat.*

24. See six articles by Ruben Salazar in the *Los Angeles Times:* "Spanish-Speaking Angelenos: A Culture in Search of a Name," February 24, 1963; "Leader Calls Effort to Aid Mexican-Americans a Failure," February 25, 1963; "Serape Belt Occupies City's Heart," February 26, 1963; "Mexican-Americans Lack Political Power," February 27, 1963; "Mexican-Americans Succeeding," February 28, 1963; "Mexican-Americans Have Culture Protected by 1848 U.S. Treaty," March 1, 1963. Although Salazar later became a powerful advocate for the Chicano people, his political awakening had not occurred at this point and his views largely coincided with the views of L.A.'s affluent Anglo community. For more on Salazar's odyssey, see the documentary *Ruben Salazar: Man in the Middle* (dir. Phillip Rodriguez, Public Broadcasting Service, 2014).

25. David Halberstam, notes from second interview of Frank McCullough for *The Powers That Be,* n.d. (circa 1976), from the David Halberstam Collection, box 193, folder 19, Howard Gotlieb Archival Research Center, Boston University.

26. Paul Weeks, "Negroes to Press Civil Rights Here," *Los Angeles Times,* June 5, 1963.

27. Both series began on a Sunday. The first article in the Mexican-American series ran prominently on page one of the second section, and the five subsequent articles ran on page one of the front section in the weekday paper. The first article in the African-American series ran on page three of the front section, and the three subsequent articles ran on page two of the front section. See four articles by Paul Weeks in the *Los Angeles Times:* "L.A. Integration Test Approaches," June 23, 1963; "Housing Equality Major Negro Aim," June 24, 1963; "Law Enforcement Hit by Negroes," June 25, 1963; "Two Concepts on Equality Offered," June 26, 1963.

28. Otis Chandler biographer Dennis McDougal writes that the third series McCullough planned was to be on L.A.'s Asian community, not its Jewish community: Dennis McDougal, *Privileged Son: Otis Chandler and the Rise and Fall of the L.A. Times Dynasty* (Cambridge, MA: Perseus, 2001), 283–284. In January 1978 the *Los Angeles Times* published a three-part series entitled "The Jews of Los Angeles," by Robert Scheer, but this seems to have been unrelated to any planned 1963 project.

29. Layhmond Robinson, "New York's Racial Unrest: Negroes' Anger Mounting," *New York Times,* August 12, 1963.

30. Charles Grutzner, "New York's Racial Unrest: Whites Are of Two Minds," *New York Times,* August 13, 1963.

31. Newkirk, *Within the Veil,* 80. The *New York Times* had a policy in place since 1946 to not mention a news subject's race unless it was "germane" to the story: Susan E. Tifft and Alex S. Jones, *The Trust: The Private and Powerful Family behind the New York Times* (Boston: Little, Brown, 1999), 275–276. The *Los Angeles Times* generally did not mention the race of criminal suspects either. However, both newspapers sometimes identified alleged criminals as "Negro" if the police wanted the public's help in apprehending the suspects, if the case was explicitly related to race, or if the story was unusually in-depth. For instance, based on the addresses given for the suspects in these two stories, they were almost certainly black, but they were not identified as

such: "Retired Man Dies in Hallway Attack; 2 Youths Arrested," *New York Times,* December 18, 1965; "Suspect Fires at Detectives; Shot to Death," *Los Angeles Times,* January 5, 1965. These two front-page stories do identify the suspects as "Negro": "Two Killed in Wilshire Shootout," *Los Angeles Times,* August 24, 1965; Emanuel Perlmutter, "Suspect Gives Up in IND Killing; Sister Calls Him Black Extremist," *New York Times,* March 18, 1965.

32. *Report of the National Advisory Commission on Social Disorders,* 210–211.

33. Thomas Hrach, *The Riot Report and the News: How the Kerner Commission Changed Media Coverage of Black America* (Amherst: University of Massachusetts Press, 2016), 137.

34. Theodore Bernstein to Clifton Daniel, April 29, 1968, Theodore M. Bernstein Papers, box 4, folder 16, New York Times Company Records, Manuscripts and Archives Division, New York Public Library.

35. Gelb, *City Room,* 444–445.

36. "Alexander Ave.—Island in the Bronx," *New York Times,* February 1, 1969. See also Joseph P. Fried, "Bedford-Stuyvesant Has Bright Side, Too," *New York Times,* February 1, 1969.

37. Gelb, *City Room,* 541–542.

38. See three articles by Charlayne Hunter in the *New York Times:* "7,000 Books on Blacks Fill a Home," March 18, 1972; "Giver of Advice to Harlem Housewives," October 19, 1970; "An Entrepreneur's Trucks Bring Southern Soul Food to Harlem," December 20, 1971.

39. Transcript of "News Conference," KNBC-TV, November 29, 1969, Los Angeles Times Records, box 232, folder 10, Huntington Library, San Marino, CA (hereafter cited as LATR). A search of the *Los Angeles Times* digital archive on ProQuest from 1967 to 1969 did not turn up either of the articles Chandler referenced, so he may have provided an inaccurate summary of the articles' contents. He referred to the same two articles—"a black dress shop down in Watts . . . a foster mother who takes in ten kids"—at a May 1969 Los Angeles Times Executive Conference. Packet titled, "Los Angeles Times Executive Conference: Editorial Excellence," May 17, 1969, LATR, box 85, folder 5.

40. Jack Jones, "Watts Girls Trained as Dental Aides by Dedicated Housewife," *Los Angeles Times,* September 25, 1967, pt. 2, p. 1.

41. "Carmichael Says the Time Has Come for Guns," *New York Times,* April 13, 1968; "Carmichael Denies in Court that He Began Atlanta Riot," *New York Times,* October 2, 1966; Eric Pace, "Carmichael Tells of Meeting Cleaver in Algiers," *New York Times,* July 25, 1969.

42. "Rap Brown Again Tells Negroes to Arm Selves," *Los Angeles Times,* August 21, 1967; Earl Caldwell, "Rap Brown: A Tough Sentence," *New York Times,* May 26, 1968.

43. Nick Williams to Otis Chandler, March 7, 1968, LATR, box 448, folder 15.

44. Nick Williams to Robert D. Nelson, July 20, 1967, LATR, box 444, folder 8.

45. Nick Williams to Frank Haven, March 19, 1969, LATR, box 453, folder 9. Although the memo was addressed only to Haven (the managing editor), Williams asked him to pass it on to the national editor (Ed Guthman), metropolitan editor (Bill Thomas), editorial-page editor (James Bassett), and soft-news editor (James Bellows).

46. Transcript of William F. Thomas commencement address at Delta College (Michigan), April 28, 1968, LATR, box 408, folder 4.

47. See Chapter 4 for explanation of the non-dupe column.

48. William J. Drummond, "Eldridge Cleaver: A Black Militant Forged by Life," *Los Angeles Times,* November 29, 1968.

49. Douglas Kneeland to Claude Sitton, May 27, 1968, Salisbury Papers, box 540, folder 31.

50. Among the *New York Times* articles by Earl Caldwell: "Black Panthers: 'Young Revolutionaries at War,'" September 6, 1968; "Black Panthers Growing, but Their Troubles Rise," December 7, 1968; "Black Panthers Serving Youngsters a Diet of Food and Politics," June 15, 1969; "Panthers: They Are Not the Same Organization," July 27, 1969; "Panthers Await Newton's Return," July 8, 1970. The *New York Times Magazine* also published a lengthy article about Eldridge Cleaver, but it focused on him mainly as a literary figure and did not include an interview: Harvey Swados, "Old Con, Black Panther, Brilliant Writer, and Quintessential American," *New York Times Magazine,* September 7, 1969.

51. When Caldwell refused to turn over his notebooks to the FBI, the government sued him. His case was eventually decided by the Supreme Court in *Branzburg v. Hayes* (1972).

52. "TV Network Officials Give Answer to Senator over Coverage of Riots," *Los Angeles Times,* August 19, 1967; "Sen. Scott Urges Code for Reporting on Riots," *Boston Globe* (UPI wire), August 2, 1967.

53. Harrison Salisbury to Turner Catledge, January 10, 1968, Salisbury Papers, box 540, folder 26.

54. James Reston to Arthur Ochs Sulzberger, April 11, 1973, James B. Reston Papers, box 2, folder 11, New York Times Company Records, Manuscripts and Archives Division, New York Public Library (hereafter cited as Reston Papers).

55. Steven V. Roberts, "Angela Davis: Flight but Not Fight Is Over," *New York Times,* October 18, 1970.

56. Jenkin Lloyd Jones to Clifton Daniel, October 29, 1970, Clifton Daniel Papers, box 30, folder 3, New York Times Company Records, Manuscripts and Archives Division, New York Public Library.

57. Nick Williams to Jim Bellows, August 21, 1968, LATR, box 464, folder 12.

58. Nick Williams to Jim Bellows, May 28, 1968, LATR, box 464, folder 9.

59. Memorandum from Frank Haven, n.d. (circa 1969 or early 1970), LATR, box 440, folder 3.

60. Nick Kotz, "The Minority Struggle for a Place in the Newsroom," *Columbia Journalism Review,* March/April 1979, 24.

61. JoEllen Kitchen to Bill Thomas, August 13, 1981, "Analysis Sheets on Minority Employment," LATR, box 426, folder 3. By 1981 the paper had one minority employee in such a position.

62. Kotz, "The Minority Struggle," *Columbia Journalism Review,* March/April 1979, 25.

63. Charlayne Hunter-Gault turned down an offer to become assistant metropolitan editor and Roger Wilkins turned down an offer to edit the Week in Review section.

Gelb, *City Room,* 542; Roger Wilkins, *A Man's Life: An Autobiography* (New York: Simon and Schuster, 1982), 355.

64. Transcript of *Behind the Lines* TV program, WNET/Channel 13 New York, February 21, 1972, A. M. Rosenthal Papers, box 15, folder 1, New York Times Company Records, Manuscripts and Archives Division, New York Public Library (hereafter cited as Rosenthal Papers).

65. Kotz, "The Minority Struggle," *Columbia Journalism Review,* March/April 1979.

66. Wilkins, *A Man's Life,* 355.

67. David Shaw, "What's the News? White Editors Make the Call," *Los Angeles Times,* December 13, 1990.

68. David Shaw, "Amid L.A.'s Ethnic Mix, the Times Plays Catch-Up," *Los Angeles Times,* December 14, 1990.

69. Earl Caldwell, interview with author, October 3, 2014. A search of the *New York Times* database on ProQuest shows that Caldwell had seven page-one bylines between April 5 and May 3, 1968.

70. Kotz, "The Minority Struggle," *Columbia Journalism Review,* March/April 1979, 28.

71. Michele Willens, *"The Los Angeles Times:* Catching Up with the Times," *California Journal,* April 1979, 121–123, clipping in LATR, box 594, folder 16.

72. Ibid.; Richard Reeves, "Mr. Otis Regrets," *Esquire,* April 10, 1979, 14–15; Joel Kotkin, "Upstart Paper Challenges 'Juggernaut' Los Angeles Times," *Washington Post,* November 23, 1979.

73. Reeves, "Mr. Otis Regrets," 14.

74. Transcript of Otis Chandler interview with Michael Jackson for KCET–Los Angeles, March 23, 1978, LATR, box 235, folder 22.

75. He wrote, "I wish we did attract this audience but, for various reasons, many minority people turn elsewhere for their news and entertainment." This gave him an opening to say he would try harder to attract a minority audience, but he declined to do so. Otis Chandler to Thelma Summers, May 11, 1978, LATR, box 235, folder 22. This is one of many form letters Chandler sent.

76. See Chapter 4 for a discussion of these sections.

77. Jane Levere, "Suburban Editions Edited for Psychographic Types," *Editor & Publisher,* February 19, 1977, 13. Memorandum from Ruth Clark of Yankelovich, Skelly and White, Inc., to Charles Greenberg, February 21, 1978, Rosenthal Papers, box 108, folder 1.

78. Nick Williams to Hernando Courtright, December 27, 1968, LATR, box 448, folder 8.

79. On suburbanites' disengagement from inner-city issues, see Kevin Kruse, *White Flight: Atlanta and the Making of Modern Conservatism* (Princeton, NJ: Princeton University Press, 2005), 234–258; and Thomas Byrne Edsall and Mary D. Edsall, *Chain Reaction: The Impact of Race, Rights, and Taxes on American Politics* (New York: W. W. Norton, 1992), 227–229. As the Edsalls write, "The accelerated growth of suburbs has made it possible for many Americans to fulfill a basic drive toward civic participation—involvement in schools, cooperation in community endeavors, a willingness to support and pay for public services—within a smaller universe, separate and apart from the consuming failure, crime, welfarism, decay—and blackness—of the older cities" (228).

80. Many authors have documented the treatment of women in newsrooms and in news coverage. See especially Patricia Bradley, *Women and the Press: The Struggle for Equality* (Evanston, IL: Northwestern University Press, 2005); Maureen H. Beasley and Sheila J. Gibbons, *Taking Their Place: A Documentary History of Women and Journalism* (Washington, DC: American University Press, 1993); Kay Mills, *A Place in the News: From the Women's Pages to the Front Page* (New York: Dodd, Mead, 1988); Nan Robertson, *The Girls in the Balcony: Women, Men and the New York Times* (New York: Random House, 1992); Helen Thomas, *Front Row at the White House* (New York: Scribner, 1999).

81. McDougal, *Privileged Son*, 126.

82. Valerie J. Nelson, "Dorothy Townsend Dies at 88; L.A. Times Reporter Broke Newsroom Barrier," *Los Angeles Times*, March 21, 2012.

83. Harrison Salisbury to Clifton Daniel, March 4, 1965, Salisbury Papers, box 669, folder 47.

84. "Females in the Newsroom," *BASNE*, February 1966, 10–12.

85. Gwyneth Mellinger, "American Society of Newspaper Editors," in *Encyclopedia of American Journalism*, ed. Steven L. Vaughn (New York: Routledge, 2007), 21.

86. Joseph C. Goulden, *Fit to Print: A. M. Rosenthal and His Times* (Secaucus, NJ: Lyle Stuart, 1988), 376–377.

87. Marlene Cimons, interview with author, October 30, 2014.

88. Theodore "Ted" Jones, "Essay: I Was Going to Be a Timesman," Robert C. Maynard Institute for Journalism Excellence, Oral History Project, n.d., http://mije.org /historyproject/Essay-IWasGoingtoBeaTimesman.

89. On the *Newsweek* suit, see Lynn Povich, *The Good Girls Revolt: How the Women of Newsweek Sued Their Bosses and Changed the Workplace* (New York: Public Affairs, 2012).

90. U.S. Bureau of the Census, *Census of Population: 1960. Subject Reports: Occupational Characteristics* (Washington, DC: U.S. Government Printing Office, 1963), 1–2; U.S. Bureau of the Census, *Census of Population: 1970. Subject Reports: Occupational Characteristics* (Washington, DC: U.S. Government Printing Office, 1973), 1; U.S. Bureau of the Census, *Census of Population: 1980. Subject Reports: Occupation by Industry* (Washington, DC: U.S. Government Printing Office, 1984), 1.

91. David R. Bowers, "More Women in Newsrooms," *BASNE*, October 1979, 8.

92. Nan Robertson, a longtime *New York Times* reporter, wrote the definitive book on women's fight for equality at the paper: Robertson, *Girls in the Balcony*. I rely heavily on Robertson's work while trying to augment it with archival sources that may not have been available to her.

93. Ibid., 132–135.

94. Women on the News Staff of the New York Times to Arthur O. Sulzberger et al., n.d., New York Times Women's Caucus Papers, folder 3, Schlesinger Library, Radcliffe Institute, Harvard University (hereafter cited as Women's Caucus Papers). The same document can be found in Rosenthal Papers, box 95, folder 7. This copy has the date "May 1972" written in pencil at the top of the first page.

95. A. O. Sulzberger to All Employees of the New York Times and Its Subsidiaries, January 11, 1973, Women's Caucus Papers, folder 17.

96. Robertson, *Girls in the Balcony,* 157.

97. Summary of New York Times Women's Caucus meeting of September 11, 1974, Women's Caucus Papers, folder 5; Robertson, *Girls in the Balcony,* 164–169.

98. Robertson, *Girls in the Balcony,* 182–183, 195–196.

99. Although both sides claimed the settlement as a victory, on balance it favored the plaintiffs: it allowed them to appeal to the court if the *Times* did not fulfill its affirmative-action goals and it awarded them back pay. However, the amount of back pay was very small, and the *Times* insisted that it was not back pay at all but "annuities"; the *Times* also claimed (implausibly) that the affirmative-action plan to which it agreed was simply a continuation of its existing policies. See Robertson, *Girls in the Balcony,* 207–210; and New York Times Company press release, October 6, 1978, Rosenthal Papers, box 95, folder 7.

100. Betsy Wade to A. M. Rosenthal, June 29, 1972, Rosenthal Papers, box 95, folder 7.

101. Recommendations from the National Organization for Women for Better Representation of Women in the *New York Times,* June 1972, Rosenthal Papers, box 122, folder 2.

102. For example, an October 1971 article referred to a female judge as having a "bathing beauty figure." When a reader wrote that she was "astounded and infuriated" to see that description, Rosenthal replied, "I was astounded and infuriated myself at the description of Judge Lillee. It was entirely out of place and I regret it." But he seems to have taken no further action, apart from copying the responsible editor on his response. A. M. Rosenthal to Stacie Jacob, October 21, 1971, and Jacob to Rosenthal, October 14, 1971, Rosenthal Papers, box 122, folder 2.

103. A. M. Rosenthal to Seymour Topping and 15 others, June 21, 1972, and A. M. Rosenthal to John Oakes, Daniel Schwartz, and Mark Senigo, June 21, 1972, Rosenthal Papers, box 122, folder 2.

104. A. M. Rosenthal to Jim Roach, July 5, 1972, Rosenthal Papers, box 122, folder 2.

105. Fred Tupper, "Misses Evert, Goolagong Win, Meet Tomorrow," *New York Times,* July 4, 1972.

106. A. M. Rosenthal to Rona L. Shamoon, July 17, 1972, Rosenthal Papers, box 122, folder 2.

107. In addition to the example of the "three top-ranked girls" above, see Rosenthal Papers: A. M. Rosenthal to Jim Roach, June 26, 1972, box 95, folder 7; A. M. Rosenthal to Bullpen, October 29, 1973, box 122, folder 2; A. M. Rosenthal to Julia Graham Lear, January 17, 1974, box 122, folder 1.

108. A. M. Rosenthal to Jacqueline Ceballos, June 5, 1974, Rosenthal Papers, box 122, folder 1.

109. Grace Lichtenstein et al. to A. M. Rosenthal, August 6, 1973, Rosenthal Papers, box 122 folder 2. The article: Ned Burks, "City Traffic Cop Takes on New Image: Small, Friendly, and Curvy," *New York Times,* August 2, 1973.

110. Mitchel Levitas to A. M. Rosenthal, August 30, 1973, Rosenthal Papers, box 122, folder 2.

111. A. M. Rosenthal to Kristin Booth Glen, June 8, 1973, A. M. Rosenthal Papers (personal papers), box 4, Manuscripts and Archives Division, New York Public Library.

112. Untitled typescript of remarks, n.d., Women's Caucus Papers, folder 2.

113. Copy of flyer titled "Make Trouble for the Sexist New York Times," Rosenthal Papers, box 122, folder 1.

114. A. O. Sulzberger to Barbara Fultz Martinez, March 8, 1974, John B. Oakes Papers, box 14, folder labeled "Sulzberger, Arthur Ochs, General Memos: 1974–1992," Rare Book and Manuscript Library, Columbia University Library (hereafter cited as Oakes Papers).

115. A. O. Sulzberger memorandum for Reading File, March 8, 1974, Oakes Papers, box 14, folder labeled "Sulzberger, Arthur Ochs, General Memos: 1974–1992.

116. "Editor's Note," *New York Times,* June 20, 1986, B1.

117. Carol R. Richards, "The Right to Choose Ms., Miss, or Mrs.," *BASNE,* September 1976, 6–7.

118. Author's survey of *Los Angeles Times* back issues on microfilm and via ProQuest online database.

119. Richards, "Right to Choose Ms."

120. Barbara Saltzman, interview with author, August 28, 2014.

121. "FEPC Orders Probe of Times Job Policies," *Los Angeles Times,* August 4, 1972; Robert L. Flannes to Otis Chandler et al., August 8, 1972, LATR, box 440, folder 3.

122. George Cotliar to Bill Thomas, December 18, 1974, and report titled "Meeting with Editorial Women's Caucus," n.d., LATR, box 440, folder 3; Claudia Luther, interview with author, September 12, 2014.

123. Ibid.; James W. Duncan to Marilyn Hearnton, January 7, 1975, LATR, box 440, folder 3.

124. Carol F. Schiller to Claudia Luther, May 30, 1975, LATR, box 440, folder 3.

125. Claudia Luther, interview with author, September 12, 2014.

126. A. M. Rosenthal to Scotty Reston, March 25, 1971, Reston Papers, box 2, folder 8.

127. A. M. Rosenthal to A. O. Sulzberger et al., July 5, 1972, Rosenthal Papers, box 95, folder 7.

128. A. M. Rosenthal to A. O. Sulzberger, John Mortimer, and Peter Millones, March 2, 1971, Rosenthal Papers, box 95, folder 1.

129. Tom Johnson, Los Angeles Times Management Bulletin, September 13, 1983, and Noel Greenwood to Bill Thomas, report on METPRO, June 12, 1986, both LATR, box 425, folder 5.

130. Kotz, "The Minority Struggle," 31.

131. Gerald M. Boyd, *My Times in Black and White: Race and Power at the* New York Times (Chicago: Lawrence Hill Books, 2010), 119. Boyd later became the first non-white managing editor of the *New York Times.* Roger Wilkins, the first African-American to join the *New York Times* editorial board, tells a similar story in his memoir: Wilkins, *A Man's Life,* 348–349.

132. Tom Collins, "'We're Going to Have It All,'" *BASNE,* July–August 1975, 7.

133. "The Affirmative Action Program of the Los Angeles Times," May 17, 1973, LATR, box 170, folder 4.

134. At the *New York Times* in 1978, women constituted 23 percent of newsroom professionals and 28 percent of managers, while minorities constituted 9 percent of

newsroom professionals and 5 percent of managers: Peter Millones to A. M. Rosenthal, July 17, 1980, Rosenthal Papers, box 95, folder 1. At the *Los Angeles Times* in 1977, women constituted 19.5 percent of newsroom professionals and minorities constituted 6.1 percent (figures for newsroom managers were not given): Los Angeles Times Employment Statistics, LATR, box 421, folder 4.

135. See, for example, Kathleen R. Rutherford to George Cotliar, October 4, 1979, LATR, box 351, folder 1; and Susan Jacoby to A. M. Rosenthal, March 18, 1976, and Julia Mutti to A. M. Rosenthal, July 26, 1977, both Rosenthal Papers, box 122, folder 1.

136. Julia Mutti to A. M. Rosenthal, July 26, 1977, Rosenthal Papers, box 122, folder 1.

137. Gaye Tuchman, *Making News: A Study in the Construction of Reality* (New York: Free Press, 1978), 149. One reporter on the *New York Times* national staff told Tuchman, "I never mind a story of mine appearing there [on the Family / Style page instead of page one]. You get good play, sensitive editing, and it will be well read."

138. Jean Sharley Taylor to Kathleen R. Rutherford, October 8, 1979, LATR, box 351, folder 1.

139. A. M. Rosenthal to Susan Jacoby, March 29, 1976, Rosenthal Papers, box 122, folder 1.

140. Betty Friedan to A. M. Rosenthal, June 6, 1978, Rosenthal Papers, box 122, folder 1.

141. Pamela Newkirk has argued that even after newsrooms become racially integrated, they usually "still perpetuate a racial hierarchy that devalues the lives and experiences of blacks and other people of color" because in order to succeed in a mostly white newsroom, journalists of color must adapt to the prevailing (white) values and perspectives; Newkirk, *Within the Veil*, 1–37, quotation at 37.

142. Kotz, "The Minority Struggle," 28.

143. Janet Cooke, "Jimmy's World: 8-Year-Old Heroin Addict Lives for a Fix," *Washington Post*, September 28, 1980.

144. The most thorough account of how the Cooke scandal unfolded at the *Washington Post* came from the paper's ombudsman, Bill Green, whose multipart report appeared on April 19, 1981.

145. Newkirk, *Within the Veil*, 164–168, 171.

146. David L. Eason, "On Journalistic Authority: The Janet Cooke Scandal," *Critical Studies in Mass Communication* 3 (1986): 434–436; Newkirk, *Within the Veil*, 170–171.

147. Mike Sager, "Janet's World," *GQ*, June 1996, 200–211, quotation at 207.

148. Ibid.

149. The series ran between August 10 and August 31, 1980. For an overview, see Bill Boyarsky, "An Assessment: Lack of Jobs Is at Root of Watts Malaise," *Los Angeles Times*, August 31, 1980, 1.

6. The Press and the Powerful: From Allies to Adversaries

1. Transcript of Los Angeles Times Executive Conference: Editorial Excellence, May 17, 1969, Los Angeles Times Records (hereafter cited as LATR), box 85, folder 5, Huntington Library, San Marino, CA.

2. See Chapter 1 for more details about the rise of interpretive reporting.

3. As Herbert Gans has argued, "moderatism" is a core journalistic value: Herbert Gans, *Deciding What's News* (New York: Vintage Books, 1980), 51–52 (orig. pub. 1979). See also Chapter 3 of this book.

4. Daniel Okrent, "Is the New York Times a Liberal Newspaper?," *New York Times,* July 25, 2004. Although the *Times* gave Okrent and his successors the title "public editor," their role was essentially that of ombudsman.

5. Eric Alterman, *What Liberal Media? The Truth about Bias and the News* (New York: Basic Books, 2003), 104–117 (on "social bias") and passim.

6. David S. Broder, *Behind the Front Page* (New York: Simon and Schuster, 1987), 332.

7. Gans, *Deciding What's News,* 68–69.

8. Many of the Progressives' social attitudes, by contemporary standards, were more conservative. The nature of Progressivism has been a topic of considerable debate among historians. See, for example, Michael McGerr, *A Fierce Discontent: The Rise and Fall of the Progressive Movement in America* (New York: Free Press, 2003); Elizabeth Sanders, *Roots of Reform: Workers, Farmers, and the American State, 1877–1917* (Chicago: University of Chicago Press, 1999); William Link, *The Paradox of Southern Progressivism, 1880–1930* (Chapel Hill: University of North Carolina Press, 1992); Robyn Muncy, *Creating a Female Dominion in American Reform, 1890–1935* (New York: Oxford University Press, 1991); Daniel T. Rodgers, "In Search of Progressivism," *Reviews in American History* 10, no. 4 (December 1982): 113–132.

9. Richard H. Rovere, *The American Establishment and Other Reports, Opinions, and Speculations* (New York: Harcourt Brace, 1962), 10.

10. Nick Williams to Mrs. William Colhoun, August 15, 1968, LATR, box 464, folder 12. Each of the three major works about the *L.A. Times* emphasizes that it was a vehicle for the business interests of the Chandler family and their allies: Robert Gottlieb and Irene Wolt, *Thinking Big: The Story of the Los Angeles Times, Its Publishers, and Their Influence on Southern California* (New York: G. P. Putnam's Sons, 1977); David Halberstam, *The Powers That Be* (New York: Knopf, 1979); Dennis McDougal, *Privileged Son: Otis Chandler and the Rise and Fall of the L.A. Times Dynasty* (Cambridge, MA: Da Capo Press, 2001).

11. Clifton Daniel, "Responsibility of the Reporter and Editor," *Nieman Reports,* January 1961, 13.

12. Tad Szulc, "Anti-Castro Units Trained to Fight at Florida Bases," *New York Times,* April 7, 1961; Gay Talese, *The Kingdom and the Power: Behind the Scenes at the New York Times, the Institution That Influences the World* (New York: Random House, 1969), 23; Harrison E. Salisbury, *Without Fear or Favor: The New York Times and Its Times* (New York: Times Books, 1980), 152–160.

13. John F. Stacks, *Scotty: James B. Reston and the Rise and Fall of American Journalism* (Lincoln: University of Nebraska Press, 2006), 226; David Halberstam, *The Making of a Quagmire* (New York: Random House, 1965), 268.

14. Bruce Schulman makes a similar argument in *The Seventies: The Great Shift in American Culture, Society, and Politics* (New York: Free Press, 2001).

15. Clifton Daniel to Harrison Salisbury, October 23, 1964, Harrison E. Salisbury Papers, box 536, folder 18, Rare Book and Manuscript Library, Columbia University Library (hereafter cited as Salisbury Papers).

16. Claude Sitton to Robert Phelps, November 18, 1966, and Tom Wicker to Claude Sitton, November 28, 1966, both Tom Wicker Papers, box 20, folder 12, Manuscripts and Archives Division, New York Public Library. The article concerned a trip that Dayan made to Saigon to observe U.S. military efforts in Vietnam. Dayan later wrote about his observations in a syndicated newspaper article. The U.S. Information Agency (USIA) had paid for the trip, as part of a policy of paying for foreign journalists to travel to Vietnam. As an illustration of the fact that Sitton was out of step with current journalistic standards, Wicker noted that the *Washington Post* ran a story about the USIA having paid for Dayan's travel. The *Post* also wrote an editorial condemning the U.S. government's practice of sponsoring foreign journalists' trips to Vietnam. See "Israeli Writer Given Saigon Trip by USIA," *Washington Post,* November 3, 1966; "Huckstering," *Washington Post,* November 4, 1966.

17. Jack Anderson, "LBJ the Boss," *Parade,* May 1, 1966. Although Anderson also wrote that LBJ could be extremely caring and generous with his staff, the article gives the overall impression that he was a tyrant.

18. Robert B. Semple Jr., "Johnson Scatters Cattle on Ranch," *New York Times,* May 31, 1965.

19. John Averill, "Big Advantage of Ranch Life," *Los Angeles Times,* November 30, 1966.

20. "The Widening No-Man's Land: President vs. the Press," *Life,* May 7, 1965, 36.

21. "Editor's Decision on Cuba Related" and "Excerpts from Speech on Coverage of Bay of Pigs Buildup," *New York Times,* June 2, 1966.

22. Roger Kahn, "The House of Adolph Ochs," *Saturday Evening Post,* October 9, 1965, 54.

23. See the following *New York Times* articles: "C.I.A.: Maker of Policy, or Tool?," April 25, 1966; "How C.I.A. Put 'Instant Air Force' into Congo," April 26, 1966; "Electronic Prying Grows," April 27, 1966; "C.I.A. Operations: A Plot Scuttled," April 28, 1966; "The C.I.A.: Qualities of Director Viewed as Chief Rein on Agency," April 29, 1966.

24. Salisbury, *Without Fear or Favor,* 522–524. McCone served as CIA director from 1961 to 1965, and many of the CIA activities discussed in the *New York Times* series occurred under his leadership.

25. Seymour Hersh, "Huge C.I.A. Operation Reported in U.S. against Antiwar Forces, Other Dissidents in Nixon Years," *New York Times,* December 22, 1974.

26. Outright lies were not necessarily the most pernicious aspect of the government and military's manipulation of the media. Journalist Frances Fitzgerald gave the following example during a 1968 panel discussion: "They [military officials] say that pacification is going terribly well. And you say pacification is *not* going terribly well. But the real issue is, what does pacification mean, anyway? The very word itself is a sort of nonsense. There's an entire debate going on that really is absolutely meaningless. As Orwell said, it's not a lie. It doesn't have that direct a relationship to the truth." "Symposium: Journalism and Mischief," *American Scholar,* Fall 1968, 630. See also

Daniel C. Hallin, *The "Uncensored War": The Media and Vietnam* (New York: Oxford University Press, 1986).

27. Dennis Britton, interview with author, September 26, 2014. Some sympathy toward the demonstrators is apparent in the main *L.A. Times* article on the protest on November 15, which described it as a "march against death" in the subheadline and twice more in the text: John J. Goldman, "Massive Capital Protest Grows; Sporadic Violence Mars Dignity," *Los Angeles Times,* November 15, 1969.

28. Max Frankel to A. M. Rosenthal, October 17, 1969, A. M. Rosenthal Papers, box 70, folder 2, New York Times Company Records, Manuscripts and Archives Division, New York Public Library (hereafter cited as Rosenthal Papers). There were two major moratorium-day protests, one on October 15 and one on November 15. Frankel was referring, of course, to the earlier one.

29. Edwin Diamond, "'Reporter Power' Takes Root," *Columbia Journalism Review,* Summer 1970, 13–14.

30. Stanford Sesser, "Journalists: Objectivity and Activism," *Wall Street Journal,* October 21, 1969.

31. Seymour M. Hersh, "An Absence of Instinct," *BASNE,* February 1970, 4–5, 9; "News Tip Starts Quest for Facts of 'Massacre,'" *Los Angeles Times* (UPI), December 11, 1969; Seymour M. Hersh, "New Viet Murder Charge," *Boston Globe,* November 13, 1969. The November 13 article was the first in a series by Hersh, and the subsequent articles—based on interviews with soldiers who had participated in the killing—were even more damning. Many other news organizations, including the CBS Evening News, also procured interviews with the participants.

32. Peter Braestrup and Stephen Klaidman, "Three Vietnam Veterans Tell of Hamlet Slayings," *Washington Post,* November 20, 1969; Christopher B. Daly, *Covering America: A Narrative History of a Nation's Journalism* (Amherst: University of Massachusetts Press, 2012), 357.

33. Mary McGrory, "Reaction to Vietnam Massacre Story Varies Widely," *Boston Globe* (syndicated column), November 25, 1969.

34. Hersh, whose article appeared on November 13, 1969, did not scoop every newspaper. The *Detroit News* and the *Alabama Journal* each published a story about My Lai and Lieutenant Calley on November 12, and the *New York Times* wrote about the massacre based on its independent reporting on November 13. But those stories did not match the depth of the Hersh article. "News Tip Starts Quest for Facts of 'Massacre,'" *Los Angeles Times* (UPI), December 11, 1969.

35. Roger Tartarian, "The Press Is Still at the Considerable Mercy of Military Information Officers," *BASNE,* February 1970, 5.

36. Nick Williams to J. Edward Murray, January 12, 1970, LATR, box 466, folder 4.

37. Judith Coburn and Geoffrey Cowan, "The Fourth Estate as Fourth Branch," *Village Voice,* January 1, 1970, 18–19.

38. Hersh, "Absence of Instinct," 4. See also "A Probe into Motives of Man Who Exposed My Lai Killings," *Los Angeles Times,* May 31, 1970.

39. See Chapter 2 for a discussion of Agnew's criticism of the media.

40. Robert M. Smith, "G.I. Says He Saw Vietnam Massacre," *New York Times,* November 20, 1969; Peter Braestrup and Stephen Klaidman, "Three Vietnam Veterans

Tell of Hamlet Slayings," *Washington Post,* November 20, 1969; "3 Vietnam Veterans Say They Saw U.S. Troops Kill Civilians," *Los Angeles Times* (AP), November 20, 1969.

41. Daly, *Covering America,* 369–371.

42. See David Rudenstine, *The Day the Presses Stopped: A History of the Pentagon Papers Case* (Berkeley: University of California Press, 1996); Sanford J. Ungar, *The Papers and the Papers: An Account of the Legal and Political Battle over the Pentagon Papers* (New York: Columbia University Press, 1989); Kevin M. Lerner, "Abe Rosenthal's Project X: The Editorial Process Leading to the Publication of the Pentagon Papers," in *Media Nation: The Political History of News in Modern America,* ed. Bruce J. Schulman and Julian E. Zelizer (Philadelphia: University of Pennsylvania Press, 2017).

43. Lerner, "Abe Rosenthal's Project X," 154.

44. William Greider, "The Press as Adversary," *Washington Post,* June 27, 1971.

45. Nicholas Gage, interview with author, April 24, 2013; Halberstam, *The Powers That Be,* 888.

46. Bob Woodward and Carl Bernstein, "White House Maintained List of Political Enemies in '71–'72," *Washington Post,* June 28, 1973.

47. Dennis Britton, interview with author, September 26, 2014.

48. Edwin Diamond, "The Cabal at 'The New York Times': Which Way to the Revolution?," *New York,* May 18, 1970, 42–45; Joseph Lelyveld, interview with author, September 5, 2014.

49. Peter Millones (identified as P. M.) to A. M. Rosenthal, April 17, 1970, Rosenthal Papers, box 70, folder 2.

50. Transcript of James B. Reston speech to American Society of Newspaper Editors, April 21, 1972, James B. Reston Papers, box 4, folder 10, New York Times Company Records, Manuscripts and Archives Division, New York Public Library.

51. For the press corps' views of Nixon, see David Greenberg, *Nixon's Shadow: The History of an Image* (New York: W. W. Norton 2003), 126–179.

52. James Keogh, *President Nixon and the Press* (New York: Funk and Wagnalls, 1972), 2.

53. "Press Must Be Probing, Adversary, Agnew Says," *Los Angeles Times* (AP), March 20, 1971.

54. Herbert G. Klein, "Freedom of the Press in the United States," *New York Times,* December 27, 1972.

55. Richard Reeves, "Nixon, Inc.—Corporation-Style Politics," *New York,* September 4, 1972, 39.

56. The biographical details about Salazar in this paragraph come from several sources: *Ruben Salazar: Man in the Middle* (dir. Philip Rodriguez, 2014, Public Broadcasting Service); Gottlieb and Wolt, *Thinking Big,* 421–425; Juan Gonzalez and Joseph Torres, *News for All the People: The Epic Story of Race and the American Media* (London: Verso, 2011), 313–315.

57. *Ruben Salazar: Man in the Middle* (dir. Rodriguez).

58. McDougal, *Privileged Son,* 283.

59. Gottlieb and Wolt, *Thinking Big,* 423; Ruben Salazar, "Reds Sell Propaganda Right under GI Noses," *Los Angeles Times,* October 4, 1965.

60. Ruben Salazar, "Yorty Binds Up His 'War Wound' and Leaves Saigon for Bangkok," *Los Angeles Times,* December 2, 1965.

61. "Yorty Accuses LA Times of Lies," clipping from *West Los Angeles Independent,* December 16, 1965, LATR, box 463, folder 3.

62. *Ruben Salazar: Man in the Middle* (dir. Rodriguez).

63. Ruben Salazar, "Militants Fight to Retain Spanish as Their Language," *Los Angeles Times,* January 14, 1969; Ruben Salazar, "Mexican Border Life and Trade Hit Hard by Operation Intercept," *Los Angeles Times,* September 28, 1969.

64. "Chicano Columnist," *Newsweek,* June 22, 1970, 61. Salazar's first column appeared on February 6, 1970, under the headline "Who Is a Chicano? And What Is It the Chicanos Want?" In it he explained that "Mexican-Americans, though indigenous to the Southwest, are on the lowest rung scholastically, economically, socially and politically. Chicanos feel cheated. They want to effect change. Now."

65. See, for instance, Ruben Salazar, "Latin Newsmen, Police Chief, Eat . . . But Fail to Meet," *L.A. Times,* March 13, 1970; Salazar, "Police-Community Rift," *L.A. Times,* April 3, 1970; and Salazar, "Mexican-Americans' Problems with the Legal System Viewed," *L.A. Times,* May 1, 1970; *Ruben Salazar: Man in the Middle* (dir. Rodriguez); Gottlieb and Wolt, *Thinking Big,* 425.

66. *Ruben Salazar: Man in the Middle* (dir. Rodriguez).

67. Gottlieb and Wolt, *Thinking Big,* 257–258.

68. Ibid., 362–364.

69. Sam Yorty to Otis Chandler, March 29, 1965, LATR, box 463, folder 3. In this letter, Yorty enclosed clippings from three Republican-oriented newspapers that covered press conferences he and his opponent had given, implying that the *Times* coverage was out of balance. Otis Chandler forwarded the letter to editor-in-chief Nick Williams with a handwritten note that said, "Oh, nuts—I'm getting fed up with this stuff. He must not have enough to do."

70. Transcript of Sam Yorty press conference, June 9, 1966, LATR, box 463, folder 4.

71. "In Harbor Inquiry: Four Indictments," *Los Angeles Times,* December 29, 1971; "Yortytoons," *Newsweek,* February 12, 1968, 67; Gottlieb and Wolt, *Thinking Big,* 393.

72. Transcript of "George Putnam News," KTLA-TV, October 15, 1968, LATR, box 463, folder 6.

73. Rudy Villasenor, "Yorty's $2 Million Libel Suit against the Times Dismissed," *Los Angeles Times,* February 19, 1969.

74. Notes from David Halberstam phone interview with Nick Williams, June 1977, from the David Halberstam Collection, box 194, folder 1, Howard Gotlieb Archival Research Center, Boston University (hereafter cited as Halberstam Collection). Williams did not indicate when this occurred, but Davis became police chief in 1969 and Williams retired in 1971, so it must have taken place during that two-year span.

75. Gottlieb and Wolt, *Thinking Big,* 394–395; Noel Greenwood, "Chancellor Says Police Overreacted at UCLA," *Los Angeles Times,* May 9, 1970.

76. Bill Thomas, "A Concise Biography of William F. Thomas," unpublished memoir, May 13, 1996, 49, provided courtesy of Michael W. Thomas.

77. Gottlieb and Wolt, *Thinking Big,* 535.

78. Bill Thomas, "The Press: Is It Biased against the Establishment?," *Los Angeles Times,* March 30, 1975.

79. "Letters to the Times: Chief Davis Cancels His Subscription," *Los Angeles Times,* August 20, 1975.

80. Thomas, "A Concise Biography," 49.

81. Gottlieb and Wolt, *Thinking Big,* 536.

82. Talese, *Kingdom and the Power,* 75.

83. Gelb, *City Room,* 154.

84. Edwin Diamond, *Behind the Times: Inside the New New York Times* (New York: Villard Books, 1994), 50.

85. Gelb, *City Room,* 367; Martin Arnold, "Narcotics a Growing Problem of Affluent Youth," *New York Times,* January 4, 1965.

86. Harrison Salisbury to Clifton Daniel, March 3, 1966, Salisbury Papers, box 537, folder 35.

87. Ibid.

88. Gelb, *City Room,* 542–544; David Burnham, "Some Policemen Are Found to Be Sleeping on Duty," *New York Times,* December 16, 1968.

89. See David Burnham, "Graft Paid to Police Here Said to Run into Millions," *New York Times,* April 25, 1970; David Burnham, "Gamblers' Links to Police Lead to Virtual 'Licensing,'" *New York Times,* April 26, 1970; David Burnham, "Police Corruption Fosters Distrust in the Ranks Here," *New York Times,* April 27, 1970.

90. John Corry, *My Times: Adventures in the News Trade* (New York: G. P. Putnam's Sons, 1993), 103–107; Gelb, *City Room,* 427–429.

91. Gelb, *City Room,* 405.

92. Corry, *My Times,* 103, 113; Joseph Goulden, *Fit to Print: A. M. Rosenthal and His Times* (Secaucus, NJ: Lyle Stuart, 1988), 108–110.

93. Corry, *My Times,* 113.

94. Gelb, *City Room,* 492–496, 502–503.

95. Richard E. Mooney to A. M. Rosenthal, August 28, 1969, Rosenthal Papers, box 92, folder 14; Martin Tolchin, "Mayor Took Company Plane; Impropriety Denied," *New York Times,* August 21, 1969. The staff's "anger" was intensified, Mooney wrote, because the delay caused the paper to lose out on a scoop. As Tolchin's article noted, the flight had first been reported by the *New York Post* and *Women's Wear Daily.*

96. This according to Richard Bergholz, who worked at the *Times*'s sister paper, the *Los Angeles Mirror,* from 1954–1962 and received the same press releases. David Halberstam notes for *The Powers That Be,* interview with Dick Bergholz, Halberstam Collection, box 192, folder 7.

97. See three articles from the *Bulletin of the American Society of Newspaper Editors,* June 1967: Roy M. Fisher, "The World of Finance Does Not Begin and End on Wall Street," 3; Al Neuharth, "How Should You Interest Readers in Business News?," 7; Paul Neville, "How to Handle the Pressures to Grab Space in the Business Section," 8.

98. See Chapter 4 for more on the consumer movement and business coverage.

99. David Halberstam notes for *The Powers That Be,* interview with Harry Bernstein, Halberstam Collection, box 192, folder 7.

100. Robert D. Nelson to Otis Chandler, and Bill Thomas to Otis Chandler, both November 18, 1974, LATR, box 440, folder 1; Mike Royko, "'It's Time to Buy a New Car'—Oh, Yeah?," *Los Angeles Times,* November 17, 1974.

101. George H. Whittlesey to Bill Thomas, October 1, 1975, and Bill Thomas to George H. Whittlesey, October 3, 1975, both LATR, box 416, folder 2; Peter Gruenstein, "Northrop Feted Key Legislators," *Los Angeles Times,* September 30, 1975.

102. Arthur R. Taylor, "Business and the Press: Who's Doing What to Whom and Why?," speech delivered at the Financial Executives Institute, New Orleans, October 21, 1975, *Vital Speeches of the Day,* December 1, 1975, 124.

103. Samuel Butler to A. M. Rosenthal, April 8, 1977, Rosenthal Papers, box 29, folder 37.

104. Louis Banks, "Memo to the Press: They Hate You Out There," *Atlantic,* April 1978, 35.

105. Arthur Ochs Sulzberger, "Business and the Press: Is the Press Anti-Business," speech delivered at the Economic Club of Detroit, March 14, 1977, *Vital Speeches of the Day,* May 1, 1977, 426.

106. Ibid.

107. Taylor, "Business and the Press," 123.

108. Diamond, *Behind the Times,* 121.

109. Max Frankel to A. O. Sulzberger, December 11, 1974, Rosenthal Papers, box 69, folder 13.

110. Leonard Silk and Mark Silk, *The American Establishment* (New York: Basic Books, 1980), 92; Chris Argyris, *Behind the Front Page* (San Francisco: Jossey-Bass, 1974), 173; Diamond, *Behind the Times,* 119–120.

111. "Behind the Profit Squeeze at the New York Times," *BusinessWeek,* August 30, 1976, 42.

112. Several authors have discussed this episode: see especially Susan E. Tifft and Alex S. Jones, *The Trust: The Private and Powerful Family behind the New York Times* (Boston: Little, Brown, 1999), 520–527; and Diamond, *Behind the Times,* 124–137. For John Oakes's perspective, see John B. Oakes Papers, box 15, folder labeled "Arthur Ochs Sulzberger: Memos Re 1976 Transition," Rare Book and Manuscript Library, Columbia University Library.

113. Max Frankel, interview with author, September 9, 2014.

114. Irving Kristol, "Crisis for Journalism: The Missing Elite," in *Press, Politics and Popular Government,* ed. George F. Will (Washington: American Enterprise Institute, 1972), 43–44.

115. See *All the President's Men* (dir. Alan J. Pakula), Warner Bros., 1976.

116. Prominent examples include David Halberstam, Neil Sheehan, and Malcolm Browne.

117. Irving Kristol, "Is the Press Misusing Its Powers?," *Chicago Tribune,* January 11, 1975.

118. Ibid.

119. On the press's treatment of Carter, see Mark J. Rozell, *The Press and the Carter Presidency* (Boulder, CO: Westview Press, 1989).

120. Gelb, *City Room,* 626.

121. Wick Temple, "Sportswriting: A Whole New Ballgame," *BASNE,* September 1977, 3–6.

122. Kristol, "Is the Press Misusing Its Powers?"

123. Transcript of Otis Chandler speech at the University of Kansas, April 30, 1975, LATR, box 234, folder 10. It is possible that his sensitivity to "jumping all over" alleged participants in illegal or unethical acts stemmed from the fact that Chandler himself was mired in a scandal over having accepted hundreds of thousands of dollars in finder's fees associated with a fraudulent investment scheme orchestrated by one of his college buddies. Regarding the "Geotek" scandal, see McDougal, *Privileged Son*, 299–302; and Halberstam, *The Powers That Be*, 881–883.

124. Halberstam, *The Powers That Be*, 562–563, 883–884, 1003–1004.

125. David Halberstam, notes for *The Powers That Be*, third interview with Otis Chandler, n.d., Halberstam Collection, box 192, folder 12.

126. Tom Braden, "To Whom Does the Truth Matter?," *Washington Post* (syndicated column), April 24, 1976.

127. Louis Banks, "Memo to the Press: They Hate You Out There," *Atlantic*, April 1978, 40. Although this article was published in 1978, Banks explained in a subsequent article that around 1974 he had begun writing articles and making speeches about the media's poor coverage of business—presumably the *Atlantic* article was adapted from those earlier articles and speeches.

128. Louis Banks, "Marching Up the Down Staircase," *BASNE*, October 1980, 4–6.

129. Kim Phillips-Fein, *Invisible Hands: The Making of the Conservative Movement from the New Deal to Reagan* (New York: W. W. Norton, 2009), 185–206.

130. Bethany Moreton, "Make Payroll, Not War," in *Rightward Bound: Making America Conservative in the 1970s*, ed. Bruce J. Schulman and Julian E. Zelizer (Cambridge, MA: Harvard University Press, 2008), 52–70.

131. Banks had formerly been managing editor of *Fortune* and editorial director of Time Inc.

132. Banks, "Marching Up the Down Staircase," 4–5.

133. Diamond, *Behind the Times*, 173–174.

134. David Halberstam, notes for *The Powers That Be*, interview with Bill Greider, n.d., Halberstam Collection, box 193, folder 8.

135. Text of Otis Chandler speech at Los Angeles Ad Club, March 31, 1976, LATR, box 234, folder 19.

136. Ibid. See Bill Thomas, "The Press: Is It Biased against the Establishment?," *Los Angeles Times*, March 30, 1975, which is discussed in greater detail in Chapter 3.

137. Nick Williams to Jack Nightscales, October 15, 1969, LATR, box 466, folder 1.

138. John Corry, *My Times: Adventures in the News Trade* (New York: G. P. Putnam's Sons, 1993), 19. Although Corry was more conservative than most journalists, and more blasé about racism, sexism, gay right, and the environment than most journalists would be, reporters of all political stripes occasionally pined for the old days of "man bites dog" stories.

139. Harris Survey press release, "Record Lows in Public Confidence," October 6, 1975, available at http://media.theharrispoll.com/documents/Harris-Interactive-Poll-Research -RECORD-LOWS-IN-PUBLIC-CONFIDENCE-1975-10.pdf.

140. The exception to the downward trend is the military, which steadily increased in public confidence beginning a few years after the U.S. withdrawal from Vietnam. See

Harris Interactive press release, "Big Drop in Confidence in Leaders of Major Institutions," February 28, 2008, available at http://media.theharrispoll.com/documents /Harris-Interactive-Poll-Research-Big-Drop-in-Confidence-in-Leaders-of-Major -Institutions-2008-02.pdf.

7. American Journalism and Its Values, 1980–2018: Validation, Devastation, Alteration

1. Robert W. McChesney, *Rich Media, Poor Democracy: Communication Politics in Dubious Times* (Urbana: University of Illinois Press, 1999), 2.
2. American Society of Newspaper Editors, 2015 Newsroom Census, Table A, available at http://asne.org/content.asp?pl=140&sl=129&contentid=129. To be clear, ASNE did not stop keeping track of newsroom employment because the figures were so depressing. They did so because the increasing use of freelancers and subcontractors made it too difficult to measure employment accurately. Rick Edmonds, "ASNE Stops Trying to Count Total Job Losses in American Newsrooms," Poynter Institute blog, September 9, 2016, http://www.poynter.org/2016/asne-stops-tryting-to-count-total -job-losses-in-american-newsrooms/429515/.
3. On Trump, see, for example, Nicholas Kristof, "My Shared Shame: The Media Made Trump," *New York Times,* March 27, 2016; David Folkenflik, "Weary Press Corps Celebrate Election's End, Then Survey Wreckage," NPR.org, November 8, 2016, http://www.npr.org/2016/11/08/501033242/weary-press-corps-can-celebrate-election -s-end-then-survey-wreckage; Mathew Ingram, "Here's Proof That the Media Helped Create Donald Trump," fortune.com, June 14, 2016, http://fortune.com/2016/06/14 /media-trump/. On McCarthy, see Chapter 1.
4. Nicholas Confessore and Karen Yourish, "Measuring Trump's Big Advantage in Free Media," *New York Times,* March 17, 2016.
5. Two of the most noteworthy journalistic expressions of this view of Trump came from *New Yorker* editor-in-chief David Remnick and from the *Los Angeles Times* editorial board: David Remnick, "An American Tragedy," NewYorker.com, November 9, 2016, https://www.newyorker.com/news/news-desk/an-american-tragedy-2; "Why We Took a Stand on Trump" (introduction to six-part series of editorials), *Los Angeles Times,* April 2–April 9, 2017, http://www.latimes.com/projects/la-ed-trump-series/.
6. Ironically, the *Los Angeles Times* and its parent company, Times Mirror, represented an exception to this trend, as major cost-cutting and layoffs began in the mid-1990s. But that resulted from the company's overly ambitious expansion in the 1970s and 1980s; the core business of the *Los Angeles Times* remained highly profitable. See Dennis McDougal, *Privileged Son: Otis Chandler and the Rise and Fall of the L.A. Times Dynasty* (Cambridge, MA: Perseus Publishing, 2001), 406–428.
7. *Los Angeles Times* media reporter David Shaw summed up these worrisome business trends in a 1991 article: David Shaw, "Inventing the 'Newspaper' of Tomorrow," *Los Angeles Times,* June 2, 1991.
8. Mark J. Perry, "Free-Fall: Adjusted for Inflation, Print Newspaper Advertising Revenue in 2012 Was Lower than in 1950," Carpe Diem blog, American Enterprise Insti-

tute, April 8, 2013, https://www.aei.org/publication/free-fall-adjusted-for-inflation
-print-newspaper-advertising-revenue-in-2012-was-lower-than-in-1950/.

9. Ben H. Bagdikian, "The Media Monopoly," *Television Quarterly* 28, no. 4 (1997): 29–40.

10. Ben H. Bagdikian, *The New Media Monopoly* (Boston: Beacon Press, 2004). The five corporations were Time Warner, Disney, News Corporation, Viacom, and Bertelsmann.

11. Marvin Kalb, "The Rise of the 'New News': A Case Study of Two Root Causes of Modern Scandal Coverage," October 1998, Joan Shorenstein Center on the Press, Politics, and Public Life, John F. Kennedy School of Government, Harvard University. Available at https://shorensteincenter.org/root-causes-of-modern-scandal-coverage/.

12. McDougal, *Privileged Son,* 418–419. The main edition of *Newsday* (based in Long Island) and the morning edition of the *Baltimore Sun* continued to publish.

13. Ibid., 436.

14. Michael A. Hiltzik and Sallie Hofmeister, "Times Publisher Apologizes for Staples Center Deal," *Los Angeles Times,* October 28, 1999.

15. Narda Zacchino, "Readers Notice Ethical Lapses," *Quill,* May 2000, 28–29.

16. McDougal, *Privileged Son,* 427.

17. James Fallows, *Breaking the News: How the Media Undermine American Democracy* (New York: Pantheon Books, 1996), 52–53, 57.

18. The growth of interpretive reporting is discussed in detail in Chapter 1.

19. Alex S. Jones, "Pulitzer Prizes in Journalism Are Expanded," *New York Times,* November 22, 1984.

20. For two early articles about the phenomenon, see David Shaw, "New Media Playing Field Opens Way to More Errors," *Los Angeles Times,* August 6, 1998; and Brian Lowry, "In 24-Hour News Era, Delay Spells Doom," *Seattle Times,* December 19, 1998. A Google Ngram search shows mentions of the term "24-hour news cycle" increasing tenfold from 1994 to 2000.

21. Ken Auletta, *Backstory: Inside the Business of News* (New York: Penguin Press, 2003), 217–218.

22. Paul Starobin, "The Conceptual Scoop," *Columbia Journalism Review,* January/February 1996, 21–25.

23. Fallows, *Breaking the News,* 130.

24. Ibid., 161.

25. Ibid., 10–16.

26. Jonathan Alter, "The Media in the Dock," *Newsweek,* October 22, 1984, 66.

27. Bill Peterson, "Helms Says 'Elite Media' Out of Step with People," *Washington Post,* March 2, 1985.

28. Rusher used the quotation as the epigraph for a book in which he assailed the media for liberal bias: William A. Rusher, *The Coming Battle for the Media* (New York: William Morrow, 1988), 11.

29. Michael Barone, "Clinton's Good Press and the Mono-Partisan Media," *Weekly Standard,* October 7, 1996, 26; L. Brent Bozell III, Lynne Cheney, and S. Robert Lichter, "Press Objectivity, R.I.P.," *American Enterprise* 7, no. 2 (March 1996): 34.

30. Howard Kurtz, "A Crusade to Right Left-Leaning News Media," *Washington Post,* June 6, 1996.

31. Mike Rosen, "Media Hive Stung by Charges of Liberal Bias," *Denver Post,* June 21, 1996.

32. "The Media in Denial," *Investor's Business Daily,* July 21, 1998.

33. Ben H. Bagdikian, *The Media Monopoly* (Boston: Beacon Press, 1983) (and six subsequent editions from 1987–2004); Edward S. Herman and Noam Chomsky, *Manufacturing Consent: The Political Economy of Mass Media* (New York: Pantheon, 1988); Robert W. McChesney, *Corporate Media and the Threat to Democracy* (New York: Seven Stories Press, 1997); and McChesney, *Rich Media, Poor Democracy* (1999).

34. Mark Hertsgaard, *On Bended Knee: The Press and the Reagan Presidency* (New York: Farrar, Straus Giroux, 1988), 3.

35. Mark Crispin Miller, "TV's Anti-Liberal Bias," *New York Times,* November 16, 1988.

36. Paul Krugman, "To Tell the Truth," *New York Times,* May 28, 2004.

37. Hertsgaard, *On Bended Knee,* 65.

38. Joann Byrd, "73 Days of Tilt," *Washington Post,* November 8, 1992; Byrd, "Son of Objectivity," *Washington Post,* November 15, 1992. See Edmund Lambeth, *Committed Journalism* (Bloomington: Indiana University Press, 1986). Despite her gender, Byrd's title at the *Washington Post* was "ombudsman."

39. Stephen J. A. Ward, *The Invention of Journalistic Ethics: The Path to Objectivity* (Montreal: McGill-Queen's University Press, 2004), 236–237.

40. For the revisions, see the Society of Professional Journalists code of ethics: for 1996, available at https://spj.org/pdf/ethicscode.pdf; for 1987, available at http://ethics.iit.edu/ecodes/node/4340; for 1973, available at http://ethics.iit.edu/ecodes/node/3702.

41. Karen Mills, "Journalism Society Working on Update of Its Ethics Code," *Austin American-Statesman,* November 19, 1995.

42. Fred Brown, "The Nine Suggestions of Journalism," *Denver Post,* August 15, 1998.

43. Alex S. Jones, "Journalists Disagree About Press Credibility," *New York Times,* May 7, 1985.

44. Christine D. Urban, *Examining Our Credibility: Perspectives of the Public and the Press* (Reston, VA: American Society of Newspaper Editors, 2000), 45.

45. Connie Koenenn et al. to Tom Johnson, June 25, 1987, Los Angeles Times Records (hereafter cited as LATR), box 433, folder 8, Huntington Library, San Marino, CA.

46. Summary of Bill Thomas meeting with Narda Zacchino, Linda Mathews, Connie Koenenn, Merle Harpe, Sandy Banks, and Connie Stewart, July 30, 1987, LATR, box 433, folder 8.

47. Terri Schultz-Brooks, "Getting There: Women in the Newsroom," *Columbia Journalism Review,* March/April 1984, 29.

48. However, a woman (Soma Golden) did become national editor in 1987. Max Frankel, *The Times of My Life and My Life with The Times* (New York: Delta/Dell, 1989), 455.

49. Leslie Bennetts, interview with author, February 1, 2016. This story is also recounted in Nan Robertson, *The Girls in the Balcony: Women, Men and the New York Times* (New York: Random House, 1992), 220–221.

50. Susan E. Tifft and Alex S. Jones, *The Trust: The Private and Powerful Family behind the New York Times* (Boston: Little, Brown, 1999), 615.

51. Joe Hagan, "A *New York Times* Whodunit," *New York,* May 26, 2012, http://nymag .com/news/features/new-york-times-2012-6/.

52. Rebecca Traister, "Jill Abramson's Firing Was about Gender: And Also Not about Gender," newrepublic.com, May 22, 2014, https://newrepublic.com/article/117868 /jill-abramsons-firing-wasnt-sexist-was-still-tied-gender; Doina Chiacu and Jennifer Saba, "New York Times Publisher Denies Sexism, Calls Abramson Bad Manager," reuters.com, May 17, 2014, http://www.reuters.com/article/us-newyorktimes-editor -idUSBREA4DoPW20140517.

53. Ken Auletta, "Why Jill Abramson Was Fired: Part Three," NewYorker.com, May 18, 2014, http://www.newyorker.com/business/currency/why-jill-abramson-was-fired -part-three.

54. Ken Auletta, "Why Jill Abramson Was Fired," NewYorker.com, May 14, 2014, http://www.newyorker.com/business/currency/why-jill-abramson-was-fired; David Folkenflik, "'Period of Turmoil' Preceded Abramson Firing, Says Top Editor at 'Times,'" *National Public Radio Morning Edition,* May 29, 2014, http://www.npr.org/2014/05/29 /317204054/abramson-not-fired-because-of-gender-says-times-new-top-editor.

55. Jonathan Z. Larsen, "Women's Way," *Columbia Journalism Review,* November / December 2001.

56. David R. Bowers, "More Women in Newsrooms," *BASNE,* October 1979, 8.

57. "ASNE Newsroom Census: Minority Employment Inches Up at Daily Newspapers," news release posted on asne.org, May 22, 1998, http://asne.org/content.asp?contentid =166.

58. ASNE Newsroom Census 2015, Table I, http://asne.org/content.asp?pl=140&sl =129&contentid=129. The 2016 census showed a slight increase—women were 39 percent of employees and 37 percent of supervisors—but it used a different meth- odology, which makes it hard to compare with previous years.

59. Margaret Sullivan, "Still Talking About It: 'Where Are the Women?,'" *New York Times* online article, May 12, 2014, https://publiceditor.blogs.nytimes.com/2014/05 /12/still-talking-about-it-where-are-the-women/.

60. For instance, the *New York Times* began a 2013 obituary of rocket scientist Yvonne Brill with the sentence, "She made a mean beef stroganoff, followed her husband from job to job and took eight years off from work to raise three children." When in 2017 human-rights lawyer Amal Clooney (who is married to actor George Clooney) testified before the United Nations about ISIS war crimes, *Time* tweeted the headline, "Amal Clooney shows off her baby bump at the United Nations." Kara Alaimo, "Newsrooms Should Follow Two Simple Rules for Reporting on Women's Bodies," *Columbia Journalism Review,* March 14, 2017, http://www.cjr.org/analysis/amal-clooney-time -tweet-united-nations.php; Amy Davidson, "Yvonne Brill and the Beef Stroganoff Il- lusion," NewYorker.com, May 1, 2013, http://www.newyorker.com/news/amy-davidson /yvonne-brill-and-the-beef-stroganoff-illusion.

61. Eric Alterman, in his book rebutting the charge that the mainstream media has a liberal bias, concedes that reporting on abortion in elite media tends to favor the pro-choice side: Alterman, *What Liberal Media?* (New York: Basic Books, 2003),

107–109. Alterman cites a 1990 series by David Shaw in the *Los Angeles Times* in which Shaw examined news coverage of abortion.

62. Gwyneth Mellinger, "Rekindling the Fire: The Compromise That Initiated the Formal Integration of Daily Newspaper Newsrooms," *American Journalism* 25, no. 3 (Summer 2008): 97–126.

63. Noel Greenwood to Bill Thomas, report on METPRO, June 12, 1986, LATR, box 425, folder 5.

64. Ibid. The METPRO trainees were not necessarily from underprivileged backgrounds; many had attended elite universities. Indeed, according to Ron Harris, METPRO's first director, some minority staffers at the *L.A. Times* objected to METPRO—as did people associated with minority training programs elsewhere. They accused the paper of "taking overqualified people, people who would make it in the business without this program." See "Closing Remarks" of report on METPRO.

65. R. Marilyn Lee to Robert F. Erburu and others, April 6, 1988, LATR, box 425, folder 4.

66. Paul Delaney (The HistoryMakers A2005.186), interview by Jodi Merriday, June 23, 2005, The HistoryMakers Digital Archive. Session 1, tape 4, story 3, "Paul Delaney Talks about Addressing the Lack of Diversity in the *New York Times* Newsroom." Paul Delaney, "'Everyone Genuinely Seems to Care: Collectively, Not Much Changes,'" *Columbia Journalism Review*, February 22, 2017, http://www.cjr.org/first _person/diversity-new-york-times-paul-delaney.php.

67. Delaney, "'Everyone Genuinely Seems to Care.'"

68. Although one-for-one was the goal, the paper did not actually achieve it—partly because several African-American candidates declined job offers. In the first year of the policy the *New York Times* hired seven blacks and nine whites; in the second year, it hired six blacks and thirteen whites. Max Frankel, *The Times of My Life and My Life with the Times* (New York: Delta, 2000), 465–466 (orig. pub. 1999).

69. ASNE Newsroom Census, "Table A: Minority in Daily Newspapers" (1978–2015), http://asne.org/content.asp?contentid=129. The category "minorities" included blacks, Latinos, Asians, Native Americans, and mixed-race individuals.

70. Gina Barton, "Is Diversity Making a Difference?," *Quill,* March 2002, 16–20.

71. David Shaw, "What's the News? White Editors Make the Call," *Los Angeles Times,* December 13, 1990.

72. Liz Spayd, "Preaching the Gospel of Diversity, but Not Following It," *New York Times,* December 18, 2016.

73. David Shaw, "Newspapers Struggling to Raise Minority Coverage," *Los Angeles Times,* December 12, 1990.

74. David Shaw, "Negative News and Little Else," *Los Angeles Times,* December 11, 1990.

75. Frank Harris III, "Covering Race a Daily Process," *Quill,* April 1997.

76. Pamela Newkirk, *Within the Veil: Black Journalists, White Media* (New York: NYU Press, 2000), 1–37 and passim.

77. Ibid., 11–15.

78. Shaw, "Newspapers Struggling." The policy also stated that at least one of the other four photos must show a woman.

79. William McGowan, *Coloring the News: How Crusading for Diversity Has Corrupted American Journalism* (New York: Simon and Schuster, 2000).

80. Jeremy Stahl, "The Exploitation of 'Beautiful Kate,'" Slate.com, August 10, 2017, https://slate.com/news-and-politics/2017/08/the-death-of-kate-steinle-and-the-rise-of-donald-trump.html; Manuel Roig-Franzia and Paul Farhi, "Breitbart: A New Force in the Trump Era," *Washington Post,* February 20, 2017; transcript of PBS *Frontline* interview with Breitbart former editor-at-large Ben Shapiro, March 24, 2017, published as "The Frontline Interview: Ben Shapiro," May 23, 2017, http://www.pbs.org/wgbh/frontline/article/the-frontline-interview-ben-shapiro; Richard Perez-Peña, "Migrants Less Likely to Commit Crimes," *New York Times,* January 27, 2014. Although the findings in Perez-Peña's article do not differentiate clearly between migrants who came to the United States legally versus illegally, an analyst quoted in the article "concluded that undocumented immigrants had crime rates somewhat higher than those here legally, but much lower than those of citizens."

81. Anthony Faiola and Stephanie Kirchner, "'Allahu-Akbar'-Chanting Mob Sets Alight Germany's Oldest Church? Shocking Story, If It Were True," Washington Post, January 6, 2017, https://www.washingtonpost.com/world/europe/allahu-akbar-chanting-mob-sets-alight-germanys-oldest-church-shocking-story-if-it-were-true/2017/01/06/30470f58-d36a-11e6-9651-54a0154cf5b3_story.html; Wil S. Hylton, "Down the Breitbart Hole," New York Times Magazine, August 16, 2017, https://www.nytimes.com/2017/08/16/magazine/breitbart-alt-right-steve-bannon.html; Paul Farhi, "Breitbart News Seems to Be Cleaning House after Readers and Advertisers Drift Away," Washington Post, June 7, 2017, https://www.washingtonpost.com/lifestyle/style/is-breitbart-news-veering-away-from-the-farthest-far-right/2017/06/06/35f91160-4ad1-11e7-a186-60c031eab644_story.html.

82. Jonathan Galinsky, "At the Fox News Site, a Sudden Focus on Women as Sex Offenders," *New York Times,* March 14, 2018, https://www.nytimes.com/2018/03/14/business/media/fox-news-women-teachers-sexual-predators.html; David Bauder (Associated Press), "12 Hours Vs. 20 Minutes: Fox News Focuses on Weinstein Harassment, Ignoring O'Reilly," *Chicago Tribune,* October 26, 2017, http://www.chicagotribune.com/entertainment/tv/ct-fox-news-weinstein-oreilly-20171026-story.html.

83. Alex S. Jones, *Losing the News: The Future of the News That Feeds Democracy* (New York: Oxford University Press, 2009), 20.

84. Prominent newspapers that closed include the *Seattle Post-Intelligencer* and *Rocky Mountain News* (both in 2009). *Newsweek* was sold for $1 in 2010 and laid off most of its staff prior to shuttering the print edition in 2012; the print edition has since been revived.

85. ASNE, 2015 Newsroom Census, Table A.

86. Robert G. Kaiser, "The Bad News about the News," Brookings Institution Essay, October 26, 2014, available at http://csweb.brookings.edu/content/research/essays/2014/bad-news.html.

87. Michael Hirschorn, "End Times," *The Atlantic,* January / February 2009.

88. Nikki Usher, *Making News at the New York Times* (Ann Arbor: University of Michigan Press, 2014), 5.

89. Jones, *Losing the News,* 189–190; Jack Shafer, "Len Downie Calls Arianna Huffington a Parasite," Slate.com, September 23, 2010, http://www.slate.com/articles/news_and _politics/press_box/2010/09/len_downie_calls_arianna_huffington_a_parasite .html. The Associated Press even sued a news aggregator (successfully) over what it called a "parasitic business model": David Kravets, "AP Sues Aggregator Over 'Parasitic Business Model,'" Wired.com, February 14, 2012, https://www.wired.com/2012 /02/ap-meltwater-lawsuit/.

90. The panel, called "Media Armageddon: What Happens When the New York Times Dies?," was held at the 2010 South by Southwest Festival. Video excerpt from Andrew Rossi (dir.), *Page One: Inside the New York Times* (Magnolia Pictures, 2011), at 35:43.

91. Bill Keller, "Is Glenn Greenwald the Future of News?," nytimes.com, October 27, 2013, http://www.nytimes.com/2013/10/28/opinion/a-conversation-in-lieu-of-a -column.html.

92. Margaret Sullivan, "Lodestars in a Murky Media World," *New York Times,* March 9, 2014.

93. Margaret Sullivan, "When Reporters Get Personal, *New York Times,* January 6, 2013.

94. James W. Hopson, "The Answer Is: Nobody Knows," *American Editor,* summer 2006; James W. Hopson, "Is There Still a Winning Strategy?," *American Editor,* summer 2008. *The American Editor* is the new name adopted in 2005 for the magazine formerly titled *The Bulletin of the American Society of Newspaper Editors.*

95. Clay T. Shirky, "Newspapers and Thinking the Unthinkable," Clay Shirky blog, March 13, 2009, http://www.shirky.com/weblog/2009/03/newspapers-and-thinking -the-unthinkable/.

96. The metered paywall differs from the "hard" or "firm" paywall, which some specialized publications like the *Wall Street Journal* and the *Financial Times* have long used. A hard paywall does not allow nonsubscribers to view the full text of any news content.

97. Jack Murtha, "How the Times Have Changed for the *Washington Post,*" *Columbia Journalism Review,* December 1, 2015, http://www.cjr.org/analysis/washington_post _vs_new_york_times.php.

98. Dan Kennedy, "The Bezos Effect: How Amazon's Founder Is Reinventing the *Washington Post*—and What Lessons It Might Hold for the Beleaguered Newspaper Industry," discussion paper for the Shorenstein Center on Media, Politics, and Public Policy, June 2016, available at https://shorensteincenter.org/bezos-effect -washington-post/.

99. Sandra G. Boodman, "This Woman's Labored Breathing Alarmed Her Friends: Doctors Were Startled to Find the Cause," WashingtonPost.com, March 20, 2017, https:// www.washingtonpost.com/national/health-science/this-woman-was-breathless—but -why/2017/03/20/66604114-e273-11e6-a453-19ec4b3d09ba_story.html.

100. Ravi Somaiya, "Where Clicks Reign, Audience Is King," *New York Times,* August 17, 2015.

101. Cited in Murtha, "How the Times Have Changed"; Lucia Moses, "How the Washington Post Leapfrogged the New York Times in Web Traffic," Digiday.com, December 1, 2015, http://digiday.com/media/washington-post-leapfrogged-new-york -times-web-traffic/; Gabriel Sherman, "Good News at the *Washington Post*," *New York,* June 28, 2016.

102. "Journalism That Stands Apart: The Report of the 2020 Group," New York Times Company, January 2017, https://www.nytimes.com/projects/2020-report/.

103. Ibid.

104. Mark Bulik, "Which Headlines Attract Most Readers?," Times Insider on nytimes .com, June 13, 2016, https://www.nytimes.com/2016/06/13/insider/which-headlines -attract-most-readers.html; Jack Marshall, "Washington Post's 'Bandito' Tool Optimizes Content for Clicks," *Wall Street Journal,* February 8, 2016, https://www.wsj .com/articles/washington-posts-bandit-tool-optimizes-content-for-clicks -1454960088.

105. The former article, by Laurie Goodstein, appeared on February 17, 2017; the latter, by Farhad Manjoo, appeared on February 22, 2017.

106. These stories were all promoted on the nytimes.com homepage on April 6, 2017.

107. Art Swift, "Americans' Trust in Media Sinks to New Low," Gallup.com, September 14, 2016, http://www.gallup.com/poll/195542/americans-trust-mass-media -sinks-new-low.aspx.

108. See Chapter 3 for a more in-depth discussion of Hallin's "spheres" concept.

109. David T. Z. Mindich, an authority on the history of objectivity in American journalism, has also noted the way Hallin's concept of spheres applies to Trump: David T. Z. Mindich, "For Journalists Covering Trump, a Murrow Moment," *Columbia Journalism Review,* July 15, 2016, http://www.cjr.org/analysis/trump_inspires _murrow_moment_for_journalism.php.

110. Jim Rutenberg, "The Challenge Trump Poses to Objectivity," *New York Times,* August 8, 2016.

111. Shafer himself may not have written those precise words, but it was the subheadline on his article: Jack Shafer, "Trump Was Not a Media Fail," Politico.com, November 9, 2016, http://www.politico.com/magazine/story/2016/11/donald-trump-wins-2016 -media-214442.

112. The idea of Hillary Clinton as a normal candidate and Trump as abnormal first gained prominence in July 2016 on Vox: Ezra Klein, "This Election Isn't Just Democrat vs. Republican: It's Normal vs. Abnormal," Vox.com, July 28, 2016, http://www .vox.com/2016/7/28/12281222/trump-clinton-conventions.

113. See, for example, Margaret Sullivan, "A Call to Action for Journalists Covering President Trump," WashingtonPost.com, November 9, 2016, https://www.washingtonpost .com/lifestyle/style/a-call-to-action-for-journalists-in-covering-president-trump /2016/11/09/a87d4946-a63e-11e6-8042-f4d111c862d1_story.html; Masha Gessen, "Autocracy: Rules for Survival," *New York Review of Books* online, November 10, 2016, http://www.nybooks.com/daily/2016/11/10/trump-election-autocracy-rules-for -survival/; Jelani Cobb, "Protecting Journalism from Donald Trump," NewYorker .com, November 29, 2016, http://www.newyorker.com/news/daily-comment/protecting -journalism-from-donald-trump.

114. Jessica Toonkel, "Newspapers Aim to Ride 'Trump Bump' to Reach Readers, Advertisers," Reuters, February 16, 2017, https://www.reuters.com/article/us-newspapers-trump-campaigns-analysis/newspapers-aim-to-ride-trump-bump-to-reach-readers-advertisers-idUSKBN15V0GI.

115. Author's notes.

116. Paul Farhi, "The Washington Post's New Slogan Turns Out to Be an Old Saying," WashingtonPost.com, February 24, 2017, https://www.washingtonpost.com/lifestyle/style/the-washington-posts-new-slogan-turns-out-to-be-an-old-saying/2017/02/23/cb199cda-fa02-11e6-be05-1a3817ac21a5_story.html.

117. Available at www.youtube.com/watch?v=gYoFdz350GE.

118. Jeff Jarvis, "Trump and the Press: A Murder-Suicide Pact," BuzzMachine.com, February 19, 2017, http://buzzmachine.com/2017/02/19/trump-press-murder-suicide-pact/.

119. Using LexisNexis, the author compared coverage of President Bush in February 2001 in the *Washington Post* and the *New York Times* with coverage of President Trump in February 2017. The news stories about Trump were far more negative, on balance.

120. Joe Pompeo, "Kellyanne Conway Was on TV Last Night—More Good News for Colbert's 'Late Night'—A 'Big Deal' 'Huge Loss' for WSJ," Politico.com, February 23, 2017, http://www.politico.com/media/tipsheets/morning-media/2017/02/kellyanne-conway-was-on-tv-last-nightmore-good-news-for-colberts-late-nighta-big-deal-huge-loss-for-wsj-001220.

121. Keller, "Is Glenn Greenwald the Future of News?"

122. Dan Barry, "In Swirl of 'Untruths' and 'Falsehoods,' Calling a Lie a Lie," *New York Times,* January 26, 2017; Sheryl Gay Stolberg, "Many Politicians Lie: But Trump Has Elevated the Art of Fabrication," *New York Times,* August 8, 2017.

123. David Leonhardt and Stuart A. Thompson, "Trump's Lies," *New York Times,* June 23, 2017. The list has since been updated online and is accessible at https://www.nytimes.com/interactive/2017/06/23/opinion/trumps-lies.html, accessed October 22, 2017.

124. Callum Borchers, "10 Ways the Media Described Trump's 'False,' 'Bogus' Voter Fraud 'Lie,'" WashingtonPost.com, January 24, 2017, https://www.washingtonpost.com/news/the-fix/wp/2017/01/24/10-ways-the-media-described-trumps-false-bogus-voter-fraud-lie/; Jason Del Rey, "Marty Baron Explains What It Will Take for the Washington Post to Call a Trump Lie a Lie," Recode.net, February 14, 2017, https://www.recode.net/2017/2/14/14613714/marty-baron-washington-post-trump-lie.

125. Steve Adler, "Covering Trump the Reuters Way," reuters.com, January 31, 2017, https://www.reuters.com/article/rpb-adlertrump/covering-trump-the-reuters-way-idUSKBN15F276.

126. Ken Doctor, "The New York Times' Dean Baquet on Calling Out Lies, Embracing Video, and Building a More Digital Newsroom," NiemanLab.org, October 6, 2016, http://www.niemanlab.org/2016/10/the-new-york-times-dean-baquet-on-calling-out-lies-embracing-video-and-building-a-more-digital-newsroom/.

127. Transcript of Dean Baquet interview on National Public Radio, *Fresh Air,* December 8, 2016, http://www.npr.org/2016/12/08/504806512/new-york-times-executive-editor-on-the-new-terrain-of-covering-trump.

128. A. M. Rosenthal, speech at University of Alabama, March 30, 1976, transcript in A. M. Rosenthal Papers (personal papers), box 15, folder 6, Manuscripts and Archives Division, New York Public Library.

Acknowledgments

Seven years ago, the prospect of researching, writing, and publishing a book seemed unimaginably far off. I could not have done it without the tremendous support I received from mentors, colleagues, family, and friends. My thanks go first to Bruce Schulman. As my adviser at Boston University, he guided this project from when it was an ill-formed idea about "when American journalism became contemporary" until the moment I was sending off a book proposal. At each stage, he pushed me to make bolder, broader claims, and to link my specific story about the press to the bigger story of politics and public life in the contemporary United States. To the extent that I have succeeded in doing so, it is thanks in large part to his suggestions.

For a work about journalism history, I could not have asked for a better sounding board than Chris Daly, who helped me situate this work within the longer sweep of American journalism's historical development. Several others at Boston University also provided crucial insights and advice, especially Sarah Phillips, Lou Ferleger, Jon Roberts, and Bill McKeen (and from Rutgers, David Greenberg). I also thank the Boston University History Department for funding my early visits to archives to collect some of the research material for this book.

Seton Hall University's College of Communication and the Arts has been wonderfully supportive of my efforts on this book from the moment I joined the faculty in 2016. Dean Deirdre Yates has shown great enthusiasm for this project, and I am grateful to her for having approved release time from my teaching commitments so that I could complete my manuscript. Jon Radwan, as chair of the Department of Communication, Journalism, and Public Relations, has provided me with invaluable guidance and support, in moving toward the publication of this book and in every other aspect of my work. The College of Communication and the Arts and the Department of Communication, Journalism, and Public Relations provided generous funding that allowed me to travel to archives and to license the images that appear in this book. My thanks go also to the Seton Hall colleagues who have given me feedback on this book and on my other research projects, especially Amy Nyberg and James Kimble.

It would have been impossible to research this book without the rich archival material that is preserved in the New York Times Company Records and the Los Angeles Times Records—housed at the New York Public Library and the Huntington Library, respectively. Both of these magnificent institutions are staffed by extremely helpful, knowledgeable archivists who provided me with invaluable assistance. At the New York Public Library's Manuscripts and Archives Division, Tal Nadan and the rest of the staff always made me feel welcome and remembered me even though many months (sometimes years) passed in between my visits. They were still in the process of cataloguing the New York Times Company Records at the time, and I greatly appreciated that they asked me which individuals' collections I would most like to use, then made those a priority. At the Huntington Library, Jennifer Goldman, Li Wei Yang, and Clay Stalls made sure I was thoroughly prepared for my visits before traveling to California; they and the rest of the efficient Huntington staff helped me make the most of my limited time there. Shortly after I began my research, the Huntington archivists completed a remarkably thorough finding aid for the enormous Los Angeles Times collection, which proved a great help.

The personal papers of David Halberstam, housed at the Howard Gotlieb Archival Research Center at Boston University, provided another key archival resource for this book. I thank the Gotlieb Center staff, especially Charles Niles, for their kind assistance. I am also grateful to the staff at Columbia University's Rare Book and Manuscript Library and at the Schlesinger Library (at Harvard

University's Radcliffe Institute for Advanced Study) for making it easy and efficient to consult their archival collections.

One of the most enjoyable aspects of this project was interviewing some of the talented journalists who worked at the *New York Times* and the *Los Angeles Times* during the 1960s and 1970s. It would have been easy for them to decline or ignore my interview requests; but not only did they agree to talk with me, most did so at great length and with great candor. I am particularly grateful to Elizabeth Mehren, former *L.A. Times* correspondent and current professor of journalism at Boston University. In providing me with introductions to several of her former colleagues, she spoke so highly of me and my work that they had little choice but to agree to an interview! I also thank Michael W. Thomas, who graciously provided me with the manuscript of an unpublished memoir by his father, the late *L.A. Times* editor-in-chief Bill Thomas. Given that I was unable to interview the elder Mr. Thomas before his passing in 2014, this was the next best thing.

I am grateful to the editors at Harvard University Press for seeing the potential in this book and for working with me to improve it. My editor, Andrew Kinney, gave my manuscript the kind of thorough attention every writer wishes for, providing excellent recommendations on everything from titles to analytical arguments to line edits. And as a first-time author, I was fortunate to have him to guide me through the ins and outs of the publishing process. I also thank Joyce Seltzer of Harvard University Press for her interest in my book and for her suggestions on how to refine my arguments, HUP's peer reviewers for their constructive criticism, and HUP editorial assistant Olivia Woods for helping me stay on top of administrative details.

Most of all, I would like to thank my family. My parents, Arlene and Kurt Pressman, always nurtured my intellectual curiosity, and they have been thoughtful, encouraging readers of my work ever since I began writing papers in elementary school. Many other family members have shown great interest in and enthusiasm for my work. But my wife, Lauren, deserves my gratitude more than anyone else. Her patience, love, and support are beyond measure. She and our wonderful sons, Owen and Caleb, provided the inspiration for this and all my work.

Index